Landmark Essays

Landmark Essays

on

ESL Writing

Edited by

Tony Silva
Purdue University

Paul Kei Matsuda
Miami University

 **Hermagoras Press**
An Imprint of Lawrence Erlbaum Associates, Publishers

Landmark Essays Volume Seventeen

Cover design by Kathi Zamminer

Lawrence Erlbaum Associates, Inc., Publishers
10 Industrial Avenue
Mahwah, New Jersey 07430

Library of Congress Cataloging-in-Publication Data

Landmark essays on ESL writing / edited by Tony Silva,
Paul Kei Matsuda
     p.cm — (Landmark essays : v.17)
  Includes bibliographical references and index.
  ISBN 1-880393-18-2 (pbk. : alk. paper)
  1. English language—Study and teaching—Foreign speakers. 2. English lanugage–Rhetoric–Study and teaching. 3. Report writing–Study and teaching. I. Silva, Tony J. II. Matsuda, Paul Kei. III. Series.
PE1128.A2 L293 2000
428.0071–dc21   00-040933

Printed in the United States of America

10 9 8 7 6 5 4 3 2

For Jeannie and Big Tony

Acknowledgements

We would like to thank Lawrence Erlbaum Associates, and Jerry Murphy and Linda Bathgate in particular, for their support, encouragement, and help in putting this book together; the authors whose work is reprinted here and their publishers for their generosity and cooperation; and Carlann Scholl for an outstanding job on the indexes.

About the Editors

Paul Kei Matsuda is Assistant Professor of English at Miami University (Ohio), where he teaches undergraduate and graduate courses in composition, rhetoric and linguistics. He has taught undergraduate and graduate writing courses for both native and nonnative speakers of English as well as graduate courses for ESL writing teachers. With Tony Silva, Paul founded and chairs the Symposium on Second Language Writing, and edited *On Second Language Writing.* At the Conference on College Composition and Communication, Paul has chaired several workshops and the Special Interest Group on Second Language Writing, and currently serves as the chair of the Committee on Second Language Writing. His articles appear in journals such as *College Composition and Communication, Composition Studies,* the *Journal of Second Language Writing* and *Written Communication* as well as in a number of forthcoming edited collections.

Tony Silva is Associate Professor of ESL at Purdue University, where he directs the Program in English Language and Linguistics and the ESL Writing Program and teaches undergraduate and graduate courses for ESL students and ESL teachers. With Ilona Leki he founded and edits the *Journal of Second Language Writing*; with Paul Kei Matsuda he founded and hosts the Symposium on Second Language Writing and edited *On Second Language Writing*; and with Colleen Brice and Melinda Reichelt he compiled the *Annotated Bibliography of Scholarship on Second Language Writing; 1993-1997.* He currently serves on the editorial boards of *Assessing Writing, Journal of Basic Writing, TESL Canada Journal,* and *Writing Program Administration.*

Table of Contents

Introduction

Paul Kei Matsuda and Tony Silva   xiii

Essays

1. *Anita Pincas.* Structural Linguistics and Systematic Composition
        Teaching to Students of English as a Foreign Language. (1962)   1

2. *Robert B. Kaplan.* Cultural Thought Patterns in Inter-Cultural Educa-
        tion. (1966)   11

3. *Vivian Zamel.* Teaching Composition in the ESL Classroom: What We
        Can Learn from Research in the Teaching of English. (1976)   27

4. *Ann Raimes.* What Unskilled ESL Students Do as They Write: A Class-
        room Study of Composing (1985)   37

5. *John Hinds.* Reader-Writer Responsibility: A New Typology. (1987) 63

6. *Ulla Connor.* Research Frontiers in Writing Analysis. (1988)   75

7. *Ruth Spack.* Initiating ESL Students into the Academic Discourse
        Community: How Far Should We Go? (1988)   91

8.   *Daniel Horowitz.*   Fiction and Nonfiction in the ESL/EFL Classroom:
Does the Difference Make a Difference? (1990)   **109**

9.   *Ann M. Johns.*   Interpreting an English Competency Examination: The
Frustrations of an ESL Science Student. (1991)   **117**

10.   *Joan G. Carson.*   Becoming Biliterate: First Language Influences.
(1992)   **137**

11.   *Terry Santos.*   Ideology in Composition: L1 and ESL. (1992)   **159**

12.   *Ilona Leki.*   Reciprocal Themes in ESL Reading and Writing. (1993)   **173**

13.   *Tony Silva.*   Toward an Understanding of the Distinct Nature of L2
Writing: The ESL Research and Its Implications. (1993)   **191**

14.   *Joy Reid.*   Responding to ESL Students' Texts: The Myths of Appropriation. (1994)   **209**

15.   *Liz Hamp-Lyons* and *Barbara Kroll.*   Issues in ESL Writing Assessment: An Overview. (1996)   **225**

16.   *Paul Kei Matsuda.*   Contrastive Rhetoric in Context: A Dynamic
Model of L2 Writing. (1997)   **241**

Indexes   **257**

Introduction
by Paul Kei Matsuda and Tony Silva

In recent years, the number of nonnative speakers of English in colleges and universities in North America has increased dramatically. According to the Institute of International Education, the number of international students—who are on student or exchange visas—in the United States exceeded 480,000 in the 1997-1998 academic year and is continuing to increase (Davis, 1998). In addition, there are equally significant numbers of immigrant and refugee bilingual students as well as native-born citizens of the United States and Canada who grew up speaking languages other than English. As a result, more and more writing teachers have found themselves working with these English as a Second language (ESL) students in writing classes that are designed primarily with monolingual, native-English-speaking students in mind. Because the majority of institutions require these students to enroll in writing courses at all levels, it is becoming increasingly important for all writing teachers to be aware of the presence and special linguistic and cultural needs of ESL writers. This increase in the ESL population has, over the last forty years, been paralleled by a similar growth in research on ESL writing and writing instruction—research that writing teachers need to be familiar with in order to work effectively with ESL writers in writing classrooms of all levels and types. Until recently, however, this body of knowledge has not been very accessible to writing teachers and researchers who do not specialize in second language research and instruction.

One of the reasons that second language writing scholarship has been relatively unknown to writing specialists in general is that second language writing since the mid-1960s has, for the most part, evolved separately as a subfield of Teaching English to Speakers of Other Languages (TESOL). During the last decade of the twentieth century, however, the continuing increase of ESL writers in writing classrooms has exposed the limitations of the "disciplinary division of labor" (Matsuda, 1998, 1999) between composition studies and TESL (Teaching English as a Second language), and the relationship between composition studies and second language studies has come to attract significant attention (Atkinson & Ramanathan, 1995; Matsuda, 1998, 1999; Roy, 1988; Santos, 1992; Silva, Leki, & Carson, 1997; Valdés, 1992). Despite the efforts of some writing specialists and ESL specialists to fill the gap between first- and second language writing scholarship and pedagogy, the differences between the perceptions and expectations of specialists in these two intellectual formations that have evolved separately over the last four decades have not been easy to reconcile.

The present volume is an attempt to narrow this gap by providing a sense of how ESL writing scholarship has evolved over the last four decades. It brings together 15 articles that address various issues in second language writing in general and ESL writing in particular. In selecting articles for inclusion, we tried to take a principled approach. The articles included in this volume have been chosen from a large database of publications in second language writing. We looked for works that mirrored the state of the art when they were published and made a conscious effort to represent a wide variety of perspectives, contributions, and issues in the field. It goes without saying that there are many other articles that would have been appropriate for this collection, but there simply wasn't enough room to include everything that deserved to be included. To direct readers to further readings on some of the issues highlighted by the articles—as well as to provide some historical contexts—will be the goal of this introduction. In order to provide a sense of the evolution of the field, this collection is arranged in chronological order. The following review of historical developments generally follows that order, although, as we move closer to the present, it gradually shifts to a more thematic organization to show how these articles are related to one another.

The Early Years

We begin our journey with "Structural Linguistics and Systematic Composition Teaching to Students of English as a Foreign Language" by Anita Pincas (1962), which represents how writing was conceived of and taught to ESL students in the late 1950s and the early 1960s. Because of the strong influence of structural linguistics and behavioral psychology—as well as the view of language teaching as a mere application of linguistics—the goal of second language instruction before the early 1960s was considered to be the mastery, mostly through pattern drills, of the sentence structure and the sound system of the target language, and writing was regarded as but a secondary representation of language (Brooks, 1960; Fries, 1945; Lado, 1964; Rivers, 1968; for a detailed analysis of the status of second language writing before the 1960s, see Matsuda, 1999, in press). For this reason, second language specialists were not prepared when, partly because of the professionalization of TESL, ESL writing instruction became part of their responsibility in the 1960s. To develop a theoretically grounded approach to the teaching of second language writing, ESL specialists attempted to apply the principles of the existing pedagogical approaches to the teaching of writing. Pincas' article represents one such attempt. In this article, she presents a view of writing that grew out of the combination of structural linguistics and behavioral psychology. A result of this combination was controlled composition—a writing exercise in which students manipulated elements of sentences in order to master correct sentence patterns. (See Erazmus, 1960, for a different pedagogical application of a similar set of principles.)

It soon became clear, however, that students who were able to produce correct sentences still produced texts that were considered by native-English-speaking readers to be incoherent. While incoherent texts were sometimes considered by writing specialists as "nothing more than the outward and visible sign of bad thinking" (Campbell, 1939, p. 179), Robert B. Kaplan, in "Cultural Thought Patterns in Inter-Cultural Education" (1966), posited that the apparent disorganization of texts written by ESL students came not from the lack of well organized thoughts but from different ways of organizing thoughts that were related to the writer's linguistic and cultural backgrounds. Although this piece has become one of the most frequently cited and reprinted—as well as most frequently criticized—articles in the history of second language writing, we felt the need to reproduce this article once again in this collection because not many people seem to have read this article closely enough to notice Kaplan's careful disclaimers or his egalitarian motives. In fact, the overwhelming popularity of this article can be attributed to the "doodles" (Kaplan, 1987, p. 9), or the diagrams of what Kaplan (1966) called the "cultural thought patterns," which have also made this article a popular target for its critics. Still, this article has contributed significantly to the development of second language writing research and pedagogy by helping to shift the focus of ESL writing beyond the sentence and by initiating a research agenda that has survived and prospered to date (e.g., Connor & Johns, 1990; Connor & Kaplan, 1987; Kaplan, 1983; Purves, 1988; for historical overviews, see Connor, 1996; Leki, 1991.)

ESL Writing Process Research

The late 1960s and the early 1970s saw the introduction of a new emphasis in composition scholarship and instruction which focused on the process of writing. Reacting against the traditional preoccupation with correcting grammar, organization and other textual features, composition specialists began to develop new pedagogical approaches that emphasized, among other things, invention, revision, and formative feedback. To understand the nature of composing, writing researchers began to conduct empirical research on writing, providing insights into how students went about the business of composing. Although, by the mid-1970s, composition and ESL had evolved into two distinct professions (Matsuda, 1999), enthusiasm for this new pedagogical and research agenda was brought to the attention of ESL specialists by Vivian Zamel. In "Teaching Composition in the ESL Classroom: What We Can Learn from Research in the Teaching of English" (1976), Zamel lamented that existing pedagogical approaches to ESL writing—which tended to rely either on frequent writing assignments or on controlled manipulation of sentence or paragraph structures—lacked an empirical basis and argued that ESL writing instruction at the advanced level can profitably incorporate insights provided by composition research. Zamel also called for second language writing research that seeks "to discover what writing is, what it involves and what differentiates the good from the bad writer" (Zamel, 1976, p. 74).

As a result, second language writing teachers began to borrow from composition specialists in developing a new, process-based approach to the teaching of ESL writers (e.g., Raimes, 1983; Spack, 1984; Spack & Sadow, 1983; Taylor, 1981; Watson, 1982; Zamel, 1982, 1983, 1987). In the early years of second language writing process research, researchers focused on how research findings on native English speakers might also be applicable to advanced second language writers (e.g., Zamel, 1976, 1983). In contrast, Ann Raimes (1985) argued that, in order to meet the unique instructional needs of ESL writers, it was necessary to examine the writing processes of less-proficient ESL writers. In "What Unskilled ESL Students Do as They Write: A Classroom Study of Composing," Raimes studied the composing processes of "unskilled" ESL writers by using methodological tools developed by composition researchers. These early studies by Raimes and others inspired a new research agenda that sought to provide an understanding of second language composing processes and other characteristics of second language writers and writing, contributing to the emergence of second language writing as a field of inquiry. (For a review of research on second language writing processes in the 1980s, see Krapels, 1990; Silva, 1993.)

Analyzing Second Language Texts

Although the growth of composing process research was sometimes described as a "paradigm shift" (Hairston, 1982; Raimes, 1983)—suggesting that the field no longer dealt with textual issues—the effort to understand the nature of second language texts, which continued to be an important issue in the classroom, was not completely abandoned. In fact, the development of process-oriented research was paralleled by advances in linguistic research, which, by the late 1970s, had begun to expand its scope to the study of written discourse features, and the advancement of discourse analysis and text linguistics (e.g., Brown & Yule, 1983; de Beaugrande, 1980; de Beaugrande & Dressler, 1981; Enkvist, 1973, 1987; van Dijk, 1972, 1980) provided theoretical and methodological tools for examining the features of second language texts. Yet, the popular and exaggerated dichotomy between process and product (Horowitz, 1986a) had created a tension among researchers of second language writing. In "Research Frontiers in Writing Analysis" (1988), Ulla Connor described advances in theoretical and methodological tools by categorizing them into sentence-based and process-centered approaches. She then argued that both types of text analysis are needed in order to develop a comprehensive theory of second language writing and that both have implications for ESL writing instruction.

The advances in the analysis of written discourse also fueled cross-linguistic and cross-cultural research in written discourse in the 1980s. In addition to the tradition of contrastive rhetoric research, which generally followed the path that was originally set by Kaplan's 1966 study, alternative traditions of cross-linguistic and cross-cultural study of discourse were developed, such as the study of discourse grammar (Longacre, 1983) and textual coherence (Halliday & Hasan, 1976;

Connor & Johns, 1990). In a series of studies on Japanese written discourse, John Hinds (1983, 1987, 1990) brought alternative traditions of research—namely, linguistic typology and discourse grammar—to the attention of second language writing researchers. In "Reader-Writer Responsibility: A New Typology" (1987), Hinds made a unique attempt to develop a typological distinction between writer-responsible and reader-responsible languages. He argued that English is a writer-responsible language, which requires the writer to avoid ambiguity, while Japanese is a reader-responsible language, which requires more interpretation by the reader, a distinction that resonates with the notion of high-context and low-context cultures (Hall, 1976). Although he based his conclusions on a limited set of data, and his claim that reading Japanese texts was more cognitively demanding than reading English texts has been challenged (McCagg, 1996), Hinds's study made a unique contribution by suggesting how the role of the writer and the reader may vary across languages and cultures, an area that continues to be underexplored.

Purposes and Contexts of ESL Writing Instruction

During the 1980s, the purpose of second language writing instruction was reconsidered at many institutions. In the early years, ESL writing courses were considered to be remedial, with the goal of preparing ESL writers for "free composition"—the production of extended written discourse—in required composition courses. As the number of ESL students increased, however, the writing needs of ESL students in various academic disciplines began to attract significant attention (e.g., Bridgeman & Carlson, 1984; Kroll, 1981; Ostler, 1980; Horowitz, 1986b). With the influence of English for Specific Purposes—an approach to the study and teaching of domain-specific English that was born in Europe—the goal of second language writing courses at many institutions began to shift from preparation for writing courses to preparation for academic writing tasks across the disciplines. As a result, English for Academic Purposes became a major emphasis, and second language writing researchers began to examine the nature and characteristics of academic written discourse as well as the context of academic discourse practices (e.g., Belcher & Braine, 1995; Johns, 1998; Swales, 1990).

At many other institutions, where the goal of first-year composition—for native speakers or nonnative speakers—was to provide humanistic education in the liberal arts tradition, the tendency to focus on the preparation of students for writing in other contexts were considered inappropriate. In a series of publications, Ruth Spack and others articulated the principles of this philosophical orientation (e.g., Gajdusek, 1988; Spack, 1984, 1988; Spack & Sadow, 1983). In "Initiating ESL Students into the Academic Discourse Community: How Far Should We Go?" (1988), Spack problematized the emphasis on disciplinary writing in first-year composition courses by proponents of Writing Across the Curriculum and English for Academic Purposes. Pointing out the limitations of the existing knowledge about writing in various disciplinary contexts, she questioned English teachers' ability to address domain-specific language issues and argued for a focus on general principles of inquiry and rhetoric rather than on disciplinary writing.

Daniel Horowitz cautioned, however, that these values—as well as values upheld by proponents of English for Academic Purposes—need to be approached critically. In "Fiction and Nonfiction in the ESL/EFL Classroom: Does the Difference Make a Difference?" (1990), Horowitz analyzed three claims about the use of literature commonly employed by ESL educators with humanistic orientations—the "training versus education" claim, the "interpretive richness" claim, and claims related to the connection between reading and writing about literature. (For further discussion of literary texts and ESL writers, see Belcher & Hirvela, 2000; Gajdusek & vanDommelen, 1993; Hirvela, in press; Spack, 1984). He concluded by making a plea that the curriculum be constructed according to an understanding of students' needs and wants. These articles by Spack, Horowitz and others have raised fundamental issues with regard to the purpose and context of second language writing instruction that continue to challenge teachers, researchers, and administrators.

The Emergence of a Field

During the 1970s and the early 1980s, second language writing research and instruction developed significantly by borrowing disciplinary and instructional practices from composition studies. Yet, insights from composition studies were not always directly applicable to the teaching of second language writers because, while second language writers are similar to first-language writers in many important ways, there also were some differences that had to be addressed in order to provide appropriate instruction. For this reason, the emphasis in second language writing research during the late 1980s and the early 1990s shifted from the application of first-language composition theory to the examination of the distinct characteristics of second language writing and writers. In "Toward and Understanding of the Distinct Nature of L2 Writing: The ESL Research and Its Implications" (1993), Tony Silva synthesized the findings of 72 reports of empirical research comparing first-language and second language writing. He identified a number of salient differences between first- and second language writing in terms of both composing processes and textual features.

With the increasing awareness of the uniqueness of its instructional and research issues, second language writing came to be recognized as a field of inquiry with its own goals, philosophical orientations, and the disciplinary infrastructure—including a journal, conferences, and several annotated bibliographies (e.g., Silva, Brice, & Reichelt, 1999; Tannacito, 1995). In "Ideology in Composition: L1 and ESL" (1992), Terry Santos considered the differences between the fields of composition studies and ESL writing, focusing on the differing emphases placed on ideological issues in the two fields. Santos's article was one of the first explicit discussions of political and ideological issues in second language writing. Although her claim that second language writing is not ideological has been questioned from a number of different perspectives (Benesch, 1993, 1994, in press; Johns, 1993; Matsuda, 1998; McKay, 1993; Severino, 1993; see also Santos, in press), this article has contributed to the field by creating a space for the discussion of ideological and political issues, which had traditionally been overlooked in the field. It also helped to raise the awareness of the interdisciplinary relationship between composition studies and second language writing, which continues to be an important issue (Atkinson & Ramanathan, 1995; Matsuda, 1998, 1999; Severino, in press; Silva, Leki & Carson, 1997).

Another relationship that has come to receive significant attention is the relationship between reading and writing. In "Reciprocal Themes in ESL Reading and Writing" (1993), Ilona Leki points out that, in spite of findings in second language reading and writing research that echo each other in many ways, teaching practices have continued to be separated. Examining the consequences of the separation on reading instruction, she argues for an integration of reading and writing instruction to promote a more social and interactive view of reading and writing. (For further discussion of the reading-writing relationship, see Carson & Leki, 1993; Belcher & Hirvela, in press).

Understanding ESL Writers

One of the central goals of the field of second language writing has been to provide an understanding of ESL writers. As a number of researchers have shown, first-language literacy education can also influence students' second language literacy experience (Liebman, 1992; Mohan & Lo, 1985). For this reason, an understanding of students' first-language literacy background can provide useful insights for the writing teacher. In "Becoming Biliterate: First Language Influences" (1992), Joan G. Carson examined three aspects of literacy acquisition in Japan and China, including the social context of schooling, cognitive considerations of the written code, and pedagogical practices. Although care must be taken to guard against the danger of overgeneralization (Kubota, 1999; Spack, 1997; Susser, 1998)—a danger which is inherent in any attempt to describe cultural practices—Carson's article provides a useful starting point for further inquiries that seek to generate a richer understanding of students' literacy backgrounds.

In recent years, an increasing number of studies have explored the writing experience of ESL students in academic settings using qualitative research methodologies (Casanave, 1995; Currie, 1993, in press; Leki, 1995, in press; Prior, 1995; Spack, 1997). While these studies provide valuable insights into the characteristics and experiences of second language writers, the understanding of second language writers is still far from adequate, especially because the ESL student population in institutions of higher education across North America is becoming increasingly diverse. Second language writers now include a significant number of refugees and permanent residents as well as naturalized and native-born citizens of the United States and Canada. (For further discussion on the issue of the increasing diversity of the ESL student population, see Harklau, Losey, & Siegal, 1999; Severino, Guerra & Butler, 1997; Valdés, 1992.)

Interacting with Second language Texts

Since the introduction of the notion of writing process, formative feedback has been one of the key elements of both first- and second language writing instruction, and efforts have been made to examine the use and effects of feedback—both teacher feedback (e.g., Ferris, 1995; 1999b; Severino, 1993) and peer feedback (e.g., Mangelsdorf, 1992; Nelson & Murphy, 1992, 1993). However, some researchers have raised concerns about the use of peer feedback for second language writers (Carson & Nelson, 1994, 1996; Zhang, 1995, 1999). More recently, the efficacy of grammar correction has been questioned (Truscott, 1996), generating a renewed interest in the issue of whether, when and how grammar issues should be addressed in teaching ESL writers (Byrd & Reid, 1998; Ferris, 1999a; Truscott, 1999).

Furthermore, with an increasing awareness of the issues of authority and power in the classroom, some teachers have come to struggle with the possibility of appropriating student texts. In "Responding to ESL Students' Texts: The Myths of Appropriation" (1994), Joy Reid discusses the issue of appropriation in the context of ESL writing instruction. After reviewing the origin of what she calls the "myth of appropriation," she resituates the issue of teacher feedback in the social context of academic writing instruction and considers how teachers may help ESL students without appropriating their texts.

Another issue that arises in working with second language texts is assessment, which can have a significant impact on students' academic career and beyond. In "Interpreting an English Competency Examination: The Frustration of an ESL Science Student" (1991), Ann M. Johns provides a detailed look at the implications of writing assessment practices. In this article, she presents a case study of a Vietnamese ESL student who, despite his success in courses in his major, was enrolled in a "remedial" composition class for the third time because he was not able to pass the English competency examination. She concludes by posing a series of questions that have significant implications for designing writing exams that are appropriate for the student population that is becoming increasingly diverse both linguistically and culturally.

How, then, can writing assessment be made more equitable for students from various linguistic and cultural backgrounds? Liz Hamp-Lyons and Barbara Kroll (1996) provide an answer to this important question. In "Issues in ESL Writing Assessment: An Overview," they discuss various factors that influence the complex issue of writing assessment design and suggest that careful attention to these factors are essential in developing assessment practices that are appropriate for the linguistically and culturally diverse student population. (For further discussion of ESL writing assessment issues, see also Byrd & Nelson, 1995; Hamp-Lyons, 1991, in press; Haswell, 1998; Kroll, 1998.)

Toward a General Theory of Second language Writing

Second language writing research and pedagogy were limited because they tended to focus on one or two aspects of writing—for example, contrastive rhetoric research tended to focus on the text; process research was concerned primarily with the writer; English for academic purposes privileged the reader, and so on (Silva, 1990). The need for a theory of second language writing that considers various elements of second language writing—including the writer, the reader, the text, and the context as well as the interaction of these elements—was increasingly felt, and some researchers began to develop integrative theories of second language writing (e.g., Grabe & Kaplan, 1996; Matsuda, 1997).

In "Contrastive Rhetoric in Context: A Dynamic Model of L2 Writing" (1997), Paul Kei Matsuda identifies what he calls the *static model* of second language writing that underlies existing pedagogical applications of contrastive rhetoric research. He then proposes a *dynamic model* of second language writing, which articulates how second language writers' linguistic, cultural and educational backgrounds may be negotiated in the process of writing. (See Zamel, 1997, for an alternative conception of the negotiation of students' background in second language writing.) Matsuda's theoretical model also provides a conceptual framework for research that examines how second language writers may negotiate their backgrounds through the use of textual features in the process of writing.

Conclusion

What we have presented here is a brief historical sketch of developments in the field of second language writing since 1960. We hope this introduction provides a sense of how the field has evolved over the last four decades. We also hope that the readers will continue to deepen their understanding of second langauage writing and writers by reading the primary scholarship in the field—both here and elsewhere.

Bibliography

Atkinson, D., & Ramanathan, V. (1995). Cultures of writing: An ethnographic comparison of L1 and L2 university writing/language programs. *TESOL Quarterly, 29,* 539-568.

Belcher, D., & Braine, G. (Eds.). (1995). *Academic writing in a second language: Essays on research & pedagogy.* Norwood, NJ: Ablex.

Belcher, D., & Hirvela, A. (2000). Literature in the teaching of L2 composition. *Journal of Second Language Writing, 9,* 21-39.

Belcher, D., & Hirvela, A. (Eds.). (in press). *The reading/writing connection: Perspectives on second language literacies.* Ann Arbor: University of Michigan Press.

Benesch, S. (1993). ESL, ideology, and the politics of pragmatism. *TESOL Quarterly, 27,* 705-717.

Benesch, S. (1994). The author responds. *TESOL Quarterly, 28,* 623-624.

Benesch, S. (in press). Critical pragmatism: A politics of L2 composition. In T. Silva & P. K. Matsuda (Eds.), *On second language writing.* Mahwah, NJ: Erlbaum.

Bridgeman, B., & Carlson, S.B. (1984). Survey of academic writing tasks. *Written Communication, 1,* 247-280.

Brooks, N. (1960). *Language and language learning: Theory and practice.* New York: Harcourt, Brace and Company.

Brown, G., & Yule, G. (1983). *Discourse analysis.* New York: Cambridge University Press.

Byrd, P., & Nelson, G. (1995). NNS performance on writing proficiency exams: Focus on students who failed. *Journal of Second Language Writing, 4*, 273-285.

Campbell, O. J. (1939). The failure of freshman English. *English Journal: College Edition, 28*, 177-185.

Carson, J. G. (1992). Becoming biliterate: First language influences. *Journal of Second Language Writing, 1*, 37-60.

Carson, J., & Nelson, G. (1994). Writing groups: Cross-cultural issues. *Journal of Second Language Writing, 3*, 17-30.

Carson, J., & Nelson, G. (1996). Chinese students 'perceptions of ESL peer response group interaction. *Journal of Second Language Writing, 5*, 1-19.

Casanave, C. P. (1995). Local interactions: Constructing contexts for composing in a graduate sociology program. In D. Belcher & G. Braine (Eds.), *Academic writing in a second language: Essays on research & pedagogy* (pp. 83-110). Norwood, NJ: Ablex.

Connor, U. (1966). *Contrastive rhetoric: Cross-cultural aspects of second language writing*. New York: Cambridge University Press.

Connor, U. (1988). Research frontiers in writing analysis. *TESOL Quarterly, 21*, 677-696.

Connor, U., & Johns, A. (Eds.). (1990). *Coherence in writing: Research and pedagogical perspectives*. Alexandria, VA: TESOL.

Connor, U., & Kaplan, R. B. (Eds.). (1987). *Writing across languages: Analysis of L2 texts*. Reading, MA: Addison-Wesley.

Currie, P. (1993). Entering a disciplinary community: Conceptual activities required to write for one introductory university course. *Journal of Second Language Writing, 2*, 101-117.

Currie, P. (in press). On the question of power and control. In T. Silva & P. K. Matsuda (Eds.), *On second language writing*. Mahwah, NJ: Erlbaum.

Davis, T. (1998). *Open doors*. New York: Institute of International Education.

de Beaugrande, R. (1980). Text, discourse, and process: Toward a multi-disciplinary science of texts. Norwood, NJ: Ablex.

de Beaugrande, R., & Dressler, W. (1981). *Introduction to text linguistics*. London: Longman.

Enkvist, N. E. (1973). *Linguistic Stylistics*. The Hague: Mouton.

Enkvist, N. E. (1987). Text linguistics for the applier: An orientation. In U. Connor & R. B. Kaplan (Eds.), *Writing across languages: Analysis of L2 text* (pp. 23-43). Reading, MA: Addison-Wesley.

Erazmus, E. T. (1960). Second language composition teaching at the intermediate level. *Language Learning, 10*, 25-31.

Ferris, D. R. (1995). Student reactions to teacher response in multiple-draft composition classrooms. *TESOL Quarterly, 29*, 33-53.

Ferris, D. (1999a). The case for grammar correction in L2 writing classes: A response to Truscott (1996). *Journal of Second Language Writing, 8*, 1-11.

Ferris, D. R. (1999b). One size does not fit all: Response and revision issues for immigrant student writers. In L. Harklau, K. M. Losey, & M. Siegal (Eds.), *Generation 1.5 meets college composition: Issues in the teaching of writing to U.S.-educated learners of ESL* (pp. 143-157). Mahwah, NJ: Erlbaum.

Fries, C. C. (1945). *Teaching and learning English as a foreign language*. Ann Arbor: University of Michigan Press.

Gajdusek, L. (1988). Toward wider use of literature in ESL: Why and how. *TESOL Quarterly, 22*, 227-257.

Gajdusek, L., & vanDommelen, D. (1993). Literature and critical thinking in the composition classroom. In J. Carson & I. Leki (Eds.), *Reading in the composition classroom: Second language perspectives* (pp. 197-217). Boston: Heinle & Heinle.

Grabe, W., & Kaplan, R. B. (1996). *Theory and practice of writing: An applied linguistic perspective*. London: Longman.

Hairston, M. (1982). The winds of change: Thomas Kuhn and the revolution in the teaching of writing. *College Composition and Communication, 33*, 76-88.

Hall, E. T. (1976). *Beyond culture*. Garden City, NY: Anchor Books.

Halliday, M. A. K., & Hasan, R. (1976). *Cohesion in English*. London: Longman.

Hamp-Lyons, L. (Ed.). (1991). *Assessing second language writing in academic contexts*. Norwood, NJ: Ablex.

Hamp-Lyons, L. (in press). Fourth generation writing assessment. In T. Silva & P. K. Matsuda (Eds.), *On second language writing*. Mahwah, NJ: Erlbaum.

Hamp-Lyons, L., & Kroll, B. (1996). Issues in ESL writing assessment: An overview. *College ESL, 6*, 52-72.

Harklau, L., Losey, K. M., & Siegal, M. (Eds.). (1999). *Generation 1.5 meets college composition: Issues in the teaching of writing to U.S.-educated learners of ESL*. Mahwah, NJ: Erlbaum.

Haswell, R. H. (1998). Searching for Kiyoko: Bettering mandatory ESL writing placement. *Journal of Second Language Writing, 7,* 133-174.

Hinds, J. (1983). Contrastive rhetoric: Japanese and English. *Text, 3,* 183-195.

Hinds, J. (1987). Reader-writer responsibility: A new typology. In U. Connor & R.B. Kaplan (Eds.), *Writing across languages: Analysis of L2 text* (pp. 141-152). Reading, MA: Addison-Wesley.

Hinds, J. (1990). Inductive, deductive, quasi-inductive: Expository writing in Japanese, Korean, Chinese, and Thai. In U. Connor & A. M. Johns (Eds.), *Coherence in writing: Research and pedagogical perspectives* (pp. 89-260). Alexandria, VA: TESOL.

Hirvela, A. (in press). Connecting reading and writing through literature. In D. Belcher & A. Hirvela (Eds.), *The reading/writing connection: Perspectives on second language literacies.* Ann Arbor: University of Michigan Press.

Horowitz, D. (1986a). Process, not product: Less than meets the eye. *TESOL Quarterly, 20,* 141-144.

Horowitz, D. (1986b). What professors actually require: Academic tasks for the ESL classroom, *TESOL Quarterly, 20,* 445-462.

Horowitz, D. (1990). Fiction and nonfiction in the ESL/EFL classroom: Does the difference make a difference? *English for Specific Purposes, 9,* 161-168.

Johns, A. M. (1993). Too much on our plates: A response to Terry Santos "'Ideology in composition: L1 and ESL." *Journal of Second Language Writing, 2,* 83-88.

Johns, A. M. (1991). Interpreting an English competency examination: The frustrations of an ESL science student. *Written Communication, 8,* 379-401

Kaplan, R. B. (1966). Cultural thought patterns in inter-cultural education. *Language Learning, 16,* 1-20.

Kaplan, R. B., Jones, R. L., & Tucker, G. R. (Eds.). (1983). *Annual Review of Applied Linguistics (Vol. 3).* Rowley, MA: Newbury House.

Kaplan, R. B. (1987). Cultural thought patterns revisited. In U. Connor & R. B. Kaplan (Eds.), *Writing across languages: Analysis of L2 texts* (pp. 9-21). Reading, MA: Addison-Wesley.

Krapels, A. R. (1990). An overview of second language writing process research. In B. Kroll (Ed.), *Second language writing: Research insights for the classroom* (pp. 37-56). New York: Cambridge University Press.

Kroll, B. (1981). A survey of the writing needs of foreign and American college freshmen. *ELT Journal, 33,* 219-227.

Kroll, B. (1998). Assessing writing abilities. *Annual Review of Applied Linguistics, 18,* 219-240.

Kubota, R. (1999). Japanese culture constructed by discourse: Implications for applied linguistics research and ELT. *TESOL Quarterly, 33,* 9-35.

Lado, R. (1964). *Language teaching: A scientific approach.* New York: McGraw-Hill.

Leki, I. (1991). Twenty-five years of contrastive rhetoric: Text analysis and writing pedagogies. *TESOL Quarterly, 25,* 123-143.

Leki, I. (1993). Reciprocal themes in ESL reading and writing. In J. Carson & I. Leki (Eds.), *Reading in the composition classroom: Second language perspectives* (pp. 9-32). Boston: Heinle & Heinle.

Leki, I. (1995). Coping strategies of ESL students in writing tasks across the curriculum. *TESOL Quarterly, 29,* 235–260.

Leki, I. (in press). Hearing voices: L2 students' academic writing experiences in English medium settings. In T. Silva & P. K. Matsuda (Eds.), *On second language writing.* Mahwah, NJ: Erlbaum.

Liebman, J. D. (1992). Toward a new contrastive rhetoric: Differences between Arabic and Japanese rhetorical instruction. *Journal of Second Language Writing, 1,* 141-165.

Longacre, R. E. (1983). *The grammar of discourse.* New York: Plenum Press.

Mangelsdorf, K. (1992). Peer reviews in the ESL composition classroom: What do the students think. *ELT Journal, 46,* 274-84.

Matsuda, P. K. (1997). Contrastive rhetoric in context: A dynamic model of L2 writing. *Journal of Second Language Writing, 6,* 45-60.

Matsuda, P. K. (1998). Situating ESL writing in a cross-disciplinary context. *Written Communication, 15,* 99-121.

Matsuda, P. K. (1999). Composition studies and ESL writing: A disciplinary division of labor. *College Composition and Communication, 50,* 142-164.

Matsuda, P. K. (in press). Reexamining audiolingualism: On the genesis of reading and writing in L2 studies. In D. Belcher & A. Hirvela (Eds.), *The reading/writing connection: Perspectives on second language literacies.* Ann Arbor: University of Michigan Press.

McCagg, P. (1996). If you can lead a horse to water, you don't have to make it drink: Some comments on reader and writer responsibilities. *Multilingua, 15,* 239-256.

McKay, S. L. (1993). Examining L2 composition ideology: A look at literacy education. *Journal of Second Language Writing, 2,* 65-81.

Mohan, B. A., & Lo, W. A.-Y. (1985). Academic writing and Chinese students: Transfer and developmental factors. *TESOL Quarterly, 19,* 515-534.

Nelson, G. L., & Murphy, J. M. (1992). An L2 writing group: Task and social dimensions. *Journal of Second Language Writing, 1,* 171-193.

Nelson, G., & Murphy, J. (1993). Peer response groups: Do L2 writers use peer comments in revising their drafts? *TESOL Quarterly, 27,* 135-141.

Ostler, S. E. (1980). A survey of the academic needs for advanced ESL. *TESOL Quarterly, 14,* 489-502.

Pincas, A. (1962). Structural linguistics and systematic composition teaching to students of English as a foreign language. *Language Learning, 7,* 185-194.

Prior, P. (1995). Redefining the task: An ethnographic examination of writing and response in graduate seminars. In D. Belcher & G. Braine (Eds.), *Academic writing in a second language: Essays on research & pedagogy* (pp. 47-82). Norwood, NJ: Ablex.

Purves, A. C. (Ed.). (1988). *Writing across languages and cultures: Issues in contrastive rhetoric.* Newbury Park, CA: Sage.

Raimes, A. (1983). Tradition and revolution in ESL teaching. *TESOL Quarterly, 17,* 535-552.

Raimes, A. (1985). What unskilled ESL students do as they write: A classroom study of composing. *TESOL Quarterly, 19,* 229-258.

Reid, J. (1994). Responding to ESL students 'texts: The myths of appropriation. *TESOL Quarterly, 28,* 273-292.

Rivers, W. (1968). *Teaching foreign language skills.* Chicago: University of Chicago Press.

Roy, A. (1988). ESL concerns for writing program administrators: Problems and policies. *Writing Program Administration, 11,*17-28.

Santos, T. (1992). Ideology in composition: L1 and ESL. *Journal of Second Language Writing, 1,* 1-15.

Santos, T. (1993). Response to Ann Johns. *Journal of Second Language Writing, 2,* 89-90.

Santos, T. (in press). The place of politics in second language writing. In T. Silva & P. K. Matsuda (Eds.), *On second language writing.* Mahwah, NJ: Erlbaum.

Severino, C. (1993). The sociopolitical implications of response to second language and second dialect writing. *Journal of Second language Writing, 2,* 181-201.

Severino, C. (in press). Dangerous liaisons: Problems of representation and articulation. In T. Silva & P. K. Matsuda (Eds.), *On second language writing.* Mahwah, NJ: Erlbaum.

Severino, C., Guerra, J. C., & Butler, J. E. (Eds.). (1997). *Writing in multicultural settings.* New York: Modern Language Association.

Silva, T. (1990). Second language composition instruction: Developments, issues and directions in ESL. In B. Kroll (Ed.), *Second language writing: Research insights for the classroom* (pp. 11-23). New York: Cambridge University Press.

Silva, T. (1993). Toward an understanding of the distinct nature of L2 writing: The ESL research and its implications. *TESOL Quarterly, 27,* 657-675.

Silva, T., Brice, C., & Reichelt, M. (1999). *An annotated bibliography of scholarship in second language writing, 1993-1997.* Stamford, CT: Ablex.

Silva, T., Leki, I., & Carson, J. (1997). Broadening the perspective of mainstream composition studies: Some thoughts from the disciplinary margins. *Written Communication, 14,* 398-428.

Spack, R. (1984). Invention strategies and the ESL college composition student. *TESOL Quarterly, 18,* 649-670.

Spack, R. (1988). Initiating ESL students into the academic discourse community: How far should we go? *TESOL Quarterly, 22,* 29-51.

Spack, R. (1997). The rhetorical construction of multilingual students. *TESOL Quarterly, 31,* 765-774.

Spack, R., & Sadow, C. (1983). Student-teacher working journals in ESL freshman composition. *TESOL Quarterly, 17,* 575-593.

Susser, B. (1998). EFL's othering of Japan: Orientalism in English language teaching. *JALT Journal, 20,* 49-82.

Tannacito, D. J. (1995). *A guide to writing English as a second or foreign language: An annotated bibliography of research and pedagogy.* Alexandria, VA: TESOL.

Taylor, B. (1981). Content and written form: A two-way street. *TESOL Quarterly, 15,* 5-13.

Truscott, J. (1996).The case against grammar correction in L2 writing classes. *Language Learning, 46,* 327-369.

Truscott, J. (1999). The case for "The case against grammar correction in L2 writing classes": A response to Ferris. *Journal of Second Language Writing, 8,* 111-122.

Valdés, G. (1992). Bilingual minorities and language issus in writing: Toward professionwide responses to a new challenge. *Written Communication, 9,* 85-136.

van Dijik, T. A. (1972). *Some aspects of text grammars: A study of theoretical linguistics and poetics.* The Hague: Mouton.

van Dijik, T. A. (1980). *Macrostructures: An interdisciplinary study of global structures in discourse, inter-action, and cognition.* Hillsdale, NJ: Erlbaum.

Watson, C. B. (1982). The use and abuse of models in the ESL writing class. *TESOL Quarterly, 16,* 5-14.

Zamel, V. (1976). Teaching composition in the ESL classroom: What we can learn from research in the teaching of English. *TESOL Quarterly, 10,* 67-76.

Zamel, V. (1982). Writing: The process of discovering meaning. *TESOL Quarterly, 16,* 195-209.

Zamel, V. (1983). The composing process of advanced ESL students: Six case studies. *TESOL Quarterly, 17,* 165-187.

Zamel, V. (1987). Recent research on writing pedagogy. *TESOL Quarterly, 22,* 520-524.

Zamel, V. (1997). Toward a model of transculturation. *TESOL Quarterly, 31,* 341-352.

Zhang, S. (1995). Reexamining the affective advantage of peer feedback in the ESL writing class. *Journal of Second Language Writing, 4,* 209-222.

Zhang, S. (1999). Thoughts on some recent evidence concerning the affective advantage of peer feedback. *Journal of Second Language Writing, 8,* 321-326.

Structural Linguistics and Systematic Composition Teaching to Students of English as A Foreign Language
by Anita Pincas

The Problem

The teaching of composition to foreign language learners has not yet been as thoroughly overhauled as have other language teaching techniques in the last twenty years. Although new teaching methods, based on the findings of structural linguistics, recognise the students' need for systematic and rigidly controlled teaching of pronunciation and grammar, they have not yet recognised the equal need in the field of composition teaching. The belief that grammar and guided reading are sufficient preparation for "free composition" is widespread and quite wrong. For the ability to write well in the *English* way can no more be picked up casually than can correct pronunciation or correct grammar.

The assumptions underlying modern second language teaching theories require an emphasis on controlled habit-formation. For the foreign learner, any free, random, hit-or-miss activity is eliminated wherever possible, so that errors arising from the native-to-target language transfer can be avoided. The learner is deprived of any opportunity to use his own automatic native language habits in the target language. He is made to mimic and repeat in drills the phonetic and syntactic patterns of the target language. He is not allowed to "create" in the target language at all.

Since free composition[1] relies on inventiveness, on creativeness, it is in direct opposition to the expressed ideals of scientific habit-forming teaching methods which strive to prevent error from occurring. One is therefore astonished to find that

Reprinted from *Language Learning, 12*(3), Pincas, A., Structural linguistics and systematic composition teaching to students of English as a foreign language, 1962, with permission from Blackwell Publishers.

writers putting forward the above premises, fall back on naive traditional views when they think about composition writing.[2] The reverence for original creativeness in writing dies hard. People find it difficult to accept the fact that the use of language is the manipulation of fixed patterns; that these patterns are learned by imitation; and that not until they have been learned can originality occur in the manipulation of the patterns or in the choice of variables within the patterns.

Suggestions

For the teaching of these patterns, systematic training of a special kind is necessary. Consideration of familiar techniques has led me to one important solution to the problem. This is the concept of multiple substitution, which I wish to expound later in this article. It is a method of controlled habit forming which can be used in a composition class to provide organised systematic imitation of models. It is neither mere substitution of items in a frame nor completely free sentence creation. It lends itself to careful programming of the kind used in teaching machines. The students can be taken from one stage to the next, having been led to give only correct responses at each stage. They are led gradually to more and more complex and difficult work, and in all their practice desirable language habits are built up. Finally, they can write "free compositions". Multiple Substitution fits into an organised scheme of composition training, which should include:

1. Practice in *recognition* of the different vocabulary and sentence constructions used in writing and in speech. For example, whereas "a lot of" is common in speech, "much" and "many" are still preferred in writing.[3]
2. Practice in *production* contrasting the usages of speech and writing. Here and in No. 4 below it is important that only when the students' recognition of the various features of English writing is fairly reliable should he begin to reproduce. There is every reason why recognition practice of this type should be as systematic and thorough as that which is given in aural-oral drills, and why, when production is reached, there should be as much avoidance of error as possible.[4]
3. Practice in *recognition* of different styles of writing for different purposes.
4. Systematic and controlled *production* practice of these different styles. This practice should be given with multiple substitution.

Practice of type 1 is fairly simple to organise. Short stories containing narration and dialogue will present contrasts of the kind to be taught. They can be drawn to the students' attention, the students can practise finding them, and so on. If no suitable stories are available, the teacher can use whatever material he has to demonstrate how narration is converted to dialogue and *vice versa*.

Practice of type 2 is given by allowing the student to make such conversions himself. It is hardly necessary to suggest that a conversion from narration to dialogue is best done orally, while a conversion from dialogue to narration is best done in writing.

Practice of type 3 is given by presenting students with contrasting styles, (for example persuasive versus descriptive, or business jargon versus personal writing, etc.) and teaching them to recognise the different styles.

No. 4 is composition writing itself. Apart from specific difficulties of usage, the general problem which most frequently confronts a teacher is that of students' weakness in spontaneous sentence building. Often, students who are able to handle complex as well as simple sentence patterns in set (either oral or written) exercises, just do not produce them spontaneously as the need arises. Their compositions may consist of monotonous sequences of simple sentences, or of different sentence types sequenced in a "jerky" or "clumsy", i.e. un-English, way. The teacher's task is to foster the ability to produce complex structures spontaneously, and, later, to teach the sequencing of sentence types in a smooth, i.e. English, flow.

I do not know of any text-book that quite solves this problem or the problems of usage for foreign learners. There are many exercises which appear to offer training in spontaneous sentence creation and the use of complex sentence structures. Exercises like "Answer the following questions in a complete English sentence.", "Use the following words in sentences.", "Express the sense of the following in your own words," and "State the meaning of the following words." But they are quite uncontrolled and leave wide scope for error. Transformation and recall exercises certainly increase the student's familiarity with sentence structures, but do not allow sentence creation. Further, these drills usually do not provide practice with sequenced sentences.[5]

A good compromise between freedom and control is in the exercises used by V. French Allen in *People in Fact and Fiction*[6] ("Pronounce Pattern Sentence No.1. ... Construct other sentences in this pattern. . . . Include such combinations as. . . .") although this practice is still with isolated sentences. Imitation is the basis of this exercise. The belief that one way to write well is to imitate suitable models is hardly a new one.[7] But if imitation can be systematized, i.e. controlled, this would be an important advance. It can be found in a combination of imitation and substitution frame technique. The substitution method can make the imitation systematic, and the imitation of a model adds the element of creativity to otherwise mechanical substitution practice.

In texts like French, *English in Tables*,[8] using substitution frames for foreign learners, students are required to make substitutions usually at one, infrequently at two or more, positions in a frame. Such drills usually rely on the teacher, or the text, to provide the items to be substituted in the frame, and to indicate the spots at which they are to be substituted. Roberts, *Patterns of English*,[9] goes much further towards sentence creation, but relies very heavily on the native speaker's ability to handle basic structures and to "feel" what substitutions are possible within a given frame. Roberts is justified in expecting the students to enjoy the puzzles of sentence frames given entirely in symbols, and to be able to make correct substitutions for the symbols. Foreign learners need more guidance (often especially geared to the difficulties arising from their native language background), preferably without the added confusion of symbols. They need a compromise between Roberts and the usual type of substitution drills. And this compromise is multiple substitution:

Students should progress from substitution at one or two positions in a frame, to substitution at many, even all, positions.

Students need to become familiar with the concept (if not the term) of the tagmeme[10] or the principle of variables within a fixed pattern. If they are being trained with substitution tables in their grammar lessons they will understand the fact that there are positions and functions (or spots) in a sentence pattern and that there is a class of mutually substitutable items for each spot. Students who are trained by traditional methods with traditional classifications are not, of course, excluded from this teaching.

When the concept is understood, it can be used to teach the use of words and constructions appropriate to different topics and types of writing. Then it can be broadened to include ever wider categories. The variables can be words, or clauses, sentences, paragraphs, or literary devices in essays and stories. In each case the frame is broadened and the items to be substituted change in number and complexity. The students have to learn to abstract the pattern from a given *concretum* (whether sentence, paragraph, essay, etc.) and to distinguish between it and the variables which can find a place in it. A composition course most profitably begins, however, with multiple substitution of words in sentences, at first isolated and then in paragraphs.

Teaching Composition

Multiple substitution practice should not be begun before the students are accurate in recognising different patterns and isolating spots where variables can be substituted. The value of the exercise lies in the production of an accurate structural counterpart of the original. It should, however, be treated as practice in *making new sentences* on given models, not as mechanical substitution.

The data which is given to the student is the model sentence, and a list of words which are to be used in writing the new sentence. At first, the positions at which variations on the model are to occur should be clearly indicated. In the early stages, also, the list of words to be used in the new sentence should be given in the order in which they will appear there. In short, everything should be done to ensure that the students will write a correct sentence when they make their own construction following the model. There is little point in complex tricks even for very advanced students. The aim of the exercise is to elicit correct sentences, to give practice in the writing of correct sentences.[11]

For example, if the model is:

(a) The *boys* in the *class speak English correctly.*

the list of words for the new sentence might be:

(b) players; team; play; football; roughly.

If this exercise is given to a class with the appropriate background there should be little difficulty in producing:

(c) The players in the team play football roughly.

After a sufficient amount of practice with other lists of words, the exercise should be made more difficult. There are two main ways of doing this.

(1) Scramble the word list. The students must then try various substitutions until they find the right one. They should not be allowed to write anything until they have the complete sentence in mind. The teacher may, of course, wish to drill the exercise orally before letting the students write at all. Or, while he is dealing with separate sentences, he may wish to make the exercise entirely oral. Because of the number of substitutions he will need the aid of the blackboard or of stencilled handouts to the students.

(2) Give the list of new items without the morphemic changes necessary for the sentence. List (b) would be given as:

(d) football; team; player; rough; play.

When the students show sufficient speed and accuracy in the above exercises, the difficulty and student initiative are increased by allowing the students to find their own list of substitution items. This advance should, however, be used with caution. It can waste a great deal of time as students sit with their minds blank, waiting for inspiration. The students should always be given an appropriate topic to guide their train of thought.[12] And the teacher is advised to come to the lesson with adequate preparation, since not even a native speaker can always quickly find topics which lend themselves to specific types of sentence construction. The teacher's burden of preparation is balanced by the negligible marking involved, since there is so little scope for error.[13]

With more complex sentence structures, the procedure is almost the same as for simple sentences like the above. For example, a teacher may have a class which is able to write correctly sentences of the form:

(e) The man who came yesterday was angry.

and (f) The man was angry because you deceived him.
but has difficulty in constructing a sentence like:

(g) *The man* who *came yesterday* was angry *because you deceived him.*

The procedure is to give substitution drill orally, making a variety of substitutions in turn at the italicised spots, substituting a word group at a time. This familiarises the students with the sentence structure. Then the students practise multiple substitution from word lists like:

(h) client; phoned; today; worried; insulted.

or (i) today; insult; client; phone; worry.

The next step is to suggest only the new topics, e.g. "an angry teacher", "a generous friend", etc., and to let the students find the appropriate words for substitution.

Practice of model (g) can be associated with teaching another type, perhaps:

(j) The book which made him famous was successful because it dealt with modern problems.

When both have been practised individually, a short passage using them both and one or two others the students know can be constructed. Multiple substitution is then made in the passage as a whole. The students are given, first, word lists, then simply topics or outlines of subjects suitable for the passage.

Questions

There are two interrelated problems facing the teacher in the organisation of multiple substitution exercises. One is to decide which aspects of a structure are to be brought to the class' attention for recognition and copying in any particular exercise. The other is to decide what items are acceptable as substitutions in any particular position in a frame. In sentences (g) and (j) above "who came yesterday" and "which made him famous" are structurally equivalent in their relation to the surrounding sentence. But they are different in their internal structure. The question is whether the teacher should accept any sort of internal structure here, so long as the student produces an acceptable adjectival clause. A similar problem might have arisen with model sentence (a) above. Would a substitution of a phrase line "in Indonesia" or "in January" be accepted in the position "in the class"? The answer to these questions must be that it depends on what the teacher wishes to teach and what he has taught in the past. If he is interested in the construction exactly as it stands in the model, and would anticipate difficulties irrelevant to and distracting from his lesson if he allowed the introduction of another type, then strict adherence to the model should be insisted upon. The important point is that the students should at all times be quite clearly told what they are expected to give as a substitution, and the teacher must carefully arrange his own word lists so as not to infringe his own instructions.

Further Development

As the course progresses, emphasis will shift from the substitution of words in sentences of different patterns to the substitution of sentences in paragraphs of different types, and finally to the substitution of different literary devices in whole essays, stories, etc. This is not to imply that less advanced students are at one end of the hierarchy, practising only multiple substitution of word units, while the most advanced students are at the other end, practising only stylistic and literary devices. Differences of style can be taught at a quite elementary level. And there are, of course, levels of difficulty within each type of substitution in the hierarchy. Thus, there are, in terms of vocabulary, difficulty grades in word and phrase substitution exercises, and in terms of morphology and sentence patterns, difficulty grades in clause or sentence substitutions.

The following is an example of multiple substitution exercise in which both the substitution of sentence types in a paragraph, and the use of two different literary devices are practised. In (a) the subject is stated at the start and described or developed in the rest of the paragraph. In (b) the sentences gradually build up to a climactic statement of the subject in the last sentence. Each is appropriate for a different purpose.

(a) My sister is a very generous girl. She often gives money to friends who have less than she has. In fact she is a very expensive daughter for her parents because she hardly keeps anything they give her.

(b) I earn £16 a week and support my wife and two children with this meagre income. We pay £3 a week for rent, while food and clothing, without any luxuries, cost about £9 a week. We need another £2 for fares and entertainments, etc. This leaves £2 which is all swallowed by the Taxation Department. My savings amount to the depressing sum of £0. The taxes in this country are exorbitant!

The pattern of (a) can be analysed:

1. Simple sentence—statement of subject.
2. Complex sentence (principal clause + adjectival clause)—illustration of subject.
3. Complex sentence (principal clause + adverbial clause of reason—consequence of subject.

In (b) the pattern is:

1. Compound sentence with *and*—statement of fact supporting subject.
2. Compound sentence with *while*—support of subject.
3. Simple sentence—further support of subject.
4. Complex sentence (principal clause + adjectival clause)—further support of and first reference to subject.
5. Simple sentence—further support of subject, consequence of sentences 1, 2, 3 and 4.
6. Simple sentence—statement of subject.

Following such an analysis students can be given a list of new sentences, on the above models, but presented in a different order. After practice in putting such sentences together to form paragraphs like the model, students can be given word substitution drills from lists like:

teacher; kind; man; he; encouragement; have; less ability than others; he; popular; person; in my school; he; never; punishes; anyone; who makes mistakes.

As in previous examples, the words can be scrambled, endings left off. When the students have become quite familiar with the structure, they can be given suitable topics and asked to make paragraphs containing the same over-all sentence patterns and arrangement, without necessarily giving word-for-word imitations.

As well as the over-all pattern, the teacher might wish to point out the difference in the vocabulary of the two paragraphs. Whereas the first is quite colourless, the second is in somewhat emotive prose *(meagre, luxuries, swallowed, depressing, exorbitant)*. And in making substitutions, students can be asked to substitute a colourless word for a colourless original, and an emotive word for an emotive original. After some time, the repeated associations of given structures and words with certain types of context will develop the so-called "feeling for style", and develop the students' ability to make correct choices independently.[14]

From the paragraph, students can move on to copying models of whole essays (expository, persuasive, auto-biographical etc.) or narratives, or letters, or character sketches, etc. And in each case there will be different types of vocabulary and structure and literary devices to abstract from the *concretum* and bear in mind when copying. Some examples of the last might be: in an essay—the organisation of the subject with special reference to main facts and illustrations; in a narrative—the point of view, the withholding of information, the alternation of narration with dialogue, the time shifts, etc.; in a character sketch—the development from externals to internals or *vice versa*; and so on. Sometimes the teacher might wish the students to copy for practice in choice of vocabulary, sometimes for practice in the use of sentences, or of paragraph types, or literary devices, sometimes for practice in all of these.[15]

A final commendation which should be made of the multiple substitution technique is that it can go far towards relieving the tedium which many learners find in even the briskest "habit-forming" drills. An ideal exercise is one which poses a problem for the learner in such a way that he feels stimulated and yet is led to the correct solution. Ordinary substitution frame drills, question-and-answer drills and others of the modern type, are certainly superior to traditional translation exercises and free composition in eliciting correct language responses. But whether they pose as interesting a challenge to the learner is an important question. Multiple substitution in composition training seems to fulfil both requirements.

Notes

1. Encouraging the "invention and consequent learning of unacceptable forms"—Nelson Brooks, *Language and Language Learning* (1960) Harcourt Brace & Co., New York, p. 197.
2. A recent example is the article by E. T. Erazmus—"Second Language Composition Teaching at the Intermediate Level" *Language Learning X* (1960) 25ff.
3. The usages of speech and writing are too frequently confused in both old and new books. J. H. McGillivray's *Life with the Taylors* (1959) American Book Co., New York, furnishes many examples. Utterances like "It seems to me that he was a baby only yesterday" and the reply to this: "The time goes fast, Mother," are presented as colloquial idiom.
4. And, as every teacher knows, it is only too frequently that a student makes in his composition the very errors against which drills have just previously been aimed and which the student performed correctly.

5. See L. R. H. Chapman, *English Composition for Beginners* (1959) Longmans Green & Co., for examples of completion and recall exercises. E. W. Stevick, *Supplementary Lessons in American English for Advanced Students* (1956) Abington Press, New York, offers a series of graded lessons claiming to "lead from rote memorisation to free composition." The completion and recall exercises are well planned, but in the transition to free composition, control is relinquished. Other writers use a variation of the recall and completion exercises, namely the use of nonsense words to indicate the sentence patterns and to act as items for substitution. (See Paul Roberts, *Patterns of English*, (1956) Harcourt Brace & Co., New York, p. 153.) But there seems little point in adding unreal words to the foreign learner's burden.

6. (1953) Thos. Crowell, New York, p. 42.

7. Teachers have been recommending the imitation of models for centuries. Among recent advocates, see Nelson Brooks, *op. cit.*, p. 198, F. L. Billows, The Techniques of Language Teaching (1961) Longmans Green & Co., and Professor Warfel, "Structural Linguistics and Composition" *College English XX*, v, (1959) p. 205, H. R. Fuller and F. F. Wasell, *Advanced English Exercises* (1961) Saxon Press, N. Y. Section on "Model Composition," and Thos. Lee Crowell. Jr., *Modern English Workbook* (1961) Saxon Press, New York, viii. None of them, however, give a detailed method for carrying out the copying process.

8. (1960) Oxford University Press.

9. See note 5.

10. For a clear explanation of the concept "tagmeme," see B. Elson, and V. B. Pickett *Beginning Morphology Syntax* (1960) Summer Institute of Linguistics, Santa Anna, California, p. 16.

11. The difference between teaching foreign learners and native speakers is crucial. For the latter, the emphasis is on making them aware of the structures they use automatically. See H. B. Allen, Ed., *Readings in Applied Linguistics* (1958) Appleton Century Crofts, New York, Part V., "Linguistics and the teaching of Grammar and Composition." p. 295-371.

12. Another method of control is to give pictures that lead to the telling of a story. L. A. Hill's *Picture Composition Book* (1960) Longmans Green & Co., gives opportunity to control subject and structure, but leaves the student a great deal of freedom.

13. The tremendous problem of grading compositions will be eased too. Teachers will have a basis of reference for their marking. See T. A. Koclanes, "Can we Evaluate Compositions?", a reprint from *The English Journal* in the *M.S.T. English Quarterly* XI, ii (1961) A publication of the Association of Manila Secondary Teachers of English.

14. See R. R. Campbell *English Composition for Foreign Students* (1946) Longmans Green & Co., Chapter 7, for an excellent word by word analysis of some different prose styles. Another attempt to teach different styles is in Ruth D. G. de Pruna, *A Workbook in English Composition*, Mimeograph (1954) Universidad Central "Marta Abreu," Santa Clara, Puerto Rico. Miss de Pruna's method is substitution of selected content words, i.e. paraphrase—a suitable introduction to multiple substitution.

15. It is true that not enough is known about style and the process of composition. A. H. Marckwardt, e.g., points out that the composition teacher needs far more information on the relationship between punctuation and the suprasegmentals, on the relative incidence of simple, compound, and complex sentences, of appositive constructions, and on positions of modifying elements, etc. ("Linguistics and English Composition" *Language Learning Special Issue* No. 2 (1961) p. 17. Even if it does not solve such problems, the substitution method is, at the very least, a good way of avoiding students' unanswerable questions.

Cultural Thought Patterns
in Inter-Cultural Education
by Robert B. Kaplan

The teaching of reading and composition to foreign students does differ from the teaching of reading and composition to American students, and cultural differences in the nature of rhetoric supply the key to the difference in teaching approach.

> ... Rhetoric is a mode of thinking or a mode of "finding all available means" for the achievement of a designated end. Accordingly, rhetoric concerns itself basically with what goes on in the mind rather than with what comes out of the mouth. ... Rhetoric is concerned with factors of analysis, data gathering, interpretation, and synthesis. ... What we notice in the environment and how we notice it are both predetermined to a significant degree by how we are prepared to notice this particular type of object. ... Cultural anthropologists point out that given acts and objects appear vastly different in different cultures, depending on the values attached to them. Psychologists investigating perception are increasingly insistent that what is perceived depends upon the observer's perceptual frame of reference.[1]

Language teachers, particularly teachers of English as a second language, are late-comers in the area of international education. For years, and until quite recently, most languages were taught in what might be called a mechanistic way, stressing the prescriptive function of such teaching. In recent years the swing has been in the other direction, and the prescriptive has practically disappeared from language teaching. Descriptive approaches have seemed to provide the answer. At the present moment, there seems to be some question about the purely descriptive technique, and a new compromise between description and prescription seems to be emerging. Such a compromise appears necessary to the adequate achievement of

Reprinted from *Language Learning, 16*(1-2), Kaplan, R. B., Cultural thought patterns in intercultural education, 1966, with permission from Blackwell Publishers.

results in second-language teaching. Unfortunately, although both the prescriptivists and the descriptivists have recognized the existence of cultural variation as a factor in second-language teaching, the recognition has so far been limited to the level of the sentence—that is, to the level of grammar, vocabulary, and sentence structure. On the other hand, it has long been known among sociologists and anthropologists that logic *per se* is a cultural phenomenon as well.

> Even if we take into account the lexical and grammatical similarities that exist between languages proceeding from a common hypothetical ancestor, the fact remains that the verbal universe is divided into multiple sectors. Sepir, Whorf, and many others, comparing the Indian languages with the Occidental languages, have underlined this diversity very forcefully. It seems, indeed, as if the arbitrary character of language, having been shown to be of comparatively little significance at the level of the elements of a language, reasserts itself quite definitely at the level of the language taken as a whole. And if one admits that a language represents a kind of destiny, so far as human thought is concerned, this diversity of languages leads to a radical realitivism. As Peirce said, if Aristotle had been Mexican, his logic would have been different; and perhaps, by the same token, the whole of our philosophy and our science would have been different.
>
> The fact is that this diversity affects not only the languages, but also the cultures, that is to say the whole system of institutions that are tied to the language . . . [and] language in its turn is the effect and the expression of a certain world view that is manifested in the culture. If there is causality, it is a reciprocal causality. . . .
>
> The types of structures characteristic of a given culture would then, in each case, be particular modes of universal laws. They would define the Volksgeist. . . .[2]

Logic (in the popular, rather than the logician's sense of the word) which is the basis of rhetoric, is evolved out of a culture; it is not universal. Rhetoric, then, is not universal either, but varies from culture to culture and even from time to time within a given culture. It is affected by canons of taste within a given culture at a given time.

> Every language offers to its speakers a ready-made *interpretation* of the world, truly a Weltanschauung, a metaphysical word-picture which, after having originated in the thinking of our ancestors, tends to impose itself ever anew on posterity. Take for instance a simple sentence such as 'I see him. . . .' This means that English and, I might say, Indo-European, presents the impressions made on our senses predominantly as human *activities*, brought about by our *will*. But the Eskimos in Greenland say not 'I see him' but 'he appears to me. . . .' Thus the Indo-European speaker conceives as workings of his activities what the fatalistic Eskimo sees as events that happen to him.[3]

The English language and its related thought patterns have evolved out of the Anglo-European cultural pattern. The expected sequence of thought in English is essentially a Platonic-Aristotelian sequence, descended from the philosophers of ancient Greece and shaped subsequently by Roman, Medieval European, and later Western thinkers. It is not a better nor a worse system than any other, but it is different.

... As human beings, we must inevitably see the universe from a centre lying within ourselves and speak about it in terms of a human language by the exigencies of human intercourse. Any attempt rigorously to eliminate our human perspective from our picture of the world must lead to absurdity.[4]

A fallacy of some repute and some duration is the one which assumes that because a student can write an adequate essay in his native language, he can necessarily write an adequate essay in a second language. That this assumption is fallacious has become more and more apparent as English-as-a-second-language courses have proliferated at American colleges and universities in recent years. Foreign students who have mastered syntactic structures have still demonstrated inability to compose adequate themes, term papers, theses, and dissertations. Instructors have written, on foreign-student papers, such comments as: "The material is all here, but it seems somehow out of focus," or "Lacks organization," or "Lacks cohesion." And these comments are essentially accurate. The foreign-student paper is out of focus because the foreign student is employing a rhetoric and a sequence of thought which violate the expectations of the native reader.

A personality is carved out by the whole subtle interaction of these systems of ideas which are characteristic of the culture as a whole, as well as of those systems of ideas which get established for the individual through more special types of participation.[5]

The fact that sequence of thought and grammar are related in a given language has already been demonstrated adequately by Paul Lorenzen. His brief paper proposes that certain linguistic structures are best comprehended as embodiments of logical structures.[6] Beyond that, every rhetorician from Cicero to Brooks and Warren has indicated the relationship between thought sequence and rhetoric.

A paragraph, mechanically considered, is a division of the composition, set off by an indentation of its first sentence or by some other conventional device, such as extra space between paragraphs. . . . Paragraph divisions signal to the reader that the material so set off constitutes a unit of thought.

For the reader this marking off of the whole composition into segments is a convenience, though not a strict necessity. . . . Since communication of one's thought is at best a difficult business, it is the part of common sense (not to mention good manners) to mark for the reader the divisions of one's thought and thus make the thought structure visible upon the page. . . .

Paragraphing, obviously, can be of help to the reader only if the indicated paragraphs are genuine units of thought. . . . For a paragraph undertakes to discuss one topic or one aspect of a topic.[7]

The thought patterns which speakers and readers of English appear to expect as an integral part of their communication is a sequence that is dominantly linear in its development. An English expository paragraph usually begins with a topic statement, and then, by a series of subdivisions of that topic statement, each supported by example and illustrations, proceeds to develop that central idea and relate that

idea to all the other ideas in the whole essay, and to employ that idea in its proper relationship with the other ideas, to prove something, or perhaps to argue something.

> A piece of writing may be considered unified when it contains *nothing* superfluous
> and it omits nothing essential to the achievement of its purpose. . . . A work is consid-
> ered coherent when the sequence of its parts . . . is controlled by some principle which
> is meaningful to the reader. Unity is the quality attributed to writing which has all its
> necessary and sufficient parts. Coherence is the quality attributed to the presentation
> of material in a sequence which is intelligible to its reader.[8]

Contrarily, the English paragraph may use just the reverse procedure; that is, it may
state a whole series of examples and then relate those examples into a single statement at the end of the paragraph. These two types of development represent the
common *inductive* and *deductive* reasoning which the English reader expects to be
an integral part of any formal communication.

For example, the following paragraph written by Macaulay demonstrates normal
paragraph development:

> Whitehall, when [Charles the Second] dwelt there, was the focus of political intrigue
> and of fashionable gaiety. Half the jobbing and half the flirting of the metropolis went
> on under his roof. Whoever could make himself agreeable to the prince or could se-
> cure the good offices of his mistress might hope to rise in the world without rendering
> any service to the government, without even being known by sight to any minister of
> state. This courtier got a frigate and that a company, a third the pardon of a rich of-
> fender, a fourth a lease of crown-land on easy terms. If the king notified his pleasure
> that a briefless lawyer should be made a judge or that a libertine baronet should be
> made a peer, the gravest counsellors, after a little murmuring, submitted. Interest,
> therefore, drew a constant press of suitors to the gates of the palace, and those gates al-
> ways stood wide. The King kept open house every day and all day long for the good
> society of London, the extreme Whigs only excepted. Hardly any gentleman had any
> difficulty in making his way to the royal presence. The levee was exactly what the
> word imports. Some men of quality came every morning to stand round their master,
> to chat with him while his wig was combed and his cravat tied, and to accompany him
> in his early walk through the Park. All persons who had been properly introduced
> might, without any special invitation, go to see him dine, sup, dance, and play at haz-
> ard and might have the pleasure of hearing him tell stories, which indeed, he told re-
> markably well, about his flight from Worcester and about the misery which he had
> endured when he was a state prisoner in the hands of the canting meddling preachers
> of Scotland.[9]

The paragraph begins with a general statement of its content, and then carefully de-
velops that statement by a long series of rather specific illustrations. While it is discur-
sive, the paragraph is never digressive. There is nothing in this paragraph that does
not belong here; nothing that does not contribute significantly to the central idea. The
flow of ideas occurs in a straight line from the opening sentence to the last sentence.

Without doing too much damage to other ways of thinking, perhaps it might be
possible to contrast the English paragraph development with paragraph development in other linguistic systems.

For the purposes of the following brief analysis, some seven hundred foreign student compositions were carefully analyzed. Approximately one hundred of these were discarded from the study on the basis that they represent linguistic groups too small within the present sample to be significant.[10] But approximately six hundred examples, representing three basic language groups, were examined.[11]

In the Arabic language, for example (and this generalization would be more or less true for all Semitic languages), paragraph development is based on a complex series of parallel constructions, both positive and negative. This kind of parallelism may most clearly be demonstrated in English by reference to the King James version of the Old Testament. Several types of parallelism typical of Semitic languages are apparent there because that book, of course, is a translation from an ancient Semitic language, a translation accomplished at a time when English was in a state of development suitable to the imitation of those forms.

1. Synonymous Parallelism:	The balancing of the thought and phrasing of the first part of a statement or idea by the second part. In such cases, the two parts are often connected by a coordinating conjunction.
Example:	His descendants will be mighty in the land *and* The generation of the upright will be blessed.
2. Synthetic Parallelism:	The completion of the idea or thought of the first part in the second part. A conjunctive adverb is often stated or implied.
Example:	Because he inclined his ear to me *therefore* I will call on him as long as I live.
3. Antithetic Parallelism:	The idea stated in the first part is emphasized by the expression of a contrasting idea in the second part. The contrast is expressed not only in thought but often in phrasing as well.
Example:	For the Lord knoweth the way of the righteous: But the way of the wicked shall perish.
4. Climactic Parallelism:	The idea of the passage is not completed until the very end of the passage. This form is similar to the modern periodic sentence in which the subject is postponed to the very end of the sentence.
Example:	Give unto the Lord, O ye sons of the mighty, Give unto the Lord glory and strength[12]

The type of parallel construction here illustrated in single sentences also forms the core of paragraphs in some Arabic writing. Obviously, such a development in a modern English paragraph would strike the modern English reader as archaic or awkward, and more importantly it would stand in the way of clear communication.

It is important to note that in English, maturity of style is often gauged by degree of subordination rather than by coordination.

The following paper was written as a class exercise by an Arabic-speaking student in an English-as-a-second-language class at an American university:

> The contemporary Bedouins, who live in the deserts of Saudi Arabia, are the successors of the old bedouin tribes, the tribes that was fascinated with Mohammad's massage, and on their shoulders Islam built it's empire. I had lived among those contemporary Bedouins for a short period of time, and I have learned lots of things about them. I found out that they have retained most of their ancestor's characteristics, inspite of the hundreds of years that separate them.
>
> They are famous of many praiseworthy characteristics, but they are considered to be the symbol of generosity; bravery; and self-esteem. Like most of the wandering peoples, a stranger is an undesirable person among them. But, once they trust him as a friend, he will be most welcome. However, their trust is a hard thing to gain. And the heroism of many famous figures, who ventured in the Arabian deserts like T. E. Lawrence, is based on their ability to acquire this dear trust!
>
> Romance is an important part in their life. And "love" is an important subject in their verses and their tales.
>
> Nevertheless, they are criticized of many things. The worst of all is that they are extremists in all the ways of their lives. It is there extremism that changes sometimes their generosity into squandering, their bravery into brutality, and their self-esteem into haughtiness. But in any case, I have been, and will continue to be greatly interested in this old, fascinating group of people.

Disregarding for the moment the grammatical errors in this student composition, it becomes apparent that the characteristics of parallelism do occur. The next-to-last element in the first sentence, for example, is appositive to the preceding one, while the last element is an example of synonymous parallelism. The two clauses of the second sentence illustrate synonymous parallelism. In the second "paragraph" the first sentence contains both an example of antithetic parallelism and a list of parallel nouns. The next two sentences form an antithetic pair, and so on. It is perhaps not necessary to point out further examples in the selection. It is important, however, to observe that in the first sentence, for example, the grammatical complexity is caused by the attempt to achieve an intricate parallelism. While this extensive parallel construction is linguistically possible in Arabic, the English language lacks the necessary flexibility. Eight conjunctions and four sentence connectors are employed in a matter of only fourteen "sentences." In addition, there are five "lists" of units connected by commas and conjunctions.

Another paper, also written by an Arabic-speaking student under comparable circumstances, further demonstrates the same tendencies:

> At that time of the year I was not studying enough to pass my courses in school. *And* all the time I was asking my cousin to let me ride the bicycle, *but* he wouldn't let me. *But* after two weeks, noticing that I was so much interested in the bicycle, he promised

me that if I pass my courses in school for that year he would give it to me as a present. So I began to study hard. *And* I studying eight hours a day instead of two.

My cousin seeing me studying that much he was sure that I was going to succeed in school. So he decided to give me some lessons in riding the bicycle. After four or five weeks of teaching me and ten or twelve times hurting myself as I used to go out of balance, I finally knew how to ride it. And the finals in school came *and* I was very good prepared for them so I passed them. My cousin kept his promise *and* gave me the bicycle as a present. And till now I keep the bicycle in a safe place, *and* everytime I see it, It reminds me how it helped to pass my courses for that year.

In the first paragraph of this example, four of the five sentences, or 80% of the sentences, begin with a coordinating element. In the second paragraph, three of the six sentences, or 50% of the total, also begin with a coordinating element. In the whole passage, seven of the eleven sentences, or roughly 65%, conform to this pattern. In addition, the first paragraph contains one internal coordinator, and the second contains five internal coordinators; thus, the brief passage (210 words) contains a total of thirteen coordinators. It is important to notice that almost all of the ideas in the passage are coordinately linked, that there is very little subordination, and that the parallel units exemplify the types of parallelism already noted.

Some Oriental[13] writing, on the other hand, is marked by what may be called an approach by indirection. In this kind of writing, the development of the paragraph may be said to be "turning and turning in a widening gyre." The circles or gyres turn around the subject and show it from a variety of tangential views, but the subject is never looked at directly. Things are developed in terms of what they are not, rather than in terms of what they are. Again, such a development in a modern English paragraph would strike the English reader as awkward and unnecessarily indirect.

The following composition was written, as a class exercise, by a native speaker of Korean, under the same circumstances which produced the two previous examples. Obviously, this student is weaker in general English proficiency than the students who produced the two prior examples.

Definition of college education

College is an institution of an higher learning that gives degrees. All of us needed culture and education in life, if no education to us, we should to go living hell.

One of the greatest causes that while other animals have remained as they first man along has made such rapid progress is has learned about civilization.

The improvement of the highest civilization is in order to education up-to-date.

So college education is very important thing which we don't need mention about it.

Again, disregarding the typically Oriental grammar and the misconception of the function of "parts of speech," the first sentence defines college, not college education. This may conceivably be a problem based upon the student's misunderstanding of the assignment. But the second sentence appears to shoot off in a totally different direction. It makes a general statement about culture and education, perhaps as *results* of a college education. The third sentence, presented as a separate "paragraph," moves still farther away from definition by expanding the topic to "man" in a generic sense, as opposed to "non-man." This unit is tied to the next, also presented as a separate paragraph, by the connecting idea of "civilization" as an aspect of education. The concluding paragraph-sentence presents, in the guise of a summary logically derived from previously posited ideas, a conclusion which is in fact partially a topic sentence and partially a statement that the whole basic concept of the assignment is so obvious that it does not need discussion. The paper arrives where it should have started, with the added statement that it really had no place to go to begin with.

The poorer proficiency of this student, however, introduces two other considerations. It is possible that this student, as an individual rather than as a representative native speaker of Korean, lacks the ability to abstract sufficiently for extended definition. In the case under discussion, however, the student was majoring in mathematics and did have the ability to abstract in mathematical terms. While the demands of mathematics are somewhat different from the demands of language in a conventional sense, it is possible to assume that a student who can handle abstraction in one area can also probably handle it at least to some extent in the other. It is also possible that the ability to abstract is absent from the Korean culture. This appears quite unlikely in view of the abundance of Korean art available and in view of the fact that other native speakers of Korean have not demonstrated that shortcoming.

The examples cited so far have been student themes. The following example is from a professional translation. Essentially, the same variations can be observed in it. In this case, the translation is from French.

> The first point to which I would like to call your attention is that nothing exists outside the boundary of what is strictly human. A landscape may be beautiful, graceful, sublime, insignificant, or ugly; it will never be ludicrous. We may laugh at an animal, but only because we have detected in it some human expression or attitude. We may laugh at a hat, but we are not laughing at the piece of felt or straw. We are laughing at the shape that men have given to it, the human whim whose mold it has assumed. *I wonder why a fact so important has not attracted the attention of philosophers to a greater degree. Some have defined man as an animal that knows how to laugh. They could equally well have defined him as an animal which provokes laughter;* for if any other animal or some lifeless object, achieves the same effect, it is always because of some similarity to man.[14]

In this paragraph, the italicized portion constitutes a digression. It is an interesting digression, but it really does not seem to contribute significant structural material to the basic thought of the paragraph. While the author of the paragraph is a philosopher, and a philosopher is often forgiven digressions, the more important fact is that the example is a typical one for writers of French as well as for writers of philosophy. Much greater freedom to digress or to introduce extraneous material is available in French, or in Spanish, than in English.

Similar characteristics can be demonstrated in the writing of native French-speaking students in English. In the interests of keeping this report within some bounds, such illustrations will be inserted without comment. The first example was written under circumstances similar to those described for the preceding student samples. The writer is a native speaker of French.

American Traffic law as compared with
Traffic law in Switzerland

At first glance the traffic law in United States appeared to me simpler than in Switzerland.

The American towns in general have the disposition of a cross, and for a driver who knows how to situate himself between the four cardinal points, there is no problem to find his way. Each street has numbers going crecendo from the center of the town to the outside.

There are many accidents in Switzerland, as everywhere else, and the average of mortality comparatively to the proportion of the countries is not better than in United States. We have the problem of straight streets, not enough surveillance by policemen on the national roads, and alcohol. The country of delicious wines has made too many damages.

The following illustration, drawn from the work of a native speaker of Latin American Spanish, was produced under conditions parallel to those already cited:

The American Children

In America, the American children are brought differently from the rest of the children in other countries. In their childhood, from the first day they are born, the parents give their children the love and attention they need. They teach their children the meaning of Religion among the family and to have respect and obedience for their parents.

I am Spanish, and I was brought up differently than the children in America. My parents are stricter and they taught me discipline and not to interrupt when someone was talking.

The next and last example is again not a piece of student writing, but a translation. The original was written in Russian, and the translation attempts to capture the structure of the original as much as possible, but without sacrificing meaning completely.

On the 14th of October, Kruschev left the stage of history. Was it a plot the result of which was that Kurschev was out of business remains not clear. It is very probable that even if it were anything resembling a plot it would not be for the complete removal of Kruschev from political guidance, but rather a pressure exerted to obtain some changes in his policies: for continuations of his policies of peaceful co-existence in international relations or making it as far as possible a situation to avoid formal rupture with the Chinese communist party and at any rate not to go unobstructed to such a rupture—and in the area of internal politics, especially in the section of economics, to continue efforts of a certain softening of "dogmatism," but without the hurried and not sufficiently reasoned experimentation, which became the characteristic traits of Kruschev's politics in recent years.[15]

Some of the difficulty in this paragraph is linguistic rather than rhetorical. The structure of the Russian sentence is entirely different from the structure of the English sentence. But some of the linguistic difficulty is closely related to the rhetorical difficulty. The above paragraph is composed of three sentences. The first two are very short, while the last is extremely long, constituting about three quarters of the paragraph. It is made up of a series of presumably parallel constructions and a number of subordinate structures. At least half of these are irrelevant to the central idea of the paragraph in the sense that they are parenthetical amplifications of structurally related subordinate elements.

There are, of course, other examples that might be discussed as well, but these paragraphs may suffice to show that each language and each culture has a paragraph order unique to itself, and that part of the learning of a particular language is the mastering of its logical system.

> ... One should join to any logic of the language a phenomenology of the spoken word. Moreover, this phenomenology will, in its turn, rediscover the idea of a logos immanent in the language; but it will seek the justification for this in a more general philosophy of the relations between man and the world. ... From one culture to another it is possible to establish communication. The Rorschach test has been successfully applied to the natives of the island of Alor.[16]

This discussion is not intended to offer any criticism of other existing paragraph developments; rather it is intended only to demonstrate that paragraph developments other than those normally regarded as desirable in English do exist. In the teaching of paragraph structure to foreign students, whether in terms of reading or in terms of composition, the teacher must be himself aware of these differences, and he must make these differences overtly apparent to his students. In short, contrastive rhetoric must be taught in the same sense that contrastive grammar is presently taught. Now not much has been done in the area of contrastive rhetoric. It is first necessary to arrive at accurate descriptions of existing paragraph orders other than those common to English. Furthermore, it is necessary to understand that these categories are in no sense meant to be mutually exclusive. Patterns may be derived for *typical* English paragraphs, but paragraphs like those described above as being atypical in English do exist in English. By way of obvious example, Ezra Pound writes paragraphs which are circular in their structure, and William Faulkner writes paragraphs which are wildly digressive. The paragraph being discussed here is not the "literary" paragraph, however, but the expository paragraph. The necessities of art impose structures on any language, while the requirements of communication can often be best solved by relatively close adhesion to established patterns.

Superficially, the movement of the various paragraphs discussed above may be graphically represented in the following manner:

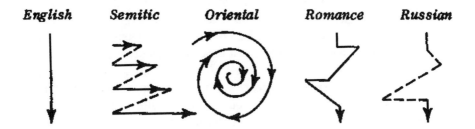

English   *Semitic*   *Oriental*   *Romance*   *Russian*

Much more detailed and more accurate descriptions are required before any meaningful contrastive system can be elaborated. Nonetheless, an important problem exists immediately. In the teaching of English as a second language, what does one do with the student who is reasonably proficient in the use of syntactic structure but who needs to learn to write themes, theses, essay examinations, and dissertations? The "advanced" student has long constituted a problem for teachers of English as a second language. This approach, the contrastive analysis of rhetoric, is offered as one possible answer to the existing need. Such an approach has the advantage that it may help the foreign student to form standards of judgement consistent with the demands made upon him by the educational system of which he has become a part. At the same time, by accounting for the cultural aspects of logic which underlie the rhetorical structure, this approach may bring the student not only to an understanding of contrastive grammar and a new vocabulary, which are parts of any reading task, but also to a grasp of idea and structure in units larger than the sentence. A sentence, after all, rarely exists outside a context. Applied linguistics teaches the student to deal with the sentence, but it is necessary to bring the student beyond that to a comprehension of the whole context. He can only understand the whole context if he recognizes the logic on which the context is based. The foreign student who has mastered the syntax of English may still write a bad paragraph or a bad paper unless he also masters the logic of English. "*In serious expository prose, the paragraph tends to be a logical, rather than a typographical, unit.*"[17] The understanding of paragraph patterns can allow the student to relate syntactic elements within a paragraph and perhaps even to relate paragraphs within a total context.

Finally, it is necessary to recognize the fact that a paragraph is an artificial thought unit employed in the written language to suggest a cohesion which commonly may not exist in oral language. "Paragraphing, like punctuation, is a feature only of the written language."[18] As an artificial unit of thought, it lends itself to patterning quite readily. In fact, since it is imposed from without, and since it is a frame for the structuring of thought into patterns, it is by its very nature patterned. The rhetorical structures of English paragraphs may be found in any good composition text.[19] The patterns of paragraphs in other languages are not so well established, or perhaps only not so well known to speakers of English. These patterns need to be discovered or uncovered and compared with the patterns of English in order to arrive at a practical means for the teaching of such structures to non-native users of the language.

In the interim, while research is directed at the rhetorics of other languages, certain practical pedagogical devices have been developed to expedite the teaching of rhetorical structures to non-native speakers of English. An elementary device consists simply of supplying to the students a scrambled paragraph. A normal paragraph, such as the one cited from Macaulay above, may be arbitrarily scrambled, the sentences numbered, and the students asked to rearrange the sentences in what appears to them to be a normal order. Frequently, the results of such an assignment will demonstrate the diversity of views or cultures represented in the classroom. The exercise can be used effectively to point out the very disparity. The students must then be presented with the original version of the paragraph, and the instructor must be able to explain and justify the order of the original.

[INSTRUCTIONS: Arrange the sentences below into some normal order.]

[This is the order in which the author arranged his sentences. Can you detect his reason?]

Scrambled Order

1. A jackass brays; a turkey cock gobbles; a dog yelps; a church bell clangs.

2. The narrow streets and lanes leading into the market are crammed with Indians, their dark skins glistening like copper or bronze in the bright sun, their varicolored cloaks looking like a mass of palette colors smeared together.

3. There is the smell of animal dung mingled with the odor of carnations and heliotrope from the flower stalls.

4. In the open plaza outside the market the crowd mills about.

5. Mothers sit on the curb nursing their babies.

6. A kind of blending of Indian talk in various dialects creates a strange droning noise.

7. On the narrow sidewalks, merchandise is spread so haphazardly that in order to pass, pedestrians have to press against the wall or leap the displays.

8. Wrinkled old women squat over charcoal braziers cooking corn cakes, or black beans, or pink coconut candy.

Normal Order

The narrow streets and lanes leading into the market are crammed with Indians, their dark skins glistening like copper or bronze in the bright sun, their varicolored cloaks looking like a mass of palette colors smeared together. In the open plaza outside the market the crowd mills about. A kind of blending of Indian talk in various dialects creates a strange droning noise. A jackass brays; a turkey cock gobbles; a dog yelps; a church bell clangs. On the narrow sidewalks, merchandise is spread so haphazardly that in order to pass, pedestrians have to press against the wall or leap the displays. Wrinkled old women squat over charcoal braziers cooking corn cakes, or black beans, or pink coconut candy. Mothers sit on the curb nursing their babies. There is the smell of animal dung mingled with the odor of carnations and heliotrope from the flower stalls.[20]

[This paragraph is descriptive, presented in the present tense, and arranged perceptually in the orfer of sight, hearing, and smell.]

A second device consists of giving the students carefully written topic sentences, arranged in some convenient way such as that suggested below, and then asking the students to fill out the subdivisions of the topic sentence with examples and illustrations chosen to support the point. Depending upon the relative difficulty of the topic, the examples may be supplied by the instructor in scrambled order.

American Television

American commercial television appears to consist of three principle classes of material: programs of serious interest, such as news broadcasts and special features; programs intended primarily as entertainment, such as variety shows, situation comedies, and adventure tales; and the advertisements which link all of these.

I. Programs of serious interest:
    A. News Broadcasts:
        1. _____
        2. _____
    B. Special Features:
        1. _____
        2. _____
II. Programs intended primarily as entertainment:
    A. Variety Shows:
        1. _____
        2. _____
    B. Situational Comedies:
        1. _____
        2. _____
    C. Adventure Tales:
        1. _____
        2. _____
III. Advertising:
    A. _____
        1. _____
        2. _____
    B. _____
        1. _____
        2. _____
IV. [Conclusion:]

[INSTRUCTIONS: The student is to supply contrasting examples for each of the spaces provided under items I and II. In item III the student must also supply the main subdivisions, and in item IV the point of the whole essay must also be supplied by the student. Obviously, item IV will vary considerably depending upon the kinds of illustrations selected to fill the blanks.]

The illustration constitutes a very simple exercise. Greater sophistication may be employed as the student becomes more familiar with the techniques. Obviously, too, the outline must be introduced and taught simultaneously. A simple technique for teaching the outline may be found illustrated in a number of texts for both American and foreign students.[21]

It is important to impress upon the student that "A paragraph is *clear* when each sentence contributes to the central thought ... [and that] clarity also demands coherence, that is, an orderly flow of sentences marked by repetition of key ideas."[22]

While it is necessary for the non-native speaker learning English to master the rhetoric of the English paragraph, it must be remembered that the foreign student, ideally, will be returning to his home country, and that his stay in the United States is a brief one. Under these circumstances, English is a means to an end for him; it is not an end in itself. Edward Sapir has written:

> An oft-noted peculiarity of the development of culture is the fact that it reaches its greatest heights in comparatively small, autonomous groups. In fact, it is doubtful if a genuine culture ever properly belongs to more than such a restricted group, a group between the members of which there can be said to be something like direct intensive spiritual contact. This direct contact is enriched by the common cultural heritage on which the minds of all are fed. . . . A narrowly localized culture may, and often does, spread its influence far beyond its properly restricted sphere. Sometimes it sets the pace for a whole nationality, for a far flung empire. It can do so, however, only at the expense of diluting the spirit as it moves away from its home, of degenerating into an imitative attitudinizing."[23]

He is absolutely correct in pointing out the dangers of spreading a culture too thin and too far from home. However, in the special case of the foreign student learning English, under the conditions stipulated above, the imitation which would be an error in most cases is the sought aim. The classes which undertake the training of the "advanced" student can aim for no more. The creativity and imagination which make the difference between competent writing and excellent writing are things which, at least in these circumstances, cannot be taught. The foreign student is an adult in most cases. If these things are teachable, they will already have been taught to him. The English class must not aim too high. Its function is to provide the student with a form within which he may operate, a form acceptable in this time and in this place. It is hoped that the method described above may facilitate the achievement of that goal.

Notes

1. Robert T. Oliver, "Foreword," *Philosophy, Rhetoric and Argumentation*, ed. Maurice Nathanson and Henry W. Johnstone, Jr. (University Park, Pennsylvania, 1965), pp. x-xi.
2. Mikel Dufrenne, *Language and Philosophy*, trans. Henry B. Veatch (Bloomington, 1963), pp. 35-37.
3. Leo Spitzer, "Language—The Basis of Science, Philosophy and Poetry," *Studies in Intellectual History*, ed. George Boas et al. (Baltimore, 1953), pp. 83-84.
4. Michael Polanyi, *Personal Knowledge: Towards a Post-Critical Philosophy* (Chicago, 1958), p. 9.
5. Sapir, "Anthropology and Psychiatry," *Culture, Language and Personality* (Los Angeles, 1964), p. 157.
6. *Logik und Grammatik* (Mannheim, Germany, 1965).
7. Cleanth Brooks and Robert Penn Warren, *Modern Rhetoric*, 2nd ed. (New York, 1958), pp. 267-68.

8. Richard E. Hughes and P. Albert Duhamel, *Rhetoric: Principles and Usage* (Englewood Cliffs, New Jersey, 1962), pp. 19-20.
9. From *The History of England from the Accession of James the Second* (London, 1849-61).
10. The following examples were discarded: Afghan-3, African-4, Danish-1, Finn-1, German-3, Hindi-8, Persian-46, Russian-1, Greek-1, Tagalog-10, Turk-16, Urdu-5; Total-99.
11. The papers examined may be linguistically broken down as follows: Group I—Arabic-126, Hebrew-3; Group II—Chinese (Mandarin)-110, Cambodian-40, Indochinese-7, Japanese-135, Korean-57, Laotian-3, Malasian-1, Thai-27, Vietnamese-1; Group III—(Spanish-Portugese) Brazilian-19, Central American-10, South American-42, Cuban-4, Spanish-8, (French) French-2, African-2 (Italian) Swiss-1. Group I total-129; Group II total-381; Group III total-88; TOTAL-598. These papers were accumulated and examined over a two year period, from the beginning of the Fall 1963 semester through the Fall 1965 academic semester.
12. I am indebted to Dr. Ben Siegel for this analysis.
13. *Oriental* here is intended to mean specifically Chinese and Korean but not Japanese.
14. From *Laughter, An Assay on the Meaning of the Comic*, Trans. Marcel Bolomet (Paris, 1900).
15. From S. Schwartz, "After Kruschev," trans. E. B. Kaplan, *The Socialist Courier* (April, 1965), p. 3.
16. Dufrenne, pp. 39-40.
17. Hans P. Guth, *A Short New Rhetoric* (Belmont, California, 1964), p. 205.
18. Edward P. J. Corbett, *Classical Rhetoric for the Modern Student* (New York, 1965), p. 416.
19. Important work in the rhetoric of the paragraph is being done by Francis Christensen, among others. See especially "A Generative Rhetoric of the Paragraph," *College Composition and Communication* (October, 1965), pp. 144-156.
20. Hudson Strode, "The Market at Toluca," *Now in Mexico* (New York, 1947).
21. At the risk of being accused of immodesty, I would recommend in particular the section entitled "Outlining" in Robert B. Kaplan, *Reading and Rhetoric* (New York, 1963), pp. 69-80.
22. Francis Connolly, *A Rhetoric Casebook* (New York, 1953), p. 304.
23. Edward Sapir, "Culture, Genuine and Spurious," *Culture, Language and Personality*, (Los Angeles 1964), pp. 113-14.

Teaching Composition in the ESL Classroom: What We Can Learn from Research in the Teaching of English
by Vivian Zamel

If one were to look through the literature on the teaching of composition in second language classrooms, one would find a multitude of suggestions as to how to teach it. The various approaches are generally based on the experiences of the authors and their theories on what the teaching of writing entails. While much can certainly be learned from these experts and methodologists, it is disappointing to find that, except for one pilot study (Brière 1966) almost no research has been done in the teaching of composition to learners of a second language. Thus, the success of a particular method or approach may have been due to a number of factors that are only partially or minimally related to a particular technique, such as the level of intelligence, motivation or affective considerations. The point is that without research and some of the answers it could provide us, a teacher is faced with the practically impossible task of deciding which approach (and/or text) to adopt. This is not to say that he or she will not teach composition effectively; rather, he or she will probably do so only after experiencing the long and often frustrating process of trial and error.

More distressing than the lack of research being done, however, is the fact that we have ignored some of the answers that have been provided by research in the teaching of English. We have acted as if teaching composition to ESL students is something totally unrelated to the teaching of composition in regular English classes and have thus deprived ourselves, I believe, of much valuable information. It seems that many of the assumptions held by teachers of ESL parallel those of English teachers; teachers of both fields have made some erroneous conclusions as to what the teaching of writing is. But, while the field of English seems to be gaining from their research evidence, we continue to suggest unfounded, though well-intentioned, practices. What we have failed to realize is that by the time our students are ready to write compositions, that is, create and express their own thoughts and ideas in the second language, they need the same kind of instruction that students in English classrooms need. To believe otherwise seems to indicate that the student has really not developed competence in the second language, still requires a great deal of control and is therefore ill-prepared to compose. If, however, students in the ESL classroom are in fact ready to write, as defined above, we can learn a great deal from the research already carried out in the field of English; just as it has provided evidence undermining well-established theories on the teaching of composition in the English classroom, it has important ramifications for the ESL classroom as well.

Methodology on the Teaching of Composition in the Second Language Classroom

The literature on the teaching of composition in a second language seems to indicate that there is a consensus as to how writing should be taught: while grammatical exercises are rejected as having little to do with the act of writing, there is, at the same time, a great concern with control and guidance. Despite the agreement that learning to write entails actual practice in writing, this practice is often no more than the orthographic translation of oral pattern practice or substitution drills. There are those that are critical of these pseudo-writing exercises, encouraging the elimination of total control, thus coming closer to identifying what composing is really all about. These, however, are the exception. The majority of approaches emphasize and focus upon practices that have very little to do with the creative process of writing.

Maintaining that writing is a culmination of the other language skills and that composition is therefore dependent on the mastery of listening, speaking and reading, foreign language methodologists describe stages or sequences of exercises which theoretically bring the student from total control to freedom. Allen and Valette (1972: 217-238), Rivers (1968: 240-260), Finocchiaro (1958: 156-162), Chastain (1971: 220-238) and Billows (1961: 181-209) all indicate the necessity of these stages, warning of the danger of asking students to write expressively too early. While I do not argue with these approaches in terms of the kind of preparation ESL students need, I take issue with the fact that the exercises described are identified with the skills of composing. Teachers are aware that their students must have a basic linguistic competence in order to write creatively. Advising them to provide interesting and meaningful topics during the "last stage," that of free composition, is of little value.

Picking up this theme on the need for control and guidance, methodologists have devised particular exercises which, while not based on learning grammar *qua* grammar, are in fact based on the grammatical manipulations of models, sentences or passages. For them, writing seems to be synonymous with skill in usage and structure, and the assumption is that these exercises will improve the students' ability to compose. Influenced by audio-lingual methodology, writing is seen as a habit-formed skill, error is to be avoided and correction and revision are to be provided continuously. Christina Bratt Paulston (1972) suggests the use of models and the manipulation of their patterns upon which to base one's writing. Dykstra (1964) likewise provides a series of model passages which students are to manipulate according to a series of steps, Spencer's (1965) manipulations entail the recasting of whole sentences following a single pattern, and Rojas' (1968) drill type exercises of copying, completion and substitution clearly reflect concern with the prevention of error. Ross's (1968) combinations and rearrangements of patterns are based on a transformational grammar approach, and both Pincas (1962) and Moody (1965) emphasize the need for rigid control by endorsing the habitual manipulation of patterns. Thus, while the teaching of grammar is expressly rejected by these methodologists as having little to do with writing, the kinds of exercises they suggest are based on the conceptualization that writing entails grammatical proficiency. Implicitly, grammatical facility means writing ability.

Taking issue with the notion that writing is orthographic speech and insisting that composition is not synonymous with producing correct responses, are those who recognize factors that have heretofore largely been ignored. Organization, style and rhetoric become the crucial aspects of skill in writing, but, here again, control and guidance are essential; drill predominates, but on a rhetorical level. Rather than sentences to manipulate, whole reading passages become the models that students are to differentiate and imitate. Kaplan (1967), pointing out the effect that cultural differences have upon the nature of rhetoric, suggests the study and imitation of paragraphs. Pincas (1964) creates a multiple substitution technique that involves habituation in the use of certain styles. Arapoff (1969) concentrates on the importance of discovering, comparing and imitating stylistic differences. Carr (1967) stresses the importance of reading, studying and analyzing the organization and logical arrangement of passages, and Green (1967) reiterates the practice needed in specific varieties of written language. While this group of methodologists approaches more closely what writing, in the sense of creating, truly entails, they still, like the first group, insist upon control. Rejecting the notion that writing is the mastery of sentence patterns, they nevertheless put restraints on the composing process. Writing for the ESL student is still essentially seen as the formation of a habit. The imitation of various styles and organization patterns may be helpful for students who are still coping with the acquisition of language. This kind of practice, however, is hardly the expression of genuine thoughts and ideas.

It is obvious that there is a predominating concern with the quality of the students' output; because the students are attempting to compose in a language other than their own, control and guidance are paramount. Furthermore, it is felt that once the imitative stages are mastered, expression will somehow automatically take place. Opposed to this position are those who believe that the composing process necessitates a lack of control; rather than emphasize the need to write correctly, the proponents of this approach stress the need to write much and often. In other words, it is quantity, not quality, that is crucial. Erazmus (1960) claims that the greater the frequency, the greater the improvement, and Brière's (1966: 146) pilot study seems to indicate that, when the emphasis is upon writing often rather than error correction, students write more and with fewer errors. Povey (1969) reiterates this theme, underlining the importance of providing opportunities to say something vitally relevant.

It is no wonder, in the light of the foregoing discussion, that ESL teachers are confused and still searching for answers. They face the decision of having to choose one of several approaches. These approaches can be seen as points along a spectrum ranging from total control to total freedom:

total control	(increase in complexity →)	free composition
substitution, manipulation or transformation of sentences & patterns	imitation & differentiation of stylistic patterns	frequent, uncontrolled writing practice

While it is easy to take a middle of the road position and advocate that what is needed is a mixture of quantity and quality, with weight given to one or the other, dependent on the individual learners (Cave 1972), this hardly clarifies the issue. Some teachers will go on teaching composition as if it were a matter of correct grammatical usage. Others will insist that rhetorical considerations must be taken into account and thus will provide longer models to manipulate and imitate. And others still will claim that it is frequency of writing that will lead to improvement and fluency. While each position may have certain merits, each represents a rather narrow view of the writing process.

In our efforts to upgrade ESL instruction and provide more effective approaches, we have failed to recognize that we can learn from research that has already been done in related fields, such as the teaching of English. After all, if ESL teachers can share the methodologies of foreign language teachers, why should they not likewise borrow from well-established approaches in the teaching of English composition? If we are dealing with students who are truly ready to express and compose, not ones who are still dealing with the patterns and structures of the language, we must rid ourselves of the belief that they need to be taught any differently than students learning to compose in regular English classes. Once we accept the notion that the two classroom situations are parallel, we can begin to learn from information which we seem to have totally ignored and which undermines many of the approaches that have been advocated.

Methodology on the Teaching of English Composition

Research in the teaching of English composition is still at a stage where findings are far from definitive and often contradictory. It has, however, provided enough evidence in some areas, areas that have important ramifications for the teaching of composition to ESL students. If we hope to make any progress, and if we are to halt the proliferation of different approaches and answers, none of which, I believe, are very satisfactory, we should begin to look at and learn from this evidence.

One such area is the issue of frequency of writing and how effective this kind of practice is. Brière and Erazmus, alluded to earlier, feel committed to the idea that one learns to write by writing. What, however, does research tell us about the factor of frequency? Can writing great quantities provide the practice necessary for improvement? If so, the role of the teacher seems to be reduced to one of assigning topics and correcting errors. Can this after-the-fact instruction really be called the teaching of composition?

The answers to these questions become quite apparent when one looks through the results of experiments that set out to demonstrate that frequency was crucial to the improvement of writing. Repeatedly, the research has indicated that frequency in and of itself is fruitless; mere practice in writing will not improve student composition. While this may sound rather obvious, a great deal of effort has been invested to prove just the opposite. The classic review of the research in the teaching of composition by Braddock et al. (1963: 35) alludes to some of these studies concluding that "it does not seem reasonable that doubling the number of aimless writing assignments which are then marked in a perfunctory manner would necessarily stimulate students to improve their writing." A more critical review of recent studies of the effect of writing frequency on writing improvement by Robert Hunting (1967) reiterates this notion. Moreover, this review, concentrating on one experiment in particular, informs us that "practice which is merely frequent, unaccompanied by instruction or motivation, may hurt writing more than improve it" (Hunting 1967: 31). Other experiments substantiate that writing frequently can in fact have detrimental effects (see, e.g., Dressel et al. 1952).[1] Thus, in the light of this research evidence, we cannot help but agree that "English teachers . . . should not assign or elicit any writing for the purpose of developing composition unless the writing becomes the vehicle for functional instruction" (Hunting 1967: 39-40).

If the number of compositions written has no effect or even detrimental effect upon the quality of writing, and if there are other factors that are related to the improvement of writing, then the issue becomes one of determining what this "functional instruction" should be. Let us eliminate error correction from the outset since by instruction we mean the teaching that will prepare students to write, not the proof-reading on which teachers waste so much of their time and which probably has little effect upon the students' ability to compose. When we look at the kind of instruction that has been recommended in the past, however, we find that it is not very much better than the grading of papers with red pencil marks. Just as the ESL approach to teaching composition has largely been based on grammatically-oriented instruction, the study of grammar and usage has long been synonymous with the teaching of composition in the field of English. One needs only to look at the great number of experiments seeking to establish the effect of grammar on the improvement of writing to realize that "for over a century teachers had been teaching grammar and expecting, indeed assuming, that it would help their students write better" (O'Hare 1973: 6).

The evidence of the research clearly undermines the case for grammar and thus has tremendous implications for the ESL teacher who provides extensive practice with the manipulation and imitation of patterns and even longer passages. While it is true that no direct teaching of grammar may be taking place, the ESL teacher is nevertheless assuming that these exercises are the key to unlocking the creative process. Extensive research, however, has shown us otherwise: over and over again, the study of grammar, whether formal or not, has been found to have little, no or even harmful influence upon the students' writing ability.

At first, studies were carried out to demonstrate the futility of formal grammar study (see, e.g., Frogner 1939 and Kraus 1957). Harris' classic study (see Braddock et al. 1963: 83) established for once and for all that the systematic study of traditional grammar has a "negligible or even a harmful effect upon the correctness of writing." With the new approaches to grammar study, however, came new attempts to show their effects upon students' writing ability. Thus, researchers influenced by Charles Fries sought to demonstrate the progress made by students receiving instruction based on a structural approach to grammar (see, e.g., Suggs 1961, O'Donnell 1963, Klauser 1964, White 1964 and Henderson 1967). Not surprisingly, the results were contradictory and the question of instruction was left unresolved. Even when students were receiving practice in the recognition and manipulation of structures, rather than the formal study of grammatical terminology, writing ability was not affected. O'Donnell (1963: 26-27) took an important step in the right direction when he realized that, while a knowledge of grammatical structures may be an important factor, writing is a complex process and involves more than the manipulation and recognition of basic elements; it seems likely that the awareness of basic structures is essential to written composition, but it is obvious that such awareness is not always accompanied by proficiency in writing.

With the advent of a still newer grammar, researchers committed themselves to studying the effects of generative-transformational grammar on the writing ability of students. Kellogg Hunt (1970) explained how the knowledge of transformational rules would help students generate sentences, while Bateman and Zidonis (1966) investigated the effects of such grammar study. The experimental treatment led to an increase in the number of grammatically correct sentences, and the skill of writing was again being identified with correct sentence structure. Soon, however, evidence appeared contradicting the findings of Bateman and Zidonis (see, e.g., Wardhaugh 1967 and Fry 1971), and the whole notion of systematically teaching rules, even those of a newer grammar, came under attack (see, e.g., Lester 1967).

Rejecting the notion that transformational rules had to be learned, John Mellon's study (1969) involved the manipulation of transformations, that is, sentence-combining practice. He concluded that it was this process, rather than learning transformational grammar, that resulted in syntactic fluency. More importantly, in the light of this discussion, was the differentiation he made between syntactic fluency and the rhetorical skill of composing: he reminded us not to assume that facility in sentence-combining had anything directly to do with the complexities of organization and expression. It should be noted that Mellon's experimental group received systematic grammar study in addition to practice in transformational sentence-combining. It was really not clear, therefore, whether it was the practice alone that led to the observed improvement. Thus, O'Hare (1973) set out to prove just that, abandoning entirely the formal study of grammar. The results indicated an improvement in overall quality of students' compositions, thus leading O'Hare to conclude that grammar-free sentence-combining does in fact affect the rhetorical aspects of writing. While it may be true that the syntactic skills that the students had acquired provided them with more alternatives for expression, it does not seem likely that that skill in and of itself was responsible for the successful performances. As a matter of fact, though Mellon's group wrote more systematically mature sentences, their compositions were judged qualitatively inferior. It appears then that syntax and rhetoric are complementary yet separate aspects of the writing process, neither one being responsible for improvement in the other. To believe otherwise refutes that which evidence has already substantiated. Moreover, it allows us to continue in our futile search for the right grammar or the most effective practice, simplistic solutions to a very complex problem.

Where Do We Go From Here?

The results of the research in the teaching of composition has had its impact. In order to discover what writing really entails, instead of looking for pat answers, different kinds of questions are being asked. Rather than approach the issue from the "grammar side," investigators are beginning to approach it from the "composition side," forcing us "to rethink the problems involved" (Potter 1967: 20). Rather than ask how to teach composition, we are trying to discover what writing is, what it involves and what differentiates the good from the bad writer. Janet Emig (1971), Terry Radcliffe (1972) and others have already demonstrated how naive our past assumptions and how oversimplified our traditional models have been. We are beginning to abandon our simplistic approaches, consisting of either providing frequent assignments or grammatically-based practice. Our whole attitude toward what the writing act represents should drastically change; like British teachers and their approach, we should become more concerned with the individual's purpose and desire for writing, while providing stimulation, a minimum of interference and correction and some indirect instruction (Squire and Applebee 1969: 118-153). The act of composing should become the result of a genuine need to express one's personal feeling, experience or reaction, all this within a climate of encouragement (Loban et al. 1961: 485-541). Once this has been established, and the fear of writing has been removed, students will have much greater facility with the other types of writing assignments they may be expected to do in school. Finally, teachers of writing, whether ESL or English, should continuously strive to provide that instruction which best meets the real needs and abilities of individual students. While this instruction might still entail some indirect teaching concerning particular structural problems, language study and rhetorical considerations, the primary emphasis should be upon the expressive and creative process of writing. The experience of composing could in this way have a purpose, that of communicating genuine thoughts and experiences. ESL students could begin to appreciate English as another language to use, rather than just a second language to learn.

Note

1. While there has been some experimental support for the positive effects of writing frequency (see, e.g., Lokke and Wykoff 1948, Maize 1954, McColly and Remstad 1963 and Wolf 1966), one should bear in mind that these results were most probably due to factors unrelated to the issue of frequency, such as the kind of instruction and learning activities provided, the process and method of correction or the criteria for evaluation.

Works Cited

Allen, Edward D. and R. M. Valette. 1972. *Language classroom techniques*. New York, Harcourt Brace Jovanovich.

Arapoff, Nancy. 1969. A method of teaching writing to foreign students. *TESOL Quarterly 3*, 4, 297-304.

Bateman, D. R. and F. J. Zidonis. 1966. *The effect of a study of transformational grammar on the writing of ninth and tenth graders*. Champaign, Ill., NCTE.

Billows, F. L. 1961. *The techniques of language teaching*. London, Longmans, Green & Co.

Braddock, Richard et al. 1963. *Research in written composition*. Champaign, Ill., NCTE.

Brière, Eugenie J. 1966. Quantity before quality in second language composition. *Language Learning 16*, 141-151.

Carr, Donna H. 1967. A second look at teaching reading and composition. *TESOL Quarterly 1*, 1, 30-34.

Cave, George N. 1972. From controlled to free composition. *English Language Teaching 26*, 262-269.

Chastain, Kenneth. 1971. *The development of modern language skills*. Philadelphia, Center for Curriculum Development.

Dressel, Paul et al. 1952. The effects of writing frequency upon essay-type writing proficiency at the college level. *Journal of Educational Research 46*, 285-293.

Dykstra, Gerald. 1964. Eliciting language practice in writing. *English Language Teaching 19*, 23-26.

Emig, Janet. 1971. *The composing process of twelfth graders*. Urbana, Ill., NCTE.

Erazmus, Edward. 1960. Second language composition teaching at the intermediate level. *Language Learning 10*, 25-31.

Finocchiaro, Mary. 1958. *Teaching English as a second language*. New York, Harper & Row.

Frogner, Ellen. 1939. Grammar approach versus thought approach in teaching sentence structure. *English Journal 28*, 518-526.

Fry, Danny J. 1971. The effects of transformational grammar upon the writing performance of students of low socio-economic backgrounds. *Dissertation Abstracts International 32/09*, 4835A.

Green, J. F. 1967. Preparing an advanced composition course. *English Language Teaching 21*, 141-150

Henderson, Charles A. 1967. A study of the relationship between awareness of basic structural relationships in English and increased ability in written composition. *Dissertation Abstracts International 29/01*, 184A.

Hunt, Kellogg W. 1970. How little sentences grow into big ones. *Readings in applied transformational grammar*, ed. Mark Lester, 170-186. New York, Holt, Rinehart & Winston.

Hunting, Robert. 1967. Recent studies of writing frequency. *Research in the Teaching of English 1*, 29-40.

Kaplan, Robert B. 1967. Contrastive rhetoric and the teaching of composition. *TESOL Quarterly 1*, 3, 10-16.

Klauser, Eva L. 1964. A comparison of a structural approach and a traditional approach to the teaching of grammar in an Illinois junior high school. *Dissertation Abstracts International 25/10*, 5633.

Kraus, Silvey A. 1957. A comparison of three methods of teaching sentence structure. *English Journal 46*, 275-281.

Lester, Mark. 1967. The value of transformational grammar in teaching composition. *College Composition and Communication 18*, 227-231.

Loban, Walter. et al. 1961. *Teaching English and literature*. New York, Harcourt, Brace & World.

Lokke, V. L. and G. S. Wykoff, 1948. Double writing in freshman composition—an experiment. *School and Society 68*, 437-439.

Maize, Roy C. 1954. Two methods of teaching composition to retarded college freshmen. *Journal of Educational Psychology 45*, 22-28.

McColly, William and Robert Remstad. 1963. *Comparative effectiveness of composition skills learning activities in the secondary school*. Madison, Wisconsin, ERIC Document Reproductive Service, ED 003 279.

Mellon, John C. 1969. *Transformational sentence-combining: a method for enhancing the development of syntactic fluency in English composition*. Champaign, Ill., NCTE.

Moody. K. W. 1965. Controlled composition frames. *English Language Journal 19*, 146-155.

O'Donnell, Roy C. 1963. *The correlation of awareness of structural relationships in English and ability in written composition*. North Carolina, ERIC Document Reproductive Service, ED 003 280.

O'Hare, Frank. 1973. *Sentence combining: improving student writing without formal grammar instruction*. Urbana, Ill., NCTE.

Paulston, Christina B. 1972. Teaching composition in the ESOL classroom: techniques for controlled composition. *TESOL Quarterly 6*, 1, 33-59.

Pincas, Anita. 1962. Structural linguistics and systematic composition teaching to students of English as a foreign language. *Language Learning 12*, 185-194.

Pincas, Anita. 1964. Teaching different styles of written English. *English Language Teaching 18*, 74-81.

Potter, Robert R. 1967. Sentence structure and prose quality: an exploratory study. *Research in the Teaching of English 1*, 17-28.

Povey, John F. 1969. Creative writing in BIA schools. *TESOL Quarterly 3*, 4, 305-308.

Radcliffe, Terry. 1972. Talk-write composition: a theoretical model proposing use of speech to improve writing. *Research in the Teaching of English 6*, 187-199.

Rivers, Wilga M. 1968. *Teaching foreign Language skills*. Chicago, University of Chicago Press.

Rojas, Pauline M. 1968. Writing to learn. *TESOL Quarterly 2*, 2, 127-129.

Ross, Janet. 1968. Controlled writing: a transformational approach. *TESOL Quarterly 2, 4*, 253-261.

Spencer, D. H. 1965. Two types of guided composition. *English Language Teaching 19*, 156-158.

Squire, James R. and Roger K. Applebee. 1969. *Teaching English in the United Kingdom*. Champaign, Ill., NCTE.

Suggs, Lena R. 1961. Structural grammar versus traditional grammar in influencing writing. *English Journal 50*, 174-178.

Wardhaugh, Ronald. 1967. Ability in written composition and transformational grammar. *Journal of Educational Research, 60*, 427-429.

White, Robert H. 1964. The effect of structural linguistics on improving English composition compared to that of prescriptive grammar or the absence of grammar instruction. *Dissertation Abstracts International 25/09*, 5032.

Wolf, Melvin. 1966. *Effect of writing frequency upon proficiency in a college freshman course*. Amherst, Mass., ERIC Document Reproductive Service, ED 003 384.

What Unskilled ESL Students Do as They Write: A Classroom Study of Composing
by Ann Raimes

What We Know About Composing in a First Language

Since the 1960s, researchers studying the composing processes of native speakers of English have been assembling, out of the idiosyncratic variety of writers' activities they observe, a composite picture of a process that is far from idiosyncratic. This is what experienced writers do: They consider purpose and audience. They consult their own background knowledge. They let ideas incubate. They plan. As they write, they read back over what they have written to keep in touch with their "conceptual blueprint" (Beach 1979), which helps them plan what to write next. Contrary to what many textbooks advise, writers do not follow a neat sequence of planning, organizing, writing, and then revising. For while a writer's product—the finished essay, story, or novel—is presented in lines, the process that produces it is not linear at all. Instead, it is recursive, a "cyclical process during which writers move back and forth on a continuum discovering, analyzing, and synthesizing ideas" (Hughey, Wormuth, Hartfiel, and Jacobs 1983:28). With such "retrospective structuring" (Perl 1979:331), writers inevitably discover new ideas as they write and then change their plans and goals accordingly. Writing, therefore, does not serve just to record preformed ideas; it helps create and form ideas, too. The view of writing as a tool for learning and not just a means to demonstrate learning is one of the major contributions of the research into the writing process (Emig 1977).

As well as studying experienced, professional writers (Emig 1975, Della-Piana 1978, Murray 1978, Sommers 1980) to derive a model of the process of skilled writers, researchers have examined other groups of writers: "traditional" college freshmen (Pianko 1979, Sommers 1980), high school students (Emig 1971, Mischel 1974, Stallard 1974, Matsuhashi 1981), children (Graves 1975, Calkins 1980), technical writers (Selzer 1983), teachers (Perl 1980), and those with writer's block (Rose 1980). Unskilled writers writing in their first language have also been examined. Perl (1978, 1979), for instance, audiotaped five unskilled writers, college students who were native speakers of English, as they composed aloud while writing on two course-related topics, one objective, the other more personal. Her coding system (1978, 1979, 1981) made possible a quantitative analysis of the behaviors exhibited. Perl concludes that unskilled writers display "stable composing processes" (1979:328), though these consistent processes are very different from those of skilled writers.

What sets apart the unskilled writers? They take less time to plan (Pianko 1979), and their plans are less flexible than the good writers' (Rose 1980). They re-scan large segments of their work less often than skilled writers do, and when they do re-scan, it is usually more for the purpose of correcting surface-level errors than for assessing the fit between their plans and the product (Perl 1979, Sommers 1980, Faigley and Witte 1981, Flower and Hayes 1981). Their revising is really mostly editing; the changes they make focus on form rather than content. They are overly and prematurely concerned with accuracy (Perl 1979). Once they put ideas on the page, they seldom rework them. The first draft either becomes the final draft or resembles it very closely. In addition, inexperienced writers spend little time considering the reader: They find it difficult to move from their "writer-based prose" to prose that conveys a message unequivocally to the reader (Flower 1979).

For these unskilled writers, a process approach to teaching is developing—one which stresses generating ideas, writing drafts, producing feedback, and revising—in an attempt to make their behavior, and ultimately their products, more like those of skilled writers. Research into the effectiveness of such a process approach to teaching L1 writers, while limited, has so far yielded positive results (Odell 1974, Hilgers 1980).

What We Know About Composing in a Second Language and What We Need to Know

A similar shift can be observed in the teaching of ESL writing, too, as teachers learn from recent studies of L2 composing processes (Edelsky 1982, Jacobs 1982, Jones 1982a, 1982b, 1983, in press, Lay 1982, 1983, Zamel 1982, 1983, Tetroe and Jones 1983, 1984, Gaskill 1984a, 1984b, Heuring 1984, Pfingstag 1984, Raimes 1984, Jones and Tetroe in press). While the number of studies gives us little reason to lament that "studies of second language writing are sadly lacking" (Krashen 1984:41), the fact that many are case studies with a limited number of subjects makes it difficult to form conclusive generalizations. However, some patterns are emerging. Studies of the ESL composing process have largely noted the similarities between composing in L1 and L2 (Jones 1982b, 1983, Lay 1982, 1983, Zamel 1982, 1983, Tetroe and Jones 1983). Lay, for example, found that her five Chinese subjects "used many of the strategies used by native language students in composing" (1983:19); Jones and Tetroe found for their five Venezuelan students "strong, direct data for the transfer of first language skill to second language" in writing and concluded that "second language composing is not a different animal from first language composing" (in press). Similarities between unskilled L1 and L2 writers have been pointed out, too. Unskilled ESL writers were found not to revise efficiently, to focus on local concerns in their texts (Heuring 1984), and "like inexperienced or basic native language writers . . . to have a very limited and limiting notion of what composing involves" (Zamel 1984: 198-199).

However, before we base our pedagogy on observations of similarities between unskilled L1 and L2 writers, we need to be cautious for two reasons. First, there is at present no consensus on valid criteria for measuring skill in writing and thus no clear agreement on the meaning of *unskilled*. Jones and Tetroe see language proficiency as a factor in "the effectiveness of the process," with lower proficiency level reducing "the quantity, though not quality of planning" (in press). Zamel, on the other hand, plays down the role of language proficiency in determining skill: "While ESL students must certainly deal with concerns that are linguistic-specific, it seems that it is their writing strategies and behaviors and not primarily language proficiency that determine composing skill" (1984:198). Yet most assessments of skill in writing look at the written products and thus inevitably take language proficiency into account. In fact, the ESL Composition Profile developed by Jacobs, Zingraf, Wormuth, Hartfiel, and Hughey (1981) devotes three of its five subheads to linguistic-specific assessment: Vocabulary, Language Use, and Mechanics. Furthermore, the writing skill of Zamel's (1983) own subjects was judged not by their strategies and behaviors, but by holistic assessment of their papers. On that basis, two of her six writers were judged as unskilled, even though they had taken and passed two semesters of freshman composition courses! Any examination of unskilled writers must therefore clearly address the question, Unskilled relative to whom and according to what criteria? For generalizations from several studies can be made only if the same criteria are used.

Second, we must be cautious about letting a pedagogical shift in the teaching of L1 writing determine what we look for in ESL research. Until recently, teaching procedures for ESL writers were clear: They were moved in lockstep fashion from the sentence to the paragraph, from controlled composition to guided essays, and only when they had achieved near-native proficiency were they allowed to really compose. The recent shift in composition theory and research has changed this pedagogy; now teachers ask their ESL students to write journals (Spack and Sadow 1983), to do written brainstorming and free writing (Taylor 1981, Knepler 1984), to delay attending to error (Zamel 1984), and to respond to each other's writing in a collaborative workshop setting (Keyes 1984, Stokes 1984). We should not, however, swing too far in the direction of treating students like native speakers of the language. If ESL writing courses in our institutions are to be taught by trained ESL teachers and not just by writing teachers, then we need to know what our students do differently from what basic writers do. We need to know what characterizes them as writers grappling not only with a written code but with a linguistic code that is still being acquired. Despite research findings, all of us who have tried to write something in a second language (which all ESL writing teachers should attempt periodically) sense that the process of writing in an L2 is startlingly different from writing in our L1.

These concerns initiated the design of a classroom study which would look for features of composing specific to unskilled ESL writers. Findings from such a study might contribute to a refined definition of the term unskilled and might very possibly have implications for instruction.

The Classroom Study

Purposes

The study was designed to explore three questions:

1. What are the composing processes of unskilled ESL student writers performing a classroom task?
2. How does the specification of audience and purpose affect the composing behaviors of ESL students?
3. Is think-aloud protocol analysis—more specifically, Perl's (1978, 1979, 1981) scheme for coding unskilled L1 writers' processes—an effective tool for analyzing the composing behaviors of ESL students?

Procedures

Students were asked to think aloud into a tape recorder as they composed, so that the resulting protocols (the taped record of the composing aloud) could be analyzed. This method of research was selected despite the reservations that have been expressed about whether composing aloud is similar to the process of composing silently (Perl 1980, Cooper and Holzman 1983) and whether it might in fact interfere with writers' "normal composing processes, interrupting their trains of thought" (Faigley and Witte 1981:412). Retrospective self-reports were rejected as an alternative: They might seem less intrusive, but they are also incomplete, since not all of the information involved in performing a task enters short-term memory. People tend, as Gestalt psychologists have found, to "forget goals and subgoals once they have been accomplished" (Hayes and Flower 1983:215); in addition, when questioned about their behavior after the fact, they often try to provide the expected answer to help the experimenter. Ericsson and Simon's (1980) thorough review of the literature on tracing mental processes concluded that when information which is already verbal is reported audibly, the performance of the task itself is not visibly affected. Only when subjects are asked to report information that they would not normally pay attention to is the performance of the task changed. Hayes and Flower, who use the think-aloud method of investigation extensively, report that Ericsson and Simon (1980) "found no evidence that thinking-aloud protocols change the course or the structure of the task being studied" (1983:216).

While there is demonstrated reason to trust in the efficacy of think-aloud protocol analysis as a tool in composition research, one which would reveal writers' behaviors as a clue to their underlying psychological processes, it has only recently been used as a research tool in language learning studies. To test the feasibility of this approach for ESL students still struggling with the language, I asked two ESL students at Hunter College to compose aloud on an assigned essay topic as I observed and made notes. I instructed them to voice what they were thinking: to plan aloud, to say the words as they wrote them, to read aloud, and to make changes aloud. I did not ask them to analyze or explain what they were doing. Such an activity is too intrusive and "changes the subject's focus by imposing an additional task" (Swarts, Flower, and Hayes 1984:55). Not unexpectedly, the thinking aloud did not come easily to them at first, but both adapted to it surprisingly quickly. When it became apparent what the resulting protocols would yield about both speech and writing and how much more they revealed about the students as writers than mere analysis of products or observation of the writing process, I decided that think-aloud composing was simply too good a tool not to be used. From what these two students said and did, I could build a picture of two remarkably different writers. Certainly the differences between them as writers were revealed far more clearly in the protocols than in the products alone.

Once I had decided to use verbal protocols, I tried to cut down on other new contexts that might influence behavior, since I did not want the students to have to cope with a vast array of experimental conditions. So I asked my own students to compose aloud on tape in the language laboratory in regular class time, with a timed, on-the-spot writing assignment that was familiar to them. As the regular classroom teacher, I would be in the room to answer questions. Many of my students were already familiar with the language laboratory, having used it for foreign language classes or for ESL supplementary instruction. Thus, they would not be intimidated by the lab or by tape recorders.

Subjects

All of the subjects were students in my six-hour-a-week developmental ESL composition course at Hunter College in the Spring 1983 semester. This is the second in a series of three courses that students take before they enter the required course in freshman composition. Completion of the sequence is accomplished by satisfactory performance on the City University of New York Writing Assessment Test, a 50-minute essay required of all City University students, which is read and rated by two or, in the case of disagreement, three readers trained in holistic evaluation. Placement into the course is by the same method. Thus students are placed into the course according to an assessment of their writing, not according to any assessment of their overall language proficiency. Discounting students who were absent for one or more of the data-collecting tasks or who failed to tape correctly, eight complete sets of data were obtained: from four speakers of Chinese, two of Greek, one of Spanish, and one of Burmese.

Measures

The data came from four sources:

1. Scores on the grammar, vocabulary, and reading sections of the multiple-choice *Michigan Test of English Language Proficiency* (1962). I wanted an inexpensive, easy-to-administer, and objectively scored test based on the norms of entering college students.
2. Holistic scores on the essays. I wanted judgments of skill comparable in type to Zamel's (1983) and Perl's (1979), so I asked three readers trained in holistic evaluation of essays for the City University of New York Writing Assessment Test to rate the students' essays on a 6-point scale. From the sum of the three scores, a ranking of the written products could thus be obtained.
3. Answers to a 12-page questionnaire, which focused on the students' background, education, and experience with and attitude toward English and writing.
4. Responses to the think-aloud composing. Think-aloud writing was discussed in class to prepare the students for their own composing aloud. I demonstrated composing aloud with a topic they gave me, and I played them the tape of one of the students in the pilot study. Then they tried composing aloud in small groups and were asked to practice at home with their next assignment. Most reported that they did. Then, a few days later, I took the whole class into the language laboratory, seated all the students before tape recorders with the privacy of headphones and cubicles, gave them an assigned topic, and asked them to compose aloud as the tape ran. The composing session yielded the students' written products and the tapes of what they said as they wrote.

The Writing Task

I chose a type of narrative task that had been used before with ESL students (Jones 1982a, in press) and with unskilled L1 writers (Pianko 1979). However, since I was interested in exploring whether the students, if given a framework of a specific purpose and audience to consider, would refer to this in their think-aloud protocol and take it into account as they planned and wrote, I added a variation to the narrative task. Half of the class, at random, was asked to write on a topic with no specification of purpose or audience: "Tell about something unexpected that happened to you" (Topic A). This topic was used previously with ESL students by Jones (1982a) to elicit narrative. The other half of the class was assigned a similar topic, but the directions, which were worded differently, specified both a clear audience and purpose (Topic B):

A Hunter College student, Maria Chen, is writing a term paper for a psychology course on what people do when something unexpected happens to them. She is collecting information for this paper and would like your help. Tell her about something unexpected that happened to you. (She thanks you for your help, and she will use the information that you give her in the paper, but without using your name.)

Of the eight students finally selected for this study, five wrote on Topic A and three on Topic B.

Coding and Analysis of the Tapes

The tapes were coded, minute by minute, on a time line, using a slightly modified version of Perl's (1981) coding scheme (see Figure 1). Reliability checks with another coder, an ESL graduate research assistant who was working with me on the project, indicated an 84 percent rate of agreement across three tapes, averaged across all coding categories. The coding sheets were analyzed for the duration, frequency, and position of various writing behaviors. An example of the coding of the first ten minutes of composing time for one of the students can be found in the Appendix, along with the transcribed text of the corresponding think-aloud composing tape and the actual text of the finished essay.

FIGURE 1

Coding Categories*

A	Assessing (+ = positive, − = negative)	Rh	Rehearsing (developing content, trying out ideas)
C	Commenting	RI	Researcher intervention
E	Editing	R^T	Reading the assigned topic
Pl	Planning structure or strategy	RV	Revising
Q	Questioning	R^W	Reading the whole draft (after Sentence 4)
R	Reading sentence or part of sentence (followed by number of sentence)	s	Silence
re	Repeating a word, phrase, or part of sentence	U	Unintelligible remark
		W	Writing

Surface-Level Editing Changes (Indicated as Subscripts of E and Rh)		Revising Changes Affecting Meaning (Indicated as Subscripts of RV)	
a	addition	a	addition
d	deletion	d	deletion
gr	grammar	sub	substitution
p	pronunciation	wc	word choice
sp	spelling		
ss	sentence structure		
v	verb form or tense		
wf	word form		

* Adapted from Perl (1981).

Findings

Language Proficiency Test Scores

Although students had been placed in the same class according to their skill in writing, they demonstrated a wide range of scores on language proficiency. The equated score on the *Michigan Test of English Language Proficiency* is derived from adding the raw scores on the three subtests: grammar, vocabulary, and reading (*Michigan Test of English Language Proficiency Manual* 1962:6). The students in this course for unskilled writers had scores ranging from 54 to 80 (see Table 1). The proficiency recommendations included in the test's manual suggest that a student with a score of 69 or below is not proficient enough in English to take any academic work, that a student with 70 to 79 could take from one fourth to one third the normal academic load plus an intensive ESL course of at least ten hours per week, and that a student with 80 to 84 could take up to one half the normal academic load plus a four-hour per week ESL course (1962:7).

My students' wide range of language proficiency test scores did not seem to correspond with demonstrated writing ability, since they had all been placed in the same course; nor did the scores correspond with the number of years the students had lived in the United States and been exposed to the language. In fact, the two students with the longest exposure to the language (11 and 13 years) had the most disparate language proficiency scores (Table 1). In an urban setting like New York, with large immigrant populations, it is, however, not uncommon for some students to continue to use their first language at home, at work, and often at school and thus to be deprived of much opportunity for natural language acquisition.

TABLE 1
Subject Characteristics

Subject	Language Proficiency Score	Essay Evaluation Scores		Years in U.S.
		Scores of 3 Readers	Total	
Johnny (M)	80	2/2/2	6	11.0
Harriet (F)	76	3/3/4	10	5.0
Chih-Hwa (F)	73	3/4/4	11	3.0
Maria (F)	72	3/3/3	9	.5
Watch-Lin (F)	65	3/2/2	7	4.0
Bo-Wen (M)	58	2/2/2	6	3.0
Yin Ping (F)	55	1/2/2	5	3.0
José (M)	54	2/2/3	7	13.0

Evaluation of the Written Products

Three trained evaluators rated the students' essays on a scale of 1 (low) to 6 (high); the individual scores and the total scores are shown in Table 1. Some correspondence can be seen between language proficiency and writing skill in that the students with the three highest ratings all scored above 70 in the language proficiency test, while most of the students with lower ratings scored in the 50s. Interestingly enough, though, one student with relatively low ratings (2/2/2) had the highest proficiency score (80). Johnny thus shows us that it is possible for a student to have many years of exposure to English, to attain a high score in a language proficiency test, and yet still be unskilled in writing.

Selected Questionnaire Responses

Table 2 presents selected student responses to the questionnaire about prior writing experience and instruction. With the exception of Johnny, all the students reported that they sometimes wrote in their Ll and that when they were reading or writing, they sometimes turned to their Ll to help them out. Only two students had not studied how to write an essay in their L1. When asked which language they preferred to write in, L1 or L2, three students chose L1, three sometimes preferred L1 to L2, and two always preferred to write in L2. What emerged from the questionnaire was a picture of most of these students easing their way from L1 to L2, with L1 very much an active part of their academic life. Again, Johnny stood out as the one most detached from L1 in general and especially from L1 writing.

The Composing Session Tapes

Awareness of audience and purpose. Only one of the three students who wrote on Topic B, the assignment with a specified audience and purpose, mentioned the sup-

TABLE 2
Selected Responses to Questionnaire

Student	First Language	Sometimes Writes in L1	Sometimes Seeks Out L1 During L2 Writing	Studied Writing in L1	Preferred Language for Writing
Johnny	Chinese	no	no	no	L2
Harriet	Greek	yes	yes	yes	L1/L2
Chih-Hwa	Chinese	yes	yes	yes	L1
Maria	Greek	yes	yes	yes	L2
Watch-Lin	Burmese	yes	yes	yes	L1/L2
Bo-Wen	Chinese	yes	yes	yes	L1
Yin-Ping	Chinese	yes	yes	yes	L1
José	Spanish	yes	yes	no	L1/L2

posed reader (the fictional psychology student). When my student Maria referred to her specific reader, it was a strategy to find a conclusion. She read her essay through, said, "I don't know how to continue," and then solved her problem by simply concluding her essay with "I hope that my information will help you with your term paper." At no other point did the presence of a specific purpose or reader appear to influence the planning, content, or approach to the essay. The assignment was, despite its wording, justifiably seen by the students as merely another "school-sponsored" topic (Emig 1971:91).

Total time spent composing. The students had a possible 65 minutes of composing time. While in principle, composing tapes tell us how long it is from the time writers are told to begin and the time they judge that they are finished, some students in this study continued to write after the language laboratory tape, which lasted only 45 minutes, had run out (see Table 3). Since they could not turn the tape over and did not ask for a new one, it was not possible to determine how much time they actually spent beyond the 45 minutes. Four of the eight students wrote for longer than 45 minutes. Only one wrote for less than 30 minutes. In her study of 17 native-English writers, Pianko (1979) found less involvement with the task: Even though her students were given a whole afternoon for their assignment, the mean composing time was 38.85 minutes. Perl's (1979) five basic writers, who wrote on course-related topics, showed a longer mean composing time of 76.5 minutes, with individual students showing a range from 24.5 to 120 minutes.

Pre-writing: time spent and activities. Pre-writing was defined as all the activities (such as reading the topic, rehearsing, planning, trying out beginnings, making notes) that students engaged in before they wrote what was the first sentence of their first draft. For three students there were no data (*nd* in Table 3) for the pre-writing time, since they did not turn on the tape until they were ready to put pen to paper. Four of the others devoted a short time to pre-writing—from .75 to 2.2 minutes. This is comparable to Perl's (1979) subjects, for whom pre-writing lasted an average of 4 minutes.

Again, there was one exceptional case: Yin Ping, with 17.5 minutes of pre-writing activities. From just looking at numbers, we might be tempted to think that this student had spent a long time making notes, planning carefully, and exploring all kinds of options before writing what was to be the first sentence of this draft. But the tape and the coding sheet present quite a different story: The long pre-writing time was linked to the number of times the student reread the topic—11 times. Why did she do that? Simply because she did not understand the meaning of the word expected. A teacher looking at her finished product would not necessarily have guessed this, though there was evidence of a few false starts. Although I was in the room the whole time, circulating from student to student, Yin Ping did not once ask for help with the meaning of the word that was so troublesome. Independence? Shyness? Or determination to work out the challenge of the linguistic problem? Whichever it was, the difficulty did not make her give up.

Like Perl's (1979) Tony, who returned to read or rephrase the assignment 19 times in the course of one essay, Yin Ping kept going back to the topic to clarify it

TABLE 3

Composing Session: Time Spent, Pre-Writing, Planning, Repeating, Reading, Rehearsing

	Johnny	Harriet	Chih-Hwa	Maria	Watch-Lin	Bo-Wen	Yin Ping	José
Total Time Spent (Minutes)	37.00	23.00	45+	39.00	45+	41.00	45+	45+
Time Spent Pre-Writing, Before Sentence 1 (Minutes)	nd	nd	2.20	nd	1.20	.75	17.50	2.00
Occurrences of Rereading of Topic	1	0	0	0	0	0	11	0
Occurrences of Planning	1	0	3	0	0	1	12	0
Occurrences of Repeating of Words or Phrases	3	0	68	46	75	40	35	38
Occurrences of Reading of Sentences or Parts of Sentences	10	3	51	53	14	29	55	17
Occurrences of Reading of Whole Draft After Sentence 4	4	0	2	3	1	0	0	1
Occurrences of Rehearsing	1	6	19	6	4	50	22	50

and to find a way to begin writing about it: "Tell about something unexpected that happened to you, something unexpect that happen to me, unexpect that happen to me . . . Does it mean it already happen or I don't want it happen?" Perl hypothesizes that her subjects might have been trying to link the topic with their own experience as they returned to it continually. For Yin Ping, however, the return to the topic in the pre-writing stage seemed to be little more than a desperate attempt to decode and comprehend the question. The other ESL writers in this study understood the vocabulary of the assignment and seldom used the wording of the topic to help them generate ideas.

Planning. The mapping out of strategies for writing—"Now, the next paragraph" or "I'll cross out that sentence and put it in the second Paragraph"—and the discussions of how to proceed, whether for the whole essay or for the next sentence, were coded as Planning (Pi). There were few instances of articulated planning operations: a total of 17 for all eight writers, and 12 of those belonged to Yin Ping as she wrestled with the meaning of the topic. The missing data for the three students who did not turn on the tape until they were ready to write could of course account for the lack of incidents of planning. However, a comparison with Perl's basic writers shows that they, too, frequently "began writing without any secure sense of where they were heading" (1979:330). They did not make lists or outlines or jot down notes. These ESL students, too, with the notable exception of Yin Ping, all decided quite early on what event to describe and then put their energies into how best to describe it in L2.

Reading. As the students were writing, they frequently read back over phrases and sentences just written—a kind of ploy to gain time or, as Perl says, "a waiting, paying attention to what is still vague and unclear" (1980:365). We could, of course, speculate that the constant reading aloud was a feature of the process of composing aloud, a way for a student to fill up tape time. If that had been the case, we would anticipate similar behavior from all the writers. However, as Table 3 shows, Johnny and Harriet, the two students with the highest language proficiency scores, did not continually go back to read and repeat what they had just written. While most of these ESL students showed similarities to Perl's native speakers in the amount of reading and repeating of sentences or parts of sentences, an interesting difference emerges with respect to their reading of the whole draft. Tony, the basic writer Perl (1979) reported on in detail, read his entire draft through (after Sentence 4) 25 times in one writing episode. The eight students in this study read the whole draft through only 11 times in all, with three students not doing it at all. These ESL students read single sentences or the preceding two or three sentences, rather than whole chunks of text. This could perhaps be attributed to the nature of the narrative task. When students are dealing with exposition or argument, they might be more likely to re-read chunks to establish the course of their argument.

Rehearsing. One of the most common activities, both while writing sentences and between writing sentences, was rehearsing (voicing ideas on content and trying out possible ideas). While all the ESL writers rehearsed at some point or other during the composing session, some used verbal rehearsal much more than others; it was used frequently by Bo-Wen and José, in particular, and also by Chih-Hwa and Yin Ping. Johnny rehearsed only once, but since he deleted his first ten sentences and began his draft again, we can conclude that he was rehearsing his ideas on paper, rather than before setting them down.

Rehearsing appeared to serve two different purposes, not indicated by the coding. Some writers rehearsed to search for grammatically acceptable forms, as with José:

> They ask me, they ask me that I, no, that they want, they asked me that they want to go, no, they asked that, that, if they can, they ask me that if, that if, I can, I could, if I could take them to 115 Street.

Others talked out ideas, tried things out, and tested on an audience words and phrases that were never put on paper. Bo-Wen seemed to be regarding *me* as the listener/audience, if not as the reader, as he talked out his ideas. He said, "I just want to tell you about Chinese culture revolution." Then he wrote part of a sentence, "When it was in the Chinese culture revolution . . ." and stopped for a kind of aside to the listener, a rehearsal of what was in his mind: "In Chinese, the culture revolution, I went to countryside, because at that time there was no school and no people working so many students graduated from school, but not really . . ." He laughed and went on, "I just wanted to say that they didn't learn anything in school." This rehearsal of text, which explained fully what he meant, then somehow got reduced as it was translated into written composition. Bo-Wen now left out himself and many of the details. After his opening of "When it was the Chinese culture revolution," he continued by adding rather drily: "schools were closed and factories didn't product." It was as if he saw the audience for the tape as having different requirements from the audience for the piece of writing.

Writing. The mean number of sentences the students wrote for this assignment was 24; the mean number of words was 309 (see Table 4). Tony, Perl's (1979) basic writer, spent 91.2 minutes on his first assignment, yet ended up with a second draft of only 10 sentences and 170 words. Of this group of low-level ESL writers, only one—Yin Ping, who had trouble understanding the wording of the topic—wrote fewer words and sentences than Tony.

The number of sentences the students wrote without interruption, or without engaging in other activities such as reading back or rehearsing, ranged from 0 to 28. For the most part, the students with the highest language proficiency scores exhibited the most occasions of such "fluency" in their writing. The same students who engaged in other activities during sentence writing also engaged in other behaviors between the writing of sentences. That is, fluency of producing text within the sentence was for the most part extended to fluency from sentence to sentence.

For some of the writers with lower proficiency scores, however, a smooth passage from one sentence to the next was somewhat less troublesome than completing an individual sentence without hesitation. Watch-Lin, for instance, wrote only 8 out of 31 sentences "fluently" but began 18 of her sentences without hesitation after finishing the preceding sentence. Other writers, too, would begin with the flourish of a *however* or an *although* and would then stall. Yin Ping, for instance, began a new

TABLE 4

Composing Session: Writing, Revising, Editing

	Number of Occurrences								
	Johnny	Harriet	Chih-Hwa	Maria	Watch-Lin	Bo-Wen	Yin Ping	José	Total
Sentences in Final Draft	23	28	18	34	31	29	8	19	
Words in Final Draft	292	394	291	371	398	287	126	316	
Sentences Written Without Interruption (No More than One s and/or re)	28	27	1	11	8	5	0	2	
Sentences Written Immediately, with No Activities After Previous Sentence	16	23	5	16	18	11	1	10	
Revisions									
Within Sentences	0	2	2	3	1	5	4	1	18
Between Sentences	0	0	2	1	1	2	5	1	12
While Reading Over	4	0	0	2	6	1	0	0	13
TOTAL	4	2	4	6	8	8	9	2	43
Editing Operations									
Within Sentences	4	1	3	4	8	2	12	12	46
Between Sentences	0	0	3	3	0	0	2	0	8
While Reading Over	2	0	0	0	3	0	0	1	6
TOTAL	6	1	6	7	11	2	14	13	60

paragraph immediately after finishing the previous one. With no hesitation, she plunged in with "I remember," and then she paused and asked, "I remember what? What I have to talk about now?" At this point, caught in the middle of something not quite expressed, she fled for safety back to the security of what had already found form and been committed to paper—the previous paragraph, which she now read twice and edited. Then she could continue with her essay, having now come up with something to follow "I remember." It may well be that even for those who have difficulty writing L2 sentences, the act of producing L2 writing is so exponentially generative that their creativity, once engaged, carries them on; plans for more text creation may come more easily than the actual means of carrying out those plans.

Revising and editing. The act of producing L2 writing in this study seemed to be so involving and exhausting that production of a new draft was rare. Only one of these ESL writers, Johnny, began again—and his new beginning was not very different from his old. Out of Perl's (1978) 20 writing sessions, however, single drafts occurred in only 4. Of course, even though Perl's subjects were nontraditional students and unskilled writers, they still had a great deal of fluent spoken language at their disposal. Witness Stan, who says that when a good writer "writes about something, you can actually read it and visualize it exactly as he has written it." He explains that "a writer is trying to capture the reader's attention and to do this, he has to put in certain things, not necessarily the truth" (181). This student may be a basic writer, but his use of English generally is far in advance of many ESL students.

While neither these students nor Perl's (1979) made major reformulations of their texts, they went about revising and editing in different ways. Perl's Tony made a total of 234 changes in his 4 writing sessions, and 210 of these (90 percent) concentrated on surface form. Altogether, Perl's five students made 617 changes in 4 writing sessions (a total of 20 sessions), or an average of 31 changes per session; again, a large number of these changes (89 percent) addressed features of surface form. Perl thus concludes that "editing intrudes so often and to such a degree that it breaks down the rhythms generated by thinking and writing" (333). Zamel (1983:174), too, reported that her unskilled ESL writer paused often, was "distracted by local problems," and rarely made changes that affected meaning.

The mean number of revisions and editing changes that these ESL writers made was 13; the range was from 3 to 23 (see Table 4). The total number of changes they made in the eight essays was 103, and only 60 of those (58 percent) concentrated on surface form. Sixty-two percent (64/103) of the changes they made took place during the writing of a sentence, rather than between sentences or while reading over the draft.

For the most part, then, editing and revising took place during the working out of an idea and not as a cleanup operation. Indeed, clarifying an idea as it emerged appeared to be the main motive for making changes in the text. The nature of the narrative task could account for this, since the students were using vocabulary and sentence structure they felt comfortable and secure with. Alternatively, it could be that when writing takes place in L2, students are not as concerned with accuracy as we thought they were, that their primary concern is to get down on paper their ideas on a topic. Or, indeed, maybe it was the act of composing aloud that took their attention away from errors and editing and focused it more on the flow of ideas and the communication of content.

Conclusions and Implications

These findings lead to tentative conclusions about the research questions posed at the beginning of the study, at least with respect to the eight students in this study, and have implications for both pedagogy and research.

As the students wrote, they exhibited not only attention to the task but commitment to it. The students' attention was riveted on their writing. The essays were not "written as quickly as possible," as Pianko (1979:10) found with her native-speaker freshman writers. None counted words as Pianko's subjects did, who perhaps were prompted to do so by the instruction to write a 400-word essay! None dealt with the assignment in a perfunctory way. Perhaps their own dual purpose—to learn how to write and to learn English—made this commitment possible, with language learning being a more concrete aim in their minds than writing.

Compared to Perl's (1979) Tony, who produced only ten sentences of finished text, these students wrote a great deal. That such an unprepared-for, teacher-initiated assignment can produce so much original language from ESL students can be seen as testimony to our students' creativity and should be taken advantage of in any ESL class, not just in a writing course. In a short time, these students produced enough text to provide material for many discussions of ideas, content, culture, audience, organization, rhetorical form, syntax, vocabulary, grammar, spelling, and mechanics. While some unskilled students might find it frustrating to produce such a piece of writing on demand, they consider it justified if their writing then becomes the raw material, the "comprehensible input," as Krashen (1981) calls it, for other class activities. And for classroom input, surely student-generated material is more valuable—and more valued by the students—than textbook sentences about the tiresome Mr. Smith.

The students did not, as a group, seem preoccupied with error and with editing. Contrary to my expectations, they edited less than Perl's basic writers, whose "premature and rigid attempts to correct and edit their own work" seemed to "truncate the flow of composing" (1979:328). The ESL writers in this study appeared to go back in order to read, to let an idea gel and find its form and voice, and to get a "running start" on the next sentence (William Gaskill, personal communication). Sometimes in the course of reading back, they edited, but very often they did not. Are we perhaps doing our ESL writers a disservice if we ask them to do rapid free writing, if we try to cut down on those pauses and backtrackings, all in the name of "fluent writing"? If recursiveness is not being used so much for correction, what are the writers using it for? Do some ESL writers need that time and that recursiveness to generate not only ideas but the L2 with which to express the ideas to another? And if some need it, which ones? This study raised these questions but did not answer them.

One possibility is that unskilled ESL writers do not go back to edit as often as the unskilled native speakers because they are not so intimidated by the thought of error. They know that they are language learners, that they use the language imperfectly. They expect the teacher to correct the language they produce, and that is why many of them have enrolled in a class. Since they expect errors and do not see them as stigmatizing in the way that L1 errors are, they are not preoccupied with them. Instead, they concentrate on the challenge of finding the right words and sentences to express their meaning. Zamel was concerned that, for her skilled ESL writers, "perhaps too much attention to meaning alone kept these students from carefully examining certain surface features of writing" (1983:176). If in fact our students are focusing on meaning anyway, we should consider the need to attend to product as well as process. Our students should be taught not only heuristic devices to focus on meaning, but also heuristic devices to focus on rhetorical and linguistic features after the ideas have found some form.

Even for students with a low level of language proficiency, the act of writing, however recursive and retrospective, served to generate language. While the think-aloud tapes and the transcribed protocols give the impression of composing being laborious and painful for some students, none gave up. All found a way to approach the topic and produced some coherent ideas to communicate to a reader. For many of these unskilled students, what they wrote in one sentence completely determined what they wrote in the next. The language they produced—a word or a phrase initiating some inchoate idea—then had to serve as the prod to get the meaning out.

The pattern that held for many, though not all, of these ESL writers was something like this: create text—read—create text—read—edit—read—create text—read—read—create text, and so on. Thus, language and the ideas expressed in that language emerged out of the student writers' own creativity, not out of textbook instruction or teacher-supplied input. All of these student writers, even those laboring to produce text, were uncovering the language they needed to express ideas and at the same time discovering new ideas.

To take advantage of this extraordinary generative power of language, we need to give our students what is always in short supply in the writing classroom—time. The time *they* need to write has to take precedence over the time we need to complete a syllabus or cover the course material. That time is needed, too, for attention to vocabulary. To generate, develop, and present ideas, our students need an adequate vocabulary. This is also true of native speakers:

Our analyses . . . suggest that the writers of the low-rated papers do not have working vocabularies capable of extending, in ways prerequisite for good writing, the concepts and ideas they introduce in their essays. Indeed, skill in invention, in discovering what to say about a particular topic, may depend in ways yet unexplored on the prior development of adequate working vocabularies (Witte and Faigley 1981:198).

The acquisition of an adequate vocabulary does not necessarily have to precede writing. If ESL students are given enough time, shown enough ways to explore topics, and given enough feedback, they will discover and uncover the English words they need as they write. When I hear Yin Ping's struggles with the possible meanings of the word *unexpected*, I perceive how essential the acquisition of vocabulary is for ESL writing and how much the task of writing can contribute to that acquisition, even when pre-writing activities are not provided. Yin Ping got closer and closer to the meaning of the word as she wrote. As she grappled with the meaning, she explored the concept and in so doing found something to write about.

Despite some similarities observed among the behaviors of my eight subjects, no clear profile of the unskilled ESL writer emerged from this study of behaviors during composing. When Perl (1979) examined her unskilled writers, she found common features that characterized them as a group. These ESL writers revealed some similarities to that group and to each other, but the patterns of behavior that emerged were not consistent enough for unskilled ESL writers to be described as a definable group with as much confidence as Perl described unskilled L1 writers. There were too many anomalies. Johnny and Harriet did not write as recursively as the others. They rarely rehearsed, read back only occasionally, and made few changes in their texts. Chih-Hwa, Maria, and Yin Ping read back over their sentences a great deal. Rather than reading back, José played with rehearsing, trying out what to write next and repeating a few words over and over to test if they sounded all right together.

Nor can the various behaviors observed be grouped neatly according to level of language proficiency or number of years in an English-speaking environment. Yin Ping, with a low proficiency level and low rating of written product, read back over her sentences as much as Chih-Hwa did. Yet Harriet, whose proficiency level and essay rating scores were close to Chih-Hwa's, showed far less recursiveness and far more fluency: Harriet read back over sentences 3 times; Chih-Hwa did it 51 times. From the background data of years in the United States and language proficiency score, we might expect Johnny to fit the profile of Perl's unskilled writers more closely than others in this group. Johnny, however, seemed to write with more ease than Perl's Tony did. He revealed a profile more like a Monitor underuser (Krashen 1981, Jones in press) and a fossilized ESL learner (Selinker 1974). A teacher would have to approach Johnny's case very differently from Chih-Hwa's, even though both were accurately placed in the same class.

Such variety among L2 writers judged as unskilled is no doubt due in part to the number of variables that contribute to that judgment. Some of the variables which this study confirmed as important—for example, language proficiency, the quality of written products, self-evaluation of L1 and L2 writing, knowledge of writing in L1 and L2 (through instruction, experience, and reading), and writing behavior (compared with what is known about skilled writers)—can be a useful basis for a teacher's formative evaluation of L2 writers, who can be judged as skilled, moderately skilled, or unskilled in each of these variables.

For students evaluated as unskilled, Zamel cautions that "we need to find out if a minimum level of language competence is required before students are able to view writing in a second language as a process of discovering meaning" (1984:198). This study shows us that students whose proficiency is judged as insufficient for academic course work generate language and ideas in much the same way as more proficient students. In other words, they use what they have and move on from there.

With context, preparation, feedback, and opportunities for revision, students at any level of proficiency can be engaged in discovery of meaning.

The study thus shows that while some of the ESL writers were similar to unskilled L1 writers in their lack of planning and their largely recursive processes at the sentence level, there were some interesting differences: The L2 unskilled writers showed commitment even to an in-class essay, and they did not seem preoccupied with finding errors but were more concerned with getting ideas down on the page.

Such findings indicate that we should neither use the same pedagogical strategies for ESL students in writing classes as for native speakers nor should we treat our students simply as learners who need large doses of language instruction to improve their writing. Some middle ground is called for. What the less proficient writers need, compared with the more proficient and compared with unskilled L1 writers, is more of everything: more time; more opportunity to talk, listen, read, and write in order to marshal the vocabulary they need to make their own background knowledge accessible to them in their L2; more instruction and practice in generating, organizing, and revising ideas; more attention to the rhetorical options available to them; and more emphasis on editing for linguistic form and style. Attention to process is thus necessary but not sufficient.

In addition, the study shows that a specified audience and purpose made no apparent difference to the students' processes and products on this teacher-initiated, timed assignment. Perl found that her subjects wrote "from an egocentric point of view," frequently taking "the reader's understanding for granted" (1979:332). Similarly, these ESL writers tended to focus on textual rather than discoursal matters (Widdowson 1983). Their primary concern was to get ideas down and to find them out for themselves in a "writer-based" way (Flower 1979). Their purpose was not to communicate with a reader. This contrasts with Zamel's skilled ESL writers, who "understood the importance of taking into account a reader's expectations" (1983: 178). We should note, however, that her writers were given unlimited time (and researcher attention) for a course-related writing task; thus the experimental conditions encouraged discoursal awareness. The ESL students in this study wrote within the constraints of a given, unprepared-for, timed topic.

When these ESL students did address the notion of a reader, it was not the artificial one provided in Topic B. They saw that for what it was: a teacher's attempt to dress up a mundane school-sponsored writing assignment. Instead, even with Topic A, some of them managed to establish for themselves at least a real listener, if not a real reader. Four of these writers, through their comments, laughs, and an intonation indicative of real communicative speech, showed an awareness of me, their teacher, as an audience. For Bo-Wen and Harriet especially, the rehearsal and talking out of ideas took on the tone of a personal chat, and the listener/audience they addressed seemed helpful in generating ideas.

It would be interesting to examine if writers who establish an audience for themselves (and that audience can be the teacher as reader, but not as evaluator) and view the task as one of negotiation with a reader ultimately make more progress in their writing than those who see the task solely as a linguistic problem. Certainly, Bo-Wen's tape revealed far more risk taking with language, far more attempts at communication than other students with a similarly low level of language proficiency. He seemed to see the task more as a "social activity" and less as a "language exercise," a distinction made by Widdowson (1983:44).

The study also demonstrated the value of think-aloud composing for ESL composition research; it showed, moreover, that Perl's scheme for coding behaviors can be applied to research in the composing behaviors of L2 writers. The fact that the students had few difficulties composing aloud and that their composing tapes could be coded with a system developed for native speakers made think-aloud composing and protocol analysis an effective research tool for this study. The coding scheme is relatively simple to use and is replicable, so further studies on other groups of ESL student writers are possible.

Think-aloud composing can, however, be more than an effective research tool. It can be useful in the writing classroom, too, since it tells the student and the teacher a great deal about writing and the writer, emphasizes a process that parallels the learning process itself, and illuminates the finished product dramatically. Students and teachers have a spoken record of an interactive process, the interaction between the writer and the text, and the student writer can hear and see graphically the emergence of a text from its very beginnings. For the writer, the concept of an audience is expanded to include not only a reader but a listener as well. We should therefore explore think-aloud composing as a teaching tool to provide an opportunity for the writer to reify an audience and engage in a creative dialogue.

Finally, think-aloud composing and analysis of students' language activities while writing have shown the value of writing as a language learning tool. Instead of serving merely as an adjunct to language learning, useful mainly for practice exercises and reinforcement of academic tasks, writing itself has primary value as a language teaching tool. Students can talk and write, experiment, play with language, take their time to find appropriate words and sentences, test out a text and change their minds, and guarantee a response from an audience. Nowhere else in ESL teaching are such ideal language learning conditions found.

The findings of this study thus suggest a new model for second language teaching, one that emphasizes writing, that acknowledges the value of writing for generating language, and that sees writing not just as one of the language skills to be learned, or the last skill to be learned, but as an effective way for a learner to generate words, sentences, and chunks of discourse and to communicate them in the new language.

Acknowledgments

This article is a revised version of a paper presented at the Annual Conference on College Composition and Communication in New York City, March 1984. The research was partially funded by a PSC-CUNY Research Award. I am grateful to my research assistant, Randy Russell, and to Anna Marino, Director of the Hunter College Language Laboratory, for their help with the implementation of the research; and to Martha Cummings, William Gaskill, two anonymous *TESOL Quarterly* reviewers, and the *TESOL Quarterly* editor, Stephen Gaies, for their helpful comments on earlier drafts. Special thanks go to my colleague at Hunter College, Karen Greenberg, who gave generously of her time and expertise whenever I needed it. She proved again to me how helpful it is for a writer to have friends who will listen, read, and give advice.

Works Cited

Beach, Richard. 1979. The effects of between-draft teacher evaluation versus student self-evaluation on high school students' revising of rough drafts. *Research in the Teaching of English* 13(2):111-119.

Calkins, Lucy M. 1980. Children's rewriting strategies: notes and comments. *Research in the Teaching of English* 14(4):331-341.

Cooper, Marilyn, and Michael Holzman. 1983. Talking about protocols. College *Composition and Communication* 34(3):284-293.

Della-Piana, Gabriel M. 1978. Research strategies for the study of revision processes in writing poetry. In *Research on composing: points of* departure, Charles R. Cooper and Lee Odell (Eds.), 105-134. Urbana, Illinois: National Council of Teachers of English.

Edelsky, Carole. 1982. Writing in a bilingual program: the relation of L1 and L2 texts. *TESOL Quarterly* 16(2):211-228.

Emig, Janet. 1971. *The composing process of twelfth graders*. Urbana, Illinois: National Council of Teachers of English.

Emig, Janet. 1975. The composing process: a review of the literature. In *Contemporary rhetoric: a conceptual background with readings*, R.W. Winterowd (Ed.), 49-70. New York: Harcourt Brace Jovanovich.

Emig, Janet. 1977. Writing as a mode of learning. *College Composition and Communication* 28(2):122-128.

Ericsson, K. Anders, and Herbert A. Simon. 1980. Verbal reports as data. *Psychological Review* 87(3):215-251.

Faigley, Lester, and Stephen Witte. 1981. Analyzing revision. *College Composition and Communication* 32(4):400-414.

Flower, Linda S. 1979. Writer-based prose: a cognitive basis for problems in writing. *College English* 41(1):19-37.

Flower, Linda S., and John R. Hayes. 1981. A cognitive process theory of writing. *College Composition and Communication* 32(4):365-387.

Gaskill, William H. 1984a. Problems and revisions in the composing processes of a Taiwanese ESL student. Paper presented at the 18th Annual TESOL Convention, Houston, March 1984.

Gaskill, William H. 1984b. Revision in the composing processes of Spanish-speaking ESL students. Paper presented at the 18th Annual TESOL Convention, Houston, March 1984.

Graves, Donald H. 1975. An examination of the writing processes of seven-year-old children. *Research in the Teaching of English* 9(3):227-241.

Hayes, John R., and Linda S. Flower. 1983. Uncovering cognitive processes in writing: an introduction to protocol analysis. In *Research on writing*, Peter Mosenthal, Lynne Tamar, and Sean A. Walmsley (Eds.), 206-220. New York: Longman, Inc.

Heuring, David L. 1984. The revision strategies of skilled and unskilled ESL writers: five case studies. Paper presented at the 18th Annual TESOL Convention, Houston, March 1984.

Hilgers, Thomas Lee. 1980. Training college composition students in the use of free writing and problem-solving heuristics for rhetorical invention. *Research in the Teaching of English* 14(4):293-307.

Hughey, Jane B., Deanne R. Wormuth, V. Faye Hartfiel, and Holly L. Jacobs. 1983. *Teaching ESL composition: principles and techniques*. Rowley, Massachusetts: Newbury House Publishers, Inc.

Jacobs, Holly L., Stephen A. Zingraf, Deanne R. Wormuth, V. Faye Hartfiel, and Jane B. Hughey. 1981. *Testing ESL composition: a practical approach*. Rowley, Massachusetts: Newbury House Publishers, Inc.

Jacobs, Suzanne E. 1982. *Composing and coherence: the writing of eleven pre-medical students. Linguistics and Literacy Series 3*. Washington, D. C.: Center for Applied Linguistics.

Jones, C. Stanley. 1982a. Attention to rhetorical information while composing in a second language. Paper presented at the 4th Los Angeles Second Language Research Forum, Los Angeles, April 1982.

Jones, C. Stanley. 1982b. Composing in a second language: a process study. Paper presented at the 16th Annual TESOL Convention, Honolulu, May 1982.

Jones, C. Stanley. 1983. Some composing strategies of second language writers. Paper presented at the Colloquium on Learner Strategies at the 17th Annual TESOL Convention, Toronto, March 1983.

Jones, C. Stanley. In press. Problems with monitor use in second language composing. In *Studies on writers' block and other composing process problems*, M. Rose (Ed.). New York: Guilford Press.

Jones, C. Stanley, and Jacqueline Tetroe. In press. Composing in a second language. In *Writing in real time: modelling the writing process*, Ann Matsuhashi (Ed.). New York: Longman, Inc.

Keyes, Joan Ross. 1984. Peer editing and writing success. *TESOL Newsletter (Supplement No. 1: Writing and composition)* 18(1):11-12.

Knepler, Myrna. 1984. Impromptu writing to increase fluency. *TESOL Newsletter (Supplement No. 1: Writing and composition)* 18(1):15-16.

Krashen, Stephen D. 1981. *Second language acquisition and second language learning*. Oxford: Pergamon Press.

Krashen, Stephen D. 1984. *Writing: research, theory, and applications*. Oxford: Pergamon Press.

Lay, Nancy Duke S. 1982. Composing processes of adult ESL learners: a case study. *TESOL Quarterly* 16(3):406.

Lay, Nancy Duke S. 1983. Native language and the composing process. In *Selected papers from the 1982 conference "New York Writes,"* Barry Kwalick, Marcia Silver, and Virginia Slaughter (Eds.), 17-21. New York: City University of New York, The Instructional Resource Center.

Matsuhashi, Ann. 1982. Pausing and planning: the tempo of written discourse production. *Research in the Teaching of English* 15(2):113-134.

Michigan test of English language proficiency. 1962. Ann Arbor: The University of Michigan, English Language Institute.

Mischel, Terry. 1974. A case study of a twelfth grade writer. *Research in the Teaching of English* 8(3):303-314.

Murray, Donald M. 1978. Internal revision: a process of discovery. In *Research on composing: points of departure*, Charles R. Cooper and Lee Odell (Eds.), 85-103. Urbana, Illinois: National Council of Teachers of English.

Odell, Lee. 1974. Measuring the effect of instruction in pre-writing. *Research in the Teaching of English* 8(2):228-240.

Perl, Sondra. 1978. Five writers writing: case studies of the composing processes of unskilled college writers. Doctoral dissertation, New York University.

Perl, Sondra. 1979. The composing processes of unskilled college writers. *Research in the Teaching of English* 13(4):317-336.

Perl, Sondra. 1980. Understanding composing. *College Composition and Communication* 31(4):363-369.

Perl, Sondra. 1981. Coding the composing process: a guide for teachers and researchers. Manuscript written for the National Institute of Education, Washington, D.C.

Pfingstag, Nancy. 1984. Showing writing: modeling the process. *TESOL Newsletter (Supplement No. 1: Writing and composition)* 18(1):1-3.

Pianko, Sharon. 1979. A description of the composing processes of college freshman writers. *Research in the Teaching of English* 13(1):5-22.

Raimes, Ann. 1984. Two studies of the composing process in a second language and the implications for teaching. Paper presented at the Annual Conference on College Composition and Communication, New York City, March 1984.

Rose, Mike. 1980. Rigid rules, inflexible plans, and the stifling of language: a cognitive analysis of writer's block. *College Composition and Communication* 31(4):389-401.

Selinker, Larry. 1974. Interlanguage. In *New frontiers in second language learning*, John H. Schumann and Nancy Stenson (Eds.), 114-136. Rowley, Massachusetts: Newbury House Publishers, Inc.

Selzer, Jack. 1983. The composing processes of an engineer. *College Composition and Communication* 34(2):178-187.

Sommers, Nancy. 1980. Revision strategies of student writers and experienced adult writers. *College Composition and Communication* 31(4):378-388.

Spack, Ruth, and Catherine Sadow. 1983. Student-teacher working journals in ESL freshman composition. *TESOL Quarterly* 17(4):575-593.

Stallard, C.K. 1974. An analysis of the writing behavior of good student writers. *Research in the Teaching of English* 8(2):206-218.

Stokes, Elizabeth. 1984. An ESL writing workshop. *TESOL Newsletter (Supplement No. 1: Writing and composition)* 18(1):4-5.

Swarts, Heidi, Linda S. Flower, and John R. Hayes. 1984. Designing protocol studies of the writing process: an introduction. In *New directions in composition research*, Richard Beach and Lillian S. Bridwell (Eds.), 53-71. New York: The Guilford Press.

Taylor, Barry P. 1981. Content and written form: a two-way street. *TESOL Quarterly* 15(1):5-13.

Tetroe, Jacqueline, and C. Stanley Jones. 1983. Planning and revising in adult ESL students. Paper presented at the Annual Conference on College Composition and Communication, Detroit, March 1983.

Tetroe, Jacqueline, and C. Stanley Jones. 1984. Transfer of planning skills in second language composing. Paper presented at the Annual Meeting of the American Educational Research Association, New Orleans, April 1984.

Widdowson, H.G. 1983. New starts and different kinds of failure. In *Learning to write: first language/second language*, Aviva Freedman, Ian Pringle, and Janice Yalden (Eds.), 34-47. New York: Longman, Inc.

Witte, Stephen P., and Lester Faigley. 1981. Coherence, cohesion, and writing quality. *College Composition and Communication* 32(2):189-204.

Zamel, Vivian. 1982. Writing: the process of discovering meaning. *TESOL Quarterly* 16(2):195-210.

Zamel, Vivian. 1983. The composing processes of advanced ESL students: six case studies. *TESOL Quarterly* 17(2):165-187.

Zamel, Vivian. 1984. In search of the key: research and practice in composition. In *On TESOL '83: the question of control*, Jean Handscombe, Richard Orem, and Barry P. Taylor (Eds.), 195-207. Washington, D. C.: TESOL.

APPENDIX

Coding for First 10 Minutes of Chih-Hwa's Think-Aloud Composing Tape

The numbered horizontal brackets show which sentence is being written. From the coding alone we can see, for example, that the writer moved from Sentence 1 to 2 and from 3 to 4 with relative ease, going back only to read the sentence just written. After Sentence 4, her pace slowed down. She read everything she had written so far (R^W), with some repetition of parts of a sentence that was troubling her. Then she reread her last sentence, going back to the trouble spot again, before tackling the fifth sentence. (Numbers at the right-hand margin indicate total minutes elapsed. See Figure 1 for key to coding categories.)

```
        3                                           4
     ——————————————————7     /———————————————————————————————————————7
    re  re  re  W  Rh_{sp}  W  Rh_{sp}   R^3 W re Rh_{sp} W Rh_{sp} re W Rh_{sp}   re W E_a ré re re C'R^W R^{1-4}
    —   —   —   —   —   —     —   —   —   —   —   —       —   —   —   —   —   — 9
```

```
                              5
                           /——————————————7
    re  re  re  re  R^4  re  re  Rh  re  re  Rh' W  Rh  re  W
    —    —    —    —     —     —     —                              10
```

Transcription of Tape of Chih-Hwa's
First 10 Minutes of Composing Aloud*

. . . about that unexpected that happened to you . . . <u>thing that expected,</u> expect, <u>that happened to you.</u> I can't think of now .. mmm, many things happened in . many things happened unexpected in lives, many things happen unexpect-in life . . . What am I going to say? There is . . . care about this . . . that happened to you .. There was, <u>there were many things happened,</u> unexpected,—petted, there were many things happened unexpectedly, there were many things happened unexpectedly,<u> in my life,</u> many things that happened unexpected in my life.

<u>The most remarkable,</u> remarkable <u>thing, was happened,</u> the most remarkable thing happened—[RAIMES: Louder.] Louder, okay. The most remarkable thing happened, was happened <u>when I was in junior high,</u> jun—, junior high <u>school.</u> There were many things happened unexpectedly in my life. The most remarkable thing was happened when I, cross out the was, the most remarkable thing happened when I was in junior high school, ahm, . . . when I was in junior high school. Mmm, there were many things happened unexpectedly in my life. The most remarkable thing happened when I was in high, in junior high school, in junior high school, happened when I was in junior high school.

<u>I was in my own country,</u> I was in my own country, I was in my own country, I was in my own country, <u>and just graduate, U-A-T-E-D,</u> and just graduated <u>from ele-mentary</u> school, E-L-E-M-T, elementary, T-A-R-Y, <u>school.</u> I was in my own country and just graduated from elementary school. <u>I was,</u> I was <u>interested,</u> T-E-R-E-S-T-E-D, I was interested in <u>sports,</u> S-P-O-R-T, in sports, especially, especially, <u>E-S-P-E-C-I-A-L-L-Y</u> especially, ah, especially baseball, <u>B-A-S-E-B-A-L-L,</u> especially in baseball, in, especially in baseball, especially in baseball. Ahh, so, ah, especially in baseball, and, why I was . . .

There were many things happened unexpectedly in my life. The most remarkable thing happened when I was in junior high school. I was in my own country and just graduated from elementary school. I was interested in sports, especially baseball, especially baseball in, ah, especially in baseball, especially in baseball, I was,

---

*Underlined sections indicate when she was writing as she was talking.

especially in baseball. Mmm, I was interested in sports, especially in baseball, in baseball. When I, when I went to, when I went to, when I went to junior high, my junior high school, my junior high school had, had many school teams, had many school teams, had many, many ...

Chih-Hwa's Written Product (First 10 Minutes)

"Tell about something that ??? unexpected that happened to you." There were many things happened unexpectly in my life. The most remarkable thing was happened when I was in junior high school. I was in my our own country, and just graduated from elementary school. I was interested in sports, especially in baseball. My junior high school had many [sports teams] . . .

Reader Versus Writer Responsibility:
A New Typology[1]
by John Hinds

This paper investigates the notion of reader responsibility, in contrast to writer responsibility. Its focal point is that there are different expectations with regard to the degree of involvement a reader will have, and that this degree of involvement will depend on the language of the reader. In this sense, this paper is concerned with language typology.

The concern with language typology, in its modern sense, dates from Greenberg's (1963) classic article in which he postulated a typology that involves certain basic factors of word order. Greenberg (1963:77) proposed that there are three common word order types, illustrated in Table 1.

The significance of Greenberg's typology is that it allowed him to postulate a number of "implicational universals." That is, by knowing that a language is SOV, for instance, it follows that that language will have postpositions rather than prepositions, that there will be no invariant rule for fronting question words, and so on.

TABLE 1 Basic Word Orders		
SVO	*SOV*	*VSO*
English	Japanese	Tagalog
Fulani	Korean	Welsh
Thai	Burmese	Zapotec

Another typology has been suggested in Li and Thompson (1976). They suggest that languages display different characteristics depending on whether grammatical subject or grammatical topic is more prominent. They identify four basic types of languages, shown in Table 2.

In subject-prominent languages, the structure of sentences favors a description in which the grammatical relation *subject-predicate* assumes primary importance. In topic-prominent languages, the grammatical role *topic-comment* is most important. For languages like Japanese and Korean, both constructions are reputed to be equally important, while for languages like Tagalog, subject and topic are said to have merged and to be indistinguishable in all sentence types.

Other typologies have been suggested as well. Thompson (1978), for instance, has discussed a typology in which languages differ in the way they utilize word order. Languages like English typically use word order to indicate grammatical relationships, while languages like Spanish, in which the movement of constituents is fairly free of grammatical restrictions, use word order to indicate pragmatic relationships, such as theme-rheme distinctions.

Monane and Rogers (1977), in a much more restricted study, have suggested that Japanese and English differ with respect to whether sentences are typically "situation-focus" or "person-focus." That is, for Japanese speakers, it appears to be enough simply to state that a situation has occurred. For English speakers, not only the situation but also the persons involved in the situation are typically stated. Monane and Rogers (1977:135) offer convincing examples, several of which are presented in Table 3.

TABLE 2

Subject-prominent Languages	Topic-prominent Languages
Indo-European	Chinese
Niger-Congo	Lahu (Lolo-Burmese)
Finno-Ugric	Lisu (Lolo-Burmese)
Subject-prominent and Topic-prominent Languages	**Neither Subject-prominent nor Topic-prominent Languages**
Japanese	Tagalog
Korean	Ilocano

TABLE 3

Situation-focus	Person-focus
sakebigoe ga shita zo. (lit.) A shouting voice occurred.	I just heard someone shout.
yama ga mieru (lit.) The mountain can be seen.	I can see the mountain.

In this paper, I suggest a typology that is based on speaker and/or writer responsibility as opposed to listener and/or reader responsibility. What this means is that in some languages, such as English, the person primarily responsible for effective communication is the speaker, while in other languages, such as Japanese, the person primarily responsible for effective communication is the listener. The lexical hedge "primarily" in the previous two clauses is important since the phenomena under discussion constitute tendencies rather than exceptionless "rules." This means, of course, that there may be circumstances in which English listeners are responsible for effective communication, in which Japanese speakers are responsible for effective communication, or in which that responsibility is shared by the listener and speaker. What is described here is the neutral situation.[2] The implications of this typology are discussed below with respect to specific grammatical manifestations of this distinction.

I take as a starting point the position that English speakers, by and large, charge the writer, or speaker, with the responsibility to make clear and well-organized statements. If there is a breakdown in communication, for instance, it is because the speaker/writer has not been clear enough, not because the listener/reader has not exerted enough effort in an attempt to understand.

This view has strong historical precedent. Havelock (1963, 1976), cited by Hildyard and Olson, has pointed out that:

> ... with the emphasis on literacy both in classical Greece and in post-reformation England there was a great concern to make sentences say exactly, neither more nor less than what they meant. Poetry and proverbial sayings which mean both more and less than what they say, were rejected as a means of expressing truth both by Plato and 2000 years later by members of the Royal Society of London . . . (1982:20).

Chafe, in discussing differences between speakers and writers, has reiterated this position.

> ... the speaker is aware of an obligation to communicate what he or she has in mind in a way that reflects the richness of his or her thoughts . . .; the writer [is] . . . concerned with producing something that will be consistent and defensible when read by different people at different times in different places, something that will stand the test of time (1982:45).

The desire to write or speak clearly in English permeates our culture. This point of view has even been made into an aphorism for public speaking: "Tell 'em what you're going to tell 'em, tell 'em, then tell 'em what you told 'em." It is the responsibility of the speaker to communicate a message.

In Japan, perhaps in Korea, and certainly in Ancient China, there is a different way of looking at the communication process. In Japan, it is the responsibility of the listener (or reader) to understand what it is that the speaker or author had intended to say. This difference may be illustrated quite effectively by an anecdote presented in Naotsuka *et al.* (1981:16). An American woman was taking a taxi to the Ginza

Tokyu Hotel. The taxi driver mistakenly took her to the Ginza Daiichi Hotel. She said, "I'm sorry, I should have spoken more clearly." This, I take to be an indication of her speaker-responsible upbringing. The taxi driver demonstrated his listener-responsible background when he replied, "No, no, I should have listened more carefully."

This difference in the way of looking at the act of communication permeates the thoughts of anyone who operates as a functioning Japanese-American bicultural. Yoshikawa gives considerable insight into this situation. He states that the Japanese actually have a mistrust of verbal language.

> What is often verbally expressed and what is actually intended are two different things. What is verbally expressed is probably important enough to maintain friendship, and it is generally called *tatemae* which means simply "in principle" but what is not verbalized counts most—*honne* which means "true mind." Although it is not expressed verbally, you are supposed to know it by *kan*—"intuition" (1978:228-229).

Yoshikawa attributes this ability on the part of the listener to intuit a speaker's meaning to the fact that Japan is a homogeneous country. Whether this explanation is correct is not the issue, although it is the case that most Japanese believe it is true. Yoshikawa further states that the basic principle of communication in Japan, the fact that what is verbally expressed and what is actually intended are two different things, is something that Japanese people are supposed to be aware of.

Suzuki (1975:31, ff.) addresses this same theme. He compares the French attitude toward clarity in language, exemplified by the expression *ce qui n'est pas clair n'est pas francais* (that which is not clear is not French), with the Japanese attitude. Suzuki claims that Japanese authors do not like to give clarifications or full explanations of their views. They like to give dark hints and to leave them behind nuances. Moreover, Suzuki claims that it is exactly this type of prose which gets the highest praise from readers. He states that Japanese readers "anticipate with pleasure the opportunities that such writing offers them to savor this kind of 'mystification' of language."

This attitude toward reader responsibility is not limited to Japan, but is shared at least by Classical Chinese. Li and Thompson (1982:81, ff.) discuss a Classical Chinese text in which many statements are what they call "telegraphic." Concerning this passage, they state:

> The next clause . . . then states: "The logic is profound and abstruse" without clarifying what logic or whose logic is being referred to. Thus, in order to extract the correct message . . ., the reader has to rely heavily on inference based on his/her knowledge of the world and the information provided by the earlier clauses of the paragraph (1982:83).

Of another sentence in this same passage, they state that the author "left it to the reader to extrapolate that the town was his home-town." This is especially of interest since in the present-day Mandarin translation of this passage, the translator made it clear that the town was Zichuan. In order to provide this piece of information to the reader, however, the translator had to research the life of the author and add a footnote to point out that Zichuan was the home-town of the author. . . .

Thus, there appears to be a major shift in typological style between Classical and Modern Chinese. Classical Chinese appears to be more like Japanese in that it is a reader-responsible language, while Modern Chinese is more like English in that it is a writer-responsible language.

I turn now to a discussion of the implications of this typology on current-day Japanese writing. My point of departure is that there are greater consequences for a reader-responsible language than merely tolerance for ambiguity and imprecision of statement, although this also occurs. It goes beyond attitudes toward writing, such that English-speaking writers go through draft after draft to come up with a final product, while Japanese authors frequently compose exactly one draft which becomes the finished product.

There are specific differences between English and Japanese in the way that authors present expository materials, and these differences help to demonstrate this typology. Kaplan (1966) originally suggested that there are differences in rhetorical styles from language to language. He cites a number of rhetoricians to demonstrate that good English writing is characterized by unity and coherence. Hughes and Duhamel (1962), cited by Kaplan, provide definitions for these terms:

> Unity is the quality attributed to writing which has all its necessary and sufficient parts. Coherence is the quality attributed to the presentation of material in a sequence which is intelligible to its reader (Kaplan 1966:4).

In a series of recent papers (Hinds 1980, 1983, 1984b), I have attempted to discuss differences in Japanese and English writing with respect to coherence. The area in which speaker and reader responsibility operates, however, is with respect to unity. That is, for English readers, unity is important because readers expect, and require, landmarks along the way. Transition statements are very important. It is the writer's task to provide appropriate transition statements so that the reader can piece together the thread of the writer's logic which binds the composition together.

In Japanese, on the other hand, the landmarks may be absent or attenuated since it is the reader's responsibility to determine the relationship between any one part of an essay and the essay as a whole. This is not to say that there are no transition statements in Japanese. There are. It is only to say that these transition devices may be more subtle and require a more active role for the reader.

In Japanese grammar, there is a continuing effort to determine the functions of two postpositional particles, *wa* and *ga*, since these two particles may frequently be interchanged. In typical analyses, *ga* is considered to be a subject marker, while *wa* is considered to be a topic marker. Kuno (1972) specifically addresses the distribution of these two particles and concludes that *ga* indicates that the subject of a sentence represents new unpredictable information, while *wa* indicates that this same noun phrase represents old, predictable information. Thus, in answer to the question "Who went to Nara?" (1), with *ga*, is appropriate since Akiko is new, or unpredictable information.

(1) *Akiko **ga** Nara e ikimashita.*
                        to went

Akiko went to Nara.

On the other hand, in answer to a question like "What did Akiko do last week?" (2) is appropriate because we have been talking about Akiko; that is, Akiko constitutes old, predictable information.

(2) *Akiko **wa** Nara e ikimashita.*

Akiko went to Nara.

While Kuno's characterization of the distribution of these particles is generally correct [but see Maynard 1981, Hinds 1984b], there is a systematic violation of this general tendency in certain types of Japanese expository writing. This may best be seen through an examination of an expository essay. The essay to be examined was taken from the *Asahi Shimbun's* daily column *Tensei Jingo* "Vox Populi, Vox Dei." The English translation of this column appears one day later in the English language version of *Asahi Shimbun*. New paragraphs are indicated by a number in parentheses preceding the sentence.

(1) *shokudoo de waribashi o tsukau.*
      We use "waribashi" (half-split throw away chopsticks) to eat.

      tsukaisute de aru.
      After use, they are thrown away.

      suterareta hashi wa ittai doo naru no daroo.
      What happens to them after they are thrown away?

      mottainai na, to omou no wa senchuuha no ijimashisha daroo ka.
      Is it merely the stinginess of those who lived through the war to feel
         that it is a waste?

(2) *aru shokudoo no hanashi de wa, mikka de ichimanbon no waribashi
         o tsukaisuteru to iu.*
      According to the owner of one restaurant, his restaurant uses and
         throws away 10,000 pairs of chopsticks every three days.

      *nihon-zentai de wa, ki no waribashi wa ichinen ni yaku 100-oku-zen
         mo tsukawareru soo da.*
      In Japan as a whole, about 10,000 million pairs of wooden chopsticks
         are used each year.

      *sore dake no ryoo no mokuzai ga ichido tsukawareta dake de, suterareru.
      kangaete mireba zeitaku na hanashi de aru.*

That much wood is used just once and thrown away.

kami no genryoo ni suru tame kaishuu shi, saisei sareru to i hanashi wa kikanai.
We have never heard about wooden chopsticks being collected and reused as raw
  material to make paper.

kaishuuhiyoo ga kakarisugite saisan ga awanai, to iu koto daroo ka.
Is it because it would not be a paying proposition since collecting the chopsticks
  would cost too much money?

(3) *tabemono o kuchi ni hakobu no ni hashi o tsukau iwayuru hashibunkaken wa
      chuugoku, choosenhantoo, betonamu, soshite nihon, to natte iru.*
The so-called "chopsticks culture" sphere includes China, the Korean Peninsula,
  Vietnam, and Japan.

sono naka de mo nihon-igai no kuni wa hashi to saji no heiyoo de aru.
But all these other countries use spoons as well as chopsticks.

hashi o kihon to suru nihon-ryoori wa kiwamete tokui na sonzai na no da.
Japanese cooking which is based on chopsticks, is a very special thing.

(4) *mukashi wa waribashi to ieba yoshino-san no sugi-bashi datta.*
Before the war, "waribashi" were Japanese cedar chopsticks from Yoshino.

yoshino no akasugi no hashi o te ni toru to, mizumizushii sugi no kaori ga suru.
When you pick up a pair of chopsticks made of red Japanese cedar from Yoshino,
  you can smell the fresh odor of the cedar.

karukute, yawarakami ga aru.
They are light and smooth to the touch.

masame ga sutto tootte ite sugata ga ii.
They are straightgrained and look good to the eye.

ichizen no sugibashi ni wa nihonjin no biishiki ga komerarete iru yoo ni omou.
We feel that the aesthetic feelings of the Japanese are concentrated in a pair of Japanese cedar chopsticks.

(5) *rikyuu wa, kyaku o motenasu hi no asa, akasugi no hashizai o toridashi, ninzuu ni
      oojite hashi o kezuri, kezuritate no sugi no kaori o kyoo shita to iu densetsu ga
      aru.*

On the mornings of those days on which he was expecting visitors, the tea ceremony
  master Rikyu got out some red Japanese cedar wood and whittled just enough
  pairs of chopsticks for the expected number of visitors. He then presented the
  guests with the odor of freshly-cut Japanese cedar.

sore ga rikyuu-bashi no umare da.
This is the origin of the "Rikyu-bashi" (Rikyu chopsticks).

nihonjin wa hashi no atarashisa, kiyoraka sa o motmeta.
The Japanese demanded freshness and purity in their chopsticks.

(6) *jibun no hashi ga tanin ni tsukawareru koto, hito no hashi o tsukau koto o kirau
      no wa, keppekikan dake de wa nai.*

It is not just out of fastidiousness that the Japanese do not like others to use their chopsticks and also do not like to use the chopsticks of others.

mukashi no hito wa hashi ni wa sore o tsukau hito no reiryoku ga yadoru to shinjita. dakara jibun no reiryoku ga yadotta hashi o tanin ni tsukawaseru koto o kiratta no da, to iu setsu mo aru. (Honda Soichiro: *Hashi no Hon*.)

In ancient times, people believed that the spirit of the person resided in the chopsticks that he used and it is said that this is why people hated to have their chopsticks used by others. (*Hashi no Hon*—Book on Chopsticks—by Soichiro Honda.)

(7) *saikin wa hokkaidoo-san no, ezomatsu, kaba, shina nado de tsukurareta waribashi no zensei jidai de aru.*

It is now the heyday of "waribashi" made from the silver firs, birches and Japanese lindens of Hokkaido.

korera no waribashi ga tairyoo ni seisan sarehajimeta no wa koodoseichooki ni haitte kara da.

These "waribashi" made from Hokkaido wood began to be produced in large quantities after the age of high economic growth started.

ima, demawatte iru waribashi no hanbun wa hokkaidoo-san da to omotte ii.

Half the "waribashi" used now are produced in Hokkaido.

(8) *waribashi no tsukaisute sono mono o hitei suru tsumori wa nai.*

We have no intention of condemning the use-and-throw-away system in connection with "waribashi."

shikashi nenkan 100-okuzen-bun no ki ga sono mama kieteshimau no wa ika ni mo mottainai.

But it is very wasteful when trees amounting to 10,000 millions pairs of wooden chopsticks disappear each year.

With the exception of the first paragraph, the initial noun phrase in each paragraph is marked by *wa*. There are, of course, other noun phrases marked by *wa*, but they will not be considered. The question to be asked is why each of these noun phrases can be marked by *wa*. To answer this question, it is necessary to understand the rhetorical pattern that organizes this essay.

The essay is organized according to a pattern known as *ki-shoo-ten-ketsu* [see Hinds 1983, 1984b]. This rhetorical style is described by Takemata (1976).

A. *ki* 起 First, begin one's argument.

B. *shoo* 承 Next, develop that.

C. *ten* 転 At the point where this development is finished, turn the idea to a subtheme where there is a connection, but not a directly connected association [to the major theme].

D. *ketsu* 結 Last, bring all of this together and reach a conclusion.

TABLE 4			
(1)	*ki*	(5)	*ten*
(2)	*shoo*	(6)	*ten*
(3)	*ten*	(7)	*ten*
(4)	*ten*	(8)	*ketsu*

The version of the rhetorical pattern which is used in this essay has a proliferation of *ten*. This means that there are a number of tangentially related subtopics brought up with few overt transition markers. The function of each paragraph in this essay is listed in Table 4.

I will focus my remarks on paragraph 5. The overall topic of the essay is *waribashi*, or throwaway chopsticks. This topic is introduced and expanded in paragraphs 1 and 2. In paragraph 3, a different perspective on chopsticks is given; that is, that there are other "chopsticks cultures," but that Japan is unique in using only chopsticks and no other utensils. The theme of paragraph 4 is the material that goes into desirable chopsticks.

Paragraph 5 begins with the phrase *rikyuu wa*, which can perhaps be translated literally as "As for Rikyu." Rikyu is certainly not old, predictable information. The appearance of this noun phrase is unpredictable, yet it is marked by *wa*.

The function of *wa* in this case is a signal to the reader that the noun phrase so marked has some kind of connection with the overall theme of the essay. It informs the reader that there is in fact some connection, and that the reader should make an effort to place this noun phrase in its proper perspective in the essay as a whole. It tells the reader, in effect, that this noun phrase should be treated as if it were old, predictable information, even though it is not. In this respect, the function of *wa* when it marks the first noun phrase of a *ten* is very similar to English transition statements such as, "The following may seem to be unrelated to the major point, but the connection between Rikyu and chopsticks will become clear in due time."

Japanese readers, then, are required to build transitions themselves in the course of reading an essay organized along these lines. The responsibility for creating the bridge lies with the reader in Japanese, while it lies with the writer in English.

This may be seen more clearly by examining statements made by Clark and Haviland (1974) and Haviland and Clark (1974) with respect to the way information is comprehended. They claim that the primary function of language is to impart new information. Thus, the speaker's purpose is to provide new information while the listener's task is to extract this new information and to integrate it with old information already in memory. Haviland and Clark state:

> The listener's strategy, therefore, is to identify the syntactically marked Given and New information, treat the Given information as an address to information already in memory, and then integrate the New information into memory at that point (1974:513).

For Haviland and Clark, communicative success depends on how well the speaker has coded given and new information:

> The listener's success with the Given-New Strategy depends critically on whether the Given information, as so marked by the speaker, actually does match information already in memory. To borrow a term normally associated with pronominalization, the Given information must have an Antecedent in memory. If there is no Antecedent, the listener must construct one by elaborating information he already has, or he must construct one from scratch (1974:513).

Thus, for the Japanese reader, *wa* indicates that information is given, or old. This indicates that there should be an antecedent in memory. There is none, of course, in the example taken from *Tensei Jingo*. The Japanese reader, though, understands that it is the reader's responsibility to treat this noun phrase as if it were old information in order to integrate the new information in the paragraph into the appropriate place in memory.

While the facts involved in this description are straightforward, and the application to language typology relatively clear, the implications for ESL classrooms are less obvious. Numerous researchers have debated the role of transfer versus developmental processes in second language acquisition, and the findings reported here assume relevance only on the condition that transfer of native rhetorical patterns exists (cf. Kaplan 1966; Hinds 1983, 1984a). If this position is in fact correct, there are implications for classroom application. In addition to teaching students in ESL writing classes that there are differences in rhetorical styles between English and their native language, it may be necessary to take a further step and teach a new way to conceptualize the writing process. It may be necessary to instruct students from certain countries, such as Japan, that the writing process in English involves a different set of assumptions from the ones they are accustomed to working with. It is not enough for them to write with the view that there is a sympathetic reader who believes a reader's task is to ferret out whatever meaning the author has intended. Such non-native English writers will have to learn that effective written communication in English is the sole provenience of the writer.[3]

Notes

1. I would like to thank Ulla Connor and Wako Hinds for specific comments that helped to strengthen this paper. Responsibility remains with the writer for errors of fact or judgment.

2. This is not an uncommon disclaimer in typological studies. Even Greenberg's word order taxonomy admits to variant possibilities under circumscribed situations. English, for example, an SVO language, allows OSV structures in such constructions as "Beans I like." Monane and Rogers also admit that Japanese, a situation-focus language, allows a variant person-focus construction. Thus, along with the situation-focus *kuruma ga aru*, "a car exists (= I have a car)," the person-focus construction *kuruma o motte-iru*, "I have a car," also exists.

3. As simplistic as this may sound, it will be instructive for some writers from Japan to be informed that even native speakers of English frequently go through several drafts of a paper before being satisfied that information is presented in the most effective way.

Works Cited

Clark, H. H. & Haviland, S. (1974). Psychological processes as linguistic explanation. In D. Cohen (Ed.), *Explaining linguistic phenomena* (pp. 1-40). Washington, DC: V. H. Willston.

Greenberg, J. H. (1963). Some universals of grammar with particular reference to the order of meaningful elements. In J. H. Greemberg (Ed.), *Universals of language* (pp. 73-113). Cambridge, MA: MIT Press.

Haviland, S., and Clark, H. H. (1974). What's new? Acquiring new information as a process in comprehension. *Journal of Verbal Learning and Verbal Behavior, 13*, 512-521.

Hildyard, A., & Olson, D. R. (1982). On the comprehension and memory of oral vs. written discourse. In D. Tannen (Ed.), *Spoken and written language* (pp. 17-34). Norwood, NJ: Ablex.

Hinds, J. (1980). Japanese expository prose. *Papers in Linguistics, 13*, 117-158.

Hinds, J. (1983). Contrastive rhetoric: Japanese and English. *Text, 3*(2), 183-195.

Hinds, J. (1984a). Retention of information using a Japanese style of organization. *Studies in Linguistics, 8*, 45-69.

Hinds, J. (1984b, March). Thematization as a staging device in Japanese expository prose. Paper presented at the Association of Asian Studies, Washington, DC.

Hughes, R., & Duhamel, P. A. (1962). *Rhetoric: Principles and usage.* Englewood Cliffs, NJ: Prentice Hall.

Kaplan, R. B. (1966). Cultural thought patterns in intercultural education. *Language Learning, 16*, 1-20.

Kuno, S. (1972). Functional sentence perspective—A case study from Japanese and English. *Linguistic Inquiry, 3*, 269-320.

Li, C. N., & Thompson, S. A. (1976). Subject and topic: A new typology of language. In C. N. Li (Ed.), *Subject and topic* (pp. 457-489). New York: Academic Press.

Li, C. N., & Thompson, S. A. (1982). The gulf between spoken and written language: A case study in Chinese. In D. Tannen (Ed.), *Spoken and written language* (pp. 77-88). Norwood, NJ: Ablex.

Maynard, S. (1981). The given/new distinction and the analysis of the Japanese particles *-wa* and *-ga. Papers in linguistics, 14, 109-130.*

Monane, T., & Rogers, L. (1977). Cognitive features of Japanese language and culture and their implications for language teaching. In J. Hinds (Ed.), *Proceedings of the second annual meeting of the University of Hawaii-Hawaii Association of Teachers of Japanese* (pp. 129-137). Honolulu: University of Hawaii.

Naotsuka, R., et al. (1981). *Mutual understanding of different cultures.* Tokyo: Taishukan.

Suzuki, T. (1975). *Tozasareta gengo: Nihongo no sekai* [A bound language: The world of Japanese]. Tokyo: Taishukan.

Takemata, K. (1976). *Genkoo shippitsu nyuumon* [An introduction to writing manuscripts]. Tokyo: Natsumesha.

Thompson, S. A. (1978). Modern English from a typological point of view: Some implications for the function of word order. *Linguistische Berichte, 54*, 19-35.

Yoshikawa, M. (1978). Some Japanese and American cultural characteristics. In M. H. Prosser (Ed.), *The cultural dialogue: An introduction to intercultural communication* (pp. 220-230). Boston: Houghton Mifflin.

Research Frontiers
in Writing Analysis
by Ulla Connor

The past decade has witnessed a major paradigm shift in composition theory and research: The emphasis has moved from the product to the process of writing. According to Hairston (1982), the product-centered, traditional paradigm stressed expository writing, made style the most important element in writing, and maintained that the writing process is linear, determined by writers before they start to write.

The process-centered paradigm, on the other hand, focuses on writing processes; teaches strategies for invention and discovery; considers audience, purpose, and context of writing; emphasizes recursiveness in the writing process; and distinguishes between aims and modes of discourse (e. g., expressive, expository, persuasive; and description, narration, evaluation, classification). Within this paradigm, research on texts and text analysis is developing rapidly. Hairston (1982), for example, includes research in linguistics and cognitive sciences as part of the new paradigm for teaching writing and emphasizes that process theory is diverse, flexible, and still emerging.

Others have articulated various synergic relationships between process and product research and have called for theories of writing integrating the two views. Phelps (1985), for example, argues for a unified theory in which the "overarching process" is the cooperative enterprise whereby writers and readers construct meanings together. Phelps offers an analysis of the dynamic interactions between readers and writers.

An integrative theory enables us to explain the apparent paradox in some process research. Although product research has been harshly condemned by some composition theorists, descriptions of writing processes have been largely achieved by analyzing sequences of different kinds of products. Among these products have been transcripts of processes—or protocols—of writers commenting on their own writing (Flower & Hayes, 1981), analyses of students' revisions of their own writing (Beach, 1976; Bridwell, 1980; Sommers, 1980; Zamel, 1983), and studies of teacher comments on student writing (Zamel, 1985). The role of product is becoming recognized not only in writing *research*, but also in the *teaching* of writing, in which experts are calling for a renewed interest in student texts and revisions. Sommers (1987), in criticizing the recent narrow emphasis on protocol analysis exploring writers' mental processes while writing or revising, recommended that researchers and teachers start analyzing students' drafts more carefully, paying attention to the development of such features as tone and personal style.

Equally important for the argument on behalf of an integrated theory of process and product in ESL, Raimes's (1985) analyses of "think aloud" protocols of unskilled ESL writers writing essays found that ESL writers "concentrate on the challenge of finding the right words and sentences to express the meaning" (p. 247). Raimes recommends that we

> consider the need to attend to product as well as process. Our students should be taught not only heuristic devices to focus on meaning, but also heuristic devices to focus on rhetorical and linguistic features after the ideas have found some form. (pp. 247-248)

Recent developments in text analysis methodology are helping to integrate the product and process perspectives. By describing sequential texts within a process, text analyses are contributing to our understanding of the writing process. Text analyses are also improving the tools with which teachers and students can talk about student writing.

Paradigm Shifts in Linguistics and Text Analysis

The 1960s, 1970s, and 1980s have witnessed major shifts in emphases in linguistics, which have yielded valuable contributions to the study of discourse, both spoken and written. Many linguists feel that traditional morphological and syntactic tools are not enough to explain texts and that new discourse tools need to be developed for the study of communicative texts (Dressier, 1978; Kintsch & van Dijk, 1978; van Dijk, 1985).

All of these theories and models of text have concerned themselves with the processes readers and writers go through in their attempts to comprehend and be comprehended. They differ, however, in the degree of attention to the structural versus procedural elements in texts. Enkvist (1975, 1978, 1985, 1987) has developed a useful taxonomy of text-linguistic approaches to writing: sentence-based, predication-based, cognitive-based, and interactive approaches.

Enkvist points out that the first text-linguists worked with sentence-based text models and were mainly interested in what linked sentences together in paragraphs and paragraphs together into texts. Cohesion, the overt linking of sentences, is a classic example of such a sentence-based approach (Halliday, 1961; Halliday & Hasan, 1976). The theory of functional sentence perspective, developed by the Prague School linguists (Daneš, 1974; Firbas, 1966), could also be classified as a sentence-based model. Even though functional sentence perspectivists are interested in the role of utterances in the total communication process, they do begin much of their work by analyzing the sentence into parts and determining their functions in communication.

The predication-based model sees texts as particular arrangements depending on a specific text strategy and maintains that the same input can be textualized into different texts. An example of such a model is Werlich's *A Text Grammar of English* (1976), which shows how text types—narrative, descriptive, expository, and argumentative—differ in the arrangement of the same input (words, sentences, transitional phrases, voice, etc.).

Cognitive-based text models emphasize the role of cognition in text processing; for example, coherence is a function of the text and of the equipment the hearer or reader brings to its interpretation. The cognitive model, however, overlaps the interactive approach, which stresses that, to communicate successfully, writers or speakers need to be aware of their audience and either conform to expected patterns or purposely break these conventions for surprise effect. The overriding theme, then, of these two approaches is that of communicative intent. Brown and Yule (1983), for example, underscore the importance of the reader-writer interaction in discourse comprehension and contrast their *discourse-as-process* approach with a *text-as-product* view. They are interested in the function or purpose of pieces of linguistic data and also how those data are processed, both by the producer and by the receiver.

Because of the inherent overlap between these approaches, which Enkvist admits, the four categories can be collapsed into two: (a) the sentence-based approach and (b) the process-centered approach. The first category includes Enkvist's sentence-based models, whereas the process-centered approach combines Enkvist's predication, cognitive, and interactive categories. Using this dichotomy of text-linguistic approaches, the next section of this article describes theories as well as methods of analysis that have been successfully applied to the study of real texts, including student essays, or that suggest promise as useful areas of inquiry. The aim is to develop a unified theory of ESL writing, which includes both process and product while accounting for the many levels of language (e.g., syntax and discourse).

Text-Linguistic Approaches

Sentence-Based Approach

Figure 1 lists relevant empirical studies dealing with sentence-level features, intersentential relations, coherence breaks, and functional sentence perspective. Research using functional sentence perspective is described to illustrate the poten-

FIGURE 1

Sentence-Based Approach: Representative Empirical Studies

Concept	Operationalization	References	Accomplished writing	Application L1 writing	L2 writing
Functional sentence perspective	Topical structure	Lautamatti (1978, 1987)	X		
		Witte (1983a, 1983b)		X	
		Connor & Farmer (1985, 1987)		X	X
		Johns (1986)			X
		Bardovi-Harlig (1987)			X
Coherence breaks	Topic structuring and cohesion	Wikborg (1985, 1987)			X
Syntactic features	Syntactic counts	Patterson & Lindell (1976)		X	
		Taylor (1979)			X
		Biber (1984, 1985)	X		
		Grabe (1987)	X		
		Connor & Biber (1987)		X	
		Reid (1987)			X
Intersentential relations	Cohesive devices	Witte & Faigley (1981)		X	
		Connor (1984b)			X
		Evensen (1987)			X

tial benefits of this type of research for both process-oriented pedagogy and integrated writing theory.

Functional sentence perspective has proved to be of paramount importance for the study of coherence in writing. Even though coherence has been of increasing interest to teachers and researchers around the world (e.g., de Beaugrande, 1980; Carrell, 1982; Connor & Johns, 1987; Enkvist, 1985; Kintsch & van Dijk, 1978), it is still an elusive concept. The problem is not so much in distinguishing between coherence and cohesion, which has been done, as it is in finding an adequate definition of coherence. Phelps (1985), a rhetorician, defines coherence as "the experience of meaningfulness correlated with successful integration during reading, which the reader projects back into the text as a quality of wholeness in its meanings" (p. 21). The problem occurs, as Phelps admits, when one asks for a definition of *successful integration*.

Nevertheless, a few linguists have attempted, with varying degrees of success, to describe coherence, using linguistic features from the text (Connor, 1984b; Evensen, 1987; Lindeberg, 1985; Wikborg, 1985, 1987). A particularly promising attempt to describe coherence, following the theory of functional sentence perspective, was developed by Lautamatti (1978, 1987), who suggests that successful integration refers to the semantic relationships that exist between sentence topics and the discourse topic. Through topical structure analysis, these relationships can be studied by looking at sequences of sentences and examining how the topics in the sentences work through the text to build meaning progressively.

Lautamatti (1978, 1987) identifies three possible progressions that result in coherent discourse: parallel, sequential, and extended parallel. In parallel progression, the sentence topics are semantically identical. In sequential progression, the sentence topics are always different; the comment of the previous sentence becomes the topic of the next sentence and so on. And in extended parallel progression, a parallel progression may be temporarily interrupted by a sequential progression.

Topical structure was used by Witte (1983a), who felt that it would allow him to study the textual stimulus for revision. L1 students were asked to revise an expository paragraph. These revised passages were rated and analyzed using topical structure analysis. The analysis revealed that the low-scoring revisions exhibited a lack of clear focus (or coherence), indicating that the reviser was uncertain about what the discourse topic was. In another study, Witte (1983b), again using topical structure analysis, studied patterns in L1 freshman-level students' writing and compared them with the quality ratings of their essays. He found topical structure analysis to be a fair predictor of writing quality.

More recently, Connor and Farmer (1985) conducted a study to examine the effects of instruction in topical structure analysis. Because of the success of topical structure analysis, the authors felt that a modified version would be useful for students as a revision strategy to check for coherence in their *own* writing. Teaching this revision strategy for students to use when they were revising their first drafts had positive results. Even though statistically significant differences were not obtained between the control and experimental groups in terms of (a) rated coherence of their final products and (b) quality of revision (meaning-preserving versus meaning-changing), the trend supported the potential of topical structure analysis as a tool for analyzing coherence in text and as a revision tool for students.

During the past 3 years in ESL classes at Indiana University in Indianapolis, we have used topical structure analysis to teach students to revise for coherence in their writing (Connor, 1987b, 1987c, 1987d; Connor, Cerniglia, & Medsker, 1987; Connor & Farmer, 1987). Our team, consisting of a linguist, two ESL writing teachers, and an instructional media specialist, has found topical structure analysis to be a useful revision technique because it encourages students to consider and reconsider the text as a whole and allows them to gauge for themselves the relative coherence of their writing. Based upon empirical research evidence from Witte's (1983a, 1983b) and Connor and Farmer's (1985, 1987) studies as well as our experience using topical structure analysis with individual students and whole classes, we have developed an instructional sequence for teaching students how to perform a topical structure analysis and how to make it work as a revision strategy.

Following closely Lautamatti's (1978, 1987) and Witte's (1983a, 1983b) work, we have isolated three principles that are crucial for students to understand in order for them to perform a topical structure analysis: (a) identifying sentence topics, (b) determining sentence progression, and (c) "charting" the progress of sentence topics.

To be able to identify sentence topics, students need to have some familiarity with the arrangement of information within a sentence according to its topic and comment. *Topic* would be explained as simply the "main topic of the sentence," which often, but not always, coincides with the grammatical subject of the sentence. For most essays and texts, one noun or noun phrase expresses this. The noun that expresses sentence topics can occur in many places in a sentence—beginning, middle, and end, as the sample text in Figure 2 shows. *Comment* would be explained as "what is being said about the topic," which is often the grammatical predicate. For example, in sentence 4 of the sample text (see Figure 2), the sentence topic is "a child," and the comment is "is very unlikely to survive."

To be able to determine sentence progression, students need to know how topics can build meaning through either parallel, sequential, or extended parallel progression. As briefly explained earlier, in parallel progression, sentence topics are semantically identical (sentences 1-4 in the sample text, Figure 2). This kind of progression—repetition of a topic—is meant to reinforce the idea on the reader's mind. In sequential progression, the sentence topics, which are always different, are typically derived from the comment in the previous sentence (sentences 5, 6, 7, and 9). This helps to develop individual topics by adding details to an idea—a requirement for good prose. Too much development of a sentence topic (if not the main idea of the essay) may distract the reader from the main idea. In extended parallel progression, the writer returns to a topic mentioned earlier in the essay (sentences 8 and 10).

After students have identified and underlined the sentence topics in their essays, they are ready to chart the progress of the sentence topics. As the sample text in Figure 2 shows, sentence topics with parallel progression are placed exactly below each other. Sequential topics are indented, and extended parallel progression is aligned with the parallel topic to which it refers.

FIGURE 2

Sample Text and Diagram

From "Observations on the Development of the Topic in Simplified Discourse" by L. Lautamatti, in *Text Linguistics, Cognitive Learning and Language Teaching* (Publications de l'Association finlandaise de linguistique appliquée No. 22) (pp. 78, 83), edited by N. E. Enkvist and V. Kohonen, 1978, Helsinki: Akateeminen kirjakauppa. Copyright 1978 by l'Association finlandaise de linguistique appliquée. Reprinted by permission.

When *a human infant* is born into any community in any part of the world *it* has two things in common with any other infant, provided neither of them has been damaged in any way either before or during birth. Firstly, and most obviously, *new born children* are completely helpless. Apart from a powerful capacity to draw attention to their helplessness by using sound there is nothing *the new born child* can do to ensure his own survival. Without care from some other human being or beings, be it mother, grandmother, sister, nurse, or human group, *a child* is very unlikely to survive. *This helplessness of human infants* is in marked contrast with the capacity of many new born animals to get to their feet within minutes of birth and run with the herd within a few hours. Although *young animals* are certainly at risk, sometimes for weeks or even months after birth, compared with the human infant *they* very quickly develop the capacity to fend for themselves. It would seem that *this long period of vulnerability* is the price that the human species has to pay for the very long period which fits man for survival as species.

It is during this very long period in which *the human infant* is totally dependent on others that *it* reveals the second feature which it shares with all other undamaged human infants, a capacity to learn language. For this reason, biologists now suggest that *language* is 'species specific' to the human race, that is to say, they consider the human infant to be genetically programmed in such a way that it can acquire language. This suggestion implies that just as *human beings* are designed to see three-dimensionally and in colour, and just as they are designed to stand upright rather than to move on all fours, so *they* are designed to learn and use language as part of their normal development as well-formed human beings.

1. a human infant
2. new born children
3. the new born child
4. a child
5.   this helplessness
6.   young animals
7.   this long period of vulnerability
8. the human infant
9.   language
10. human beings

Note: Italics indicate sentence topic.

After students have made the diagrams, they should study them carefully to check for coherence of ideas and then make changes accordingly. To teach this, we first show students sample essays with varying levels of coherence and suggest ways to improve coherence in them. Initially, we also go over students' own coherence diagrams and essays with them to help interpret them. Students quickly become comfortable with this method and include—even if not required—topical structure diagrams as part of their regular paper "packets," along with their prewriting, drafts, and peer comments. We think that to benefit most from this method, students should use it with their first drafts. At that point in the writing process, students are still inclined to make substantive changes.

Student response has been positive, and we have seen improvement in student writing, specifically in regard to clearer focus and better development of subtopics.

We feel that topical structure analysis is a useful check of coherence in writing, which should of course be used in addition to teacher and peer comments.

Another sentence-based text-linguistic approach that explains problems of coherence in student writing is offered by Wikborg (1985, 1987) as part of a large-scale project conducted at the University of Stockholm. Working with hundreds of EFL college student essays from five different disciplines (business, literature, English, law, and journalism), Wikborg developed a comprehensive system of coherence breaks including *topic-structuring* problems and *cohesion* problems. Under the former, she lists breaks related to unspecified topic, unjustified change in topic, misleading paragraph divisions, irrelevance, and misleading disposition and headings. Under *cohesion* problems, she includes the types of cohesion described by Halliday and Hasan (1976) as well as instances of cohesion that do not work.

Wikborg's (1985, 1987) system is data based rather than theory based. In other words, the researcher read through compositions, identified coherence breaks, and then classified these breaks into categories. Although the categories can be explained by linguistic and rhetorical theories, the system needs to be verified with other student writing before it can be applied to other ESL writing situations. The research, however, is impressive and should encourage continued efforts to define coherence using linguistic and rhetorical features in students' own writing.

In summary of the contributions of the other sentence-based research listed in Figure 1, it is fair to say that these studies have emphasized the description and evaluation of written products. Patterson and Linden (1976) and Taylor (1979) have developed and applied quantitative syntactic systems for large-scale evaluations of student writing in Sweden and Australia, respectively. Biber (1984, 1985) and Grabe (1987) are interested in objective, quantifiable syntactic models geared to identifying genre types. Connor and Biber (1987) have identified preferred syntactic patterns in persuasive writing by English-speaking high school students from three different cultures. The research on cohesion (Connor, 1984b; Witte & Faigley, 1981) was prompted by questions concerning *quality* of writing, thus contributing to a better understanding of evaluation criteria.

Process-Centered Approach

The process-centered approach is concerned with the production and comprehension of texts. Unlike the sentence-based approach, in the text analyses for this approach, sentences are typically reduced to propositions (most often defined as a relationship between a predicate and its argument, as explained below). Because many of the models were developed for the purpose of assessing the text comprehended's understanding of texts, this approach emphasizes superstructures of texts over a linear representation of sentences as evidenced in the sentence-based approach.

Empirical research using the procedural approach has examined many aspects of texts that have implications for the teaching of ESL writing. This text-linguistic approach has been applied to a variety of genres, including persuasive writing and business letter writing, on both accomplished texts and student writing (see Figure 3). Research using semantic representations of text is described to illustrate the advantages of this approach for a writing theory that integrates product and process.

Influential approaches to the analysis of the semantic representations of texts include van Dijk's (1977) "topic of discourse" analysis, Kintsch's (1974) propositional analysis, and Meyer's (1975) semantic content structure analysis. All of these analyses have in common a notion of *proposition*, defined in varying ways, from the relationships between a predicate and its argument (Grimes, 1975; Meyer, 1975) to the psychological status of the semantic representation involved, that is, what the hearer or reader has in mind after hearing or reading a text (Kintsch & van Dijk, 1978; van Dijk & Kintsch, 1983).

Meyer's (1975) semantic content structure analysis (the way information is organized in a text) serves as an example of a theory of semantic representation that empirical studies have applied to the study of reading and writing. This theory views a text as a complex proposition in which each proposition fulfills some rhetorical function. As explained in more detail in Connor (1984a), the key to understanding Meyer's system is to know what a simple proposition is and how propositions may be pieced together to develop a coherent text.

In Meyer's analysis, a proposition is a meaning unit which consists of a *predicate* (relator) and one or more *arguments* belonging to the predicate. A predicate may be realized as a verb, adjective, or sentence connective, and an argument may be realized as a noun, noun phrase, or prepositional phrase. For example, in the sentence *John hit Mary*, hit is the predicate, and *John* and *Mary* are the arguments. In Meyer's semantic content structure analysis of texts, a text is viewed as a proposition. The relators are Meyer's *rhetorical predicates* (e.g., explanation, response, manner). Independent sentences serve as arguments and are linked by rhetorical predicates which come in many levels, creating a hierarchy of superordinate and subordinate ideas. For example, "response" is a top-level rhetorical predicate which can have as its arguments, "problem" and "solution." This could be called a problem-solution, top-level structure. Other top-level structures include comparison, collection of descriptions, and causation.

Several studies have used Meyer's semantic content structure to examine the recall of texts by ESL learners. Figure 4 (reproduced from Connor, 1984a, pp. 246-247) shows a content structure diagram of an expository passage with a problem/solution, top-level structure that Connor and McCagg (1983, 1987) used in a series of studies. In the analysis, the text is broken into clauses, and each clause is assigned its rhetorical function according to the role it plays in conveying the overall meaning of the text. Then a content structure diagram is constructed, identifying rhetorical predicates that show how superordinate and subordinate ideas are related. In the recall experiments, the same text analysis was applied both to the test passage and to the recall protocols. This allowed comparisons of the structure and content of the paraphrases with the structure and content of the original reading selection, both in terms of what propositions were recalled and in terms of how these propositions were sequenced.

FIGURE 3

Process-Centered Approach: Representative Empirical Studies

Concept	Operationalization	References	Accomplished writing	L1 writing	L2 writing
			Application		
Discourse-level patterns in narratives	Story grammar analysis	Mandler & Johnson (1977)	X		
		Martin & Rothery (1980)			X
		Soter (1985)			X
Discourse-level patterns in exposition	Semantic content structure analysis	Meyer (1975)	X		
		Carrell (1984, 1985)			X
		Carrell & Eisterhold (1987)			
		Connor (1984a)			X
		Connor & McCagg (1983, 1987)			X
Sentence functions	a. Inferencing	McCagg (1984, 1987)			X
	b. Speech acts	Lindeberg (1985)			X
	c. Function of initial sentences	Scarcella (1984)			X
Reader/writer responsibility in business writing	Rhetorical structure	Harris (1987)	X		
		Jenkins & Hinds (1987)	X		
Patterns in discourse	a. Argument superstructure	Tirkkonen-Condit (1984)	X		
		Connor & Takala (in press)		X	
		Connor & Lauer (in press)		X	
	b. Rhetorical appeals to the audience	Connor & Lauer (1985, 1986)		X	
		Stygall (1986)		X	
	c. Toulmin (1958) analysis of reasoning	Connor & Lauer (in press)		X	
		Connor (1987a)			X

FIGURE 4

Content Structure Diagram

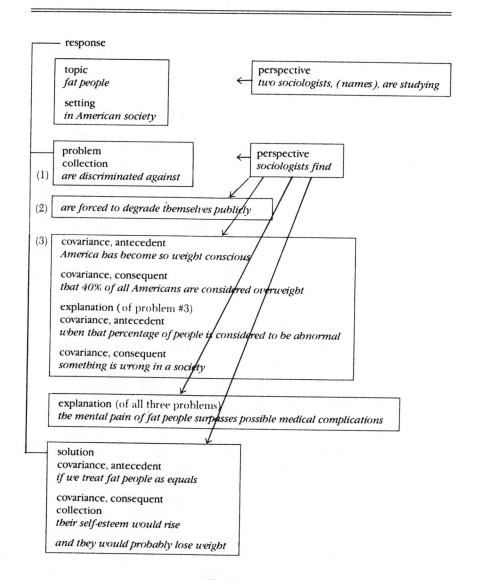

On Being Fat in America

Fat people in American society are often discriminated against in their jobs and forced to degrade themselves publicly, sociologists find. Two sociologists, Dr. Ardyth Stimson of New Jersey's Kean College and Dr. Jack Kamerman, are currently studying fat people and their role in society.

FIGURE 4—*Continued*
Content Structure Diagram

According to Dr. Stimson, "We treat people who are fat as handicapped people but we don't give them the sympathy that we give to other handicapped people. Instead, they're completely rejected and blamed for their handicap. In addition, they're expected to participate in what we sociologists call degradation ceremonies. In other words, you're supposed to stand there and say, "Hee, hee, hee, don't I look awful? Hee, hee, hee, isn't it funny I can't move around?"

"Some cities," Kamerman said, "set overweight limits for teachers, and if you exceed that limit—25 percent above what the insurance tables define as healthy—you are fired." He also said that there have been other studies that found fat people do not get promoted as easily and do not advance in a company.

Stimson recently completely a study of 40 women, and while none was even remotely medically overweight, she said 39 felt they were fat, and it caused some of them trouble in their everyday relationships.

"America has become so weight conscious," she said, "that 40 percent of all Americans are now considered overweight." She said there is something wrong in a society when that percentage of people are considered to be abnormal. "The problem is so great," she said, "that if you are overweight, people no longer think of you as a doctor, a lawyer, or a teacher but as that fat person."

In some instances, the mental pain of fat people is so severe the effect it has on their lives far surpasses the medical complications that could arise as a result of being fat. If fat men and women were treated as equals, their self-esteem would rise and they would probably lose weight.

Three pedagogical implications emerge from Connor and McCagg's research for the teaching of ESL *writing*. Based upon empirical findings concerning the quality of written paraphrases as rated by ESL teachers, the authors recommended teaching ESL writers to place their task in a proper context, to support main ideas with more details, and to revise freely without being bound by the order of ideas in the original passage. (Here we see a direct analogy with the revising process of good writers, who revise more extensively than do poor writers, who tend to revise at the surface level only.)

Carrell (1987), who has shown that findings from ESL reading comprehension research and from ESL composition research complement each other, suggests that "teaching ESL writers about the top-level rhetorical structure of texts" and "teaching them how to signal a text's organizational plan through linguistic devices would all function to make their writing more effective" (p. 55). In other words, we could train students to identify and use top-level structure and types along with appropriate signaling words. In a recent pilot study, Carrell and Eisterhold (1987) found some effects for the training of top-level rhetorical structures on students' subsequent writing quality.

Caution needs to be exercised, however, against thinking that the teaching of top-level rhetorical structures is a panacea for text analysis and for the teaching of writing. We still do not know what the proper time is to apply the knowledge of the rhetorical top-level structure in writing so that it does not restrain students' natural writing process. Even if it were established that all good expository passages followed one of Meyer's highest level organizational structures (problem/solution, comparison, collection of descriptions, and causation), we still would not know at which stage in the writing process those particular structures appear. For some writers, a top-level structure may serve as a heuristic that helps them generate and organize ideas, whereas for others, these organizational structures appear later. Or some topics may encourage earlier top-level structure appearance. To improve our instruction, future research needs to continue trying to identify the role of semantic representational structure in texts and in the writing process.

Another research method that holds promise for ESL instructional practice is McCagg's (1984, 1987) taxonomy of inferencing. McCagg developed a systematic way of accounting for propositions occurring in reading comprehension protocols that are not directly or explicitly stated in the stimulus reading passage. Based upon detailed analyses of Japanese-speaking ESL students' recall protocols, McCagg classifies propositions into text based and reader based, each with a number of subcategories. Although McCagg's focus has been limited to the analyses of reading recalls by student writers, the taxonomy could be used for examining and teaching coherence in student writing. It is based on a sound theory and has been tested on numerous texts.

Figure 3 shows that other empirical studies using the process-centered approach include analyses of story grammar, speech act analyses, examinations of reader-writer responsibility in business letter writing, and numerous recent analyses of the production and comprehension of persuasive discourse. The number of applications to L1 and L2 student writing in these analyses is impressive. This is encouraging for the teaching of ESL writing because all of these studies involve the process of interpretation by the reader and interaction between the writer and the reader. They offer insights that are useful for students and teachers in planning and revising discourse.

Conclusion

This article has shown that text analyses of writing are diverse, flexible, and still developing. Two major approaches—sentence based and process centered—were distinguished among empirical studies of writing. It is maintained that both approaches are necessary for a comprehensive theory of writing. This article has also shown that at the same time that paradigm shifts both in writing and text analysis have accelerated research into how and what students write, there has been a healthy interchange that has resulted in interdisciplinary work among rhetoricians, linguists, psychologists, and teachers. Thanks to these cooperative efforts, we are moving toward an integrated theory of writing that includes both process and product.

Acknowledgments

Preparation of this article was supported in part by a grant from the Exxon Education Foundation. I would like to thank Craig Chaudron, Janice Lauer, Nils E. Enkvist, and two anonymous reviewers for their helpful comments on an earlier draft of this article.

Works Cited

Bardovi-Harlig, K. (1987). *The role of pragmatic word order in English composition*. Unpublished manuscript.

Beach, R. (1976). Self-evaluation strategies of extensive revisors and non-revisors. *College Composition
and Communication, 27*, 160-164.

de Beaugrande, R. (1980). *Text, discourse, and process*. Hillsdale, NJ: Lawrence Erlbaum.

Biber, D. (1984). *A model of textual relations within the written and spoken modes*. Unpublished doctoral
dissertation, University of Southern California, Los Angeles.

Biber, D. (1985). Investigating macroscopic textual variation through multi-feature/multi-dimensional
analyses. *Linguistics, 23*, 337-360.

Bridwell, L. S. (1980). Revising strategies in twelfth grade students' transactional writing. *Research in the
Teaching of English, 14*, 197-222.

Brown, G., & Yule, G. (1983). *Discourse analysis*. London Cambridge University Press.

Carrell, P. L. (1982). Cohesion is not coherence. *TESOL Quarterly, 16*, 479-488.

Carrell, P. L. (1984). The effects of rhetorical organization on ESL readers. *TESOL Quarterly, 18*, 441-469.

Carrell, P. L. (1985). Facilitating ESL reading by teaching text structure. *TESOL Quarterly, 19*, 727-752.

Carrell, P. L. (1987). Text as interaction: Some implications of text analysis and reading research for ESL
composition. In U. Connor & R. B. Kaplan (Eds.), *Writing across languages: Analysis of L2 text* (pp.
45-55). Reading, MA: Addison-Wesley.

Carrell, P. L., & Eisterhold, J. (1987, April). *Training formal schemata for reading and writing ESL*. Paper
presented at the 21st Annual TESOL Convention, Miami.

Connor, U. (1984a). Recall of text: Differences between first and second language readers. *TESOL Quarterly, 18*, 239-256.

Connor, U. (1984b). A study of cohesion and coherence in English as a second language students' writing.
Papers in Linguistics: International Journal of Human Communication, 17, 301-316.

Connor, U. (1987a, April). *Analytic vs. holistic essay rating: A place for both in ESL*. Paper presented at the
Fifth Annual Conference on Writing Assessment, Atlantic City, NJ.

Connor, U. (1987b). Argumentative patterns in student essays: Cross-cultural differences. In U. Connor &
R. B. Kaplan (Eds.), *Writing across languages: Analysis of L2 text* (pp. 127-155). Reading, MA: Addison-Wesley.

Connor, U. (1987c, March). *Examining and teaching coherence in ESL*. Paper presented at the College
Composition and Communication Conference, Atlanta.

Connor, U. (1987d, June). *Examining and teaching coherence in ESL: Use of topical structure analysis*. Paper presented at the Nordtext Conference, Turku, Finland.

Connor, U., & Biber, D. (1987). *Syntactic characteristics of student persuasive writing: A cross-cultural
study*. Unpublished manuscript, Indiana University in Indianapolis, Department of English.

Connor, U., Cerniglia, C., & Medsker, K. (1987). *STAR—Studying topical analysis for revision* [Com-
puter-assisted instructional lesson]. Indianapolis: Indiana University, Department of English.

Connor, U., & Farmer, M. (1985, March-April). *The teaching of topical structure analysis as a revision
strategy: An exploratory study*. Paper presented at the meeting of the American Educational Research
Association, Chicago.

Connor, U., & Farmer, M. (1987). *Examining and teaching coherence in ESL: Use of 'topical structure analysis.'* Unpublished manuscript, Indiana University in Indianapolis, Department of English.

Connor, U., & Johns, A. M. (Eds.). (1987). *Coherence: Research and pedagogical perspectives*. Manuscript
submitted for publication.

Connor, U., & Lauer, J. (1985). Understanding persuasive essay writing, linguistic /rhetorical approach.
Text, 5, 309-326.

Connor, U., & Lauer, J. (1986, April). *Understanding persuasion essay writing*. Paper presented at the meeting of the American Educational Research Association, San Francisco.

Connor, U., & Lauer, J. (in press). Cultural variation in argument. In A. C. Purves (Ed.), *Contrastive rhetoric: Theory and application*. Beverly Hills, CA: Sage.

Connor, U., & McCagg, P. (1983). Cross-cultural differences and perceived quality in written paraphrases of
English expository prose. *Applied Linguistics, 4*, 259-268.

Connor, U., & McCagg, P. (1987). A contrastive study of English expository prose paraphrases. In U.
Connor & R. B. Kaplan (Eds.), *Writing across languages: Analysis of L2 text* (pp. 75-89). Reading,
MA: Addison-Wesley.

Connor, U., & Takala, S. (in press). Predictors of persuasive student writing. In E. Degenhart (Ed.), *Assessment of student writing in an international context* (Research Report Series B: Theory into Practice No. 9). Jyvaskyla, Finland: Institute for Educational Research.

Daneš, F. (Ed.). (1974). *Papers on functional sentence perspective.* Prague: Academia.

Dressier, W. U. (Ed.). (1978). *Current trends in text linguistics.* Berlin/New York: de Gruyter.

Enkvist, N. E. (1975). *Tekstdingvistiikan peruskasitteita* [Principles of text linguistics]. Helsinki: Oy Gaudemus Ab.

Enkvist, N. E. (1978). Some aspects of applications of text linguistics. In N. E. Enkvist & V. Kohonen (Eds.), *Text linguistics, cognitive learning and language teaching* (Publications de I'Association finlandaise de Iinguistique appliquée No. 22) (pp. 1-28). Helsinki Akateeminen kirjakauppa.

Enkvist, N. E. (1985). Introduction: Coherence, composition, and text linguistics. In N. E. Enkvist (Ed.), *Coherence and composition A symposium* (pp. 11-26). Åbo, Finland: Research Institute of the Åbo Akademi Foundation.

Enkvist, N. E. (1987). Text linguistics for an applier: An introduction. In U. Connor & R. B. Kaplan (Eds.), *Writing across languages: Analysis of L2 text* (pp. 19-43). Reading, MA: Addison-Wesley.

Evensen, L. S. (1987). *Pointers to superstructure in student writing.* Unpublished manuscript.

Firbas, J. (1966). Non-thematic subjects in contemporary English. *Travaux Linguistique de Prague, 2,* 239-256.

Flower, L. S., & Hayes, J. R. (1981). A cognitive process theory of writing. *College Composition and Communication, 32,* 365-387.

Grabe, W. (1987). Contrastive rhetoric and text-type research. In U. Connor & R. B. Kaplan (Eds.), *Writing across languages: Analysis of L2 text* (pp. 127-155). Reading, MA: Addison-Wesley.

Grimes, J. (1975). *The thread of discourse.* The Hague: Mouton.

Hairston, M. (1982). The winds of change: Thomas Kuhn and the revolution in the teaching of writing. *College Composition and Communication, 33,* 76-88.

Halliday, M. A. K. (1961). Categories of the theory of grammar. *Word, 17,* 241-292.

Halliday, M. A. K., & Hasan, R. (1976). *Cohesion in English.* London: Longman.

Harris, D. P. (1987). *The use of 'organizing sentences' in the structure of paragraphs in science textbooks.* Unpublished manuscript.

Jenkins, S., & Hinds, J. (1987). Business letter writing: English, French, and Japanese. *TESOL Quarterly, 21,* 327-349.

Johns, A. (1986). Coherence in academic writing; Some definitions and suggestions for teaching, *TESOL Quarterly, 20,* 247-266,

Kintsch, W. (1974). *The representation of meaning in memory.* Hillsdale, NJ: Lawrence Erlbaum.

Kintsch, W., & van Dijk, T. A. (1978). Toward a model of text comprehension and production. *Psychological Review, 85,* 363-394.

Lautamatti, L. (1978). Observations on the development of the topic in simplified discourse. In N.E. Enkvist & V. Kohonen (Eds.), *Text linguistics, cognitive learning and language teaching* (Publications de l'Association finlandaise de linguistique appliquée No. 22) (pp. 71-104). Helsinki: Akateeminen kirjakauppa.

Lautamatti, L. (1987). Observations on the development of the topic in simplified discourse. In U. Connor & R. B. Kaplan (Eds.), *Writing across languages: Analysis of L2 text* (pp. 92-126). Reading, MA: Addison-Wesley.

Lindeberg, A. (1985). Cohesion, coherence patterns, and EFL essay evaluation. In N.E. Enkvist (Ed.), *Coherence and composition; A symposium* (pp. 67-92). Åbo, Finland: Research Institute of the Åbo Akademi Foundation.

Mandler, J. M., & Johnson, N. S. (1977). Remembrance of things parsed: Story structure and recall. *Cognitive Psychology, 9,* 111-191.

Martin, J. R., & Rothery, J. (1980). Writing project: Report 1 (Working Papers in Linguistics). Sydney, Australia: University of Sydney, Department of Linguistics.

McCagg, P. (1984). *An investigation of inferencing in second-language reading comprehension.* Unpublished doctoral dissertation, Georgetown University, Washington, DC.

McCagg, P. (1987). *Toward understanding coherence: A response proposition taxonomy.* Unpublished manuscript.

Meyer, B. J. F. (1975). *The organization of prose and its effects on memory.* Amsterdam: North-Holland.

Patterson, A., & Lindell, E. (1976). *Om fri skrivning: Skolan. Pedagogisk-psykologiska problem* [About school writing. Pedagogical/psychological problems] (Report No. 301). Malmo, Sweden: Lärarhögskolan.

Phelps, L. W. (1985). Dialects of coherence: Toward an integrative theory. *College English, 47*, 12-29.

Raimes, A. (1985). What unskilled ESL students do as they write: A classroom study of composing. *TESOL Quarterly, 19*, 229-258.

Reid, J. (1987, April). *Does ESL writing differ qualitatively?* Paper presented at the 21st Annual TESOL Convention, Miami.

Scarcella, R. C. (1984). How writers orient their readers in expository essays: A comparative study of native and nonnative English writers. *TESOL Quarterly, 18*, 671-689.

Sommers, N. I. (1980). Revision strategies of student writers and experienced adult writers. *College Composition and Communication, 31*, 378-387.

Sommers, N. I. (1987, March). *Constructing readers—constructing texts: New directions in researching the revising process.* Paper presented at the College Composition and Communication Conference, Atlanta.

Soter, A. (1985). *Writing: A third language for second language writers.* Unpublished doctoral dissertation, University of Illinois, Champaign-Urbana.

Stygall, G. (1986). *Rating writing with Toulmin.* Unpublished manuscript, Indiana University in Indianapolis, Department of English.

Taylor, C. V. (1979). *The English of high school texts* (Educational Research and Development Commission Report No. 18). Canberra: Australian Government Publishing Service.

Tirkkonen-Condit, S. (1984). Towards a description of argumentative text structure. In H. Ringbom & M. Rissanen (Eds.), *Proceedings from the second Nordic conference on English studies* (Publications of the Research Institute of the Åbo Akademi Foundation No. 92) (pp. 221-236). Abe, Finland: Åbo Akademi.

Toulmin, S. (1958). *Uses of argument,* Cambridge: Cambridge University Press.

van Dijk, T. A. (1977). *Text and context.* London: Longman.

van Dijk, T. A. (Ed.). (1985). *Handbook of discourse analysis* (Vols. 1-4). New York: Academic Press.

van Dijk, T. A., & Kintsch, W. (1983). *Strategies of discourse comprehension.* New York: Academic Press.

Werlich, E. (1976). *A text grammar of English.* Heidelberg: Quelle and Meyer.

Wikborg, E. (1985). Types of coherence breaks in university student writing. In N. E. Enkvist (Ed.), *Coherence and composition: A symposium* (pp. 93-133). Åbo, Finland: Research Institute of the Åbo Akademi Foundation.

Wikborg, E. (1987). *Coherence breaks in Swedish student writing: Misleading paragraph division.* Unpublished manuscript.

Witte, S. P. (1983a). Topical structure and revision: An exploratory study. *College Composition and Communication, 34*, 313-341.

Witte, S. P. (1983b). Topical structure and writing quality: Some possible text-based explanations of readers' judgments of students' writing. *Visible Language, 17*, 177-205.

Witte, S. P., & Faigley, L. (1981). Coherence, cohesion and writing quality. *College Composition and Communication, 32*, 189-204.

Zamel, V. (1983). The composing processes of advanced ESL students: Six case studies. *TESOL Quarterly, 17*, 165-186.

Zamel, V. (1985). Responding to student writing. *TESOL Quarterly, 19*, 79-101.

Initiating ESL Students Into
the Academic Discourse Community:
How Far Should We Go?
by Ruth Spack

Within the last decade, numerous approaches to the teaching of writing in programs for ESL college students have been tried, and much discussion has focused on the most appropriate approach to adopt (see the *TESOL Quarterly* Forum contributions of Horowitz, 1986c/Liebman-Kleine, 1986/Horowitz, 1986b/Hamp-Lyons, 1986/ Horowitz, 1986a; Reid, 1984b/Spack, 1985a/Reid, 1985; Reid, 1984a/Zamel, 1984). Though a misleading process/product, or process-centered/content-based, dichotomy has characterized the debate, ESL writing researchers and teachers have generally agreed that the goal of college-level L2 writing programs is to prepare students to become better academic writers.

However, the achievement of this goal is complicated by at least two major factors. One is that we have not yet satisfactorily determined, despite numerous surveys, what academic writing is, an issue that this article examines. The other is that there is most often a large gap between what students bring to the academic community and what the academic community expects of them.

In the case of native English-speaking basic writers—academically disadvantaged students who have achieved only very modest standards of high school literacy—Bizzell (1982) points out that the students' social situation and previous training may hamper their ability to succeed in the academy. In other words, their problems with academic writing may not lie in a lack of innate ability but rather in the social and cultural factors that influence composing. The gap is even wider for ESL students who can be classified as basic writers, for it includes L2 linguistic and cultural differences. Even for ESL students who are highly literate in their native language, a similar gap exists: The students' lack of L2 linguistic and cultural knowledge can stand in the way of academic success.

It is clearly the obligation of the ESL college-level writing teacher, whether teaching basic writers or highly literate students, to find a way to narrow the gap. As Bizzell (1982) suggests, we must help students master the language and culture of the university; the role of the university writing teacher is to initiate students into the academic discourse community. The issue of concern in this article is the means through which we should fulfill our role.

My concern stems from what I perceive to be a disturbing trend in L2 writing instruction, a trend that has been influenced both by the Writing Across the Curriculum (WAC) movement in L1 writing instruction and the English for specific purposes (ESP) movement in L2 instruction. This trend toward having teachers of English, including teachers of freshman composition, teach students to write in disciplines other than English may lead many in the composition field to assign papers that they are ill-equipped to handle. The purpose of this article is to remind teachers of English that we are justified in teaching general academic writing and to argue that we should leave the teaching of writing in the disciplines to the teachers of those disciplines.

Defining Academic Writing

Determining what academic writing is and what ESL students need to know in order to produce it has not been an easy task for researchers and teachers. In fact, a number of L2 writing instructors, including this author, have tried several different approaches, faithfully following textbook guidelines. Early ESL writing textbooks were largely workbooks that fostered controlled composition and that did not satisfy students' need to learn how to produce their own body of work for their other university courses. Later efforts to have students create their own academic texts often resulted in absurd assignments that students could not logically fulfill. For example, one textbook (Bander, 1978) suggested that science students begin with a topic sentence such as "The importance of oxygen to mankind cannot be overstated" and that humanities students show how "the revolutions that took place in France, the United States, and Russia resulted in major changes in those countries" (p. 30). (This, according to the book, could be done in one paragraph!)

ESL writing textbooks began at this time to be modeled after textbooks for native speakers (NSs) of English, which emphasized the rhetorical patterns researchers claimed were commonly found in American academic prose. These books ask students to write whole pieces of discourse by imitating models (which are, paradoxically, often excerpts rather than whole pieces of discourse) and to describe, compare, classify, define, and determine the cause and effect of everything from religion to Chinese food.

Though still popular with many teachers, this approach has been called into question in both L2 and L1 fields because "starting from given patterns and asking students to find topics and produce essays to fit them is a reversal of the normal writing process" (Shih, 1986, p. 622) and turns attention away from the meaningful act of communication in a social context (Connors, 1981). Furthermore, a recent (though admittedly limited) survey of actual writing assignment handouts given to university students by teachers in courses other than writing (Horowitz, 1986d) reveals that these assignments do not ask students to start from patterns and produce essays to fit them. If further research bears this out, it will be safe to say that this pattern-centered approach is not suitable for a program that emphasizes academic writing.

In response to some of this criticism, and again following the model of NS writing textbooks, the ESL field has begun to publish textbooks that emphasize the cognitive process of writing. This approach is based on the research of composition specialists who have drawn on the theories of cognitive psychologists and psycholinguists to explore the mental procedures writers use to communicate ideas (see, for example, the L1 research of Flower & Hayes, 1977, 1981; the L2 research of Lay, 1982; Raimes, 1985; Zamel, 1982, 1983). The thrust of these ESL textbooks (see, for example, Hartfiel, Hughey, Warmuth, & Jacobs, 1985) is to teach students systematic thinking and writing skills so that they can use their own composing strategies effectively to explore ideas. Emphasis is on self-generated topics, with thematically organized readings usually, but not always, acting as springboards for ideas.

Yet the writing produced in such courses has not been universally accepted as academic, even though it takes place in the academy. Much of the writing is based solely on students' personal experiences or interests. Although this provides students with a drive to learn to write by focusing on what really matters to them, it has its drawbacks. As Bazerman (1980) points out, in emphasizing the writer's independent self, teachers ignore the fact that writing is "not contained entirely in the envelope of experience, native thought, and personal motivation to communicate" (p. 657).

I would argue that since the personal essay as a genre informs the discipline known as English literature, this kind of writing can be considered academic. It also serves as a vehicle for reflection and self-expression for specialists in many other fields, including science (e.g., Cole, 1985), medicine (e.g., Thomas, 1983), and engineering (e.g., Petroski, 1986). And the personal essay plays a role in students' future academic success: When they apply for transfer, for scholarships, or to graduate school, they are asked to write on personal topics in order to sell themselves and presumably to display their writing skills. Still, there is no evidence that the skills learned in this kind of writing adequately provide students with the tools they need to produce the academic writing required in other courses.

Although the cognitive process approach is admired because of its emphasis on writing as a learning process and its development of useful, teachable skills, MacDonald (1987) reveals its limitations: Its L1 research (e.g., Flower& Hayes, 1977, 1981) is based on only one kind of writing, which MacDonald describes as "composing with an undefined problem, with the writer forced to create a problem for him- or herself ... a kind of composing traditionally associated with English departments—whether interpretations of literature or personal essays" (p. 328). Other kinds of writing, such as scientific or social science writing, which have different demands and constraints, are ignored. Raimes's (1985) L2 research, based on students' personal experience essays, has been challenged on similar grounds (Horowitz, 1986c).

A further criticism of a process approach that promotes student-generated meaning and form is that it does not acknowledge that "most writing for academic classes is in response to a specific assignment or prompt" (Johns, 1986, p. 253). Shaughnessy (1977), Bizzell (1982), and Rose (1985) therefore claim that it does not prepare students to grapple with the challenges of academic life but rather postpones their confrontation with the "complex linguistic and rhetorical expectations of the academy" (Rose, 1985, p. 357).

Bizzell (1982) argues that to succeed in their university studies, students need critical training and recommends a "social-contextual approach" that "demystifies the institutional structure of knowledge" (p. 196). Researchers and textbook writers, Bizzell contends, need to focus on the conventions of academic discourse, emphasizing the relationship between discourse, community, and knowledge. In finding ways to "demystify" academic discourse, ESP researchers have been at the forefront of genre analysis, identifying and analyzing "key genres, such as Case Studies in Business, Legislative documents in Law, lab reports in Science, disease-descriptions in Medicine and Agriculture" (Swales, 1986, p. 18).

L1 and L2 researchers have conducted a number of surveys to determine what writing tasks are actually assigned across academic disciplines. Horowitz (1986d) has found fault with some of the studies (Bridgeman & Carlson, 1984; Johns, 1981, 1985; Kroll, 1979; Ostler, 1980), which, he points out, "beg the question" of what the tasks are: "Instead of trying to discover and classify university writing tasks—a logical prior endeavor—they began with a set of preconceived classifications, forcing on the respondents the particular scheme used in each survey" (p. 448). The surveys of Behrens (1980), Rose (1983), and Horowitz (1986d) take a more ethnographic view, creating classifications after examining the data. Nevertheless, the Horowitz survey has been criticized on the grounds that it is a limited study (only 38 of the 750 faculty members who were contacted responded; only 54 writing assignments were collected) (Raimes, 1987) and that it ignores the context in which the tasks were assigned (Zamel, 1987).

Until we collect more assignments, interview the teachers to learn the purposes of the assigned tasks, observe the courses in which the tasks are assigned, examine the resulting student essays, and analyze the teacher responses to and evaluations of these papers, we cannot truly understand the nature of the academic writing students are asked to produce. Furthermore, we should not forget that it is important to take a critical look at these assignments. Having seen numerous examples of writing assignments for other courses, I suspect that one reason so few faculty members responded to Horowitz is that they may have been reluctant to show English teachers their own poorly written or poorly designed texts. The fact that papers assigned by teachers in other disciplines are different from those assigned in freshman composition classes—the finding of several surveys—does not necessarily mean that the former are superior.

Still, it is impossible and perhaps foolish to ignore the implications of the surveys: The writing students do in courses other than English composition is rarely dependent solely on their own general knowledge base. Rather, "students will be confronted with either academic or professional writing tasks that surface in relation to texts of various kinds (literary, historical, psychological, legal, managerial) or *data* (computer, laboratory-testing, statistical, chemical)" (Scheiber, 1987, p. 15). These assignments are viewed as a means of promoting understanding of the content presented in subject-matter courses (Shih, 1986). Furthermore, writing academic papers involves the recursive processes of drafting, revising, and editing (Shih, 1986). Therefore, writing teachers can comfortably design process-centered courses around text-based or data-based tasks in which written language acts as a medium for learning something else. What that something else should be is the focus of this article.

Teaching Writing in the Disciplines

Until fairly recently, students wrote the various kinds of papers listed above only in classes other than English, with the obvious exception of essays related to literary texts. But there has been a growing tendency in both L1 and L2 composition instruction to add the responsibility of teaching writing in other disciplines to the other responsibilities of English department writing programs. It is beyond the scope of this article to examine all the reasons for this trend; only two of the influences are touched on in this section: Writing Across the Curriculum, an L1 movement, and English for specific or academic purposes, an L2 movement.

Writing Across the Curriculum

For a number of years, faculty have complained about weaknesses in students' ability to produce papers of high quality in subject-area courses—weaknesses attributed in part to a loosening of standards in the academy and in part to the change in the student population in the 1960s and 1970s from a somewhat elitist, homogeneous group to an academically underprepared group representing diverse cultures and educational backgrounds. Partly in response to this concern, a movement known as Writing Across the Curriculum, modeled on a British program, took hold in colleges and universities in the 1970s, its purpose to restore writing to its central place in the curricula of institutions of learning (Maimon, 1984). Though there have been several WAC models, they have shared the goal of encouraging instructors in all disciplines to make writing an inevitable part of the teaching and learning process in their courses. In faculty development seminars teachers of English have collaborated with subject-area instructors so that the latter can learn more about writing.

But WAC programs have not always met with success (Russell, 1987). Obstacles such as "increased teaching loads, large classes, administrative responsibilities, lack of collegial support, pressures to research, publish, write grants and the like"

(Fulwiler, 1984, p. 119) on teachers in other disciplines have caused some to refuse the extra burden of introducing the writing process into their courses. Furthermore, the lack of understanding on the part of English department faculty of the processes involved in writing essays that are neither personal nor interpretive has led to counterproductive faculty workshops (Applebee, 1986; Fulwiler, 1984). Collaborative faculty workshops have only recently begun to focus on the processes and strategies involved in scientific, technical, and social science writing, perhaps because researchers have only recently begun studying the writing processes of scientists (see Gilbert & Mulkay, 1984; Myers, 1985; and, for a discussion of these and other studies, Swales, 1987), engineers (Selzer, 1983), and social scientists (Becker, 1986).

Faculty development seminars now bring teachers of English together with subject-area instructors not only so that the latter can learn more about writing, but also so that the former can learn more about the subject area (Dick & Esch, 1985). In writing and planning linked courses with colleagues, the English composition teacher's general goal of strengthening students' writing skills is becoming the more specific goal of training students to handle the tasks of the other disciplines. This goal has led today to the creation of programs such as that at Beaver College (described in Maimon, Belcher, Hearn, Nodine, & O'Connor, 1981), which are built on the foundation of a cross-disciplinary, required freshman composition course. L1 textbooks designed for use in such English composition courses include instructions for writing in other disciplines—case studies in the social sciences, laboratory reports in the natural sciences, and so on (e.g., Bazerman, 1985; Maimon et al., 1981).

English for Specific Purposes/English for Academic Purposes

At approximately the same time the WAC movement was gaining prominence in L1 writing instruction, the ESP movement had taken hold in the field of L2 acquisition. ESP programs arose as a "practical alternative to the 'general' orientation of language teaching: cultural and literary emphases, education for life" (Maher, 1986, p. 113). Taking as its focus science and technology—the fields with the heaviest concentrations of international students—ESP creates courses, taught by English language teachers, whose aim is generally to fulfill the practical needs of L2 learners and specifically to produce technicians and technocrats who are proficient in English (Coffey, 1984). Collaboration, or team teaching, between the language instructor and the instructor in the other discipline is the preferred method of instruction but is possible "only where there is a high level of goodwill and mutual interest and understanding" (Coffey, 1984, p. 9).

When the students' needs consist of "the quick and economical use of the English language to pursue a course of academic study" (Coffey, 1984, p. 3), English for academic purposes (EAP) is offered. The incorporation of writing into the EAP curriculum, however, necessitates collaboration with the instructor in the other discipline, following what Shih (1986) calls the "adjunct model" of many university composition programs for native students. But the development of such programs for ESL students has been slow, and Shih recommends that we learn from existing programs:

> The potential contributions and possible limitations of the adjunct-course approach for ESL programs in general, and for preparing ESL students to handle university writing tasks in particular, remain to be evaluated. What is needed, minimally, is co-operation from subject-area instructors and ESL faculty willingness to step into sub-ject-area classrooms and keep up with class events. For ESL instructors seeking to set up adjunct courses, the experiences of composition adjunct programs already in place for native students are a rich source of information. (p. 640)

The next section of this article examines studies of these NS programs and dis-cusses the implications of the researchers' findings.

Studies of Writing Programs in the Disciplines and their Implications

Several L1 programs have been instituted to introduce students to the methods of inquiry in various disciplines. In typical programs, English teachers have collabo-rated with teachers in other disciplines, such as biology (Wilkinson, 1985), psy-chology (Faigley & Hansen, 1985), and sociology (Faigley & Hansen, 1985), linking the compositions to subject matter in the other course. Investigations of these programs reveal some obvious advantages: Students learn new forms of writ-ing which as professionals they might need; they have more time to write, since there is less reading due to the fact that one subject matter is employed for two courses; and their discussions of student papers are more informative, since knowl-edge is shared among class members.

However, the disadvantages of such a program are equally, if not more, signifi-cant, as Wilkinson (1985) and others show, and should be of great concern to the English teacher. First of all, it is difficult for a writing course to have a carefully planned pedagogical or rhetorical rationale when it is dependent on another content course; furthermore, the timing of assignments is not always optimal. Second, the program can raise false expectations among the faculty as well as among the stu-dents. English faculty, even when they collaborate with content teachers, find they have little basis for dealing with the content. They therefore find themselves in the uncomfortable position of being less knowledgeable than their students. Students likewise can resent finding themselves in a situation in which their instructor cannot fully explain or answer questions about the subject matter. Faigley and Hansen (1985) observed collaborative courses in which completely different criteria for evaluation were applied to students' papers by the two teachers because the English teacher did not recognize when a student failed to demonstrate adequate knowledge of a discipline or showed a good grasp of new knowledge.

The same phenomenon can hold true in L2 writing instruction. Pearson (1983) finds that "the instructor cannot always conveniently divorce the teaching of form from the understanding of content" (pp. 390-397). This drawback is often mentioned only in passing in articles recommending that English teachers use technical and scientific materials they are not familiar with (see Hill, Soppelsa, & West, 1982). But the lack of control over content on the part of English teachers who teach in the other disciplines is a serious problem. This concern is reflected in a state-of-the-art article on English for medical purposes (EMP):

> A sense of insecurity and uncertainty can sometimes be observed amongst EMP teachers regarding their effective roles as lay persons teaching 'medical English' among medical professionals. . . .
>
> Occasionally, the specialist informant, who is co-opted on to a teaching programme, harbours suspicions about the language teacher's motives. Consider the view of the *DUODECIM* [Finnish Medical Society] team of doctors: 'We believe that it is essential to have teachers *entirely at home* in medicine and English and who have some experience in writing and lecturing' (Collan, 1974:629), and 'Too few teachers combine enough experience in the use of the English language in general and knowledge of the speciality in particular' (Lock et al., 1975: cover). 'Is the teacher trying to teach my subject?' 'What if s/he gets the medical bits wrong and misleads the learners?' (Maher, 1986, p. 138)

In spite of these drawbacks, some investigators claim that it is possible for an English teacher to conduct a course that focuses on writing in a particular discipline if the teacher learns how a discipline creates and transmits knowledge. This is accomplished by examining the kinds of issues a discipline considers important, why certain methods of inquiry and not others are sanctioned, how the conventions of a discipline shape text in that discipline, how individual writers represent themselves in a text, how texts are read and disseminated within the discipline, and how one text influences subsequent texts (Faigley & Hansen, 1985; Herrington, 1985).

This exploration, of course, would involve a great deal of commitment, as anyone who has studied a particular field or discipline knows. Specialists in second language instruction, for example, have spent years acquiring the knowledge and understanding that enable them to recognize the issues that dominate discussion in the field (e.g., communicative competence), the methods of inquiry employed (e. g., ethnography), the structure of manuscripts focusing on those issues (e.g., the *TESOL Quarterly* format), the names associated with various issues (e.g., Krashen/Input Hypothesis; Carrell/schema theory; Zamel/writing process), and the impact a given article might have on thinking and research in the field.

It seems that only the rare individual teacher can learn another discipline, for each discipline offers a different system for examining experience, a different angle for looking at subject matter, a different kind of thinking (Maimon et al., 1981). Furthermore, whereas the transmission of a discipline within content courses primarily requires that students comprehend, recall, and display information in examinations, writing in the disciplines

> requires a complete, active, struggling engagement with the facts and principles of a discipline, an encounter with the discipline's texts and the incorporation of them into

one's own work, the framing of one's knowledge within the myriad conventions that help define a discipline, the persuading of other investigators that one's knowledge is legitimate. (Rose, 1985, p. 359)

The teaching of writing in a discipline, then, involves even more specialized knowledge and skills than does the teaching of the subject matter itself.

The difficulty of teaching writing in another discipline is compounded when we realize that within each discipline, such as the social sciences, there are subdiscipline, each with its own set of conventions. Reflection on personal events, for example, is considered legitimate evidence in sociology and anthropology, but not in behavioral psychology (Rose, 1983). Even within subdiscipline, such as anthropology, there are other subdiscipline with their own sets of conventions. The articles of physical anthropologists, for example, resemble those of natural scientists, whereas those of cultural anthropologists sometimes resemble those of literary scholars (Faigley & Hansen, 1985).

To further complicate matters, no discipline is static. In virtually all academic disciplines there is controversy concerning the validity of approaches, controversy that nonspecialists are usually unaware of until it is covered in the popular media (see, for example, Silk, 1987, for a discussion of the recent debate between political and anthropological historians). In addition, the principles of reasoning in a discipline may change over time, even in science, which is affected by the emergence of new mathematical techniques, new items of apparatus, and even new philosophical precepts (Yearley, 1981). Formal scientific papers, then, though often considered final statements of facts, are primarily contributions to scientific debate (Yearley, 1981).

And although we may be able to read and study texts from other disciplines, analyze genres, and thereby learn writing styles and conventions to teach our students, we should also be aware of any critical stance in relation to the texts. For example, Woodford (1967), editor of a scholarly scientific research journal, has mocked the state of scientific writing:

> The articles in our journals—even the journals with the highest standards—are, by and large, poorly written. Some of the worst are produced by the kind of author who consciously pretends to a "scientific scholarly" style. He takes what should be lively, inspiring, and beautiful and, in an attempt to make it seem dignified, chokes it to death with stately abstract nouns; next, in the name of scientific impartiality, he fits it with a complete set of passive constructions to drain away any remaining life's blood or excitement; then he embalms the remains in molasses of polysyllable, wraps the corpse in an impenetrable veil of vogue words, and buries the stiff old mummy with much pomp and circumstance in the most distinguished journal that will take it. (p. 743)

Woodford argues that this kind of writing is damaging to the students who read it. In his experience as a teacher of graduate students of science, he has found that it adversely affects students' ability to read, write, and think well. (English teachers, who traditionally have seen themselves as purveyors of effective prose, might do well to wonder why they should present such poorly written texts to their students.)

Even studying a finished product—whether well written or not—cannot prepare English teachers to teach students how writers in other disciplines write. A written product such as a scientific report is merely a representation of a research process, which is finally summarized for peers; it is not a representation of a writing process. To teach writing, writing teachers should teach the writing process; and to teach the writing process, they should know how to write. But English teachers are not necessarily equipped to write in other disciplines. Testimony to this truth appears in the ESP literature:

> In the author's experience, every attempt to write a passage, however satisfactory it seemed on pedagogic grounds, was promptly vetoed by the Project's scientific adviser because a technical solecism of some kind had been committed. The ESP writer, however experienced, simply does not know when a mistake of this kind is being committed. (Coffey, 1984, p. 8)

To learn to write in any discipline, students must become immersed in the subject matter; this is accomplished through reading, lectures, seminars, and so on. They learn by participating in the field, by doing, by sharing, and by talking about it with those who know more. They can also learn by observing the process through which professional academic writers produce texts or, if that is not possible, by studying that process in the type of program recommended by Swales (1987) for teaching the research paper to nonnative-speaking graduate students. They will learn most efficiently from teachers who have a solid grounding in the subject matter and who have been through the process themselves.

I do not deny that programs that instruct students to write in other disciplines can work. But a review of the L1 literature (e.g., Herrington, 1985) and the L2 literature (e.g., Swales, 1987) on successful programs reveals that the teachers are themselves immersed in the discipline. For example, Herrington's (1985) study is an observation of senior-level engineering courses taught by engineering faculty. And Swales's list of publications reveals a background in scientific discourse dating back at least to 1970.

Academic Writing Tasks for ESL College Students

English teachers cannot and should not be held responsible for teaching writing in the disciplines. The best we can accomplish is to create programs in which students can learn general inquiry strategies, rhetorical principles, and tasks that can transfer to other course work. This has been our traditional role, and it is a worthy one. The materials we use should be those we can fully understand. The writing projects we assign and evaluate should be those we are capable of doing ourselves. The remainder of this article is devoted to practical suggestions for incorporating academic writing into an English composition course designed for ESL undergraduates, without the need for linking the course with another subject-area program.

Working With Data

According to a number of surveys discussed earlier, students are often asked to work with data, either as observers or as participants. These experiences can become a part of the writing class instruction. In the L1 literature, Hillocks (1984, 1986) recommends that we engage students in a process of examining various kinds of data—either objects such as shells or photographs, or sets of information such as arguments. Students can be led to formulate and test explanatory generalizations, observe and report significant details, and generate criteria for contrasting similar phenomena.

Such programs have been shown to work in L2 writing classes. Zamel (1984) has reported on a class project in which students read published interviews with workers, then conducted and wrote up their own interviews, and later compared the data. Likewise, students have become amateur ethnographers, observing and evaluating the language in their communities (Zamel, 1986). Such tasks can produce writing that is "rich and original" (Zamel, 1984, p. 202).

But since composing in a second language is an enormously complex undertaking and because "it seems that this complexity has more to do with the constraints imposed by the writing task itself than with linguistic difficulties" (Zamel, 1984, p. 198), students need consistent teacher input in the observation and interviewing processes. They also need regular in-class collaborative workshops so that they can comment on and raise questions about each other's writing.

Writing From Other Texts

Though training in observation and interviewing can undoubtedly be useful in students' academic career, perhaps the most important skill English teachers can engage students in is the complex ability to write from other texts, a major part of their academic writing experience. Students' "intellectual socialization may be accomplished not only by interacting with people, but also by encountering the writing of others" (Bizzell, 1986, p. 65). As Bazerman (1980) says, "we must cultivate various techniques of absorbing, reformulating, commenting on, and using reading" if we want to prepare our students to "enter the written exchanges of their chosen disciplines and the various discussions of personal and public interest" (p. 658).

L1 and L2 research shows the interdependent relationship between reading and writing processes (see Krashen, 1984; Petrosky, 1982; Salvatori, 1983; Spack, 1985b): Both processes focus on the making meaning; they share the "act of constructing meaning from words, text, prior knowledge, and feelings" (Petrosky, 1982, p. 22). To become better writers, then, students need to become better readers.

Intelligent response to reading, Bazerman (1980) reminds us, begins with an accurate understanding of a text—not just the facts and ideas, but also what the author is trying to achieve. But this is not easy for second language readers. Even advanced, highly literate students struggle in a way that their NS counterparts do not. First, there are linguistic difficulties. Overcoming them is not simply a matter of learning specialists' language because often the more general use of language causes the greatest problem, as one of my freshman students pointed out in a working journal (mechanical errors corrected):

> During the last few days I had to read several (about 150) pages for my psychology exam. I had great difficulties in understanding the material. There are dozens, maybe hundreds of words I'm unfamiliar with. It's not the actual scientific terms (such as "repression," "schizophrenia" "psychosis," or "neurosis") that make the reading so hard, but it's descriptive and elaborating terms (e.g., "to coax," "gnawing discomfort," "remnants," "fervent appeal"), instead. To understand the text fully, it often takes more than an hour to read just ten pages. And even then I still didn't look up all the words I didn't understand. It is a very frustrating thing to read these kinds of texts, because one feels incredibly ignorant and stupid.

And there are cultural barriers, best expressed by another student (mechanical errors corrected):

> My last essay was about bowing in the Japanese culture. After discussing my first draft with my classmates, Ramy and Luis, I felt I could get about half of the message across. But I found it interesting that both of them were stuck at the part where I mentioned Buddhism. I was interested because I saw a similarity with my own experience; i.e., I am always stuck when any essay mentions Christianity. I am not Buddhist or Shintoist, but Japanese culture is so much influenced by those religions that it is almost impossible to talk about Japan without them. The problem is that many concepts associated with these religions are nonexistent in Christian-influenced society (Western society). I do not know how to explain something which does not exist in the English-speaking world in the English language. And I do not know how to understand something that never existed in my frame of reference. To me it is almost as hard as solving complicated math problems.

Given the complexity of reading in a second language, it is necessary for L2 writing teachers to become familiar with theories and techniques of L2 reading instruction (see, for example, Dubin, Eskey, & Grabe, 1986) if they are to guide their students to become better academic writers.

Some of those techniques are already part of L1 and L2 composition instruction. Marginal notes, note taking, working journals (see Spack & Sadow, 1983), and response statements (Petrosky, 1982) can train students to discover and record their own reactions to a text. Exercises that focus on the processes of summarizing, paraphrasing, and quoting can encourage precise understanding of an author's style and purpose. But these techniques should not be ends unto themselves. Rather, paraphrase, summary, and quotation become part of students' texts as they incorporate key ideas and relevant facts from their reading into their own writing. In this way, students can develop informed views on the issues they pursue, building on what has already been written.

Readings can be content based, grouped by themes, and can be expressive or literary as well as informative. They can be drawn from a specific field, if the area of study is one that the instructor is well versed in, or from several fields, if the articles are written by professionals for a general audience. Although these articles may not be considered academic since they were not written for academic/professional audiences, they can give students an understanding of how writers from different disciplines approach the same subject. Most important, they allow instructors to avoid placing themselves in the awkward position of presenting materials they do not fully understand. But whatever readings are chosen, teachers of ESL students should always consider the background knowledge that readers are expected to bring to written texts (e.g., knowledge of American history, recognition of the publications in which the texts originally appeared, discernment of organizational formats, etc.) and help their students establish a frame of reference that will facilitate comprehension (Dubin et al., 1986).

Writing tasks should build upon knowledge students already possess but should also be designed to allow new learning to occur. Students can initially write about their own experiences or views, then read, discuss, and respond informally in writing to the assigned readings. They can next be assigned the task of evaluating, testing the truth of, or otherwise illuminating the texts. Students can be directed to compare the ideas discussed in one or more of the readings with their own experiences, or they can be asked to agree or disagree or take a mixed position toward one of the readings. Making specific references to the readings, they can develop ideas by giving examples, citing experiences, and/or providing evidence from other texts on the subject.

By sequencing assignments, the teacher can move the students away from a primarily personal approach to a more critical approach to the readings. The goal should not be regurgitation of others' ideas, but the development of an independent viewpoint. Students can develop the ability to acknowledge the points of view of others but still "question and critique established authorities in a field of knowledge" (Coles & Wall, 1987, p. 299). This is a particularly important skill for foreign students, many of whom are "products of educational systems where unquestioning acceptance of books and teachers as the ultimate authority is the norm" (Horowitz & McKee, 1984, p. 5).

Yet other assignments, such as research projects utilizing the library and perhaps data from interviews and/or observations, can ask students to evaluate and synthesize material from a number of sources in order to establish a perspective on a given subject or area of controversy. Like the assignments discussed above, this type of assignment allows for demonstration of knowledge and prompts the "independent thinking, researching, and learning" (Shih, 1986, p. 621) often required when students write for their other university courses. Such an assignment also builds on skills students have already practiced: reading, note taking, summarizing, paraphrasing, quoting, evaluating, comparing, agreeing/disagreeing, and so on.

These skills are transferable to many writing tasks that students will be required to perform in other courses when they write for academic audiences. The content will vary from course to course, and the format will vary from discipline to discipline and within disciplines, depending on the particular constraints of individual assignments and the particular concerns of individual teachers. But students should have a fairly good sense of how to focus on a subject, provide evidence to support a point or discovery, and examine the implications of the material discussed.

The Process of Academic Writing

Although it might appear at first glance that asking students to write from other texts—a common writing assignment before research on the composing process gained prominence—is a throwback to traditional teaching methods, that is far from the case. The kinds of writing assignments described above take place within the context of a process-centered approach, with students employing appropriate inquiry strategies, planning, drafting, consulting, revising, and editing.

The students' papers become teaching tools of the course. An assigned paper is not a test of their ability to follow prescribed rules of writing, but a chance to examine and organize, and then reexamine and reorganize, their thinking. Because more than one draft is read, it is not a matter of "better luck next time," but "try again until you have communicated your ideas clearly." Students can be trained to respond productively to each other's work-in-progress; thus, they can learn how collaboration among scholars evolves. These experiences in collaborative learning help students become "socialized into the academic community" (Maimon, 1983, p. 122).

Student-teacher interaction is almost always necessary, at least initially, for learning to take place. Over time, students internalize various routines and procedures and "take greater responsibility for controlling the progress of an assigned task" (Applebee, 1986, p. 110). But first, teacher feedback on drafts guides students toward producing a more tightly organized, well-focused paper that fulfills the assignment. The final product of this effort shows them what effective writing should look like. Their own good work becomes a model for future academic papers, including essay examinations. The writing classroom is the place where students are given the time to learn how to write.

With each assignment, learning can be structured so that students are provided with useful strategies for fulfilling the task at hand. Assignments can be given in such a way that students understand from the beginning what the task requires and what its evaluative criteria will be (Herrington, 1981). Students can be helped to "'deconstruct' the assignment prompt" (Johns, 1986, p. 247). After they have done some informal writing, including invention techniques (Spack, 1984), they can be given a variety of suggestions on how to organize an academic paper that makes reference to another author's work. For example, they can be told what might go in the beginning (a summary of the author's article and an identification of the particular issue the student will respond to), middle (ideas and examples presented in logical order, never wandering from the central issue and frequently referring back to the reading), and ending (discussion of the implications of what has just been written).

The constraints of the form are meant to benefit, not hamper, the students' writing. Knowledge of what usually comes at the beginning, in the middle, and at the end of such discourse can give students another writing strategy or cognitive framework. However, rigid adherence to specific formulas is counterproductive. Students, especially those who were trained in a different culture and who are now enriched by a second culture, can create texts that may not follow explicit guidelines but that are still effective.

Indeed, Lu's (1987) discussion of her experience in writing is an example of this phenomenon. Caught between the rigid, imitative forms required at school in China and the inner-directed approach of the at-home English instruction given by her Westernized parents, she wrote a book report that was not acceptable to either her school instructors (because she sentimentally focused on the internal conflict of a character) or her at-home instructors (because she praised a "Revolutionary" book). Yet the essay was a highly original text.

As Coe (1987) points out, an understanding of the purpose of form—to enable writers to communicate accurately and effectively to readers—can "empower students to understand, use, and even invent new forms for new purposes" (p. 26). So, respect for form is encouraged—and necessary if students are to succeed in certain other courses—but flexibility is built into the course to encourage students to respect the composing process as well.

Conclusion

It is ironic that the pressure on ESL/English teachers to teach the writing of other disciplines is manifesting itself at precisely the time when influential technological institutes such as the Massachusetts Institute of Technology are funding programs to increase student exposure to the humanities in an effort to produce more well-rounded, open-minded students. The English composition course is and should be a humanities course: a place where students are provided the enrichment of reading and writing that provoke thought and foster their intellectual and ethical development.

This approach includes exploratory writing tasks that deal with making sense of thoughts and experiences. As Rose (1983) reminds us, "making meaning for the self, ordering experience, establishing one's own relation to it is what informs any serious writing" (p. 118). It also includes expository writing tasks that direct students to take an evaluative and analytical stance toward what they read. Each of these processes "makes a crucial contribution to the whole of intellectual activity" (Zeiger, 1985, p. 457).

Students will mature as writers as they receive invaluable input from numerous classroom experiences and from teachers who are conversant in other disciplines. To initiate students into the academic discourse community, we do not have to change our orientation completely, assign tasks we ourselves cannot master, or limit our assignments to prescribed, rule-governed tasks. We can instead draw on our own knowledge and abilities as we strengthen and expand the knowledge and abilities of our students.

Acknowledgments

This is a revised version of a paper presented at the 21st Annual TESOL Convention in Miami Beach, April 1987. The author would like to thank Catherine Sadow and three anonymous *TESOL Quarterly* reviewers for their valuable suggestions on earlier drafts.

Works Cited

Applebee, A.N. (1986). Problems in process approaches: Toward a reconceptualization of process instruction. In A.R. Petrosky & D. Bartholomae (Eds.), *The teaching of writing* (pp. 95-113). Chicago: The National Society for the Study of Education.

Bander, R.G. (1978). *American English rhetoric.* New York: Holt, Rinehart and Winston.

Bazerman, C. (1980). A relationship between reading and writing: The conversational model. *College English, 41,* 656-661.

Bazerman, C. (1985). *The informed writer: Using sources in the disciplines* (2nd ed.). Boston: Houghton Mifflin.

Becker, H.S. (1986). *Writing for social scientists.* Chicago: University of Chicago Press.

Behrens, L. (1980). Meditations, reminiscences, polemics: Composition readers and the service course. *College English, 41,* 561-570.

Bizzell, P. (1982). College composition: Initiation into the academic discourse community. *Curriculum Inquiry, 12,* 191-207.

Bizzell, P. (1986). Composing processes: An overview. In A.R. Petrosky & D. Bartholomae (Eds.), *The teaching of writing* (pp. 49-70.) Chicago: The National Society for the Study of Education.

Bridgeman, B., & Carlson, S.B. (1984). Survey of academic writing tasks. *Written Communication, 1,* 247-280.

Coe, R.M. (1987). An apology for form; or, who took the form out of the process? College *English, 49,* 13-28.

Coffey, B. (1984). ESP—English for specific purposes [State-of-the-art article]. *Language Teaching: The international Abstracting Journal for Language Teachers and Applied Linguists, 17,* 2-16.

Cole, K.C. (1985). *Sympathetic vibrations: Reflections on physics as a way of life.* New York: Bantam.

Coles, N., & Wall, S.V. (1987). Conflict and power in the reader-responses of adult basic writers. College *English, 49,* 298-314.

Connors, R.J. (1981). The rise and fall of the modes of discourse. *College Composition and Communication, 32,* 444-455.

Dick, J. A. R., & Esch, R.M. (1985). Dialogues among disciplines: A plan for faculty discussions of writing across the curriculum. *College Composition and Communication, 36,* 178-182.

Dubin, F., Eskey, D. E., & Grabe, W. (1986). *Teaching second language reading for academic purposes.* Reading, MA: Addison- Wesley.

Faigley, L., & Hansen, K. (1985). Learning to write in the social sciences. *College Composition and Communication, 36,* 140-149.

Flower, L. S., & Hayes, J.R. (1977). Problem-solving strategies and the writing process. *College English, 39,* 449-461.

Flower, L., & Hayes, J.R. (1981). A cognitive process theory of writing. *College Composition and Communication, 32,* 365-387.

Fulwiler, T. (1984). How well does writing across the curriculum work? *College English, 46,* 113-125.

Gilbert, G. N., & Mulkay, M. (1984). *Opening Pandora's box: A sociological analysis of scientists' discourse.* Cambridge: Cambridge University Press.

Hamp-Lyons, L. (1986). No new lamps for old yet, please [in The Forum]. *TESOL Quarterly, 20,* 790-796.

Hartfiel, V. F., Hughey, J. B., Wormuth, D. R., & Jacobs, H.L. (1985). *Learning ESL composition.* Rowley, MA: Newbury House.

Herrington, A.J. (1981). Writing to learn: Writing across the disciplines. *College English, 43,* 379-387.

Herrington, A.J. (1985). Classrooms as forums for reasoning and writing. *College Composition and Communication, 36,* 404-413.

Hill, S. S., Soppelsa, B. F., & West, G.K. (1982). Teaching ESL students to read and write experimental-research papers. *TESOL Quarterly, 16,* 333-347.

Hillocks, G., Jr. (1984). What works in teaching composition: A meta-analysis of experimental treatment studies. *American Journal of Education, 93,* 133-170.

Hillocks, G., Jr. (1986). *Research on written composition: New directions for teaching.* Urbana, IL: National Conference on Research in English/ERIC Clearinghouse on Reading and Communication Skills.

Horowitz, D.M. (1986a). The author responds to Hamp-Lyons . . . [in The Forum]. *TESOL Quarterly, 20,* 796-797.

Horowitz, D.M. (1986b). The author responds to Leibman-Kleine . . . [in The Forum]. *TESOL Quarterly, 20,* 788-790.

Horowitz, D. (1986c). Process, not product: Less than meets the eye [in The Forum]. *TESOL Quarterly, 20*, 141-144.

Horowitz, D.M. (1986d). What professors actually require: Academic tasks for the ESL classroom. *TESOL Quarterly, 20*, 445-462.

Horowitz, D. M., & McKee, M.B. (1984). Methods for teaching academic writing. *TECFORS, 7*, 5-11.

Johns, A.M. (1981). Necessary English: A faculty survey. *TESOL Quarterly, 15*, 51-57.

Johns, A.M. (1985). Academic writing standards: A questionnaire. *TECFORS, 8*, 11-14.

Johns, A.M. (1986). Coherence and academic writing: Some definitions and suggestions for teaching. *TESOL Quarterly, 20*, 247-265.

Krashen, S.D. (1984). *Writing: Research, theory and applications.* Oxford: Pergamon Press.

Kroll, B. (1979). A survey of the writing needs of foreign and American college freshmen. *English Language Teaching Journal, 33*, 219-227.

Lay, N.D.S. (1982). Composing processes of adult ESL learners: A case study. *TESOL Quarterly, 16*, 406.

Leibman-Kleine, J. (1986). In defense of teaching process in ESL composition [in The Forum]. *TESOL Quarterly, 20*, 783-788.

Lu, M. (1987). From silence to words: Writing as struggle. *College English, 49*, 437-448.

MacDonald, S.P. (1987). Problem definition in academic writing. *College English, 49*, 315-331.

Maher, J. (1986). English for medical purposes. [State-of-the-art article]. *Language Teaching: The International Abstracting Journal for Language Teachers and Applied Linguists, 19*, 112-145.

Maimon, E.P. (1983). Maps and genres: Exploring connections in the arts and sciences. In W.B. Homer (Ed.), *Composition and literature: Bridging the gaps* (pp. 110-12.5). Chicago: University of Chicago Press.

Maimon, E.P. (1984). *Writing across the curriculum: Knowledge and acknowledgment in an educated community.* Unpublished manuscript.

Maimon, E. P., Belcher, C. L., Hearn, G. W., Nodine, B. F., & O'Connor, F.B. (1981). *Writing in the arts and sciences.* Boston: Little, Brown.

Myers, G. (1985). Texts as knowledge claims: The social construction of two biology articles. *Social Studies of Science, 15*, 593-630.

Ostler, S.E. (1980). A survey of academic needs for advanced ESL. *TESOL Quarterly, 14*, 489-502.

Pearson, S. (1983). The challenge of Mai Chung: Teaching technical writing to the foreign-born professional in industry. *TESOL Quarterly, 17*, 383-399.

Petroski, H. (1986). *Beyond engineering: Essays and other attempts to figure without equations.* New York: St. Martin's Press.

Petrosky, A.R. (1982). From story to essay: Reading and writing. College *English, 46*, 19-36.

Raimes, A. (1985). What unskilled ESL students do as they write: A classroom study of composing. *TESOL Quarterly, 19*, 229-258.

Raimes, A. (1987, April). *Why write? Perspectives in purpose and pedagogy.* Paper presented at the 21st Annual TESOL Convention, Miami Beach.

Reid, J. (1984a). Comments on Vivian Zamel's "The composing processes of advanced ESL students: Six case studies" [in The Forum]. *TESOL Quarterly, 18*, 149-153.

Reid, J. (1984b). The radical outliner and the radical brainstormer: A perspective on composing processes [in The Forum]. *TESOL Quarterly, 18*, 529-534.

Reid, J. (1985). The author responds . . . [in The Forum]. *TESOL Quarterly, 19*, 398-400.

Rose, M. (1983). Remedial writing courses: A critique and a proposal. *College English, 45*, 109-126.

Rose, M. (1985). The language of exclusion: Writing instruction at the university. *College English, 47*, 341-359.

Russell, D.R. (1987). Writing across the curriculum and the communications movement: Some lessons from the past. *College English, 38*, 184-194.

Salvatori, M. (1983). Reading and writing a text: Correlations between reading and writing. *College English, 45*, 657-666.

Scheiber, H.J. (1987). Toward a text-based pedagogy in the freshman composition course—with two process-oriented writing tasks. *Freshman English News, 15*, 15-18.

Selzer, J. (1983). The composing processes of an engineer. *College Composition and Communication, 34*, 178-187.

Shaughnessy, M. (1977). *Errors and expectations.* New York: Oxford University Press.

Shih, M. (1986). Content-based approaches to teaching academic writing. *TESOL Quarterly, 20*, 617-648.

Silk, M. (1987, April 19). The hot history department. *The New York Times Magazine*, pp. 41,43,46-47,50,56,62, 64.

Spack, R. (1984). Invention strategies and the ESL college composition student. *TESOL Quarterly, 18,* 649-670.

Spack, R. (1985a). Comments on Joy Reid's "The radical outliner and the radical brainstormer: A perspective on composing processes" [in The Forum]. *TESOL Quarterly, 19,* 396-398.

Spack, R. (1985b). Literature, reading, writing, and ESL: Bridging the gaps. *TESOL Quarterly, 19,* 703-725.

Spack, R., & Sadow, C. (1983). Student-teacher working journals in ESL composition. *TESOL Quarterly, 17,* 575-593.

Swales, J. (1986). A genre-based approach to language across the curriculum. In M. Tuckoo (Ed.), *Language across the curriculum* (pp. 10-22). Singapore: RELC.

Swales, J. (1987). Utilizing the literatures in teaching the research paper. *TESOL Quarterly, 21,* 41-68.

Thomas, L. (1983). *The youngest science: Notes of a medicine-watcher.* New York: Viking Press.

Wilkinson, A.M. (1985). A freshman writing course in parallel with a science course. *College Composition and Communication, 36,* 160-165.

Woodford, F.P. (1967). Sounder thinking through clearer writing. *Science, 156,* 743-745.

Yearley, S. (1981). Textual persuasion: The role of social accounting in the construction of scientific arguments. *Philosophy of Social Sciences, 11,* 409-435.

Zamel, V. (1982). Writing: The process of discovering meaning. *TESOL Quarterly, 16,* 195-209.

Zamel, V. (1983). The composing processes of advanced ESL students: Six case studies. *TESOL Quarterly, 17,* 165-187.

Zamel, V. (1984). In search of the key: Research and practice in composition. In J. Handscombe, R. A. Orem, & B.P. Taylor (Eds.), *On TESOL '83* (pp. 195-207). Washington, DC: TESOL.

Zamel, V. (1986, March). *From process to product.* Paper presented at the 20th Annual TESOL Convention, Anaheim, CA.

Zamel, V. (1987). *Teaching composition: Toward a pedagogy of questions.* Unpublished manuscript.

Zeiger, W. (1985). The exploratory essay: Enfranchising the spirit of inquiry in college composition. *College English, 47,* 454-466.

Fiction and Nonfiction
in the ESL/EFL Classroom:
Does the Difference Make a Difference?
by Daniel Horowitz

Although one advocate of the use of literature in ESL classes recently claimed that literature is now "largely neglected" (Gajdusek, 1988, p. 227), other evidence indicates that interest in its use is now greater than ever. Recent articles in both of TESOL's publications (Gajdusek, 1988; Robson, 1989) have called for its wider use. Krakowian (1989) reports that "the role of literature in ELT was one among the many prominent topics at the 23rd international IATEFL conference, an issue further supported by . . . a plan to set up a SIG on Literature in Language Teaching" (p. 3). A group with similar objectives is seeking interest section status with TESOL as well.

It seems an appropriate time, therefore, to take a critical look at the arguments presented by these advocates. One important reason for doing so is that the last major article that argued against the use of literature in ESL (Topping, 1968) is hopelessly dated. An even more important reason is that new light has been shed on this question by recent debate about how far ESP/EAP reading/writing courses should go in initiating students into academic discourse communities (Braine, 1988; Johns, 1988; Spack, 1988a; Spack, 1988b; Spack, 1988c). This paper hopes to show that the *literature* debate is really a microcosm of the *discourse communities* debate by presenting and then analyzing the three major claims of those who advocate the use of literature in ESL. These claims are:

Reprinted from *English for Specific Purposes, 9*(2), Horowitz, D., Fiction and non-fiction in the ESL/EFL classroom: Does the difference make a difference?, 1990, with permission from Elsevier Science.

1. The "training versus education" claim;
2. The "interpretive richness" claim;
3. Claims related to the connection between reading and writing about literature.

The "Training Versus Education" Claim

Every advocate of the use of literature in ESL classes suggests that teachers have the responsibility to *educate* rather than simply *train* their students, and that literature, with its "humanizing influence" (Widdowson, 1984b, p. 161), is ideally suited for this aim. Spack (1985) claims that:

[t]he focus of their college education should not be limited to vocational skills, for such a program may impede the full development of the educated mind . . . (p. 720)

Desirable effects of this broad, humanistic interpretation of education, to which the study of literature contributes, include: the discovery that English can be a beautiful language (Spack, 1988a), "growth in emotional awareness and maturity" (Hirvela & Boyle, 1988, p. 181), development of "empathy" (Robson, 1989, p. 27), "habits of inquiry, and speculation, critical reasoning, and the conscious testing of inferences or hypotheses" (Gajdusek, 1988, p. 233). The claim is explicitly made that these latter skills are transferable: "Such training helps [students] in other courses which demand logical reasoning, independent thinking, and careful analysis of text" (Spack, 1985, p. 721).

Although this claim rests on humanistic values that are widely shared by educators, one can accept these values without accepting the claim. To begin with, the dichotomies set up by these writers are loaded. Given a choice between "training" and "education," or between "vocational skills" and "development of the educated mind," who among us would choose the former? Yet, we can fairly question whether our forced choice then commits us to teach literature—why not philosophy, art, contempory political issues, or other subjects on the humanist agenda? But, beyond these specific choices, even if we accept the general humanist agenda, and grant that education means empowering our students as human beings, does it necessarily follow that the best way to do so is to use the ESL classroom to *directly* address issues critical to human existence? Or, are there alternate, perhaps more appropriate, routes to empowerment?

The concept of "academic empowerment" (Johns, 1988, p. 706) provides just such an alternative, and it is linked to two powerful new educational metaphors, that of *teacher as initiator into the academic culture,* and that of *teachers and students as joint ethnographers of that culture.* With graduate students, this means that students and their teachers work together—teacher as language expert, students as subject specialists—to ferret out the "secrets of the trade," including the genres appropriate to the students' fields and to their quest for admission to those fields, such as academic correspondence (Swales & Horowitz, 1988). It also means that teachers must begin to feel at home "within the multifarious universes of discourse denizened by other occupations, disciplines and professions" (Swales, 1985, p. 221). For undergraduates, it means developing the ability to observe and learn from what is happening in their classes, to serve as "sources of information from the various disciplines" (Braine, 1988, p. 702), and to develop expertise in the common tasks (Braine, 1989; Horowitz, 1986a, 1986b) they must perform. In short, to discover "the specific demands of the target academic culture" (Johns, 1988, p. 706).

This new role is frightening for some teachers because if, for example, "authentic assignments brought by students [are] used as curriculum material in the English classroom" (Braine, 1988, p. 702), teachers might "find themselves in the uncomfortable position of being less knowledgeable than their students" (Spack, 1988a, p. 37). This author believes that this is a position teachers are going to have to get used to, and questions the logic which says that since few ESL teachers are qualified to teach writing in the disciplines, they are therefore under no obligation to help our students learn it themselves.

Another area that should be questioned is the claim that training in the reading and writing of literature transfers to students' other courses. Recent studies of argumentation in different fields call this claim into question. Connor and Johns (1989), for example, found major differences in the way problems are posed and arguments and data presented in three fields. The field-specific nature of argumentation is explained by Perelman (1959), who points out that "all argumentation is a function of the audience to which it is addressed" (p. 155) and to which a writer must adapt. In fact, the "entire development" of an argument depends on the assumptions or premises "acknowledged as true, as normal and probable, as valid" by a particular audience. These premises range from "common sense, as that is conceived by the audience," to "those of a particular discipline, scientific, juridical, philosophical or theological" (p. 156).

What all this means is that definitions of "logical reasoning, independent thinking, and careful analysis of text" (Spack, 1985, p. 721) have evolved. We have realized that "logical" is a relative term meaning "what is accepted by a discipline," that writers' independent thinking will remain unknown unless it is expressed according to the conventions of a discipline, and that texts are best analyzed as forms of discourse which reflect the communicative needs of a given discourse community (Swales & Horowitz, 1988).

The "Interpretive Richness" Claim

Advocates of the use of literature in ESL claim that fiction provides *richer opportunities for interpretation of discourse* than does expository prose, basing their claim on an analysis of differences between the two, whereas expository writing has *indexical* meaning (Widdowson, 1984a)—it refers to a reality outside of itself: Fiction "refashion[s] reality in the image of new ideas and new ideals" (Widdowson, 1984b, p. 169), creating a world with "*internally* [italics added] coherent meaning" (Gajdusek, 1988, p. 230). Thus, with no requirement of fidelity to things as they are commonly or socially perceived—having severed the "link to the social context that normally provides [a discourse] with its value as use,"—literature is free to "create alternative contexts of reality" (Widdowson, 1984b, p. 169).

But the same sword that cuts literature free from the bonds of common reality also cuts readers off from at least some of the procedures for interpretation of discourse that they depend on when reading expository prose. Expository prose, in addition to its external connections, contains many "contextualizing devices, such as introductions, transition words and sentences, even complex sentence grammar" (Gajdusek, 1988, p. 230). Literature makes much less use of these devices, its clues to meaning being "more consistently implicit than explicit" (Gajdusek, 1988, p. 235). And herein lies literature's "unique advantage": it makes "such a highly interactive 'demand' upon the reader" (Gajdusek, 1988. p. 230) that it engages "the human capacity for making sense, for negotiating meaning, for finding expression for new experience in metaphor" (Widdowson, 1984b, p. 169).

The claim is further made that these interpretive procedures "can be transferred to enrich the reading of expository texts as well" (Gajdusek, 1988, p. 232). Indeed, they can be applied to "a range of language uses, both literary and nonliterary, which [students] encounter inside and outside the learning situation" (Widdowson, 1975, p. 84).

Although it is true that the writer of literature has greater freedom in refashioning reality than does the writer of expository prose, studies of the *process* of the creation of scientific prose have shown that it too involves the reconstruction of reality. Knorr-Cetina (cited in Swales, 1987) shows how two descriptions of the same experiment, one in a laboratory report and one in a research paper, were presented from totally different perspectives, each with "its own processes of *literary* [italics added] reasoning and its own standards of argument" (Swales, 1987, p. 48).

Clearly, the nature of these refashionings is determined by convention, by the acceptable representations of reality that obtain in a given discipline. But, as the advocates of literature are quick to point out, there is much in the usual type of literature used in ESL—contemporary, straightforward short stories and novellas—(Spack, 1985) that is conventional as well. Gajdusek (1988), for example, suggests that teachers of literature help their students understand the following literary conventions: point of view, character, setting, style, plot, conflict, climax, turning point, theme, imagery, and symbol. These are, in a sense, the conventional framework that supports a short story writer's creativity, and they are no less conventional than the conventions of nonfiction.

We can say, then, that nonfiction is a bit more literary and fiction a bit more conventional than advocates of literature portray them. Given this understanding, and bearing in mind the type of literature recommended for use with ESL students, is there any reason to believe that the interpretive demands made by literature are in fact richer, or greater, than those of nonfiction? Or is it more accurate to say simply that they are different?

As for "making sense" and "negotiating meaning," surely the reading of nonfiction requires no less than the reading of fiction. But it should also be kept in mind that metaphor and imagery are not the exclusive property of literature. Lakoff and Johnson (1980) take the view that:

Our ordinary conceptual system, in terms of what we both think and act, is fundamentally metaphorical in nature ... Since communication is based on the same conceptual system that we use in thinking and acting, language is an important source of evidence for what that system is like (p. 3).

And Boyd (1979), discussing the use of metaphor in science, claims that "a considerable variety of sorts of metaphor . . . play a role in science, and in theory change" (p. 359). Nor is he merely talking about the use of "exegetical or pedagogical metaphors," which "play a role in the teaching or explication of theories," but also those which "constitute, for a time at least, an irreplaceable part of the linguistic machinery of a scientific theory" (p. 360).

One more example of the use of metaphor in nonfiction is provided by the following titles of articles taken from recent issues of professional journals in the field of international relations (*Foreign Affairs* and *International Organization*): "The persistent myth of lost hegemony"; "Managing an oligopoly of would-be sovereigns: The dynamics of joint control and self-control in the international oil industry past, present, and future"; "The superpowers: Dance of the dinosaurs"; "The economics of illusion and the illusion of economics." The articles themselves are rich in metaphor and imagery, though it would take this paper too far afield to provide complete evidence for this claim.

In sum, by seeing all discourse as a mixture of convention and creativity, we understand that all texts require rich interpretation, and that those readers who lack either the linguistic skills or the necessary background information will come away with impoverished interpretations.

Claims Related to the Connection Between Reading and Writing About Literature

Spack (1985) suggests that "the study of literature (fiction) and the writing of literary analyses" (p. 704) is an excellent way to make the connection between two skills (reading and writing) that *should* be taught together, but too often are not. Literature, then, provides "real content" (Gajdusek, 1988, p. 229) for an ESL course, resulting in "the production of the kinds of academic texts students need to write for college courses" (Spack, 1985, p. 703). The study of literature "convey[s] important concepts about structure in all writing, their own included" (Gajdusek, 1988, p. 251). For example, "[t]he understanding of reading can help make students aware that when they write texts, they need to consider the reader's point of view" (Spack, 1985, p. 706).

There is no argument against the contention that reading and writing should be taught together. The question is whether or not teaching our students to read and write about literature is the best reading/writing combination, and this question turns on the question of tranferability. The arguments presented in the previous two sections cast doubt on the claim that writing about literature resembles the writing required in other college courses. This is especially, and obviously, true for graduate students, but the author believes that this is also true for undergraduates in a general EAP course.

Let us begin with reading, and imagine two ESL classrooms, one using an non-fiction text (for argument's sake, a short journal article) and one a literary text (a short story). In both classrooms, teachers would try to make students aware of any essential background knowledge presupposed by the reading and design activities so that that knowledge could be shared among all students. The next step in the academic classroom, however, would be to begin sampling (or scanning) the text, looking at subheadings, tables of contents, pictures, graphs, charts, and so forth, and searching for places where the main ideas might be found in one place, such as in an abstract (labeled or unlabeled) or summary. Students might then attempt to discover the structure of the reading by scanning the beginnings of paragraphs for words and phrases which indicate enumerative structures ("First," etc.) or paragraph functions ("In short . . .," "The argument being made here is that . . .," etc.). This might be followed by chunking the article, trying to find main ideas within each subsection, and so forth.

Does this sound familiar to the teacher of literature? Probably not. As pointed out above, many of the meaning signposts present in academic writing are not used in literature. But even more fundamentally, advocates of literature insist that we should not spoil "the pleasurable literary experience of reading a masterpiece of fiction" with too much preparation (Spack, 1985, p. 710), that "we have not the right to diminish the pleasure of personal discovery by disembodying such information from the experience of the literature that contains it . . ." (Gajdusek, 1988, p. 235). Of course, the reader of literature is in the same business of developing schema, but literature is generally read from beginning to end. The "unfolding" of the plot, the "development" of character, the "building up" of tension—these pleasures are lost to those who approach a literary text in the "guerrilla warfare" style we try to teach for reading nonfiction.

Even more important differences arise when one considers what happens when reading becomes the basis for writing. The suggestion that students write "literary analyses" is a strange one indeed. The same author who claimed at one point that writing about literature resembles the writing required in other college courses claims at another that "literary analysis is a unique form of writing" (Spack, 1985, p. 710), and, at yet another, that "students write papers about stores of their choice on topics they themselves have generated . . ." (Spack, 1985, p. 719). From this description, we can conclude that students are not being taught to write as "professional" literary analysts (an absurd notion in itself), but rather being encouraged to write personal essays about literature. Yet the same author, in a later article, has apparently realized that:

> [t]here is no evidence that the skills learned in [writing personal essays] provide students with the tools they need to produce the academic writing required in other courses. (Spack, 1988a, p. 32).

The point is that if we do choose to have our students write about literature, we have two choices open to us, to have them do so as generalists, or as specialists. In the former case, their work does not fall within the domain of *any* academic discourse community, and thus cannot serve even as an example of how experts create a text in relation to the other texts in their field. In the latter case, how can we justify the time and effort spent initiating students, already overburdened by "the linguistic and cultural demands of authentic university classes" (Johns, 1988, p. 706), into a specialist community that is not—and never will be—theirs?

Conclusion

This author has tried to critically analyze the arguments put forward by those who advocate the use of literature in the ESL/EFL classroom, but not—and this may come as a surprise—in the hope of persuading others that literature has no place there at all. The point is that, as English teachers and lovers of language, we may be prone to uncritical acceptance of arguments that appeal to humanist values. Of course, we should be proud of these values and foster and defend them, but we must remain on our guard when they function simply to add luster to an otherwise dull argument.

More specifically, before teachers make the decision to use literature with their classes, they should think hard about how the actual activities performed in class fit in with their students' needs and wants. Are the students studying English as a second or as a foreign language? Are they presently enrolled in university courses or working to gain entrance to a university? Are they (to be) undergraduate or graduate students? Are they learning English for professional or vocational purposes, for personal enjoyment, or for some combination of motives? Are they in the class because they have to be or because they want to be? Do they have a strict time limit on their English studies or not? Are they a homogenous or heterogeneous group? This list of questions is neither exhaustive nor original—they are the ones we should ask before adopting any materials or method—but this author suspects that they tend to be asked less when the magic word "literature" is part of the package we are considering.

If we keep such questions in mind when we think about using literature in ESL/EFL classrooms, our profession—ever in search of *the* answer—may be able to avoid another in the series of wild swings of opinion that seem to plague us. It will be a sign of our growing maturity as a profession when new ideas—or old ones that have come calling again—are met not only with open arms but with a critical eye as well.

Works Cited

Boyd, R. (1979). Metaphor and theory change: What is 'metaphor' a metaphor for? In A. Ortony (Ed.), *Metaphor and thought* (pp. 356-408). Cambridge: Cambridge University Press.

Braine, G. (1988). A reader reacts . . . *TESOL Quarterly, 22,* 700-702.

Braine, G. (1989). Writing in science and technology: An analysis of assignments from ten undergraduate courses. *English for Specific Purposes, 8,* 3-15.

Connor, U., & Johns, A. (1989). *Introducing ESL students into academic discourse communities: Differences do exist.* Paper presented at 23rd Annual TESOL Convention, San Antonio, TX.

Gajdusek, L. (1988). Toward wider use of literature in ESL; Why and how. *TESOL Quarterly, 22,* 227-257.

Hirvela, A., & Boyle, J. (1988). Literature courses and student attitudes. *ELT Journal, 42,* 179-184.

Horowitz, D. (1986a). Essay examination prompts and the teaching of academic writing. *English for Specific Purposes Journal, 5,* 107-120.

Horowitz, D. (1986b). What professors actually require: Academic tasks for the ESL classroom. *TESOL Quarterly, 20,* 445-462.

Johns, A. (1988). Another reader reacts . . . *TESOL Quarterly, 22,* 705-707.

Krakowian, B. (1989). IATEFL: The Warwick conference. *TESOL Newsletter, 23*(4), pp. 3, 25.

Lakoff, G., & Johnson, M. (1980). *Metaphors we live by.* Chicago: The University of Chicago Press.

Perelman, C. (1963). The social context of argumentation. In C. Perelman, *The idea of justice and the problem of agrument* (J. Petrie, trans.) (pp. 154-160). London: Routledge and Paul.

Robson, A. E. (1989). The use of literature in ESL and culture-learning courses in US colleges. *TESOL Newsletter, 23*(4), 25-27.

Spack, R. (1985). Literature, reading, writing, and ESL: Bridging the gaps. *TESOL Quarterly, 19,* 703-725.

Spack, R. (1988). Initiating ESL students into the academic discourse community: How far should we go? *TESOL Quarterly, 22,* 29-51.

Spack, R. (1988a). The author responds to Braine. *TESOL Quarterly, 22,* 703-705.

Spack, R. (1988b). The author responds to Johns. *TESOL Quarterly, 22,* 707-708.

Swales, J. 1985. "ESP—the heart of the matter or the end of the affair?" In R. Quirk, & H. G. Widdowson (Eds) *English in the world* (pp. 212-223). Cambridge: Cambridge: University Press.

Swales, J. (1987). Utilizing the literatures in teaching the research paper. *TESOL Quarterly, 21,* 41-68.

Swales, J., & Horowitz, D. (1988). *Genre-based approaches to ESL and ESP materials.* Paper presented at the 22nd Annual TESOL Convention, Chicago.

Topping, D. M. (1968). Linguistics or literature: An approach to language. *TESOL Quarterly 2,* 95-100.

Widdowson, H. G. (1984a). Reference and representation as modes of meaning. In H. G. Widdowson, *Explorations in applied linguistics 2* (pp. 160-173). Oxford: Oxford University Press.

Widdowson, H. G. (1984b). The use of Literature. In H. G. Widdowson, *Explorations in applied linguistics 2* (pp. 160-173). Oxford: Oxford University Press.

Interpreting an English Competency Examination: The Frustrations of an ESL Science Student
by Ann M. Johns

This article was inspired by a question that has become important to administrators, test developers, and teachers of composition, as English-medium universities become increasingly culturally diverse (Casanova et al., 1989; Hamp-Lyons & Prochnow, 1990): Why do many ESL students who are successful in their chosen field of study fail writing competency examinations set by test developers and English departments? Examinations designed to determine entrance and exit writing proficiency present "a real obstacle course" (Bannai, 1990) for ESL students because these students often cannot enter their majors or graduate without being certified as competent in academic writing. This dilemma appears to be particularly acute among Asian immigrant students. In the nineteen-campus California State University, for example, of the Asian first-time freshmen who took the English Placement Test (a holistically scored entrance examination) in 1987, only 19.6% scored at the competency level, though the pass rate for all first-time freshmen was 43.5%. (*Report of the English as a Second Language Workgroup*, 1988, p. 1.)

At first, the reasons for ESL student failure seem obvious: (a) some students seldom use English outside of the classroom, preferring to speak and write their native languages with friends and family; (b) some have chosen to major in subjects that require high math aptitude but seldom require writing, for example, electrical engineering; (c) some have had little writing practice in their grammar-oriented ESL classes; (d) others have only recently arrived in this country. Certainly there is some truth in all of these claims. Anyone who has worked with ESL students in English-medium educational institutions can testify to their validity.

However, other factors might also explain ESL student failure to pass writing competency exams, factors relating to the tests themselves and to the diverse cultures, ideologies, and languages represented by the graders and the students. A growing body of research explores the various issues that may influence student outcomes. One avenue of exploration focuses on whether the scoring procedures currently in use are appropriate for ESL students. Homberg (1984), for example, asked whether holistic scoring is suitable for ESL compositions written in various modes, concluding that with expert training, this scoring approach can be quite reliable. Cumming (1990) investigated whether analytic scoring is superior to holistic methods in separating two fundamental constructs in ESL: writing ability and language use. He found that [in analytic scoring] "both writing and language skills are being evaluated in conjunction and are not logically distinguished from each other in evaluators' ratings" (p. 12). Cumming advocated holistic scoring because comparable results can be achieved more quickly than with analytic approaches.

Whereas Homberg and Cumming compared methods of scoring in ESL essays, others have examined the effect of readers' academic orientations on student scores. Bridgeman and Carlson (1983), while completing an extensive study that led to the development of the TOEFL (Test of English as a Foreign Language) Test of Written English (TWE), found that graders from English departments and those from academic departments representing the majority of ESL majors disagreed about the relative importance of various criteria employed in essay evaluation. English faculty ranked criteria in the following way:

1. Paper organization	6. Audience appropriateness
2. Development of ideas	7. Quality of content
3. Paragraph organization	8. Vocabulary usage
4. Addressing the topic	9. Vocabulary size
5. Sentence structure	10. Punctuation and spelling

Faculty from engineering and science departments, on the other hand, ranked evaluation criteria in a considerably different order:

1. Quality of the content	6. Overall writing
2. Assignment requirements	7. Paragraph organization
3. Addresses topic	8. Sentence structure
4. Development of ideas	9. Punctuation/spelling
5. Paper organization	10. Vocabulary size

In later research employing reader protocols, Hamp-Lyons (1990a) further substantiated the hierarchy of evaluation criteria for English faculty.

Other factors influencing essay difficulty and scoring are prompt type and construction. In a study in which prompt difficulty predicted by expert English department graders was compared to student writing scores, Hamp-Lyons and Prochnow (1990) discovered that "the commonly held assumption that essay readers and applied linguists can predict which essay prompts will be difficult for ESL writers is false" (p. 26). Whereas the readers believed that ESL students would score highest on prompts that were expository (i.e., descriptive and narrative) and private, in fact, students scored best when responding to prompts that were argumentative and required a public orientation.

The issue of prompt construction for writing competency examinations has also been discussed by those who develop general competency tests. Hoetker and Brossell (1986) attempted to create culturally fair prompts by making them "as brief as possible, as simply phrased as possible, and as similar one to the other as possible . . . [by providing] a topic about which all the examinees equally have something to say" (p. 328). Pollitt, Hutchinson, Entwistle, and DeLuca (1985), in discussing English "O" level examinations, suggested that questions "do not need to be complex" and should be worded "in such a way as to make [them] accessible to a large proportion of candidates" (p. 9).

These discussions of general competency examinations can be contrasted with comments by faculty from several disciplines about prompt construction for classroom examinations. When questioning these faculty, Hamp-Lyons (1990b) found that

> [they] cited "avoidance of ambiguity" as the most common design feature they used in their essay examination questions. The next most frequent design factor had to do with finding out what students know. Here faculty talked about allowing students to show the ability to apply knowledge to the problems in their discipline. (p. 41)

These studies suggest that English faculty and faculty within the other disciplines in which ESL students enroll in large numbers differ somewhat in their approaches to prompt construction and evaluation criteria.

Test type, grading criteria, and prompt type undoubtedly influence ESL student success and failure. However, the students themselves and their approaches to writing are now becoming equally important topics in testing research. Carey, Flower, Hayes, Schriver, and Haas (1989) examined native speaker expert and novice approaches to writing task representation in terms of content, form, audience, theme, and other goals. They found that initial planning may be the key variable in writing success, particularly with the type of "ill-defined prompt" (Flower, 1987) that often appears on English competency examinations. These researchers also discovered that native speakers who write successful texts, as judged by English composition faculty,

> appear to do proportionately less content planning in their initial task representation than do those who produce less successful texts; conversely, more successful writers'

initial plans contain proportionately more rhetorical goals for audience, theme, form, and for features such as tone and style. (p. 17)

Freedman, Dyson, Flower, and Chafe (1987) have noted that in-depth studies of student interpretations of tasks continue to be rare in the literature, however: "Few researchers have studied how students interpret (rather than how they meet the particular standards for) the writing opportunities available to them; only rarely have they followed students and events over time, investigating the sources of these interpretations" (p. 9).

The research reported here offers several possibilities for addressing the question proposed initially in this article: Why do many ESL students fail writing competency examinations set by English teachers? Expanding upon findings from previous task representation studies (Carey et al., 1989; Flower, 1987) and case studies of college writers (Berkenkotter, Huckin, & Ackerman, 1988; McCarthy, 1987), I examined one Asian ESL student's interpretation of a writing competency task and his comparison of this examination with essay tests administered in classes in his discipline.

The Subject

The subject discussed in this study was one of more than 150 Asian science and engineering students who were enrolled in "remedial" composition classes designed to prepare them for entry-level English competency at a large, comprehensive university. I selected from my "remedial" class three such students to interview; each had failed the competency examination at least once and was maintaining a B average or better in his other classes. For fourteen weeks, I met with each student individually for thirty minutes and audiotaped a discussion about the competency examination and writing required in other classes in which the students had been enrolled. During the discussions, there was an acknowledged general purpose: to discover why these ESL students were having difficulty with writing competency tests administered by English composition teachers. However, there was no predetermined script, which permitted "an openness to categories and modes of thought and behavior which may not have been anticipated" (Saville-Troike, 1982, p. 45).

In addition to talking with the students, I collected all of their writing from my class and as many examples as possible from their other classes, although collecting texts was difficult for some majors, such as electrical engineering, for which little writing was required.

"Luc," the subject of this discussion, was one of the three students interviewed. He is an intelligent, twenty-one year old junior, a biochemistry major who has attained an A- grade point average in his major and a B+ average overall. In contrast to some of my other students, he had been required to write in several classes. In biology, for example, he produced lab reports and essay examination responses.

Luc came from a large Vietnamese family that values education. Two of his brothers were biochemistry majors at another university in the area; his sister, a high school student, published poetry in Vietnamese. His parents, who chose to come to the United States to improve the family's professional opportunities, were actively pursuing their own careers: his father was a biochemist in a large firm in the area, and his mother has founded her own pharmacy, for which Luc wrote all of the business letters "because [he was] the best English writer." Their house was full of books, mostly about chemistry and biology, which Luc read for pleasure.

Luc had completed nine years of public schooling in Vietnam, where the language of instruction had been Vietnamese. During that time, he had studied one foreign language, English, using what appeared to be the Grammar-translation Method, principally to analyze nineteenth century British poetry. He remarked that although his foreign language instruction in Vietnam helped him to learn some vocabulary and grammar, it had not prepared him very well to read or write for academic purposes. He enrolled in high school when he came to the United States five years ago and completed three years there. When he began his high school studies, he was integrated immediately with other native speakers in some classes (e.g., math); however, he continued in ESL classes until the last semester of his senior year, when he was placed in an American literature class with native speaking students.

Thus, most of Luc's formal instruction in English composition had taken place since entering the university. When this study was conducted, Luc was enrolled in his third semester of "remedial" English classes designed to prepare students for freshman-level writing competency. He had failed the end-of-semester holistically scored writing competency examination twice and had taken two equivalent examinations at the test office, for which he attained holistic scores lower than the 7 required to pass. A representative composition, indicating his writing level when he entered my class, can be found in Appendix A.

The Examination

The competency examination set by the writing center in which Luc was enrolled was a reading-to-write task. This task type was selected by the test designers for two reasons: first, they assumed that good reading involves a number of processes that are also characteristic of good writing (Eisterhold, 1990; Carson, Carrell, Silberstein, Kroll, & Kuehn, 1990); and second, they believed that students provided with a reading are able to exploit the content to develop more interesting essays. Other support for the reading-to-write approach can be found in the work of Johns (1981, 1986) who, through surveys of faculty in the institution in which Luc was enrolled, found that reading-to-write assignments are common in academic classrooms. Horowitz (1986b) made the same discovery when surveying faculty at a midwestern university.

In the semester in which this study was undertaken, as in the two previous semesters, Luc was enrolled in a theme-based writing course (see Brinton, Snow, & Wesche, 1989, pp. 26-44) in which "the crisis in American education" was the required topic for all of the readings. His class was one of twenty-two "remedial" writing classes, five of which, like mine, were designated as ESL and were taught by instructors trained to deal with ESL writing. Most of the other classes, taught by instructors not trained to work with ESL students, contained a mixture of ESL students and native speakers who had been unable to meet competency requirements by passing the entrance examination.

The final competency test for these classes was designed by a committee of faculty members, the majority of whom had been educated in the humanities (especially in literature) and had been teaching composition to native speakers for a number of years. This two-hour examination consisted of reading a short article and responding to an "agree/disagree" prompt. In the previous semester, the 832-word exam article was "The Cheapening of College Education," an editorial written by Robert Samuelson for an educated American audience. The examination prompt was the following:

> Samuelson argues that since it is so easy to get admitted into college and since one doesn't have to have excellent grades to get financial aid, students aren't motivated to work hard in high school. Do you agree? Why? Support your argument with ideas and examples from the reading, as well as your own experiences and observations.

As noted earlier, the general topic of the reading, "the crisis in American education" had been the topic of the readings in all of Luc's "remedial" classes. It was argued that a number of readings on the same topic would provide students with sufficient background and vocabulary to produce an essay response of about 500 words. The particular reading upon which the examination was based was kept from the students until the day of the test because the exam committee feared that students would memorize responses and therefore not produce original essays.

The "agree or disagree" prompt was the standard prompt type for the examination, in recognition of the importance of persuasive writing at all academic levels (Black, 1989; Rubin & Rafoth, 1986).

Methodology

In order to examine Luc's "extended interpretive process" (Flower, 1987), I interviewed him weekly after his writing class. I also collected samples of his writing from other classes, making specific requests for writing in his major. (See Appendix B for a sample essay response in biology.) What I am reporting here are Luc's retrospective accounts of his academic writing experiences, including his frustrations with the writing competency examination. Although there are those who doubt the validity of such retrospective accounts, Tomlinson (1984) argues for their considerable value to researchers for what they reveal, such as

> what factors writers assume to be present at the time the processes occurred, how their composing experiences crystallize (or are mythologized) into something much less

complex, what the nature of their a priori theories is [and] the writers' representation of the writing process. (p. 442)

My discussion is organized around the task topics mentioned by Carey et al. (1989) augmented by topics suggested by Luc in our open-ended discussions. The purposes of this study are quite different from those of Carey and her colleagues, however. In this research, the purpose was to discover the reasons this student gave for his failure to pass the writing competency examinations even though his writing in other classes had attained high marks.

Topics

I have divided the discussion that follows into the topics that were central to Luc's comments about writing responses for English competency examinations and for his discipline. The topics include prompt type, the content of the required reading and essay response, the rhetorical organization required by the prompt, preparation for the writing task, and the expectations of the audience, that is, of the faculty who will read and grade the examinations.

Prompt

For Luc, the prompt type in the English competency examinations presented problems at the rhetorical and disciplinary levels. The typical competency exam prompt, cited above, consisted of an introduction, some primary instructions, and some secondary instructions (Johns, 1976). The introduction, "Samuelson argues that since it is so easy to get admitted into college and since one doesn't have to have excellent grades to get financial aid, students aren't motivated to work hard in high school," reiterated the author's argument, presenting the claim with which the students were to agree or disagree. The primary instructions indicated the required rhetorical mode for the essay, persuasion: "Do you agree?" Finally, there were secondary instructions, stating how the students should develop their essays: first, the word, "why?", indicating that development was required, followed the two possible methods of support, "with ideas and examples from the reading" and "[with] experiences of your own." Every semester the prompts varied slightly in terms of wording and embedding of instructions, so for Luc the task continued to be both complicated and vague. Despite previous practice in responding, he still had difficulty understanding how he was to follow the instructions, particularly how he was to organize his paragraphs and integrate examples from his own life ("which there aren't any") and the reading.

Luc was much more comfortable with prompts that provided little introduction and stated specifically how his response should be organized. He insisted that nearly all of the essay prompts in his three biology classes required responses with the same general organization, which he would have to modify slightly for each examination question: a overview of the characteristics of the feature/topic (e.g., a genus or species), examples of that feature or topic, and discussion of its importance to human beings or other creatures. He brought in several similarly structured prompts for me to consider, for example, "Discuss the Kingdom Monera (What it is, characteristics that define the kingdom, importance to other organism and/or to the earth, etc.) Be specific." It appeared that his considerable experience with biology classes in which topics and concepts were integrated into a classification system that provided the scaffolding for the course enabled Luc to understand what Nelson (1990, p. 365) calls "the history of the class." He could grasp the connections between the terms, concepts, and examples in the lecture and text and the organization of the prompts that appeared on his examinations. Jolliffe and Brier (1988) described the process through which Luc was going in his discipline:

> As novice writers are learning to participate in a discipline's discourse community and select and develop subject matters in its conventionally accepted ways, they are also learning the kinds of organizational patterns, arrangements, forms and genres of writing the discipline must exhibit . . . writers are systematically led to know their subject matters by systematically considering textual form. (p. 46)

However, the writing class was quite unlike the other university classes Luc had experienced. Each of the readings was organized differently and the prompt often required an organization apparently unrelated to the readings; therefore, Luc continued to struggle with the relationships among the readings, the prompt, and the essay he was to write.

There were other factors which made the English proficiency prompt challenging for Luc, related to the nature of argumentation in various disciplines (see, e.g., Myers, 1985; Connor & Johns, 1989). When I asked him about whether he had been exposed to argumentation in biology, he replied,

> Well, maybe we say this or that is true. But in biology and chemistry, it's either wrong or it's right, like we have positive and good evidence from our experiments and books. But in English, it's just an opinion, so we don't know if it's wrong or right. Who knows the answers to these things? It's like we shouldn't be talking about it.

Though the biology faculty might disagree with his statement that it's "either wrong or it's right" in their discipline, one instructor with whom I spoke accepted Luc's notion that biology requires a specific approach to argumentation. Toulmin (1958) spoke of the features of argument constructed among specific communities of readers as "field invariant." Luc had already experienced sufficient immersion in biology to understand some of its field invariant characteristics. Thus, he already knew something about the "types of knowledge claims [he] could make and what counts as a good reason to support those knowledge claims" (Herrington, 1985, p. 355) in his discipline.

Content. As Bridgeman and Carlson (1983) and Hamp-Lyons (1990a) demonstrated, the centrality of content is an issue about which English faculty and faculty from other disciplines disagree. Carey et al. (1989) and Flower (1987), representing the English composition position, maintained that the selection and presentation of content are secondary to rhetorical considerations in expert writing processes:

> inexperienced [native speaking] writers may organize their writing tasks around content rather than around rhetorical features; that is, they set themselves the goals to tell what they know about a topic rather than to adapt or transform their knowledge to meet the rhetorical constraints of audience and purpose. (Carey et al., p. 4)

Scardamalia and Bereiter (1982) have advanced a similar argument. However, Jolliffe and Brier (1988), studying writing in disciplines outside of English and composition, spoke of the centrality of content in expert writing, noting that "[experts] write about those subjects that form part of what Toulmin calls the 'language' of their rational enterprise—the concept names and key terms participants in the field read and write about" (p. 56). Luc maintained that his understanding of biology terms and their relationship to concepts in the discipline was more important to his success in his classes than his ability to organize his essay response although, undoubtedly, the two issues cannot be separated. As a first step in preparing for his examinations, he listed and memorized all of the major terms in his texts and lectures. His immersion in and knowledge of the content, augmented by his understanding of essay structure, earned him comments such as the one by his biology instructor following his essay response in Appendix B: "Wonderful paper!"

Luc argued that his knowledge of certain topics had another effect on him as well: Because he controlled the vocabulary of his discipline, when he wrote about biology, words came "naturally." Thus, he was free to concentrate on other features of the writing such as organization. Winfield and Barnes-Felfelli (1982) found that asking students to write about known content has other positive outcomes, as well: "Easing the dual cognitive processing load by having students deal with culturally familiar material increases fluency" (p. 376). Flower, Schriver, Carey, Haas, and Hayes (1989) have also commented on the fit between the writer's knowledge and successful composing: "[Success is often determined by whether] the writer has the necessary topic knowledge. If so, his attention can turn to searching knowledge and to expressing that information accurately" (p. 6).

Brandt (1990) wrote of literacy as compelling the reader/writer to become immersed in the subject matter: "[It] requires learning how to become purely and attentively entangled" (p. 67). Luc was rapidly becoming literate in his discipline, increasingly "entangled" in its content. However, because the readings in his composition class represented no discipline that he could recognize and because he could not relate to them well, he found it difficult to become sufficiently interested or adequately knowledgeable to write a passing essay on the topic:

> Luc: When I sit down with your questions, my mind goes everywhere. I don't know what to do.
> Teacher: What do you mean?
> Luc: Well, I don't get your subjects like the crisis in American education—I don't like it and I don't know how to talk about it.
> Teacher: Do you mean that you don't have enough information?

> Luc: Maybe. But my mind wanders; and, you know, I write anything on the paper. Then you give me a six [combined holistic score] because I don't stay on the subject.

Some of the responsibilities for his frustrations are Luc's own, of course; no doubt his composition teachers would argue that he needs to expand his horizons, to learn to read and understand several genres and topics outside of his discipline. However, the problem can also be seen from another perspective: It may be that the issue of the "crisis in education in America" and several other issues that are selected for theme-based courses (e.g., abortion, the status of women) are ideologically foreign and the readings are laden with the values of the majority culture. It may also be that composition teachers and competency test graders require students to accept these values in order to be certified as proficient. Whatever the case, Luc found the readings and their arguments quite foreign. For him, there was no crisis in education—"It's fine." Thus the assumptions on which the readings and prompt were based were perplexing for him.

Rhetorical organization. Luc believed that in unfamiliar writing situations, being able to see examples of successful written products is essential, perhaps because he had not had as many experiences with English discourse as native speakers. He made these comments about preparing to write the letters for his mother's pharmacy, for example:

> I first wrote my letters on my own, but they weren't good, so I bought one of those letter books. I just look at the samples, and then I think about what people want to hear. . . . I don't follow the models exactly, but sometimes I use the sentences and the organization.

Luc's remarks indicated that models for unfamiliar contexts were a necessary starting point for him. He needed them as a guide, but he could vary them for various rhetorical situations. In biology and in other courses in which he been writing, he had a sufficient sense of the discipline that models were less important.

However, in composition, he continued to feel that exact models were necessary. He complained that the examples that his composition teachers gave him were frustrating. What these various examples had in common was an introduction, two or three paragraphs of support of various kinds, and a conclusion. But he found the variety of possibilities in these sample essays confusing; they did not provide sufficiently detailed and functional models to be useful to him. Thus, although he had learned that he needed "three reasons" to support an argument, he still didn't know how to present them.

Preparation for Writing

Two general strategies had been important to Luc's success in performing English language tasks: memorization and practice. He told me that

> The first thing to [language] learning is to memorize. Because I think for the first time, nobody to show you the correct way. Every day, when I came to the US, I was watch-

ing TV and memorizing conversations. I tried memorizing from the dictionary, but there is no connection between the words. It is much easier memorizing in biology because I can make word connections and put them in a group. I memorize sentences, too. I put a model in my mind and I practice it. Then sometimes I try it on a teacher or a friend to see if it's right.

The second important element in his language learning and production was practice. Because he had been selected by his family as their best English speaker, it was his responsibility to talk on the phone to officials about his mother's pharmacy. For him, practice for this and other tasks was an issue of *face:* "I always prepare for phone conversations. I practice what I am going to say. It's embarrassing if you do it wrong and Americans don't understand you." In like manner, Luc prepared through practice for his examinations in most of his classes. He indicated that when studying for his biology essay examinations,

> I read the textbooks and go over the lectures and I know about the topics that have to be studied and the vocabulary that goes with the topics. Then I type out all of the important vocabulary and organize it on a chart. Then I think of the questions the teacher might ask and I practice on the chalk-board different ways to answer the questions. I check my answers with my notes and with the book. When I get to the test, I organize the answers to fit the questions.

As can be seen in Appendix B, memorization of terms and sentences is in evidence throughout this essay response, a response for which he received a perfect score.

Although successful in his other classes, these preparation techniques were less effective for the English competency examination because Luc could not predict the vocabulary, the organization of the reading, and the amount of "creativity" and "real information" required:

> I know the general topic (education) but I don't know the vocabulary in the reading in advance. Sometimes, it takes me a long time to read the reading. I don't know what I'm supposed to do with the topic, so I talk about anything that goes with the topic that interests me. That gets me into trouble. The teachers say "be creative," but that puts me into trouble because the teacher doesn't really show what that means. And I don't have enough real information [as in biology and chemistry] that I can put in the essay.

Thus, although memorization and practice had served him well, Luc probably would have to develop other strategies to demonstrate writing competency.

Audience

According to Carey et al. (1989), audience awareness is essential to task representation. Black (1989) noted that "Some research has suggested that audience awareness, consciously using ideas about an audience to create or revise text, could be a key factor helping to explain differences in writing ability" (p. 232; see also Berkenkotter et al., 1988; Flower, 1987). Rubin and Piche (1979), in a study comparing native English-speaking students in various grades with mature writers, concluded that with age and cognitive development, writers are able to adapt both syntax and writing strategies to their defined audiences. In the case of ESL students, audience awareness becomes a more complex issue: Understanding various American audiences requires understanding cultural backgrounds, ideologies, and attitudes toward knowledge that may not be their own and for which they may have little respect (Ballard & Clanchy, n.d.; Peck, 1991). Adapting messages "to the internal states of their receivers" (Flavell, 1981, p. 40) and creating sentences of appropriate length and complexity for these American audiences require an immersion into the majority culture that many ESL students have not achieved and may not wish to achieve.

For a variety of reasons, Luc's ability to adapt to his audiences in undergraduate biology and chemistry classes was quite good. He knew his professors personally "and what they wanted in writing." He also knew enough about the class history (Nelson, 1990) to present his written responses in a way that would appeal to these faculty. However, when it came to writing for the English competency exam, his difficulties with audience became greater because he was less familiar with the values of the discourse community (Swales, 1990) that he was addressing:

> When I write in biology or any subject, I know the instructor. But one problem with the competency exam is that I don't know who is going to read and what that person is like. Lots of "education" stuff. Well, I may have some examples and they're OK for the Vietnamese people, but for American people, I don't know if my examples are too good so I am worried.

> There are lots of examples from the education readings where we don't agree, like we don't think it's the teachers' fault that schools are bad. So we don't know what to say. So we don't know whether to agree with our points or the points that we think the Americans agree with. Will we make our readers mad?

Peter Elbow (1991) has remarked that academic discourse requires

> giving reasons and evidence, yes, but doing so as a person speaking with acknowledged interests to others whose interest and position one acknowledges and tries to understand. (p. 142)

But for Luc, knowing his English examination audience and acknowledging its position was almost impossible. Not only were the examination readers not Vietnamese, they were not in his discipline, and because the essays were scored anonymously, he never had a chance to meet them. Thus, he had little data on which to base his approach to this audience, and he found his inability to evoke it frustrating and inhibiting.

Conclusion

This study, based upon retrospective reports of an Asian science student, addressed this question: "Why do ESL students have difficulty passing writing competency examinations?" The answer, at least for Luc, is complicated. Successfully immersed in the content and texts of his chosen discipline and having also completed his institution's "breadth" requirements with good grades, he found the specifications for the English competency task difficult to grasp. The structure of the writing prompt seemed opaque, and the issues presented were difficult to argue because they required his opinions. The readings on the topic were written for a "foreign" audience, in his view. Luc found the topic of the examination, "the crisis in education," to be of little interest; his attitude and approach toward it were undoubtedly hindrances to his improvement. And finally, the strategies that had served him well in the past, memorization and practice, were not of use to him when writing the competency test.

My discussions with Luc raise a number of questions that appear to be relevant to English competency testing at all levels of education and for all types of students. Here are a few of these questions:

1. Should academic English competency examinations attempt to be fair to all students? Or should one of the purposes of the examinations be to ascertain whether students can write for a "general academic community" whose conventions and topics reflect Western European attitudes and beliefs (Benson, 1991)?
2. If fairness is an issue, are there typical university topics and tasks that can be identified and incorporated? (Horowitz, 1986b; Reid, 1989)
3. Is it necessary for students to be proficient in the academic domains with which English faculty are comfortable as well as the domains in which they plan to specialize (e.g., engineering, the sciences, and computer science)? In these days of advanced technology, should the humanities be considered the basis for all academic knowledge and thought? (Russell, 1990)
4. Can one examination suffice to certify college entrance or graduate academic proficiency? Or, as Peyton, Staton, Richardson, and Wolfram (1990) suggested, should "valid assessment of an individual student's writing ability include samples of writing across a variety of writing tasks, which contain genuine variations in topic, purpose and audience?" (p. 142)
5. Who should grade competency examinations, English instructors or other faculty? Faigley and Hansen (1985), in a study of the scoring of one student's papers by several faculty, have presented some of the problems inherent in allowing only English composition faculty to be evaluators:

> People read texts with varying expectations and their judgments of merit vary as a consequence. The English instructor evaluated Linda according to how well she met the standards of a handbook notion of an essay; the sociology teacher evaluated Linda according to the depth of her exposure to new knowledge.

> Differences in the expectations and beliefs that readers bring to a text tend to be ignored in freshman English courses and in popular testing procedures such as holistic evaluation. Teachers of courses on writing in the disciplines, however, are going to collide head on with these differences, which handbook notions of correctness and narrowly construed ideas of process cannot accommodate. (p. 148)

The comments relate well to other discussions cited in this article (e.g., Bridgeman & Carlson, 1983) about what faculty from different disciplines value in writing. Certainly we must consider these values when determining academic writing proficiency.

6. At what point and for what reasons should students' sentence-level errors be an issue in examinations that are basically first drafts, written in an in-class situation? Sweedler-Brown (1991), in a study in which she presented graders trained in English and linguistics with two sets of identical ESL essays, one of which had been "cleaned up" for sentence-level errors in syntax and morphology, discovered that the only factor that was significant in the scores designed by this group of graders was sentence-level error. "Cleaned up" papers received passing scores (i.e., a holistic score of 8 or better); the same papers with sentence-level errors failed.

Errors were very common in Luc's biology essays, as can be seen in Appendix B; however, the essays received excellent scores. Another study that focused on a Lao student enrolled in a freshman anthropology class (Johns, in press) resulted in the same finding: the faculty grader was sufficiently impressed by the ESL student's control of the content that he ignored her sentence-level errors on essay examinations.

7. Should the examination tasks at various academic levels (e.g., college entrance, upper-division, graduate) be different? If so, in what ways? For example, should the entrance examinations require simple exposition and general topics and the upper-division and graduate require argumentation in the students' disciplines?

Luc's frustrations with a competency examination quite foreign to his experience are not unique, as I have discovered in my interviews. As students in our universities become more culturally and linguistically diverse, we need to consider more carefully the character of our examinations designed to certify them as proficient in writing at each academic level. According to de Castell and Luke (1988), "literacy instruction has always taken place within a substantive context of values" (p. 159). We owe it to our culturally and linguistically diverse students to recognize the values that permeate our tests and to decide which of these values are basic—and which are not—to determining writing competency.

APPENDIX A
Luc's Response to the Samuelson Prompt

I agree with Samuelson because I think that it's easy to obtain financial aid in college. Besides, I also think that students aren't motivated to work hard in high school because the college's admission standards is low.

I strongly believe that high school students aren't motivated to work hard because the financial aid has made ^{almost} everyone overcome the expenses in college. ~~The most The reason. I . In my family, my brothers and sys sisters they all have financial aid. The reasons for~~
~~At the beginning of this semester~~
When my family migrated to the United States six years ago. When I still was in high school. my most concern ~~was that financially~~ about my futher education is that the financial. I went to the counselor office and search for the financial aid. I ~~wa~~ really surprise that them are so many financial ^{aid} ~~sources~~ avalable such as Calgrant A-B-C, pell grant, student loan, schoolarship etc. I realized that these financial aid would help me to go to college. I started my freshman year with ~~a~~ 6-000 dollard grant & loan. I really amaze that this country given me a great chance to go to college. That was my personal experience. I always ~~take in~~ wonder for myself whether the American students are getting financal aid or not on ~~bee~~ just because I am a foreing students it's so easy for me to get financial aid. I went around and talk to other friend; What's most surprising me that alot of my American friend obtain financial aid with a very low G.P.A. I ask several of them and from my own financial aid application I reallize that the requirement for obtaining finanacial aid is not the fact ~~that It~~ It's independent of G.P.A. Student is getting financial aid Because of their needy. Consider what's call a needy conditions. ~~Every one can~~ Most high school student move. away from home and become independent. So they become a desperate needy kid for financial aid. I think that ~~the rea~~ the requirement for obtain financial is pretty easy.
~~Admission standards is low~~
~~financial aid is available~~
—

So most student can get into college without working hard enough if students can can money to go to college without working hard, then why should they work hard?. Isn't this american attitute. I think that ~~the problem is that if you don't face~~ because the American attitute that if we don't face the problems, don't worry about them. Just like the problem of cholesterol in this country. I think that because they continue to eat a large amount of hamburger and McDonal & Chicken The Box still survive even though the problem with heat disease increase largely. We still doenot [?] care. So I think if somehow we put in the requirement for a fininacal aid depend on the GPA of students I think we will have a better education and High School students will work harder and more motivated.
The Second Reason that I think students aren't working hard in high school is that the admissions requirement is low ~~The R~~ The most [?] is that the transition from high school to college is very big. It's I first attend college I'm so surprise that how hard college student have to face compared with high school studens. This is surprise me that because the college admision requirement doesn't amphaising enough to create [?] pressure in high school. I think that the education system tend to have everyone graduate from high school and have a chance to get into college. Because of this system, I think student are motivate to work hard in high school. Besides, I think that GPA the requirement for admission is too low. For the state system it's below ~~3.5~~ 2.5. If we considert a student with 2.5 G.P.A. to get in to ~~school~~ college. We really said that ~~how~~ our acceptance really

encouraged student to go to college. But not encouraged student work hard in high
school. For me a student that doesn't have any advanced class would easily obtain 2.5
G.P.A. ther for going to college is not a big problem for high school student. This is why
student aren't working hard in high school.

Besides the statistic has show that

Master Basic Skill

Samuelson argues that since it is so easy to get into college and since one doesn't
have to have excellent grades to get financial aid, student aren't motivated to work hard
in High school. I agree with Samuelson's argumentation because I think that ^{the} expenses
in college are cheap. ~~Another~~ Besides, I also think reason for what I agree with
~~Samuelson is~~ that ~~I think~~ the college admission standards are low. Because of the cheap
expenses and low-admidsion requirement, ~~G P~~ I agree with Samuelson that students
aren't motivated to work hard in High school.

I agree with Salmuson that st high school students aren't motivated to work hard because it's very easy

APPENDIX B
Luc's Response to an Essay Prompt in Biology

2. (30 points). Discuss the Kingdom Fungi in regards to some of the salient characteristics contained in the Kingdom; also, name some of the Divisions and why their members are of importance to man, and a brief narrative concerning symbioses encountered within this group of organisms.

Kingdom Fungi are not Relatedto ~~main~~ plant or animals. They appear to have had multiple origin from the Protocteats. They are Eukaryoti which contain membrane bound organell and ~~miele~~ genetic material is enclosed inside the nuclei, they are mostly multicellular. Most Fungi composed of fillaments call hyphae which form a net-like mass call mycellium. The hyphae is divided in to cell by septs which usually has s pores through which <u>cell organells</u> and nutrient can pass. Cell wall is composed of chiten. The fungi can Reproduced by sexual or asexual; some by Both. When the condition is favorable they produce asexual spore which wh will germinate in the moist place and there are foods. When the condition is unfavorable—they produced sexual spore, which can withstand the harsh condition. These spores will Reproduce asexually but in to different strain (+) and (-) These haploid is unite by syngamy mid diploid zygote is produce, it undergoes meiosis to form haploid stage.

Most fungi are heterotrophic. They aquire energy by absorption of small organic molecules formed when the mycellium secrete enzym to the surrounding Media. Fungi may be ~~spo~~ saphophyte which they feed on non-living organic material as decomposer. Some ~~are~~ are ~~obtai symbiosis~~ parasitic which obtain energy from the host other are po parasitic symbionts—(Micorshizea, Lichen)—Fungi are important to main. They are the primary decomposer (zygomycetes - decay fungi)—some are used as food source such as mushroom (Basidiomycetes) other Yeast (Ascomycetes) used for Bread making, Bear and wine brewing; Penincillum (Imperfecta fungi) used as Antibiotic which kill Bacteria. ~~Some pathogenic fungi~~ ~~(Imp~~ Fungus are also important to man—they are the spoiler of wood, clothing, food. pathogenic fungi (Imperfecta Fungi) cause Athele's foot, ring worm. ~~They~~ Some Ascomycetes cause ~~Duth~~ Dutch Elm Disease and temporary lost of Insanity or death.

    Symbiosis in fungi are two form: Lichen and Micorrhizea <u>Lichen</u>—The symbiotic between fungi and green Algae or Cyanobacteria—The Fungal component is mostly the Ascomycetes The Fungi penetrate the Photosynthetic partner to absorb organic carbon. Some can even secrete chemical which command the photosynthetic partner to produce things needed by the Fungus. This is the controlled Parasitic Relationship Because the Fungi will die if they are Isolate from the Photosynthetic Partner, but the photosynthetic partner will live—This Relationship allows Both partner live in place where are inhospitable to either alone.

<u>Micorrhizea</u> (Symbiotic Mutualistic) Relationship between the Fungi and 80% green plant. The fungus component is mostly Basidiomycetes They help to transfer (translocation) of certain soil' nutrients that need by the plant such as Phosphorus, Manganese, Mg, Cu. In Return they absorp the Organic Carbon from the plant. Thus Fungi may or may not penetrate the Root of the Plants.

<u>Entemicorrhizea</u>—Fungi that penetrate the Rooth system of the plant (Most are zygomycetes)

<u>Ectomicorhizea</u>—Fungi that don't penetrate the Root system of the plant (spruce, pine)in some case this ecto type help plants to prevent heavy absorption of Metal's Acid Rain.

<u>Add-Symbiosis</u>—Fungi provide the orchids (arbereal) seeds with carbon utttill they are large enough to grows on their own.

Works Cited

Ballard, B., & Clanchy, J. (n.d.). *Assessment by misconception: Cultural influences and intellectual traditions.* Unpublished monograph, Australian National University, Canberra.

Bannai, H. (1990). *Executive summary. Asian Pacific Alliance Education Committee: ESL recommendations.* Unpublished manuscript, California State University, Long Beach.

Benson, M. J. (1991). University-level ESL reading: A content analysis. *English for Specific Purposes, 10* (1).

Berkenkotter, C., Huckin, T. N., & Ackerman, J. (1988). Conventions, conversation and the writer: Case study of a student in a rhetoric Ph.D. program. *Research in the Teaching of English, 22,* 9-44.

Black, K. (1989). Audience analysis and persuasive writing at the college level. *Research in the Teaching of English, 23,* 231-253.

Brandt, D. (1990). *Literacy as involvement: The acts of writers, readers, and texts.* Carbondale: Southern Illinois University.

Bridgeman, B., & Carlson, S. B. (1983). *Survey of academic writing tasks required of graduate and undergraduate foreign students* (Research Rep. No. 83-18). Princeton, NJ: Educational Testing Service.

Brinton, D. M., Snow, M. A., & Wesche, M. B. (1989). *Content-based second language instruction.* New York: Newbury House.

Carey, L., Flower, L., Hayes, J. R., Schriver, K. A., & Haas, C. (1989). *Differences in writer's initial task representations* (Tech. Rep. No. 35). University of California, Berkeley: Center for the Study of Writing.

Carson, J. E., Carrell, P. L., Silberstein, S., Kroll, B., & Kuehn, B. (1990). Reading-writing relationships in first and second language. *TESOL Quarterly, 24,* 245-266.

Casanova, S., C. Cepeda, R., Bennett, S., Carlson, D., Charnofsky, H., Daro, P., Merrit, K., Parker, L., Petit, S., White, L., & Wilson, J. (1989). *California's limited English language students: An intersegmental agenda.* A report to the Intersegmental Coordinating Council from the Curriculum and Assessment Cluster Committee, California State University, Long Beach.

Castell, S. de, & Luke, A. (1988). Defining "literacy" in North American schools. In E. R. Kintgen, B. M. Kroll, & M. Rose (Eds.), *Perspectives on literacy* (pp. 159-174). Carbondale: Southern Illinois Press.

Connor, U., & Johns, A. M. (1989, March). *Argumentation in the disciplines: Studies in business and engineering.* Paper presented at the Twenty-third Annual TESOL Convention, San Antonio, TX.

Cumming, A. (1990). *Application of contrastive rhetoric in advanced ESL writing.* Paper presented at the 24th Annual TESOL Conference, San Francisco.

Eisterhold, J. C. (1990). Reading-writing connections: Toward a description for second language learners. In B. Kroll (Ed.), *Second language writing. Research insights for the classroom* (pp. 88-102). New York: Cambridge University Press.

Elbow, P. (1991). Reflections on academic discourse: How it relates to freshmen and colleagues. *College English, 53,* 135-155.

Faigley, L., & Hansen, K. (1985). Learning to write in the social sciences. *College Composition and Communication, 36,* 140-149.

Flavell, J. H. (1981). Cognitive thinking. In W. P. Dickson (Ed.). *Children's oral communication skills* (pp. 35-60). New York: Academic Press.

Flower, L. (1987). *The role of task representation in reading-to-write* (Tech. Rep. No. 6). University of California, Berkeley: Center for the Study of Writing.

Flower, L., Schriver, K. A., Carey, L., Haas, C., & Hayes, J. R. (1989). *Planning in writing: The cognition of a constructive process* (Tech. Rep. No. 34). University of California, Berkeley: Center for the Study of Writing.

Freedman, S. W., Dyson, A. H., Flower, L., & Chafe, W. (1987). *Research in writing: Past, present and future* (Tech. Rep. No. 1). University of Califomia, Berkeley: Center for the Study of Writing.

Hamp-Lyons, L. (1990a). Challenging the task. *JALT Journal, 12,* 29-36.

Hamp-Lyons, L. (1990b). *Essay test strategies and cultural diversity: Pragmatic failure, pragmatic accommodation and the definition of excellence.* Paper presented at the 24th Annual TESOL Conference, San Francisco.

Hamp-Lyons, L., & Prochnow, S. (1990). *The difficulties of difficulty: Prompts in writing assessment.* Paper presented at the RELC Seminar, Singapore.

Herrington, A. (1985). Writing in academic settings: A study of the contexts for writing in two college chemical engineering courses. *Research in the Teaching of English, 19,* 331-359.

Hoetker, J., & Brossell, G. (1986). A procedure for writing content-fair essay examination topics for large-scale writing assessments. *College Composition and Communication, 37,* 328-335.

Homberg, T. (1984). Holistic evaluation of ESL compositions: Can it be validated objectively? *TESOL Quarterly, 18,* 87-108.

Horowitz, D. (1986a). Essay examination prompts and the teaching of academic writing. *English for Specific Purposes, 5,* 107-120.

Horowitz, D. (1986b). What professors actually require: Academic tasks for the ESL classroom. *TESOL Quarterly, 20,* 445-462.

Johns, A. M. (1981). Necessary English: A faculty survey. *TESOL Quarterly, 15,* 35-44.

Johns, A. M. (1986). *Writing tasks and demands in academic classrooms.* Unpublished manuscript, San Diego State University, California, Academic Skills Center.

Johns, A. M. (in press). Toward developing a cultural repertoire: The case study of a Lao college freshman. In D. E. Murray (Ed.), *Diversity as resource: Redefining cultural literacy.* Washington, DC: TESOL.

Johns, C. M. (1976). Examination questions. Unpublished handout, University of Aston, Birmingham, UK.

Jolliffe, D. A., & Brier, E. M. (1988). Studying writers' knowledge in academic disciplines. In D. A. Jolliffe (Ed.), *Writing in academic disciplines* (pp. 35-88). Norwood, NJ: Ablex.

McCarthy, L. (1987). A stranger in strange lands: A college student writing across the curriculum. *Research in the Teaching of English, 21,* 233-265.

Myers, G. (1985). The social construction of two biologists' proposals. *Written Communication, 2,* 219-245.

Nelson, J. (1990). This was an easy assignment: Examining how students interpret academic writing tasks. *Research in the Teaching of English, 24,* 362-396.

Peck, S. (1991). Recognizing and meeting student needs. In M. Celce-Murcia. (Ed.). *Teaching English as a second/foreign language* (2nd ed., pp. 363-372). Rowley, MA: Newbury House.

Peyton, J. K., Staton, J., Richardson, G., & Wolfram, W. (1990). The influence of writing task on ESL students' written products. *Research in the Teaching of English, 24,* 142-172.

Pollitt, A., Hutchinson, C., Entwistle, N., & DeLuca, C. (1985). *What makes an examination difficult?* Edinburgh: Scottish Academic Press.

Reid, J. M. (1989). English as a second language composition in higher education: The expectations of the academic audience. In D. M. Johnson & D. H. Roen (Eds.), *Richness in writing: Empowering ESL students* (pp. 220-234). New York: Longman.

Report of the English as a second language workgroup. (1988). Long Beach: Office of the Chancellor, California State University.

Rubin, D. L., & Piche, G. L. (1979). Development of syntactic and strategic aspects of audience adaptation skills in written persuasive communication. *Research in the Teaching of English, 20,* 9-21.

Rubin, D. L., & Rafoth, B. A. (1986). Social cognitive ability as a predictor of the quality of expository and persuasive writing among college freshmen. *Research in the Teaching of English, 20,* 9-21.

Russell, D. R. (1990). Writing across the curriculum in historical perspective: Toward a social interpretation. *College English, 52,* 52-73.

Saville-Troike, M. (1982). *The ethnography of communication.* London: Basil-Blackwell.

Scardamalia, M., & Bereiter, C. (1982). Assimilative processes in composition planning. *Educational Psychologist, 17,* 165-171.

Swales, J. M. (1990) *Genre analysis. English in academic and research settings.* New York: Cambridge University Press.

Sweedler-Brown, C. (1991, March). *Influence of the syntax vs. the rhetoric in holistic evaluation of ESL writing.* Paper presented at the Annual Conference on College Composition and Communication, Boston.

Tomlinson, B. (1984). Talking about the composing process. *Written Communication, 1,* 429-445.

Toulmin, S. (1958). *The uses of argument.* Cambridge: Cambridge University Press.

Winfield, F. E., & Barner-Felfelli, P. (1982). The effects of familiar and unfamiliar cultural context on foreign language composition. *Modern Language Journal, 66,* 373-378.

Becoming Biliterate:
First Language Influences
by Joan G. Carson

Many ESL learners come to the language learning task already literate in their first language. These learners have achieved varying levels of writing proficiency in their native language and are now faced with the prospect of learning to write in English. Much has been written about the difference between the forms and functions of first and second language literacy (e.g., Chang, 1983; Connor & McCagg, 1987; Eggington, 1987; Hinds, 1983; Kaplan, 1966; Ostler, 1987), and about the relationships between students' L1 and L2 literacy (e.g., Canale, Frenette, & Belanger, 1988; Carson, Carrell, Silberstein, Kroll, & Kuehn, 1990; Clarke, 1978; Cummins, 1981; Cziko, 1978; Edelsky, 1982). These studies focus on *products,* on what learners already know about writing/reading that may affect their second language acquisition efforts. However, little attention has been paid to the *process* of literacy acquisition,[1] to what second language learners have learned about LEARNING to read and write in their L1 that may affect how they approach literacy acquisition in ESL writing classrooms.

In this paper I will examine L1 writing development in two contexts: Japanese and Chinese primary and secondary educational settings. Because writing goes hand-in-hand with reading at all stages of development in these contexts, writing development must be viewed from an understanding of the total picture of literacy acquisition. Using this perspective, I will examine three aspects of literacy acquisition that affect the ways in which Japanese and Chinese students learn to read and write:

1. the social context of schooling;
2. cognitive considerations of the written code; and
3. pedagogical practices that are determined by the interaction of the social context with the cognitive demands of mastering the written code.

Reprinted from the *Journal of Second Language Writing,* *1*(1), Carson, J., Becoming biliterate: First language influences, 1990, with permission from Elsevier Science.

The literacy education that I describe is necessarily an idealized one for both Japan and China; naturally, there are regional and individual differences. In addition, available literature in English on changes in the educational system in the People's Republic of China often lags behind the changes themselves, and so current practices in the PRC may differ in some respects from the ones I describe. Nevertheless, these considerations of what it means to learn to write in Japanese and Chinese will provide insights about the pedagogical expectations that these learners, who represent two of the largest ESL student populations, bring to ESL writing classrooms.

I. The Context of Schooling: Social Aspects

The social context of schooling involves the following aspects of education in Japan and China:

1. attitudes towards literacy;
2. the structure of the educational system;
3. the underlying philosophy of education;
4. the social structure and cultural values that are reflected in classrooms; and
5. the content and perceived function of elementary and secondary school language arts curricula.

The social context influences significantly both pedagogical practices as well as students' attitudes toward literacy and literacy learning.

Japan

Japan is probably the most literate nation in the world, 99+ percent by some estimates. How do they do it? "Painfully. Exhaustingly. And yet rather naturally" (Duke, 1986, p. 61). At all levels of society literacy is valued, so that literacy acquisition is "natural" in spite of the fact that becoming literate is "painful" and "exhausting." This tradition of literacy in Japan began in the Tokugawa Era (1600s to mid 1800s) when the upper class systematically pursued reading and writing skills. Even the working class understood the practical value of literacy, voluntarily undertaking to educate their children, and this spillover from the upper classes to the lower levels of society was already well underway when Japan inaugurated a national school system (Duke, 1986). Thus, when compulsory education began in 1872, the value of literacy was already firmly established in Japanese society. By 1920, schools enjoyed 99% enrollment; now that figure is 99.9%.

Japan's schools are organized as a 6-3-3 system: 6 years of elementary school, 3 years of junior high school, and 3 years of senior high school. Elementary and junior high school are compulsory. Although students must take entrance exams for admission to senior high school, 94% go to high school, and 84% of these graduate. Of high school graduates, 29% will continue in higher education and 25% will participate in some type of vocational education (Dorfman, 1987).

The school system is regulated by the Ministry of Education which fixes the school calendar (Japanese children go to school 5½ days a week, 9½ months a year), and enforces a textbook approval system. This centralization of textbook selection results in similarity of content and difficulty and, additionally, of teaching methods, owing to the teacher's guides that accompany the texts. As Duke (1986) notes, "Literacy from the first grade is . . . an affair of state in Japan" (p. 53).

Teachers can rightly assume that their students will form a linguistically homogeneous group, all speaking Japanese natively, and it is taken for granted that *all children* will learn to read and write "kokugo." the national language.[2]

> The entire school is involved in the process of reading and writing. The teachers take it very seriously. The PTA stresses it. The parents expect it. The older brothers and sisters reinforce it. The Ministry of Education decrees it. Industry depends on it (Duke, 1986, p. 62).

The picture is one of all aspects of society conspiring in a literacy campaign. It would be difficult, given these conditions, for Japanese *not* to learn to read and write.

The philosophy underlying Japanese education derives from a Confucian and Buddhist heritage which stresses respect for learning and educational endeavors which lead to personal and societal improvement. According to Dorfman (1987), the goals of education are: academic knowledge, intellectual growth, vocational skills, moral education, and character development. Schools are expected to teach (and assume that these things are teachable)

- respect for society and established order;
- valuing group goals above individual interests:
- diligence and moral commitment;
- self-criticism;
- well-organized and disciplined study and work habits.

All aspects of education reflect these principles. Sakamoto and Makita (1973) explain that

> The main purpose of Japanese reading education is not only to make children literate, but also to enforce the understanding of the morals of stories and to promote sound personality development (p. 450).

A basic tenet of Japanese educational philosophy is that educational outcomes do not depend on intelligence so much as on time and effort. In this context difficulty and hardship are considered good; they make you strong. According to White (1987),

> The reason why Japanese industry works and why Japanese schools teach, why workers don't quit and why children don't drop out of school is that what is most wanted out of life—stability, security, and support—are acquired through effort and commitment. This lesson is taught to the young, at home and at school (p. 49).

Because time and effort are understood as the most important factors, little consideration is given to individual differences. Students are expected to keep up with the basic standard set by the Ministry of Education, a standard which is demanding and increasingly complex as one moves along the educational ladder. It is understood that in school, as in life, hard work, diligence, and perseverance lead to success.

Schools are structured to reflect the central role of the group in Japanese society and the importance of harmonious relations. Group participation is encouraged in order to develop group loyalty, minimize competition, and avoid recognition of individual relations. The group is not top-down or authoritarian; rather, it is peer-oriented, egalitarian, bound by horizontal ties. Children work in teams, or *han,* for both academic and nonacademic purposes, and each member of the group is expected to contribute to group effort. Groups serve a pedagogical as well as a socializing function.

> Though the group socializes children to see the value of cooperative teamwork, it also creates, teachers feel, an environment in which underachievers are stimulated to perform better, or at least feel fully included in what is going on (White, 1987, p. 117).

This groupwork is *by* the group, *for* the group. This contrasts with American versions—peer-tutoring, for example, which focuses on individual, not group needs.

Because of the high uniformity of instruction and the fundamental belief that effort leads to success, children are rarely divided by ability levels before high school.[3] Choral work, including choral reading, is common, and "the effect is to involve all students in the total class effort, a mutually supportive approach" (Duke, 1986, p. 65). These group activities are more than just supportive; they are also motivating in that they promote shared identity and allow individuals to influence group goals and activities. This collective action

> doesn't deny the role of an individual's skill and energies, and his (sic) personal contribution is fully noted. What motivates him (sic) to work so hard without an "individualized" reward is the promise . . . of a stable reference group and the predictable satisfaction it provides (White, 1987, p. 48).

In addition to the motivating function of group activities, teachers, parents, and schools take seriously their need to motivate students by awakening the desire to try. According to Duke (1986), the teacher's attitude is one of seriousness of purpose. The school sends letters home about what is happening at school, suggesting what parents can do to help. At home it is the mother's traditional role in Japan to do whatever she can to help with the child's education.

A final important motivator is the constant threat of exams: end of term, high school, and university entrance. Exams are taken seriously in Japan because they have lifelong consequences.[4] The *kokugo* (national language) test is at the heart of every exam.

The school curriculum reflects both the importance as well as the difficulty of learning to read and write in Japanese. In every year of elementary and junior high school, students spend more time on Japanese language than on *any other* class—32% of total class time in first grade, declining gradually to 13% of class time in 9th grade. In senior high school, students select one of two tracks, literature or science. For literature majors, the amount of time devoted to Japanese language studies (including classical literature) begins to rise again, and by the third year constitutes 24% of all classwork. For science majors, the amount of time allotted to Japanese study declines from 15% in their first year of senior high school to 9% of total class time in the third year (Dorfman, 1987).

Underlying the teaching and learning of the forms of literacy are assumptions about the functions of language. Language "is viewed less as a tool for self-expression than as a medium for expressing group solidarity and shared social purpose" (Tobin, Wu, & Davidson, 1989, p. 189). This attitude is reflected by a survey in which 80% of Japanese preschool parents, teachers, and administrators indicated that the most important thing for children to learn in preschool was sympathy, empathy, and concern for others. Only 5% indicated that communication skills were a top priority. As Tobin et al. note,

> in Japan, where successful communication is believed to depend largely on the empathic and intuitive abilities of the listeners, children are taught less to express themselves than to be sensitive to others' spoken and unspoken forms of self-expression (p. 191).

Language teaching encourages children to express what is socially shared rather than what is individual and personal. Choral recitation and memorization are pedagogical techniques for accomplishing this. Explicit training in public performance separates "performance as a skill, which anyone can learn, from responsibility for the content of one's pronouncements" (White, 1987, p. 112). Language is a useful medium for expressing social cohesion, and although there is formal group recitation, teachers feel no need to model, correct, or solicit informal speech.

To summarize, becoming literate in this highly literate country means learning to read and write in the Japanese educational system which reflects the values of Japanese society: the importance of education (and of literacy), the need to work hard to succeed, the inherent value of the group, and the primacy of shared social purpose. In this context language is understood as a medium for expressing social cohesion, and not primarily as a medium for individual expression. These values not only affect the functions of written language in Japanese society, they also define the social context of schooling in which literacy is acquired.

China

The situation in China is somewhat different.[5] Prior to 1949, only 20% of the population was literate. There was no tradition of literacy among the masses in China, but the Communists' victory "released a pent up demand for schooling by ordinary Chinese" (Cleverly, 1985, p. 112). Given the enormity of the task (for society and for the individual), enthusiasm was difficult to maintain, and the literacy movement slowed. By 1957, the literacy rate was only 37%, but by 1982 that figure had risen to 70%. Even with that progress, however, in 1984, 235 million people over the age of 12 remained illiterate or semiliterate.[6] According to the 1984 figures, 16% of the urban population was illiterate or semiliterate, compared with 34% of the rural population. Seventy percent of this total were women (Cleverly, 1985).

The slow spread of literacy in China reflects the fact that mass education is a recent phenomenon—mid-20th century—and compulsory education is even more recent. China operates the world's largest school system. In 1984, there were 182 million students in Chinese schools and universities. Officially, 94% of Chinese children attend primary school[7] (Cleverly, 1985).

The school system is organized on a 5-3-3 model: 5 years of primary school (beginning at age 7), 3 years of junior high school, and 3 years of senior high school. In some cities, Beijing and Shanghai, for example, there are 6 years of primary school. At this point in time, only primary school is compulsory nationwide, although local governments may require compulsory junior high school in some regions. In the countryside, students often complete only primary school. There is an attrition rate of nearly 30% in primary school, usually rural girls. Seventy-five percent of primary school graduates enter junior high school, and 25% of those will enter senior high school. University admissions are highly competitive, since there are places for only 500,000 students (5% of the high school graduates) nationwide.

Chinese children go to school 6 days a week, 9½ months a year. The curriculum in the lower grades of primary school is heavily weighted toward reading and language activities. Nearly 50% of the class time is devoted to Chinese; together, Chinese and math occupy $^2/_3$ of the day's schedule and in some rural areas only Chinese, math, and morals are taught. By junior high school, Chinese and math occupy 38% of the curriculum, and by senior high school, Chinese and foreign languages together constitute 30% of the curriculum (Cleverly, 1985).

The philosophy underlying Chinese education is a Confucian focus on self-improvement. Confucius was more concerned with presenting moral precepts than with advocating a method of critical thinking, and the notion that lessons should contain moral principles remains the traditional function of Chinese education. In modern China, Mao Zedong, like the dynastic leaders before him,

> prized education as a means of ordering relations on earth according to a supreme blueprint. . . . wanted a schooling devoted to ethical and collective ends, and . . . valued the combination of knowledge and action (Cleverly, 1985, p. 14).

What differs from Taiwan to Hong Kong to the PRC is not the belief that moral messages play an important role in learning to read and write, but rather the substance of these messages (Unger, 1977). The four basic moral principles that education should foster are

- love of country;
- service to others;
- willingness to abide by the group's decisions;
- respect for authority.
  (Petri, 1984)

To assure authorities that lessons are accomplishing their approved political/ideological purposes, teachers are required to have elaborate lesson plans. These lesson plans serve the additional function of ensuring that teachers, some of whom are ill-trained (some in rural areas only primary school graduates themselves), will adhere closely to the textbooks (Unger, 1977). Class size averages 40-50 pupils, and almost all teaching is whole group and very regimented, including drills, recitation, and memorization.

The primacy of the group in China results from Chinese notions of "guan"—control and regimentation (Tobin et al., 1989). The group is linked to order, is vertically organized and teacher-directed; it exists to serve the collective good. This is quite different from the Japanese notion of the group as an egalitarian unit with inherent value. For the Chinese, individualism is possible if it doesn't threaten shared acceptance of order and responsibility, and if it is directed to serve the public good and follow socially-approved channels. Selfishness threatens the collective group. The goal of the individual is to be a good citizen.

As in Japan, Chinese teachers encourage children to express what is socially shared rather than what is individual and personal. Choral recitation and memorization are used often, with an emphasis on enunciation, diction, and self-confidence in speaking and performing. Children are taught to express themselves clearly because successful communication is believed to depend largely on the clarity of expression of the speaker (Tobin et al., 1989). (This contrasts with the Japanese belief that successful communication is more a function of the listener's skill.) Oral skills are considered an academic subject, necessary to be productive members of society, and so teachers encourage public speaking, correcting mispronunciations and misusage.

To summarize, becoming literate in China involves learning to read and write in a society that values education, but that has only recently been able to develop positive attitudes among the masses towards literacy. Schools reflect the traditional function of Chinese education, which is to teach moral principles reflecting basic societal values: patriotism, the collective good, group loyalty, and respect for authority. In this context, schools are controlled and regimented, with a focus on maintaining order and authority. As in Japan, language is not thought of as primarily a medium for expressing individual meaning, although in China clear public expression is valued as a tool for successful communication. These, then, are the values and attitudes that define the social context of schooling in which literacy is acquired in China.

II. The Written Code: Cognitive Factors

Issues of the written code center around the cognitively demanding task of mastering complex orthographic systems in both Japanese and Chinese. These cognitive considerations are important because the writing system takes years to master, and until the entire system is learned, students' abilities to read and write are limited by the amount of code they control at a given time. Reading and writing, then, are skills that are developed relative to students' progress in learning the written code.

Japanese

Learning to read and write in English requires learning an alphabetic written code consisting of 26 letters and mastering the complex sound-symbol correspondences represented by these letters and their combinations. In Japanese, the situation is more complex. Readers and writers-to-be must learn four different writing systems: two phonetic syllabaries (*katakana* and *hiragana*), one system consisting of Chinese characters (*kanji*), and finally the Roman alphabet and Arabic numbers.

These systems not only differ in form, but they each also have their specific domain in the written language. The Roman alphabet and Arabic numbers are less important, accounting for only 1% of written text. More important are the two syllabaries and the Chinese characters. The *kana*—hiragana and katakana—are syllabaries,[8] with each symbol representing a Japanese syllable. The kanas consist of 46 basic symbols plus diacritics that, when added to the basic symbol, yield 71 written syllables. Kana average 3 strokes, although katakana is somewhat plainer than hiragana. Hiragana is used to write grammatical information (e.g., the subject marker *wa* as well as verb, adjective, and adverb endings) and certain native words. In written Japanese, approximately 65% of the text is written in hiragana. Katakana, is used for borrowed foreign words and represents approximately 4% of written text.

Kanji symbols are Chinese characters that are essentially morphemic. (The Japanese word *karate,* for example, consists of two morphemes/characters: *kara,* which means "empty" and *te,* which means "hand.")[9] Japanese children learn 1,850 kanji in school—996 kanji in the 6 years of elementary school, 854 in middle school—and this number is considered a substantial basic inventory, although educated adults will know more. Each of these kanji can be read or pronounced in several ways depending on context. They are generally more complex than the kana, requiring 1-20 brushstrokes each to write.[10] Kanji account for 30% of the symbols used in written text, but this percentage does not reflect the importance of kanji characters. Kanji are used for content words which stand out in a sentence as key ideas or words against a background of hiragana grammatical information. Kanji may have hiragana symbols added to them (e.g., in verbs and adjectives), and a word typically consists of a root predicate morpheme in kanji and a Japanese grammatical ending in hiragana.[11]

In written text, individual words are not visually separated from one another. Children learn to intuit which symbols group to form a word, although the hiragana grammatical endings make this process less daunting than it sounds. Text can be written either horizontally, from left to right, or vertically, from top to bottom and right to left. In school, language classes use vertical text—compositions are written this way—as do social studies texts. Japanese newspapers, books, and magazines are also written in vertical text. Arithmetic and science class texts are written horizontally and children keep their arithmetic and science notebooks this way. Technical books, scientific journals, business, and government use text that is written horizontally (Dorfman, 1987; Sakamoto & Makita, 1973).

An additional consideration of the written code in Japan is the aesthetic aspect. Writing requires an extraordinary degree of dexterity. Characters can consist of many strokes—1-24, or more—and each stroke is written in a specified order. Writing is taught not just as communication, but as art. *Shooji,* calligraphy class, involves drawing characters with an artist's brush and is part of the educational curriculum from third grade through junior high school. Contests and exhibitions are common, and all children participate. This participation in art contests "instills into the child a unique attitude toward his (sic) language . . . a feeling of deep respect for the written word, an attitude difficult to appreciate by those who write with the alphabet" (Duke, 1986, p. 74).

Chinese

Although Japanese kanji are the result of a highly intricate adaptation of Chinese characters for polysyllabic Japanese, the writing system was developed for the monosyllabic classical Chinese language. Phonetically, vowel sounds are prominent in Chinese; twenty-one consonants can occur syllable-initially, but only [ng] can occur in final position. In Mandarin there are 420 syllables, many of which are phonetically similar. This, coupled with the essentially monosyllabic nature of the language,[12] means that there are a large number of homophones. For example /i/ may mean any of 30 different words (e.g., "clothes," "idea," "one," "medicine," "easy"), although tones, context, and written forms can help disambiguate the meaning. Morphologically, Chinese is analytic; each word is a one syllable morpheme and there are few bound forms. Syntactically, Chinese is an isolating language; there are no conjugations or inflections. Because words are not marked grammatically, word order is everything.[13] The written characters (the root words) are thus the same even for verbs, nouns, adjectives, and adverbs. One character, for example, may mean "ascend" (V), "top" (N), "upper" (ADJ), and so forth.

The Chinese writing system reflects the morphological structure of the language. Each character is morphemic, although words may contain more than one character. According to Liu (1978), Chinese characters were originally pictographs in which the sign indicated the word by meaning, not sound. In the second stage of the development of the writing system, signs were combined for compounds. The signs for "pig" and "roof," for example, would combine to mean "house," "home," "family." Phonetic loaning marked the third stage. Because the essentially monosyllabic nature of Chinese results in many homophones, the same character was used to represent them all. Although this system allowed the representation of abstract terms with concrete pictographs (similar to using the picture of an eye to stand for the homophone "I" in English, for example), the problem of ambiguity remained. In the fourth stage, the homophones were disambiguated by adding a graph to the character to suggest meaning. Now the symbol consisted of two parts: a radical to indicate meaning, and a phonetic part to indicate sound. (In the English example noted earlier, the phonetic part would be a character that would be read as /ai/, and the radical would indicate whether it was to be understood as a body part or a personal pronoun.) Ninety percent of all Chinese characters are constructed according to this principle.

Radicals, the part of the character that indicates meaning, are arranged from simple to complex according to the number of strokes within each stroke category. Each radical has been given a number. (For the 6-stroke category, e.g., there would be radical 5, radical 11, etc.) The number of strokes ranges from 1-30, with the mean being around 11.6. Complexity of form does not necessarily indicate difficulty of learning, however. In one study (Leong, 1973), a relatively simple 4-stroke character was written correctly by 21% of third grade children tested, while an apparently more complex form (16 strokes) was written correctly by 73% of the children.

The authoritative Kanghsi dictionary contains 48,000 characters (Leong, 1973), of which 6-7,000 are actively used. Estimates vary on the number of characters necessary for reading and writing, but it is generally agreed that the minimum is around 3,500, about twice the number needed in Japanese. According to a sample taken by the National Publishing Bureau, 6,300 different characters are employed in ordinary publications, and of that number 2,400 make up 90% of the characters (Jiang & Li, 1985).

There is a diversity of languages spoken in China, but *Putonghua* (Mandarin), the national language, is taught and serves as the medium of instruction in schools. Putonghua utilizes the pronunciation of the Beijing dialect, the grammar of Northern Chinese dialects, and the vocabulary of modern colloquial Chinese literature. Although the spoken languages of China differ, one writing system is used to represent them all. A top priority since 1949 has been simplifying the language system by abolishing words, simplifying characters by reducing the number of strokes, and reducing the number of radicals. *Pinyin,* alphabetic writing using Roman phonetization, was introduced to facilitate the learning of characters and to speed the popularization of Putonghua.

III. Learning to Read and Write: Pedagogical Issues

Pedagogical practices in literacy instruction are very much the result of the interaction of the social context of schooling with the practical considerations of code mastery. Learning to write involves (at least in the primary school and to some extent in secondary schools) acquisition of a complex orthographic system. This demand, coupled with educational values and the perceived social functions of language, determine the way that children learn to read and write in Japan and China.

Japan

Given the fact that Japanese must master four separate codes in order to read and write, it is even more amazing that the literacy rate exceeds 99%. According to Sakamoto and Makita (1973), this phenomenon is the result of a combination of factors including:

- compulsory education from 1st through 9th grade;
- Japanese parents' attitude of respect for education (they are eager for their child to learn);
- availability of good, cheap reading materials;

- many reading stimuli including a reading movement for mothers, reading groups, book report contests, and national reading week;
- the initial use of phonetic symbols that are easy to learn.

In fact, most children begin school already knowing how to read, even though as a general practice no letters or characters are taught either in nursery schools or in kindergartens. According to one study of Tokyo children (Sakamoto & Makita, 1973), 31% of three-year-olds, 58% of four-year-olds, and 83% of five-year-olds could read all of hiragana. In another study, 64% of children surveyed could read more than 60 of the 71 symbols five months before beginning elementary school, and only 1% of the children surveyed could read no hiragana (Sakamoto, 1978). Children also know an average of 6 kanji before beginning elementary school.

Since they are not taught to read, how do children learn? Parents' concern for reading is an important factor, but they do little direct teaching. More important are the picture books written in phonetic hirigana and read by parents to their children, and the kana blocks that children are encouraged to play with. Mothers begin to read picture books and preschool magazines[14] to children at an early age (36% of Japanese mothers begin reading to their children at age 1, according to Sakamoto, 1978). Because these texts are written in hiragana—phonetic symbols with direct sound-symbol correspondence—children find them relatively easy to learn, given the exposure they have. Mothers are very much invested in this type of interaction with their children.[15]

Building on whatever proficiency they may bring with them, once in school, children are taught kana using the whole word method in which kana are presented in lexical contexts. Additionally, children are taught kana through a writing method in which the child writes the kana repeatedly with his/her fingers on a table or in the air, pronouncing the syllable as it is written. Following this kinesthetic activity, children write the symbol, tracing it on dotted lines. In first grade, children are taught all hiragana, 46 kanji, and, in the latter half of the year, they begin learning katakana, which they master by the end of second grade.

Children move from kana to Chinese characters, although kana remain functional in the writing system. First grade texts begin with stories in kana (which children can already read) and gradually introduce Chinese characters. The order of presentation of kanji in school is determined by the Ministry of Education, which arranges the symbols systematically for teaching from first through ninth grade. Specific kanji characters are introduced each year, for a total of 996 taught in the 6 years of elementary school, and 854 taught in the 3 years of junior high school. To ease the transition from hiragana to kanji, teachers use a method called furigana in which a phonetic reading of kanji is given by printing hiragana on the line above it, or on the right side of kanji written vertically. Kanji are always taught in sentences, never out of context. Learning kanji can also involve radical analysis, or the derivation method, for those kanji that are somewhat pictographic. Otherwise, the primary method for teaching kanji is to provide multiple encounters. Although kanji are complex, the biggest factor in learnability is the familiarity of the character (Sakamoto & Makita, 1973).

In Japan, traditional methods of memorization, repetition, drilling, and testing are used to teach written language. As Duke (1986) notes, "Teaching methods in the kokugo in the overwhelming number of classrooms in Japan cannot be described as creative, innovative or imaginative" (p. 64). Nevertheless, they are effective. Correctness and neatness are stressed and valued.

As students learn more of the code, they are no longer confined to material written only in hiragana (or in some combination of controlled scripts) but can begin to read more sophisticated texts, including stories, poems, and essays. The 3-step method is a traditional and widely used method for teaching reading. In this method an introduction to the text is followed by (1) reading through the text, (2) reading in detail, and (3) appreciation. In the first step, students read the text aloud with errors or pronunciation mistakes corrected by the teacher. Students then give a brief summary and discuss their own related experience. In this step, students need to read quickly to get a rough outline and to focus on the factual information. The second step is the most important, in which students think over the story for detailed comprehension by analyzing characters (kanji) as well as phrase and sentence relationships. This step clarifies details in the text, and also encourages the habit of reading between the lines for the author's intention, thought, and viewpoint. In the third step, students are led to understand the moral of the story. Reading is also a way to learn or be exposed to new kanji.

Through junior high school, the focus in writing instruction is on learning formulas for writing. Students learn the importance of composition structure: topic sentences, main ideas, supporting details,[16] conclusions. Self-expression is not important and is not encouraged. Typical themes include "Friendship," "School Life," "The Importance of Nature." Students read texts that model the structure of compositions that they write, continuing to reflect principles that have guided their literacy learning—to write what has been learned from reading, whether at the character/word level (kanji) or at the discourse level (essay structure). One important difference, however, is that in writing, students always have access to hiragana to express meaning, even if they do not yet possess the appropriate kanji.

China

According to Leong (1978), beginning readers in Chinese are advantaged by the writing system, since each character, inherently a phonemic-semantic combination, gives more information than do the more abstract letters used to write English. The disadvantage, of course, is the cost in memory. As a result, the focus in teaching is on language as a written code. As Leong (1973) notes,

> a knowledge of the nature of the Chinese language and an understanding of the reading task—its discriminatory and decoding aspects—are central to good pedagogy (p. 396).

The goal for primary schools is to teach approximately 3000 characters (compared to the 996 taught in Japanese primary schools).[17] The gradations from year to year, however, are not uniform. What facilitates the teaching of characters is pinyin, an alphabetic form of writing with grapheme-phoneme correspondence that is used to help children learn the pronunciation of characters. This set of phonetic symbols is printed alongside characters for the first several years of elementary school, and thereafter for teaching new characters.[18] In China, the parallel character/pinyin text allows learners to acquire new characters naturally in the course of reading. Utilizing pinyin means that reading can be learned by eye and by ear. With Chinese characters, "learning to read . . . is largely learning by eye and by hand" (Leong, 1978, p. 157).

In school, children are first taught pinyin, and then characters are introduced which are also given in pinyin, much the way the Japanese use hiragana to teach kanji. By the end of second grade, students have learned to spell and pronounce syllables in pinyin and to utilize pinyin to learn new words. In third grade pinyin is used to look up words in the dictionary and to read simple texts, and from the fourth grade on, students can read pinyin texts and transcribe without difficulty. By the time they have entered junior high school, they have mastered pinyin. During this time, children are simultaneously learning to write characters, using pinyin when necessary. Without pinyin, students found it difficult to read and write because they did not know enough characters. Knowing pinyin changed this, because it has allowed students to read and write more, better, and sooner (Dai & Lu, 1985). Pinyin, though, is a system to be discarded when students become proficient in writing characters.

Code mastery is an important aspect of reading and writing instruction. In the past, the difficulty of learning characters meant that most reading and writing instruction was not possible until 4th and 5th grade. But now, as Jiang and Li (1985) note, certain innovations characterize literacy instruction. Pinyin is used to teach reading, which makes character recognition much easier and which allows writing instruction to begin earlier. Character acquisition and reading are taught simultaneously, which helps interest and motivate students. A final innovation is the development of the concentrated method in which teachers concentrate on character recognition in first and second grade, teaching related (shape, sound, meaning) characters. In spite of these innovations, Jiang and Li claim that reading materials do not challenge the cognitive abilities of the students and that the quantity is insufficient to activate reading competence.

A focus of primary school reading and writing instruction is necessarily on mastery of the code. Reading is taught using the "look and say" method (Leong, 1973), which focuses on the whole character as the basic unit. Reading a passage is followed by repetition of new characters; homework is writing the new characters. Writing is valued as a way to learn characters and "writing and reading characters seem to be associated skills which reinforce each other" (Liu, 1978). Traditionally, writing has been taught by rote, using kinesthetic reinforcement and including an aesthetic component of calligraphy.

However, language instruction in primary school is more than just code mastery. According to the Shanghai, Zhejiang, Beijing, and Tianyin Joint Writing Group for the Design of Educational Materials (1985).

> The goal of elementary school language instruction is to develop in the children the ability to recognize characters, read, and write compositions and to begin to develop at a very elementary level a fresh, lively, and accurate style of writing. (p. 87).

In addition to pinyin and 3,000 Chinese characters, foundations for reading and writing include the ability to

- use pencil, pen, and brush to write;
- use a dictionary;
- understand main ideas of oral speeches and summarize;
- read and understand appropriate children's books;
- write smooth and complete sentences;
- write short simple narratives and "common practical writing with sound thought, a clear central focus, specific content, a clear sequence of development, attention to incorrectly written characters, and be able to use the ten common types of punctuation" (Shanghai et al. Joint Writing Group, 1985, p. 88).

The focus on form required by character learning is reflected in the focus on sentence and discourse forms. By second grade, students

> will accumulate good words and sentences for the text. . . . They will continue to cultivate the writing of complete sentences, the writing of smooth sentences, and attention to not making mistakes in the writing of characters or in their use. . . . They will begin practicing building sentences from a model (Shanghai et al. Joint Writing Group, 1985, p. 95).

Beginning in third grade, students practice correcting defective sentences and begin focusing on the paragraph as a unit. Students also begin developing their ability to divide text into meaningful segments, recognizing main ideas and organizational patterns, such as general to specific and specific to general. In fourth grade, students are writing main ideas of texts they have read, in addition to outlining and summarizing the reading. Fifth graders focus on elements in the text, including topics and supporting details, development, facts, and inferences. In fifth grade students are expected to be able to write good and "lively" sentences using figures of speech. By sixth grade, expectations are that close reading will allow students to

> understand the relationships between the language, bearing and psychological aspects of the people in the article (Shanghai et al. Joint Writing Group, 1985, p. 99).

A typical lesson to explain and clarify a text will begin with the teacher putting new words from the primer on the board. The whole class reads them several times and the meanings are explained several times. Then the whole class will read the passage aloud together. Questions about the text will be answered (sometimes repeated aloud together), and passages and lessons will be memorized.

> When the Chinese speak of memorization, they mean much more: the actual commitment to memory of whole passages, sometimes pages on end, word by word. The Chinese word *beishu*—the literal translation of which is "to recite the book from memory"—often means precisely that (Unger, 1977, p. 16).

Why stress memorization? According to Unger, there are several reasons. First, of course, is the burden of learning Chinese orthography, a task that is doubly difficult for non-Mandarin speakers. Second, teachers believe that memorization of texts is a good way for students to develop their writing abilities.

> What is considered a good Chinese writing style is much more of a stereotyped "formula" than is . . . written English. In Chinese the student learns through memorization the frame-work for writing that others have employed and then learns to plug in appropriate ready-made phrases such as the traditional four-character metaphorical idioms (*chengyu*) or the political idioms newly devised since Liberation (Unger, 1977, pp. 17-18).

Sheridan concurs.

> There are whole phrases which reflect a certain style in the Chinese oral and written tradition, and one often meets these phrases in conversation as well as in writing. The practice of memorization is continued so as to help students develop writing style through modeling (Sheridan, 1981, p. 807).

The focus on model compositions,[19] though, has its drawbacks. Zhang (1987) contends,

> In the training for writing a composition, what is involved is the preparation of a few sets of ready-made "model" compositions. For example, in the model titled "A person that I ..." one can substitute anything for the ellipses. . . . Nothing seems to matter anymore; just put in the right words to complete the formula (p. 41).

Nevertheless, memorization is thought to help students learn sentence patterns that they can later use flexibly. However, Unger (1977) notes that

> One end result, to a non-Chinese eye, is that the modern Chinese essays which are published often lack the imaginative word-usage and the range of personal styles that are found in the essays of other languages (p. 18).

Still, there is a strong belief that the path to lively and creative writing styles lies in internalizing others' styles. Little improvisation or creativity is allowed: creativity is seen as flowing from discipline and proficiency. "A polished but flexible use of prose is . . . to be built up from the child's memorized mastery of paragraphs from his (sic) reading texts" (Unger, 1977, p. 19).

This focus on memorization, Jiang and Li (1985) note, means that only a few brief and meager passages (20 perhaps in a half year) can be studied, and that independent reading is not encouraged. This, then, is how Chinese children learn to read and to write, "persistently writing and re-writing the words, phrases and passages being studied" (Unger, 1977, p. 32).

IV. Implications for Becoming Biliterate

Japanese and Chinese speakers come to the L2 literacy classroom with prior experience that can affect their learning to read and write in English. This prior experience often includes previous English language instruction, which undoubtedly influences any subsequent exposure. Still, I would argue that the language learning context that I have described indirectly influences the second language pedagogy in these countries, as well.[20] More importantly, then, writing teachers need to examine how aspects of L1 literacy learning might affect Japanese and Chinese speakers' expectations of and preferred learning strategies in ESL writing classrooms.

For the social context of schooling, ESL teachers might expect that Japanese learners are more conditioned to assume that they will acquire second language literacy successfully, given the "natural" (as well as extraordinary) literacy acquisition process and rate in Japan. Chinese students would not necessarily share this sense that anyone can become literate, coming from a society in which literacy acquisition occurs at some cost, and in which not everyone is successful. The Chinese and Japanese share a sense that the goal of education is personal and societal improvement, a goal that is understood only indirectly in U.S. education. In any case, both groups would find much less focus on moral lessons in reading and writing assignments. Writing topics that focus on personal opinion are likely to be most difficult, since this type of writing can be at odds with the Confucian notion of education as knowledge transmission, not as personal invention (Johns, 1991).

Although both groups share a sense that hard work will lead to success, this maxim may not play out as expected in second language learning. Endless hours of memorization and grammar drills will not necessarily lead to a more proficient second language reader and writer. The U.S. instructional version of hard work in writing classrooms more often focuses on the hard work of planning, writing, and revising, and not on the hard work of memorizing and learning the forms.

Because both the Japanese and Chinese are accustomed to groupwork, they are likely to feel initially quite comfortable with classroom methods that focus on group activities. However, because the function of the group, particularly in writing classes, is more often to serve individual needs rather than the group, these methods could be at best somewhat confusing from a pedagogical perspective. At worst, they are potentially disorienting to the extent that they fail to provide the socializing function that is so important to students who have come to expect to develop their sense of shared identity from the group. In a similar vein, in U.S. classrooms it is expected that language will be used to express individual meaning, a language function that is at odds with both groups' sense of language as a medium for expressing group solidarity and shared social purpose. Although writing in American culture can focus on collectivist ends, the discourse of the academy, as Clark and Doheny-Farina (1990) point out, is committed to individualist ethics.

Japanese students, socialized to value the ability of the listener/reader to understand, have developed the ability to read between the lines. However, these writers are somewhat disadvantaged in a context that places the responsibility for clear communication on the speaker/writer, as is true for Chinese and English. This is problematic in writing for a culture which not only values, but requires explicit and detailed prose (Hinds, 1987).

Additionally, both groups in their schooling have come to understand clearly the function of examinations as social selection devices, especially the ubiquitous language proficiency exams that are the key to academic placement. This exam focus can be quite motivating, although the disadvantage is that the students are likely to be impatient with curricula that do not address exam requirements specifically and directly. These ESL students feel acutely the need to perform well on a multitude of writing proficiency exams, not only as an exit criterion from ESL programs, but also as additional "gates" in their regular curriculum studies—freshman composition exit exams, and the minimal competency writing exams that may be administered later in their academic careers.

Issues of the written code have implications mainly for learning to read in English, and; as such, indirect implications for learning to write. Both the Japanese and Chinese bring with them to the second language literacy task the cognitive flexibility that comes with already having mastered multiple codes. Furthermore, the Japanese are accustomed to distinguishing content and function words in reading, since these are graphically marked by the writing systems. This sense that these two categories of words in a text are of different value is one that should serve a second language reader well.

An additional issue of the written code is that the match between sounds and symbols in English is not as good as it is in either hiragana or in pinyin. According to Lee, Stigler, and Stevenson (1986)

> the rules governing grapheme-phoneme correspondence in English orthography are complex, irregular, and difficult for beginning readers to master. As a result, reading English presents a host of problems related to phonemic awareness and segmentation and phonetic decoding (p. 123).

Alphabetic writing systems, they claim, are more efficient for fluent adults, but "they make greater conceptual demands on those beginning to read the language" (p. 124). Nevertheless, because both groups have learned systems that require phonetic recoding (hiragana and pinyin), they are accustomed to the practice of sound-symbol correspondence, even though their expectations are that it will be more predictable.

Finally, expectations of U.S. classrooms are likely to be very much influenced by students' experiences with pedagogical practices in both Japan and China. One consequence of the magnitude of the code-learning task is that reading and writing are inextricably linked in the six years that Chinese students are learning Chinese characters and in the nine years that Japanese students are mastering kana and kanji. Knowing these characters means that a student can correctly write the character, and this proficiency results from multiple encounters in reading and multiple tracings in writing. Learning to read and write in a very real sense is learning individual words, and one consequence of this learning is that words become extremely important, not only because the characters are taught using whole word methods, but also because the characters themselves are meaningful units. This focus on the importance of words and word meanings can result in the sense that Japanese and Chinese readers remain word bound when they read in English, translating every word and resisting urgings to use different strategies for different purposes. Because learning to read always entails *close* reading, other types of reading such as skimming and scanning, while available as reading strategies, are not part of their classroom expectations of how reading is taught and learned. ESL instructors often interpret this close reading and word boundedness as being the result of grammar-translation language learning, but it seems to me more nearly the effect of reading pedagogy. The advantage here, of course, is that Japanese and Chinese are likely to be good close readers, with the Japanese, as I have noted earlier, being particularly attuned to inferencing and reading between the lines. This reading ability is one that serves ESL academic writers well, since most academic writing tasks require analysis of textual sources.

Expectations that are unlikely to be fulfilled in U.S. classrooms are those that focus on the need for memorization, pattern practice, and drill as techniques that are useful in learning to read and write. The dependence on text memorization and on model passages as the principal techniques for learning to write encourage a focus on the written product that may be at odds with writing instruction in U.S. classrooms that is process oriented and/or that is grounded in the belief that writing should, at its core, serve as a medium for expressing personal meaning. Still, Japanese and Chinese students come to second language reading and writing classrooms with a well-developed sense that reading and writing are inextricably related in literacy development, that one learns to read by writing and to write by reading. They are thus primed to learn much from reading second language texts that they can use in writing, including words, sentence patterns, and rhetorical forms.

Conclusion

Empirical investigation is certainly warranted to examine the extent to which expectations based on ESL students' literacy backgrounds actually manifest themselves in ESL classrooms. Still, knowing about the educational background of their students can provide ESL writing teachers with insights into the ways in which ESL writers may approach the often formidable task of learning to write in English. ESL students come to second language writing classrooms with expectations of how writing is taught and learned. To the extent that their expectations do not match pedagogical practices, they are likely to be confused about the purpose and effectiveness of these methods. Their previous experiences in learning to read and write may not yield effective strategies in ESL writing classrooms where the task of learning to write differs not only in the complexity of its demands, but also in its social context and, ultimately, in its social functions. Recognizing the advantages and disadvantages of L1 instructional background for L2 literacy acquisition, ESL writing teachers can make the differences explicit where appropriate, can accommodate those differences where feasible, and can exploit those differences where possible to enhance the writing development of Japanese and Chinese second language learners.

Acknowledgments

I would like to thank Dwight Atkinson, Ulla Connor, Dong Zhe, Helene Dunkelblau, Junko Kawada, Jim Kohn, Grace Liu, Gayle Nelson, Margaret van Naerssen, and two anonymous JSLW reviewers who offered careful and constructive comments on earlier drafts of this paper.

Notes

1. The IEA study of written composition (Gorman, Purves, & Degenhart, 1988; Purves, 1988) had as its goal the description of cause and effect relationships between instructional practices and written products in 14 different countries. In addition to the fact that Japan and China (the countries described in this paper) were not included in the IEA study, the focus of that study can still be understood as having primarily a product focus: How can written products be accounted for with reference to instructional practices?

2. In the daily school schedule, the subject taught is *kokugo* (national language), not *nihongo* (Japanese).

3. Promotion is virtually automatic in Japanese schools.

4. A job is usually a lifetime commitment in Japan and hiring decisions are very much influenced by the quality of a prospective employee's university. Therefore, success in school (i.e., the ability to get into a prestigious university) is a major determinant of the economic and social status of adults.

5. By China, I mean the People's Republic of China (PRC). Where there are similarities in educational and literacy practices with other Chinese-speaking countries, I will specify those countries by name. Although I am referring specifically to the PRC, much can be generalized, including underlying traditional philosophies of education and issues of language and pedagogy.

6. Although one can write a letter with 300 characters, Cleverly (1985) defines a person as semiliterate who knows fewer than 1500 characters, cannot read a simple book, or write a simple message.

7. Cleverly (1985) suggests that the figure is probably more like 85%.

8. Syllabaries are rare as writing systems. Japanese and Cherokee are the only modern languages that use them (Sheridan, 1982).

9. Kanji have two phonetic readings, one Japanese and one Chinese, with the same meaning. This would be similar to "etc." in English, where "et cetera" would be the Latin reading and "and so on" would be the English reading.

10. There are arguments that kanji, in spite of the fact that they are complex, are easier to learn than kana, because the meaningfulness effects of the kanji overpower their visual perceptual complexity (Steinberg & Yamada, 1978-79).

11. Although kanji and hiragana mix, hiragana and katakana do not.

12. Modern Chinese is more polysyllabic than classical Chinese, due to the pervasiveness of morphological compounding (DeFrancis, 1984; Norman, 1988).

13. Chinese word order is basically SVO, although topic/comment better describes Chinese syntax.

14. In 1975, there were over 40 magazines in Japan targeting the preschool population (Sakamoto, 1978).

15. Compare this type of parent-child interaction with the interaction fostered by the type of toys (generally favored in the U.S.) that encourage educationally independent activity (White, 1987).

16. It is important to note that Japanese dislike specifying detail and prefer to "read between the lines," figure out what is unsaid. This is relatively easy for a culturally and linguistically homogeneous group (Kinosita, 1988).

17. Students are not expected to learn too many new characters after primary school. In general, a person who knows 4-5,000 characters is understood as having at least a secondary education (Jiang & Li, 1985).

18. In Taiwan, *zhuyin fuhao,* a phonetic spelling system, is also used to help in the pronunciation of characters. In Hong Kong, characters are taught with no pronunciation aids.

19. Zhao (1990) notes that writing instruction in China is just now beginning to bear signs of plurality, becoming more student-centered and more oriented toward critical thinking.

20. I am grateful to Dwight Atkinson for pointing out this relationship.

Works Cited

Canale, M., Frenette, N., & Belanger, M. (1988). Evaluation of minority student writing in first and second language. In J. Fine (Ed.)., *Second language discourse: A textbook of current research.* Norwood. NJ: Ablex.

Carson, J.E., Carrell, P.L., Silberstein, S., Kroll, B., & Kuehn, P. (1990). Reading-writing relationships in first and second language. *TESOL Quarterly, 24,* 245-266.

Chang, S.J. (1983). Linguistics and written discourse in particular languages: Contrastive studies: English and Korean. In R. B. Kaplan, et al. (Eds.), *Annual review of applied linguistics, III* (pp. 85-89). Rowley. MA: Newbury House.

Clark, G., & Doheny-Farina, S. (1990). Public discourse and personal expression. *Written communication, 7,* 456-481.

Clarke, M. (1978). Reading in Spanish and English: Evidence from adult ESL students. *Language Learning, 29,* 121-150.

Cleverly, J. (1985). *The schooling of China.* Sydney: George, Allen, and Unwin.

Connor, U., & McCagg, P. (1987). A contrastive study of English expository prose paraphrases. In U. Connor & R. Kaplan, (Eds.), *Writing across languages: Analysis of L2 text* (pp. 73-86). Reading, MA: Addison-Wesley.

Cummins, J. (1981). The role of primary language development in promoting educational success for language minority students. In *Schooling and language minority students: A theoretical framework* (pp. 3-49). Los Angeles: Evaluation, Dissemination and Assessment Center, California State University.

Cziko, G. (1978). Differences in first and second language reading: The use of syntactic, semantic and discourse constraints. *Canadian Modern Language Review, 34,* 473-489

Dai, B-Y, & Lu, J-P. (1985). Reading reform in Chinese primary schools. *Prospects, 15,* 103-110.

DeFrancis, J. (1984). *The Chinese language: Fact and fantasy.* Honolulu. HI: University of Hawaii Press.

Dorfman, C.H. (Ed.). (1987). *U.S. study of education in Japan.* Washington, DC: U.S. Government Printing Office.

Duke, B. (1986). *The Japanese school.* New York: Praeger.

Edelsky, C. (1982). Writing in a bilingual program: The relation of L1 and L2 texts. *TESOL Quarterly, 16,* 211-228.

Eggington, W.G. (1987). Written academic discourse in Korean: Implications for effective communication. In U. Connor & R. Kaplan (Eds.), *Writing across languages: Analysis of L2 text* (pp. 153-168). Reading, MA: Addison-Wesley.

Gorman, T.P., Purves, A.C., & Degenhart, R.E. (Eds.). (1988). *The IEA Study of Written Composition I: The International Writing Tasks and Scoring Scales.* New York: Pergamon.

Hinds, J. (1983). Contrastive rhetoric: Japanese and English. *Text, 3,* 183-195.

Hinds, J. (1987). Reader versus writer responsibility: A new typology. In U. Conor & R. Kaplan. (Eds.), *Writing across languages: Analysis of L2 text* (pp. 141-152). Reading, MA: Addison-Wesley.

Jiang, S., & Li, B. (1985). A glimpse at reading instruction in China. *The Reading Teacher,* 762-766.

Jie, G., & Lederman, M.J. (1988). Instruction and assessment of writing in China: The National Unified Entrance Examination for institutions of higher education. *Journal of Basic Writing, 7,* 47-60.

Johns, A. (1991). Interpreting an English competence exam: The frustrations of an ESL science student. *Written Communication, 9,* 379-401.

Kaplan, R.B. (1966). Cultural thought patterns in intercultural education. *Language Learning, 16,* 1-20.

Kinosita, K. (1988). Language habits of the Japanese. *English Today, 4,* 19-25.

Lee, S-Y, Stigler, J.W., & Stevenson, A.W. (1986). Beginning reading in Chinese and English. In B.R. Foorman & A.W. Siegel (Eds.), *Acquisition of reading skills* (pp. 123-150). Hillsdale, NJ: Erlbaum.

Leong, C.K. (1973). Hong Kong. In J. Downing (Ed.), *Comparative reading* (pp. 383-402). New York: Macmillan.

Leong, K.K. (1978). Learning to read in English and Chinese: Some psycholinguistic and cognitive considerations. In D. Feitelson, (Ed.), *Cross-cultural perspectives on reading and reading research* (pp. 157-173). Newark, DE: International Reading Association.

Liu, S.B.F. (1978). Decoding and comprehension in reading Chinese. In D. Feitelson, (Ed.), *Cross-cultural perspectives on reading and reading research* (pp. 144-156). Newark, DE: International Reading Association.

Norman, J. (1988). *Chinese.* New York: Cambridge University Press.

Ostler, S. (1987). English in parallels: A comparison of English and Arabic Prose. In U. Connor & R. Kaplan, (Eds.), *Writing across languages: Analysis of L2 text* (pp. 169-185). Reading, MA: Addison-Wesley.

Purves, A.C. (Ed.). (1988). *Writing across languages and cultures: Issues in contrastive rhetoric.* Beverly Hills: Sage.

Sakamoto, T. (1978). Beginning reading in Japan. In L.O. Ollila (Ed.), *Beginning reading instruction in different countries* (pp. 16-25). Newark. DE. International Reading Association.

Sakamoto, T., & Makita, K. (1973). Japan. In J. Downing (Ed.), *Comparative reading* (pp. 440-465). New York: Macmillan.

Shanghai, Zhejiang, Beijing, & Tianyin Joint Writing Group for the Design of Educational Materials. (1985). Six-year elementary school language program: Character, word, sentence, article, listen, speak, read, write. *Chinese Education, 18,* 86-99.

Sheridan, E.M., (1981, April). Literacy and language reform in the People's Republic of China. *The Reading Teacher* (pp. 804-808).

Sheridan, E.M. (1982). Early reading in Japan. *Reading World, 21,* 326-332.

Steinberg, D.D., & Yamada, J. (1978-1979). Are whole word *kanji* easier to learn than syllable *kana? Reading Research Quarterly, 24,* 88-89.

Tobin, J.J., Wu, D.Y.H., & Davidson, D.H. (1989). *Preschool in three cultures.* New Haven: Yale University Press.

Unger, J. (1977). Post-cultural revolution primary-school education: Selected texts. *Chinese Education, 10,* 4-34.

White, M. (1987). *The Japanese educational challenge.* New York: The Free Press.

Zhang, J. (1987). Thought-provoking and worrisome aspects of our primary and secondary education. *Chinese Education, 20,* 40-47.

Zhao, H. (1990). The teaching of writing in China: An overview. Paper presented at the Conference on College Composition and Communication. Chicago, IL.

Ideology in Composition:
L1 and ESL
by Terry Santos

Introduction

Although the writing component of ESL has been around as long as the field of ESL itself, its emergence as an independent area of specialization in applied linguistics, with the theoretical development and empirical research of a specialization, has come about only within the last decade. Like other areas in applied linguistics in their developing stages—second language acquisition, reading, vocabulary—ESL writing looked to and borrowed theories from its L1 counterpart. The transfer from L1 to L2 composition theory can be seen most plainly in the research and textbooks that appeared in the 1980s based on the process approach (Hughey, Wormuth, Hartfiel, & Jacobs, 1983; Leki, 1989: Raimes, 1985, 1987; Zamel, 1983).

And yet I would argue that process has not become nearly as central in ESL writing as it became in L1 composition, nor as it might have been expected to in ESL, given the tendency toward reliance on L1 theories. Rather, product-oriented or text-centered research (e.g., Connor, 1987; Hinds, 1987; Wikborg, 1985) has been as influential as, if not more so than, process research in writing and, moreover, it is not the process approach but the current-traditional paradigm that still holds sway in the ESL classroom. Admittedly, without a full-scale and much-needed empirical investigation (including classroom visits), this point is difficult to prove unequivocally: however, a look at the textbooks, the handouts, and the exams in writing courses as well as a look *in* writing classrooms themselves would very likely convince even doubters that, while lip-service may be paid to process, practice reverts

Reprinted from the *Journal of Second Language Writing, 1*(1), Santos, T., Ideology in Composition: L1 and ESL, 1992 with permission from Elsevier Science.

159

more to the older product paradigm. (For a thoughtful discussion of the gap between theory and practice in the teaching of L1 writing, see Hamilton-Wieler, 1988.) Rhetorical modes of development (e.g., classification, comparison/contrast) are still explicitly taught in many, if not most, ESL writing classes, with examples drawn from paragraph or essay models, and focus on form, e.g., via error analysis, is standard procedure. Probably the strongest effect the process approach has had on classroom instruction in ESL writing has been in the areas of drafting and revising (although from what I can tell, one-shot in-class essays are not an uncommon practice). Among the procedures unique to ESL writing instruction, on the other hand, are discussion and analysis of rhetorical differences between essays in English and in other languages, and, now and then, reformulation of ESL students' essays by either the instructor or proficient native-speaking writers so that students can examine in detail the ways in which their essays have been changed and improved by native writers.

To the extent that ESL writing *has* adopted a process-oriented theoretical approach from L1, it has done so primarily from two of the three perspectives within L1 process theory; namely, the cognitivist (e.g., Raimes, 1987) and the expressivist (e.g., Spack, 1988), while neglecting the third, the social constructionist. As Faigley (1986) and Johns (1990) have indicated, each of the three distinct perspectives in L1 process can be identified by its emphasis and its advocates. The *cognitivist* view (e.g., Flower, 1989; Flower & Hayes, 1980; Kroll, 1978) focuses on the intellectual analytical procedures involved in writing; the *expressivist* (e.g., Elbow, 1981; Moffett, 1982; Murray, 1982), stresses the personal voice in writing; and the *social constructionist* (e.g., Bizzell, 1987; Bruffee, 1973, 1986; Trimbur, 1985, 1989) sees writing as a social artifact with political as well as social implications. The social constructionist position is also commonly associated with critical theory and critical pedagogy, as represented in ESL methodology theory by Pennycook (1989) and Peirce (1989). It is this third, sociopolitical—and consciously ideological—view of writing that I will examine in this article as a contrast between L1 and L2 composition theory.

Ideology in Titles and Guidelines

To an outsider, one of the most striking features of L1 composition is the extent to which it sees itself ideologically. As Berlin has stated in tracing the fortunes of composition in higher education back to the nineteenth century, "The question of ideology has never been far from discussions of writing instruction in the modern American college" (1988, p. 477). The ideology implicit in current titles of books, journal articles, conference presentations, and the like is eye-catching: "Composing Ourselves: Politics, Commitment, and the Teaching of Writing" (Lunsford, 1990); *The Social Uses of Writing: Politics and Pedagogy* (Fox, 1990); *Writing as Social Action* (Cooper & Holzman, 1989); *The Social Construction of Written Communication* (Rafoth & Rubin, 1988); "Political Pedagogy" (Herzberg, 1988); "Rhetoric and Ideology in the Writing Class" (Berlin, 1988); "The Politics of

Change in Writing Instruction: Sources of the Mandate" (Bridwell-Bowles, 1988); "Politics and Practices in Basic Writing" (Lunsford, 1987); "Writing as an Act of Power: Basic Writing Pedagogy as Social Practice" (Perdue, 1984); "The Politics of Literacy" (Power, 1983); "The Politics of Composition" (Rouse, 1979); "The Politics of Research into the Teaching of Composition" (Lloyd-Jones, 1977).

If titles were not sufficient indication of the emphasis on the sociopolitical in L1 composition, the opening sentence of *College Composition and Communication*'s information for contributors makes it official: "*CCC* publishes articles dealing with the theory, practice, history, and *politics of composition* [italics added] and its teaching at all college levels."

In sharp contrast, almost nothing like this can be found in the literature on ESL writing, either in titles or in journal guidelines. A search of every established ESL/EFL journal—*TESOL Quarterly, Language Learning. Applied Linguistics, English Language Teaching Journal, ESP, RELC, SSLA, JALT*—over the last 10 years turns up no title linking ESL writing to sociopolitical concerns. As far as I know, only Land and Whitley's chapter "Evaluating Second Language Essays in Regular Composition Classes: Toward a Pluralistic U.S. Rhetoric" in Johnson and Roen (1989) raises these issues in regard to university ESL writing. (Two other chapters in the book also advocate a social view of writing, but their focus is on teaching ESL to children.)

That there should be this extreme of difference between L1 and L2 composition theory surely merits investigation. Incidentally, it is worth noting that, to my knowledge, only Johns (1990) has commented on the lack of attention to ideology in ESL writing and has called for a redress of the situation. Later in this article I will attempt to explain why ESL writing has ignored the ideological issues that have so engaged L1 composition. First, however, I want to look more closely at the theoretical and pedagogical manifestations of those issues in L1 composition.

Social Constructionism

Social constructionism rejects the traditional view that writing is the act of an individual mind attempting to express itself and communicate its message to a perceived audience. Rather, it assumes, in Bruffee's words, that "writing is primarily a social act" (1986, p. 784), which is different from saying that writing can always be placed in a social *context,* as expressivists and cognitivists would not deny. The difference, which in my opinion is not always clear on the theoretical level, though it is on the political and pedagogical levels, seems to turn on the relationship between the self and society. The traditional conception is of a separation between the two, whereas in the social constructionist view, they become one and the same, namely, social: "What we normally regard as individual, internal, and mental" is actually "social in origin" (Bruffee, p. 775). Thus, the individual qua individual is a fiction, for a person exists only as a member of a group, i.e., a community or society. "[I]n effect there is nowhere else the individual can be: consciousness is the extension of social experience inward" (Trimbur, 1989, p. 604).

It follows for social constructionists that regarding as exclusively social what has long been thought of as individual—denying in essence the very notion of individuality—requires a drastic reorientation of a wide range of ideas, including cognition (socially based), knowledge ("socially justified belief" dependent upon "social relations, not—reflections of reality" [Weiner, 1986, p. 52]), objectivity (impossible to achieve, since the social is naturally subjective. and therefore undesirable as a goal because hypocritical), and, what is central to this article, language. Language should not be thought of as residing in the minds of individual speakers; instead, it should be considered as originating from and constituted in the community. Speech and writing are seen as social constructs, the users of which are members of discourse communities in which form and function are understood and valued, with newcomers to the community needing to be initiated into the particular discourse prevailing within it.

Allied with social constructionist theory is a political ideology which is left-wing or Marxist in nature and which provides a major part of the pedagogical framework for the theory. It is "self-consciously aware of its ideological stand, making the very question of ideology the center of classroom activities" (Berlin, 1988, p. 478). The political tenets relevant here are that education must be understood as inherently political and ideological; therefore, "students must be taught to identify the ways in which control over their own lives has been denied them, and denied in such a way that they have blamed themselves for their powerlessness" (p. 490); the unequal power relations between student and teacher in the traditional classroom must be circumvented; and what is to be learned and the manner in which learning is to take place must be negotiated among students and between students and teacher. Social constructionism and its accompanying political ideology reinforce each other in devaluing both the idea and the importance of the individual. Trimbur (1989, p. 604) puts it this way:

> Pedagogies that take the individual as the irreducible, inviolate starting point of education—whether through individualized instruction, cultivation of personal voice, or an emphasis on creativity and self-actualization—inscribe a deeply contradictory ideology of individualism in classroom practice. If these pedagogies seek to liberate the individual, they also simultaneously constitute the student as a social atom, an accounting unit under the teacher's gaze, a record kept by the teacher. [They] prevent a class of students from transforming themselves from an aggregate of individuals into a participatory learning cornmunity.

Trimbur's indictment is clearly twofold: that of students as individuals and of teachers as authority figures. He and other social constructionists therefore advocate a pedagogy that does away with both.

Collaborative Learning

While some social constructionists, such as Berlin, advocate a Marxist "liberatory" pedagogy, the pedagogical concomitant to the theory and politics of social constructionism that has received the most attention at conferences and in journals is collaborative learning, one of whose earliest proponents was Bruffee in his 1973 article "Collaborative Learning: Some Practical Models." Since then, his ideas have been elaborated upon and refined by advocates such as Wiener (1986) and Trimbur (1989) to the point where we can now identify specific procedures associated with collaborative learning in the classroom.

Perhaps the most recognizable procedure is group work which operates through negotiation and consensus (two important terms in collaborative learning). "The group's effort to reach consensus by their own authority is the major factor that distinguishes collaborative learning from mere work in groups" (Weiner, p. 54). The teacher's role is initially to introduce the task, making sure it is an open-ended one—i.e., with no set answer or pre-conceived, favored result—and then to get out of the way in order to allow each group to work cooperatively through the task as it sees fit. It is "the process of intellectual negotiation that underwrites the consensus. The demand for consensus that's made by the task promotes a kind of social pressure ... to recognize and tolerate differences ..." (Trimbur, quoted by Wiener, p. 54). A composition class would proceed via group negotiation and consensus at every stage of the writing process, with the final product representing the group's best shared effort. The norms of language for the written product would likewise represent a consensus of judgment by the group. The social, political, and pedagogical elements of social constructionism thus come together in collaborative learning: the social nature of thought, knowledge, and language, the shift of power from the teacher to the students, and a product arrived at through negotiation and consensus within a group.

Other Views

To be sure, social constructionism and collaborative learning have not met with unmitigated enthusiasm. Some have decried the tendency toward "groupthink," while others, particularly Stewart (1990), have defended the idea of the development of the individual voice of the writer as something valuable to be encouraged and nurtured in the classroom. Sledd (1987) has labeled social constructionism self-serving, a ploy on the part of its proponents for gaining attention (and tenure) without addressing the structural bases of society. Bizzell (1988) favors collaborative learning, but cautions that it is difficult to achieve: "I do not know that anyone has yet articulated a truly collaborative pedagogy of academic literacy, one that successfully integrates the professor's traditional canonical knowledge and the students' non-canonical cultural resources." (p. 150). Still others find distasteful the political orientation of social constructionism which underlies collaborative learning. No less a figure in L1 composition than Hairston had this to say in a letter to *College English* (1990, pp. 694-96):

I have been reading *College English* with increasing irritation in the last several months, and finally I just have to protest. I find the magazine dominated by ... fashionably radical articles that I feel have little to do with the concerns of most college English teachers ... I'm also very concerned about the image of the profession I think the magazine would convey to the public if they read it (thank goodness they don't!): that of low-risk Marxists who write very badly, are politically naive, and seem more concerned about converting their students from capitalism than in helping them to enjoy writing and reading.

I don't think I'm just being captious. I hate to see the journal attempt to elevate its standing in English departments by publishing articles that are as opaque and dull as anything in *PMLA* or *Critical Inquiry.* And I'm very concerned that the process favors the young leftist radicals in the profession and leaves the mainstream behind ...

In response, Trimbur wrote (1990, pp. 699-70):

The fact of the matter is that the intellectual context of composition studies has changed over the past five or ten years as teachers, theorists, researchers, and program administrators have found useful some of the ideas and insights contained in contemporary critical theory, whether feminist, poststructuralist, neopragmatist, or neoMarxist.

What this means, moreover, is that the "mainstream" Maxine refers to isn't quite there anymore, at least not in the sense it was in the mid-seventies. Composition studies have grown, have discovered new lines of intellectual affiliation, and have differentiated internally. Because of this, there are all kinds of issues that need to be hashed out, but it doesn't help to try to curb or marginalize the leftists in our field by appealing to a now-mythical center occupied by "most of us." Some teachers, and I would include myself, do indeed want to do more than help students "enjoy writing and reading." I see writing and reading as powerful tools for students to gain greater control over their lives and to add their voices to the ongoing debate about our communal purposes.

Composition and Literature

Why has the ideology of social constructionism and collaborative learning in L1 composition received so little attention in ESL writing? The letters of Hairston and Trimbur point to one simple, if not sole, reason: L1 composition, residing mostly in English departments, has been highly influenced by critical literary theories, whereas ESL writing has identified itself as part of applied linguistics, accommodating itself to the prevailing standards of inquiry and research in that field. Their different backgrounds make L1 and L2 composition very different in their assumptions about language and the role of explicit sociopolitical ideology in theory and practice.

There is something ironic about the current influence of literary theory on L1 composition, given the time and effort specialists expended in the 70s and 80s attempting to establish composition as an independent academic field. At that time it was felt that literature and composition addressed different student audiences, had different intellectual interests, and less and less to say to each other. In a few universities composition was able to break away from its English department moorings and form its own department or writing center, but in most cases it remained uneasily housed in English, its practitioners feeling a lack of respect and understanding from the department's literature specialists. Indeed, the treatment of composition specialists by faculties of literature and what to do about it became a common theme in journals and at writing conferences.

Now, however, we read that "poststructuralism has . . . brought the two blocs closer together" (Moberg, 1990, p. 67). L1 composition and literature are discovering common ground: "the epistemological position which asserts that our use of language is what constructs society, that reality is not described in language—rather that there is no reality except as soaked in discourse" (p. 67). Sharing this view has meant that composition theorists are finding more in common with literary theorists than with practicing composition instructors. If there is a lesson here, it is that theorists across disciplines will often find better company among each other than among practitioners within their own disciplines.

A second facet of the renewed composition/literature relationship is what Clifford calls "[t]he influential resurgence of intellectual Marxism within English studies" (1989, p. 517). (English studies is understood as the umbrella term for literature, composition, and rhetoric.) Why it should be that, as Crews says, "only disaffected Western intellectuals appear capable of maintaining the faith" of Marxism (1986, p. 137) is open to informed speculation. (Crews himself offers two reasons: "Marxism retains its hold on the imagination only where it has not yet been put into effect" [p. 137] and "through the very process of forced etherealization, [it] has acquired a labyrinthine quality that suits a certain academic cast of mind" [p. 139]). Kimball (1990) claims that the student radicals of the 1960s grew up to become academics, bringing their radicalism inside, so to speak. Another factor could be that the influx into colleges and universities in the 1970s and 1980s of nontraditional students—mostly poor, minority, non-native or nonstandard dialect speakers—who were largely unprepared for academic reading and writing brought home to many English professors the social aspect of language and literacy and the inequalities thereof, a shock which radicalized some of them. In composition, the turn to the far left has been seen less charitably as the response to "the presumptively dreary though necessary labor of teaching composition" (Freedman, 1987, p. 76), that is, a way out via the more exalted mode of theory. Hairston considers "the call for . . . politicization . . . a self-serving excuse to avoid the hard job of teaching the basics" (Siegel, 1991, p. 38). Whatever the reasons, literary theory and composition have formed renewed associations based on shared theoretical and ideological positions.

Linguistics and Science

Science, on the other hand, has been virtually untouched by leftist theory, and it is partly for this reason that linguistics, applied linguistics, and TESOL, of which ESL writing is a branch, have likewise remained aloof from ideology. All three disciplines model themselves on the sciences in their research methodology, a methodology which has as its foundation an idealized adherence to neutrality and objectivity.[1] Students in linguistics, applied linguistics, and TESOL training programs are taught to regard all languages and dialects "as equals in the eyes of science" (Hymes, 1985, VI) and to engage in analyses unprejudiced by value judgments about the linguistic system, its speakers, and, by easy extension, the sociopolitical circumstances attached to the system. The more rigorously precise and objective the analysis, the better it is considered to be. The socioeconomic effects on the speakers of a nonstandard dialect or nonmainstream language may be noted as part of its description, but for the most part those effects are not dwelt on. The injunction in linguistics to be nothing but descriptive has carried over to its applied branch and to TESOL. ESL writing has, in consequence, adopted the research paradigm of applied linguistics, as can be seen in any survey of the literature, where the dominant studies on text analysis, contrastive rhetoric, and academic writing tend to be quantitative.

ESL Writing and Pragmatism

I said earlier that to a large extent L1 composition sees itself ideologically. In contrast, ESL writing may be characterized as seeing itself pragmatically. Consider, for example, Swales's (1990) explanation for avoiding ideology in his book *Genre Analysis:*

> In the case of *discourse community and genre* . . . I shall not consider differences that arise as a result of differing ideological perspectives . . . such as those found in the work of neo-Marxist and capitalist economists . . . A specific reason for this exclusion is that the proposed approach is not activated by a wish to make a contribution to intellectual history or to construct a schematic vision of disciplinary cultures, but rests on a pragmatic concern to help people, both non-native and native speakers, to develop their academic communicative competence. (p. 9)

Swales may be misconstruing the motivating force behind the ideological perspective in L1 composition, but his point about pragmatism is accurate enough. Nowhere in ESL writing can that pragmatism be better illustrated than in the work that has been done on writing in relation to English for academic purposes. Horowitz (1986b) was the first to protest against the process approach in ESL writing, charging that it fails to take into account the academic realities facing non-native-speaking students, especially their need to write essay exams under time pressure. Furthermore, the emphasis on topics of the students' choice, multiple drafts and revisions, and peer-group evaluation "create a classroom situation that bears little resemblance to the situations in which [writing] skills will eventually be exercised" (p. 144). Instead, writing teachers should help prepare students for the types of academic writing assignments they will be expected to carry out in other classes. "Realistic simulations" was his recommendation for the best approach to teaching ESL writing for academic purposes. Certainly, this approach comes with its own set of problems, as Spack (1988) has pointed out, but the pragmatic bent is clear.

Since then, studies on writing in EAP have investigated and analyzed professors' assignments (Horowitz, 1986c), professors' reactions to the writing of non-native-speaking students (Santos, 1988), the "deconstruction" (Johns, 1986) or "decoding" (Horowitz, 1986a) of assignment or exam prompts, the effects of topic types (Reid, 1990), differences in topic development (McKay, 1989), varieties of paraphrasing and summarizing (Campbell, 1990)—in short, the nuts and bolts of academic writing. Pursuing political goals and/or changing students' sociopolitical consciousness is not on the ESL writing agenda. Horowitz spoke, I think, for the majority in the field when he said, "[W]ho are we to try to change the value structures of our students?" (1986, p. 143). Compare this statement with Bizzell's (1990) from L1 composition: "We must help our students, and our fellow citizens, to engage in a rhetorical process that can collectively generate trustworthy knowledge and beliefs conducive to the common good—knowledge and beliefs to displace the repressive ideologies an unjust social order would inscribe in the skeptical void" (p. 671).

The ESL/EFL Distinction

The opposite viewpoints represented by Bizzell and Horowitz reflect another aspect of the L1/L2 split on ideology in composition, which is the EFL factor, or the difference between teaching English in the United States and teaching abroad. Bizzell's frame of reference, like that of other social constructionists, is American society—its inequalities, its exclusions, its power structure—of which she and her students are members. But teaching abroad makes critical pedagogy much more problematic. What can be defended as a right in this country is less easily defended in other countries, and part of the function of TESOL training programs is to help prepare graduates to teach English abroad, to serve as administrators of English language programs in other countries, or to train foreign teachers. These aims tend to be incompatible with explicit ideology in the classroom. Another way of putting it is that TESOL training programs tend toward the conservative because of the international and diplomatic nature of their role. This national/international difference in scope between L1 and L2 composition may also explain why a left wing with an express ideological agenda has developed in L1 composition and not in ESL. It is easier to focus on politics at the local and national levels than at the international, and L1 composition is markedly noninternational. Faigley (1986) has noted that the United States is all but alone in the world in offering L1 basic writing courses and programs at the university level, and one of the consequences of this phenomenon is a certain insularity in the L1 composition profession. This is especially noticeable to an ESL specialist used to an international flavor at TESOL conferences and conventions; at L1 writing conferences, one sees only Americans. The same holds true in the journals in the two fields. The international representation in ESL journals is taken for granted: it is nonexistent in the journals on L1 composition. There would seem to be something of a paradox operating here: that TESOL may be more conservative *because* international and L1 composition more radical because national.

The influence of EFL in TESOL may also help account for the fact that the question of students' "right" to their own language in writing has not been the source of controversy that it has in L1 composition. It is simply a given in ESL/ EFL writing that students have their native languages, and "right" has nothing to do with it. The point is how to help them become more proficient writers in English. One suggestion has been to focus explicitly on contrastive rhetoric, that is, the differences among cultures in rhetorical development and even style. Reid's (1989) matter-of-fact discussion of how writing teachers might present contrastive rhetoric in the classroom may be taken as a reflection of the typical attitude toward students' native languages:

> One way to begin raising students' awareness of U.S. academic prose is a frank discussion among teachers and students about rhetorical differences between English academic prose and the rhetoric—the presentation of written material—in the students' native languages. . . . A discussion about contrastive rhetoric, in which the teacher describes characteristics of languages and asks for feedback from students who speak that language, is a good stimulus for structuring discussions about coping strategies. (p. 223)

Two features in Reid's passage stand out: the respect accorded the student's native language and the unembarrassed assumption that learning academic writing is the goal of the class. However, a tacit third feature is also apparent: The students Reid is thinking of are familiar with writing in their native languages and come to the class with a fund of academic literacy to draw on. This is, in fact, the case in teaching writing to university-level ESL students, whether abroad or in intensive academic English programs for international students in the U.S. The fact does not make the teaching of writing to these students easier so much as it gives all involved an agreed-upon set of assumptions to operate from; moreover, it tends to favor the cognitive, problem-solving approach to writing.

L1 composition, on the other hand, is more ambivalent about the relationship between academic discourse and students' native dialects or languages, and the problem is compounded by being class-based in American society. As more students enter universities unprepared for the demands of academic reading and writing, more L1 composition instructors, whose basic writing classes the students enter, feel it is unfair to "impose" standards of academic writing on them. In 1972 a resolution was passed by the Executive Committee of the Conference on College Composition and Communication declaring students' right to their own language, a resolution which was accepted two years later by the members of the CCCC. As a mere affirmation, however, it gave no indication whatsoever of how it was meant to be enacted in the writing classroom, and the debate still goes on at conferences and in journal articles. Kutz (1986) states the dilemma thus:

> While politically we may affirm students' right to their own language, in our real concern for students and for their success in the academy we show our lack of faith in that position and return to argue for the primacy of academic discourse in our teaching . . . We want to validate our students as people and as language users, but we also want to teach them to use language in ways that support academic success, ways they do not

know when they enter our classes. We fear that validating their present language will lead them to believe anything goes, when we know that in the university and the world beyond there are rigid conventions, not only for correct usage, but for genre, style, and diverse other features they must use to be successful. Further, we know that many conventions of academic discourse are not arbitrary prescriptions, but have evolved as the clearest way to express the thinking done in various disciplines—even as a heuristic for that thinking. (p. 385)

Kutz seems to believe that "validat[ing] our students as people and as language users" is incompatible with "teach[ing] them to use language in ways that support academic success." In ESL and EFL writing this notion of incompatibility seems false. We are trying to help our students add written academic discourse to their linguistic repertoire. If by "validate," Kutz means simply basic respect, the point seems unexceptionable; however, if she means it as it is used in therapy and counseling, with its connotations of people suffering from psychological dysfunction and dependency, it seems both false and arrogant—false because it reduces students to the status of helpless victims and arrogant because it imputes more power to us than we have or should have.

Future Directions

Will ESL writing follow L1 composition in articulating a similar sociopolitical ideology? In this article I have claimed that the major influences in ESL—its scientific orientation in research, its pragmatism, and the conservatizing effect of EFL—work against a movement toward either left-wing ideology or radical pedagogy. If this analysis is correct, only features of collaborative learning would seem to have a chance of gaining a hold in ESL, not for the affiliation with social constructionist theory, but rather for the possible effectiveness of the groupwork procedures. What may counter the current prevailing influences on ESL writing, however, is a pattern I see developing in some American universities and community colleges: the blurring of the distinction between ESL writers and L1 basic writers. (The tendency is evident on a number of community college and state university campuses in California.) Increasingly, these formerly separate groups are merging into one. In many cases, the effects of bilingual education have amalgamated the two, while in other cases the various ages of arrival in the U.S. of immigrant children and their subsequent years of education here have placed them at different points on the continuum of English-language proficiency such that the cut-off between L1 and ESL is indeterminate. Finally, budget cuts in higher education could jeopardize existing ESL writing programs or cause administrators to fund just one, into which all basic writers would be placed. Possible consequences of these trends could be:

1. Specialists in L1 and L2 composition would come together to coordinate writing courses and programs.
2. The influence of L1 composition on ESL could then lead to a similar emphasis on ideology in ESL writing.

3. The fact that the students that ESL specialists would be working with would exhibit problems more in the nature of nonstandard dialects than second languages could encourage a shift in focus from the cognitive perspective on writing to the sociopolitical, as it has in L1 composition.

On the other hand, if ESL writing remains independent and/or housed in English-language institutes which serve primarily international students, sociopolitical ideology would be less likely to attract researchers and practitioners. Nor is it in any way inevitable that teaching writing to ESD (English as a second dialect) students would precipitate a move toward sociopolitical ideology among ESL specialists any more than teaching writing to ESL students has. In fact, knowledge of and experience in ESL might prove to be the strongest force against an ideological emphasis. Understanding what is involved in learning and teaching a second language or dialect should lead to greater emphasis on the cognitive, academic, and pedagogical rather than on the sociopolitical, which usually only gathers momentum when other explanations appear inadequate. It should not be overlooked, however, that a dominant paradigm in a field can come to seem explanatorily unsatisfying for a variety of reasons—including boredom—and the mere fact that ideology has so far been ignored could itself be the cause of its emergence in ESL writing. Those active in an area are the ones who chart its future course, ask the shaping questions, and provide ways of answering them. The direction in which the relatively new specialization of ESL writing will go will depend on those helping to chart its course.

Acknowledgments

I would like to thank Craig Chaudron, the two anonymous reviewers for the *Journal of Second Language Writing,* and most especially Ilona Leki and Tony Silva for their close reading of and thoughtful comments on earlier versions of this paper. Responsibility for the final product, however, rests with the author.

Notes

1. My characterization of the scientific method has been questioned by one of the anonymous reviewers of this article, by the editors of *JSLW,* and by at least one member of the audience at the University of Hawaii ESL faculty colloquium, where I presented a version of this paper. While acknowledging that my encapsulated characterization is stark, I nonetheless stand by it, in particular as it pertains to science research in the U.S. (On the whole, European scientists tend to worry more about the social, political, and economic aspects of their research.) Nothing I read about, say, gene-splicing or other forms of genetic research makes me change my mind about the dominance of scientific discovery procedures, which constitute a virtually autonomous realm. In this regard. I recall a recent conversation with a young graduate student completing her Ph.D. in biochemistry at Cal Tech who was very critical of the indifference she perceived to the connection between science research and social ramifications. I cite this anecdote because I believe it fairly represents the attitude of the research mainstream in science. For an in-depth consideration of science as dominant discourse and truth, see Aronowitz (1988).

Works Cited

Aronowitz, S. (1988). *Science as power: Discourse and ideology in modern society.* Minneapolis: University of Minnesota Press.

Berlin, J. (1988). Rhetoric and ideology in the writing class. *College English, 50,* 477-494.

Bizzell, P. (1987). What can we know, what must we do, what may we hope: Writing assessment. *College English, 49,* 575-586.

Bizzell, P. (1988). Arguing about literacy. *College English, 50,* 141-153.

Bizzell, P. (1990). Beyond anti-foundationalism to rhetorical authority: Problems defining "cultural literacy." *College English, 52,* 661-675.

Bridwell-Bowles, L. (1988). The politics of change in writing instruction: Sources of the mandate. Paper presented at the Conference on College Composition and Communication. St. Louis. MO.

Bruffee, K. (1973). Collaborative learning: Some practical models. *College English, 49,* 634-643.

Bruffee, K. (1986). Social construction, language, and the authority of knowledge: A bibliographical essay. *College English, 48,* 773-790.

Campbell, C. (1990). Writing with others' words: Using background reading text in academic compositions. In B. Kroll (Ed.), *Second language writing: Research insights for the classroom* (pp. 211-230). Cambridge, MA: Cambridge University Press.

Clifford, J. (1989). Discerning theory and politics. *College English, 51,* 517-532.

Connor, U. (1987). Argumentative patterns in student essays: Cross-cultural differences. In U. Connor & R.B. Kaplan (Eds.), *Writing across languages: Analysis of L2 text* (pp. 127-155). Reading, MA: Addison-Wesley.

Cooper, M., & Holzman, M. (1989). *Writing as social action.* Portsmouth: Boynton

Crews, F. (1986). *Skeptical engagements.* New York: Oxford University Press.

Elbow, P. (1981). *Writing with power: Techniques for mastering the writing process.* New York: Oxford University Press.

Faigley, L. (1986). Competing theories of process: A critique and a proposal. *College English, 48,* 527-542.

Flower, L. (1989). *Problem-solving strategies for writing.* (3rd ed). San Diego: Harcourt, Brace & Jovanovich.

Flower L., & Hayes, J.R. (1980). A cognitive process theory of writing. *College Composition and Communication, 31,* 365-387.

Fox, T. (1990). *The social uses of writing: Politics and pedagogy.* Norwood. NJ: Ablex.

Freedman, C. (1987). Marxist theory, radical pedagogy, and the reification of thought. *College English, 49,* 70-88.

Hairston, M. (1990). Comment. *College English, 52,* 694-696.

Hamilton-Wieler, S. (1988). Empty echoes of Dartmouth: Dissonance between the rhetoric and the reality. *The Writing Instructor, 8,* 29-41.

Herzberg, B. (1988). Political pedagogy. Paper presented at the Conference on College Composition and Communication, St. Louis, MO.

Hinds, J. (1987). Reader vs. writer responsibility: A new typology. In U. Connor & R.B. Kaplan (Eds.), *Writing across languages: Analysis of L2 text* (pp. 141-152). Reading, MA: Addison-Wesley.

Horowitz, D. (1986a). Essay examination prompts and the teaching of academic writing. *English for Specific Purposes, 5,* 197-220.

Horowitz, D. (1986b). Process, not product: Less than meets the eye. *TESOL Quarterly, 20,* 141-144.

Horowitz, D. (1986c). What professors actually require: Academic tasks for the ESL classroom. *TESOL Quarterly, 20,* 247-266.

Hughey, J.B., Wormuth, D.R., Hartfiel, V.F., & Jacobs, H.L. (1983). *Teaching ESL composition: Principles and techniques.* Rowley, MA: Newbury House.

Hymes, D. (1985). Preface. In N. Wolfson & J. Manes (Eds.), *Language of inequality* (pp. V-VIII). Amsterdam: Mouton Publishers.

Johns, A. (1986). Coherence and academic writing: Some definitions and suggestions for teaching. *TESOL Quarterly, 20,* 247-265.

Johns, A. (1990). L1 composition theories: Implications for developing theories of L2 composition. In B. Kroll (Ed.), *Second language writing: Research insights for the classroom* (pp. 24-36). Cambridge, MA: Cambridge University Press.

Kimball, R. (1990). *Tenured radicals: How politics has corrupted our higher education.* New York: Harper & Row.

Kroll, B.M. (1978). Cognitive egocentrism and the problem of audience awareness in written discourse. *Research in the Teaching of English, 12,* 269-281.

Kutz, E. (1986). Between students' language and academic discourse: Interlanguage as middle ground. *College English, 48,* 385-396.

Land, R.E., & Whitley, C. (1989). Evaluating second language essays in regular composition classes: Toward a pluralistic U.S. rhetoric. In D.M. Johnson & D.H. Roen (Eds.), *Richness in writing: Empowering ESL students* (pp. 284-293). New York: Longman.

Leki, I. (1989). *Academic writing: Techniques and tasks.* New York: St. Martin's Press.

Lloyd-Jones, R. (1977). The politics of research into the teaching of composition. *Conference on College Composition and Communication, 28,* 218-222.

Lunsford, A.A. (1987). Politics and practices in basic writing. In T. Enos (Ed.), *A sourcebook for basic writing teachers* (pp. 246-258). New York: Random House.

Lunsford, A.A. (1990). Composing ourselves: Politics, commitment, and the teaching of writing. *Conference on College Composition and Communication, 41* 71-82.

McKay, S.L. (1989). Topic development and written discourse accent. In D.M. Johnson & D.H. Roen (Eds.), *Richness in writing: Empowering ESL students* (pp. 253-262). New York: Longman.

Moberg, G. (1990). The revival of rhetoric: A bibliographic essay. *Journal of Basic Writing, 9,* 66-85.

Moffett, J. (1982). Writing, inner speech, and meditation. *College English, 44,* 231-244.

Murray, D. (1982). *A writer teaches writing.* (2nd ed). Boston: Houghton Mifflin.

Peirce, B.N. (1989). Toward a pedagogy of possibility in the teaching of English internationally. *TESOL Quarterly, 23,* 401-420.

Pennycook, A. (1989). The concept of method, interested knowledge, and the politics of language teaching. *TESOL Quarterly, 23,* 589-618.

Perdue, V. (1984). Writing as an act of power: Basic writing pedagogy as social practice. *DAI, 45,* University of Michigan.

Power S.G. (1983). The politics of literacy. In R.W. Bailey & R.M. Fosheim (Eds.), *Literacy for life: The demand for reading and writing.* New York: MLA.

Rafoth, B.A., & Rubin, D.L. (Eds.) (1988). *The social construction of written communication.* Norwood, NJ: Ablex.

Raimes, A. (1985). What unskilled ESL students do as they write: A classroom study of composing. *TESOL Quarterly, 19,* 229-258.

Raimes, A. (1987). Language proficiency, writing ability, and composing strategies: A study of ESL college student writers. *Language Learning, 37,* 439-468.

Reid, J.M. (1989). English as a second language composition in higher education: The expectations of the academic audience. In D.M. Johnson & D.H. Roen (Eds.), *Richness in writing; Empowering ESL students* (pp. 220-234). New York: Longman.

Reid, J.M. (1990). Responding to different topic types: A Quantitative analysis from a contrastive rhetoric perspective. In B. Kroll (Ed.), *Second language writing: research insights for the classroom* (pp. 191-210). Cambridge, MA. Cambridge University Press.

Rouse, J. (1979). The politics of composition. *College English, 41,* 1-12.

Santos, T.A. (1988). Professors' reactions to the academic writing of non-native-speaking students. *TESOL Quarterly, 22,* 69-90.

Siegel, F. (1991). The cult of multiculturalism. *The New Republic,* February 18, 1991, 34-40.

Sledd, J. (1987). Comment. *College English, 49,* 585-588.

Spack, R. (1988). Initiating ESL students into the academic discourse community: How far should we go? *TESOL Quarterly, 22,* 29-51.

Stewart, D.C. (1990). Comment. *College English, 52,* 689-691.

Swales, J.M. (1990). *Genre analysis: English in academic and research settings.* Cambridge, MA: Cambridge University Press.

Trimbur, J. (1985). Letter to H.S. Wiener (quoted in Wiener, 1986).

Trimbur, J. (1989). Consensus and difference in collaborative learning. *College English, 51,* 602-616.

Trimbur, J. (1990). Response. *College English, 52,* 696-700.

Wiener, H.S. (1986). Collaborative learning in the classroom: A guide to evaluation. *College English, 48,* 52-61.

Wikborg, E. (1985). Types of coherence breaks in university writing. In N.E. Enkvist (Ed.), *Coherence and composition: A symposium* (pp. 93-133). Abo, Finland: Research Institute of the Abo Akademi Foundation.

Zamel, V. (1983), The composing processes of advanced ESL students: Six case studies. *TESOL Quarterly, 17,* 165-186.

Reciprocal Themes
in ESL Reading and Writing
by Ilona Leki

Reading, like writing, begins in confusion, anxiety and uncertainty . . . it is driven by chance and intuition as well as by deliberate strategy and conscious intent . . . certainty and authority are postures, features of a performance that is achieved through an act of writing, not qualities of vision that precede such a performance. (Bartholomae & Petrosky, 1986, p. 21)

Over the last 10 to 20 years, research in L2 reading and writing has progressed almost entirely independently, yet their findings echo each other. Relying heavily on insights from L1 research and on psycholinguistic studies of reading and composing processes, L2 researchers have made extensive use of miscue, protocol, and think-aloud analyses of the reading and writing of proficient and less skilled L2 readers and writers. As a result of these studies, we have some idea of where L2 readers focus their attention as they try to make sense of a text—to what extent they predict upcoming text, what they do with unknown vocabulary, how they try to process incoming text and relate it to what they have already read (Carrell, 1983b; Clarke, 1979; Cziko, 1978; Devine, 1988; Hudson, 1982; Rigg, 1977). We also have an idea of what goes on in the minds of experienced and inexperienced L2 writers as they compose—how much they plan, how much they translate from their L1, where they focus their attention, how they handle vocabulary problems (see Krapels, 1990 for an overview of L2 writing research; Arndt, 1987; Cumming, 1989; Hall, 1990; Jones & Tetroe, 1987; Raimes, 1985; Zamel, 1983).

Often (but not always—see Raimes 1985) these studies reveal that less skilled readers and writers both appear to attend to the same thing, to the text on the page rather than to the meaning potential of that text, to the forms of the letters and words

---

Reprinted from *Reading in the composition classroom: Second language perspectives,* Leki, I., Reciprocal themes in ESL reading and writing, 1993, with permission from Thomson Learning.

rather than to the overarching connections between them. Inefficient L2 readers read too locally (Cohen, *et al.,* 1979), failing to link incoming text with previous text, and because they are unskilled in rapid text processing in L2, depend too heavily on bottom-up strategies to decode or extract the message assumed to exist in the text (Carrell, 1988b; Hosenfeld, 1984; McLaughlin, 1987; Stanovich, 1980).[1] Poor L2 writers focus excessively on word- and sentence-level grammatical and print code concerns (Arndt, 1987; Hatch, Polin, & Part, 1970; Silva, 1990).[2] All of this is to the detriment of meaning. Good readers and writers, on the other hand, are better able to focus on broader concerns related to communication.

Further parallels between cognitive research in reading and in writing indicate that proficient L2 readers and writers use strategies not hierarchically or linearly, but interactively in reading and recursively in writing (Carrell, 1983b; Zamel, 1983). The unifying characteristic of good readers and good writers seems to be flexibility, the ability to use and reuse different strategies as the moment calls for them.

The implications of this research have generally discouraged teachers from our previous focus on subskills of reading and writing, such as grammar and vocabulary, and encouraged us to focus on cognitive strategies that imitate those of proficient L1 readers and writers. Classrooms have turned toward teaching the processes of reading and writing.

Yet, oddly enough, until recently little in the L2 research literature has addressed reading and writing together, and despite the parallels between research findings in these domains and despite commonsense views that reading and writing have a reciprocal effect on each other, including the notion that good writers learn to write well in part by reading a great deal (see, however, Flahive & Bailey, this volume), adult ESL classrooms are only beginning to consider how to effectively integrate both reading and writing. We know that reading builds knowledge of various kinds to use in writing and that writing consolidates knowledge in a way that builds schemata to read with (Bereiter & Scardamalia, 1987; Sternglass, 1988). We also know that, for example, biology professors learn to write articles the way biology professors do by reading articles that biology professors have written. We do not have courses that teach biology professors to write like biology professors. Yet we continue to separate ESL reading courses from ESL writing courses.

This anomaly probably results from several causes. First, reading researchers themselves have urged that reading be taught in its own right and not be thought of as merely a skill in support of other language skills (Grabe, 1986). That is, reading should be thought of as more than merely a prompt for discussion or writing.

Second, writing pedagogy of the 1980s has also made the role of reading material in the ESL classroom unclear. In the past, readings that appeared in ESL writing textbooks were used as model texts; classes analyzed the structure of these texts, and students were instructed to pattern their own writing after those model structures (Raimes, 1986; Reid, this volume). Influenced by process approaches to writing instruction, teachers became reluctant to continue the use of texts as models because of the implication that form pre-exists content, that to write well students needed only to pour their content into the model forms exemplified in the reading passages. The role of reading in the writing classroom became somewhat uncertain. Were readings to be used as source material for student writing, as stimulus for ideas? How were writing teachers to treat those reading texts? Were writing teachers being asked to teach reading at the same time as writing? (See Kroll, this volume, for the argument that L2 writing teachers must also be reading teachers.) No systematic approach or consensus on how to use nonfiction readings in ESL writing classrooms has yet emerged. Up to now, discussion in the literature on using readings in writing classrooms has primarily revolved around making a case for teaching fiction (Gajdusek, 1988; Mlynarczyk, 1992; Spack, 1985).

A third reason functioning to keep reading instruction out of the advanced ESL writing classroom is related to the structure of higher education in this country. Although native English speakers take courses in freshman composition (often without readings in support of writing), reading courses are considered remedial for native students (Bartholomae & Petrosky, 1986) and as a result are typically also unavailable for nonnatives except in language institutes.[3] It is assumed that ESL students at advanced levels are already reading well independently. (See Blanton, this volume, on the error of this view.) After all, these students are reading a great deal in other content-area classes. But difficulty and inefficiency in reading are easily dissimulated. This effort is hidden from us and from our content-area colleagues. While we see and hear about our students' problems in writing, their reading problems may remain invisible, implying no problem exists.

Finally, however problematic, exit exams in writing are quite common in colleges and universities, prompting the development of writing courses to prepare students for them; this is not the case in reading.[4] As a result, we have advanced ESL writing courses but do not typically teach reading beyond the level of language institutes despite the fact that ESL students report a greater need for proficiency in reading than in any other English language skill at the university level (Carrell, 1988a; Christison & Krahnke, 1986).

The unfortunate separation of reading and writing has impoverished instruction in both domains. Without readings in ESL writing classrooms, teachers tend to rely heavily on expressivist writing assignments based on personal experience or previous knowledge (Bazerman, 1980; Horowitz, 1986b; Spack, 1988). While this form of writing is valuable, it is limited and not the type of writing typically required from ESL students in higher education (Horowitz, 1986a; Johns, 1981; Reid, 1987). Reading, a major source of new knowledge, is ignored, and students are not called upon to develop the ability to select and integrate new knowledge with knowledge and information they already possess and with their analyses and reactions to that new knowledge and information. It is this ability to integrate or internalize new information in writing that undergirds the notions both of knowledge-transforming (Bereiter and Scardamalia, 1987) and of critical literacy (Flower et al., 1990) and may in fact be what we actually mean when we speak of comprehension of a text.

Writing pedagogy in the 1980s and 1990s has remained fairly closely in line with writing research, having undergone an enormous change in the 1980s, a virtual paradigm shift, as teachers abandoned remedial models of writing instruction and incorporated research insights into their classroom. While L2 reading research has produced insights as far-reaching as those of writing research, its impact on textbooks and classrooms has been less noticeable (Grabe, 1986). Schema theory and the notion of top-down processing of text did inspire the successful incorporation of pre-reading activities into many reading classrooms (Anderson & Pearson, 1984; Carrell & Eisterhold, 1983; Goodman, 1976). But to judge by textbooks and peda-gogical articles on reading in the 1980s, researchers' exploration of the notion of the interactive nature of reading (Rummelhart, 1977; Stanovich, 1980) has had an al-most negligible impact (Grabe, 1986). As a result, the unfortunate effect of teaching reading and writing in separate courses has had dramatic consequences on reading instruction, robbing reading of its natural purpose and ignoring its social dimen-sions. The rest of this chapter will explore the implications of this situation, touch-ing on a number of themes that will be taken up again more specifically in the subsequent chapters of this book.

Isolated Reading Classes: Reading for no Real Reason

The research literature in L2 emphasizes the importance of purpose in both writ-ing and reading (Eskey, 1986; Kroll, 1991). In recent writing instruction, purpose for writing has become a central focus. Many classrooms now include, for exam-ple, unevaluated writing journals in which students can freely explore topics of personal interest to them and from which they may select entries to develop into full essays (Blanton, 1987; Spack & Sadow, 1983). Writing on topics selected in this manner goes a long way toward ensuring the kind of internal motivation for writing which presumably results in the commitment to task which, in turn, is thought to help writing and language improve. But the immediate purpose for writing about a particular subject is neither language nor even writing improve-ment. It is, rather, a more natural purpose, i.e., communication with a reader about something of personal significance to the writer. The emphasis on publishing stu-dent writing grows from the same belief in the importance of purpose; if a piece is to be published, a student has far more reason to feel intellectually committed to the writing, to both the content and form of the text. Finally, the entire thrust of writing instruction within an English for Specific Purposes context rests on the belief that students should learn to write what they will need to write and in the way they will need to write within the academic disciplines they have chosen (Horowitz, 1986a; Reid, 1987).

The literature on reading has also pointed out that readers read for different pur-poses and that those purposes affect what is attended to and with what intensity (Eskey, 1986). This concern with purpose has emerged in the L2 reading classroom most clearly in pre-reading questions intended to lend direction to reading by giving students something to read for. But this understanding of purpose is extremely nar-row. Certainly, having a purpose for reading a text should make that text easier to read, but that avoids the real question: Why is this text being read in the first place? While it is axiomatic that our L2 students learn to read by reading, it appears that in L2 reading classes this axiom has been inappropriately reversed: the reason for reading a text is to learn to read. Yet as Flower *et al.* (1990) point out,

Literacy, as Richardson, Vygotsky, and others have defined it, is not synonymous with the ability to read (decode) or write (transcribe) per se. Rather it is a "goal-directed, context-specific" behavior, which means that a literate person is able to use reading and writing in a transactional sense to achieve some purpose in the world at hand. . . . (p. 4)

The failure to provide real purposes for reading suggests that in isolated L2 reading classes (i.e., ones in which students are not reading to write), students are not reading but merely practicing reading. This "reading practice" is evident in reading selections and in pedagogical focuses in L2 reading classrooms.

Text Selection

The reading material used in many ESL reading classes both reveals and furthers the distortion of the reading class into the reading practice class. Since isolated reading classes serve no other purpose than to teach reading, there is no particular reason to read one text rather than another. In line with that reasoning, then, most readings in L2 reading classes are short texts on a variety of topics that are thought to be of high interest to our students: pollution, friendship, language, cultural differences, education, the role of women in various cultures.[5]

Short texts are selected because they conveniently fit into our class periods better than long texts, they take less time to read, and they are thought to be easier to read than longer texts. But short texts are, in fact, likely to be more difficult to read since students never read enough about the subject to build the knowledge about it that would allow them to read with ease and pleasure. (See Sternglass, 1988 on the issue of knowledge building for the purpose of knowledge making.) Like our students, we allow our intuitions to lead us astray—when our students have trouble reading, they slow down and try to decode the text word for word, operating locally, microscopically, and hoping that by simplifying and separating, they will later be able to add up all the pieces and understand. When confronted with students having difficulties reading, we have the same reaction: to break up the reading, go microscopic, and give students shorter, "easier" texts to read (Bartholomae & Petrosky, 1986).

Furthermore, we select a variety of subject matters to maintain student interest and motivation and, ostensibly, to focus attention on content. We hope that by using a shotgun approach to subject matter we will eventually hit upon at least one subject of interest to each of our students. That may or may not happen, but the result of constant shifts in subject matter is once again the same: The texts are harder to read because the students must gear up for a new subject with each reading selection. This approach to reading material also denies our students the eye-opening experience readers have when they return to a text read earlier with new knowledge structures born of reading other texts on the same subject (see Spack, this volume). The original text now literally means something new to the reader; the meaning of sections of text previously blurred by misunderstanding is clarified through the lens of new knowledge. But the possibility for such growth is eliminated by asking students to switch their attention from pollution to animal behavior to education with each new chapter.

Finally, there is the question of high interest. It is possible to argue that the subjects typically covered in ESL readers are of high interest to teachers and textbook writers, but not particularly to L2 students. The topics *might* be of high interest if these students could already read them as easily as *we* read them. But L2 reading is a struggle, and these subjects are unlikely to be of high enough personal interest to our students to compensate for the burden created by asking students to read a hodge-podge of subjects for no particular reason except to learn to read English better. (See Kroll, this volume, for a glimpse into a classroom using such an approach.) This approach to teaching reading resembles writing classes of ten years ago, when teachers struggled to divine what might be interesting, motivating topics for students to write on and came up with such assignments as "Describe your most embarrassing moment." Even if we locate high interest readings, as Bartholomae & Petrosky (1990) maintain, the issue is less what students read (i.e., the discovery of the perfect text) than what they then *do* with what they read, how we ask them to engage that text.

Pedagogical Practices

One source of the problems in isolated reading classes is confusion about what we can accomplish. If we are convinced by evidence that pleasure reading contributes to L2 reading and writing proficiency (Elley & Mangubhai, 1983; Hafiz & Tudor, 1989; Krashen, 1988, 1984; van Naerssen, 1985), one goal of a reading class might be to promote pleasure reading. Unfortunately, this goal is unrealistic; for all but the most proficient of our students, L2 reading is too difficult a chore to be engaged in simply for pleasure (Janopoulos, 1986), and to build proficiency in reading strictly through pleasure reading takes time our ESL students may not have.

Our goal then becomes to attempt to preempt reading difficulties by teaching generic strategies for reading *any* text. Our teaching strategy has been to examine the cognitive processes of proficient readers, those who presumably do read a great deal for pleasure, to isolate the strategies they use, and to teach these strategies to our students. We find that proficient readers do not read all texts in an invariable, plodding pace from word to word, dictionary in hand, as some of our less proficient students do. Instead, they skim some texts or sections of text, they scan, they read in chunks rather than word for word, they note cohesion markers, they guess vocabulary meaning from context, and they read fast (Grabe, 1986). So we direct our students to imitate these behaviors and practice skimming, scanning, guessing, and chunking texts; we tell them not to use dictionaries; we give them practice recognizing cohesion markers; and we push them to read fast (Eskey & Grabe, 1988).

The problem with teaching these cognitive strategies is that even if our students accomplish these goals, they are still not learning reading; they are learning strategies for reading, which can at best be only imitations of reading behaviors, like children turning the pages of books they cannot yet read. We seem to have assumed that these strategies are the causes of proficiency in reading. But these strategies are the *result* not the cause of reading proficiency; good readers read fast because they can. They are able to comprehend incoming text quickly. If our students use dictionaries and read slowly with an even amount of attention to every word, they do this because this is all they *can* do. They do *not* comprehend; they do not know which words are essential to meaning and which may be passed over.[6] If proficient readers skim some texts, they do so because the text, as they themselves judge it for their own internally motivated purposes, merits no more careful reading. The answer to the question of which texts should be skimmed, which scanned, which words looked up in the dictionary, or which texts abandoned altogether is determined by the reader's purpose in reading. If the purpose in reading is only to practice reading, there can be no internally motivated answers to these questions. With no purpose for reading, then skimming, scanning, or any of the other strategies we teach all become no more than artificial exercises. By taking over control of their reading through post-reading exercises and telling our students which texts to skim, which information to scan for, and how fast to read, we are preventing the very grappling with meaning that would allow students to develop their own strategies for rapid and accurate text processing. (See Devine, this volume, for discussion of the interaction between goal setting, or purpose, and metacognition.)

The problems inherent in teaching strategies to improve reading devoid of any true purpose for reading are exacerbated by textbooks that direct students to practice these techniques thoroughly, that is, with every, or nearly every, text in the book. Despite the research findings that good readers read for varying purposes and with varying degrees of attention, isolated reading courses tend in fact to direct students to do the opposite, to regard each reading selection addressed in class as equally important and eligible for similar analysis. Again we see clear parallels with the kinds of discredited writing instruction practices in which every text students write is taken to be a final draft and then corrected and evaluated.

Another nearly universal pedagogical practice in L2 reading classrooms is post-reading comprehension checks, often aimed, like standardized reading tests, at checking comprehension by asking students to identify the main idea of a text or passage. But this enterprise is problematic. First, knowing the main idea of a text does not mean understanding the text. Second, questioning students about the main idea does absolutely nothing to *show* students how to achieve comprehension, whether or not they can successfully spot the same main idea we spot. Finally, pointing out that our students' version of the main idea is or is not the same as ours, far from helping our students achieve understanding, does not even help our students identify the main idea! It is not clear that we even know exactly how we determine what the main idea of a text is. (See Parry, 1987 for an interesting discussion of factors that may have influenced a group of West African students in their construction of the meaning of a text.) If we do not know how we ourselves recognize the main idea of a text, we cannot teach it to our students and end by merely mystifying them. Yet there seems to be almost an obsession with main ideas in reading pedagogy and testing that is reminiscent of the previous exaggerated interest in topic sentences in writing and that represents a reductionist view of reading. By relying so heavily and confidently on comprehension and main idea questions, we seem to be defining—and encourage our students to define—text comprehension as correct responses to comprehension questions. Yet, many would argue that the only way to demonstrate comprehension is through extended discourse where readers become writers who articulate their understandings of and connections to the text in their responses. Response is, then, an expression and explanation of comprehension; and comprehension means using writing to explicate the connections between our models of reality—our prior knowledge—and the texts we recreate in light of them. (Petrosky, 1982, pp. 24-25, discussing David Bleich)

Typical comprehension checks also imply that the meaning of a text resides in the text and that the students' goal is to ferret out the meaning the author put there. This implication is out of tune with the notions, so pervasive in current reading research, of reading as the construction, not the deciphering, of meaning and of reading as interaction between reader and text, in which meaning depends as much on what the reader brings to the text as what the text brings to the reader. The usual comprehension check denies the role of the reader in constructing meaning. Yet Tierney & Pearson (1983) assert that "there is no meaning on the page until a reader decides there is" (p. 569).

Furthermore, exactly what do our students gain by correctly identifying the main idea in an ESL textbook article on dreams or friendship? What difference does it make if the student correctly or incorrectly identifies the same main idea as the teacher? In natural reading contexts, proficient and even less skilled readers reading for a real-world purpose not only skim, scan, or chunk for their own purposes, but they also choose to privilege either main ideas or details of a text, again depending on their purpose in reading. In a given text read by a specific reader in a real-world context, the main idea may or may not be significant. The reader may retain only a striking image or line of reasoning, or even, as is often the case with academic readers, only a citation or reference to another text. But if the purpose for reading a text is to practice reading, then students have no basis on which to privilege main ideas or details. By persistently imposing a check for comprehension of main ideas, we may in fact be training our students to read in ways characteristic of poor readers, bound to the text and lacking the purpose that would allow them to skip over information they themselves judge uninteresting or unnecessary.

Thus on one hand, a leveling process takes place such that all the texts read are given equal attention and therefore equal weight, and on the other hand, a selection process occurs whereby someone besides the reader decides what should be salient to the reader. If that which resonates for the student does not match the main idea of the text, the importance of the student's encounter with the text is undermined and the student's reading is dismissed as a failure to understand.

Attempting to Teach What Cannot be Taught

Perhaps one difficulty with the entire enterprise of teaching the construction of meaning, whether in reading or in writing, is that although it can be learned, in some important, very real sense, it cannot be taught (see Eskey, 1986). Perhaps we are unwilling to believe this. Perhaps it is because we feel we need to teach *something* in isolated reading classes that we have typically turned to teaching not reading, not text comprehension or meaning construction, but reading strategies and study skills.

One of the complaints in the early 1980s against traditional approaches to teaching L2 writing was that students were not really writing but rather manipulating language, not using language to communicate but rather to practice grammar or to practice larger components of written texts, such as rhetorical patterns (Kroll, 1991). In traditional approaches to teaching writing, we assumed that by teaching students to write a topic sentence, to select and explain three examples, and to write a conclusion, we had given students all the building blocks necessary to create virtually any expository text (Kroll, 1991).

Don't we see the same kinds of narrowly focused aims in current traditional reading courses, aims of learning vocabulary by studying prefixing and suffixing, aims of identifying main idea and supporting details, aims of recognizing discourse features? Certainly, the ability to recognize discourse features and a large number of vocabulary items helps make reading easier, but if these abilities are set as the goals for the course rather than as a means of facilitating the reading of specific texts selected for a real purpose, we are back to teaching skills. More sophisticated ones, to be sure, but for all their sophistication, they still do not get to the heart of the question of how to help L2 students read.

Ironically, it may be that both proficient and less skilled L2 readers already have and can make use of the entire gamut of skills that we teach in reading classes but use these skills to different degrees in L2 reading (Sarig, 1987). L2 reading classes may not even *need* to teach skills, which L2 readers may already possess, but could provide the opportunity for L2 readers to discover *through meaningful contact with L2 texts* which combination of skills works best for them in L2.

In the 1980s, we recognized that if the purpose of writing in a writing class is to practice writing in order to get ready for "real" assignments, students were being seriously handicapped in the development of their ability to decide what to write and how to write it. As long as reading classes have no other purpose than to develop skills, to practice reading, or to learn language, attempts to get students to read with real direction are similarly doomed. The reading class becomes a hothouse, self-referential and solipsistic, in which students spend all their time rehearsing and never performing, getting ready to read while real reading is deferred. (See Blanton, this volume, on reading as performance.) When we teach a reading or writing course as a skills course, we act as though real reading and writing will come later, once our students know where to look for the main idea of a text or how to write a topic sentence. But it makes no sense to defer real reading and writing until students are adequately prepared, because adequate preparation is itself a result of a purposeful plunge into the struggle with meaning.

Reading researchers, paralleling writing researchers, have for years indicated that reading instruction must be more concerned with meaning and less with skills. For over 20 years in the literature on teaching reading to native speakers, researchers have been calling for a focus on meaning (Goodman, 1976; Smith, 1971); for 10 years in the L2 literature (Carrell, 1983a; Hudson, 1982), researchers have emphasized the importance of text content over reading skills. Yet as lately as the December 1989 *TESOL Quarterly,* Carrell, Pharis, & Liberto must again call for approaches to teaching reading, including semantic mapping and ETR, which will aid students not in developing skills and strategies with which to confront *any* text, but in comprehending specific texts.[7] Hudson (1991) makes a similar plea for ESL reading. Isolated L2 reading classes seem to have allowed us to get lost in details, not of decoding skills as in the past, but of main idea hunting and learning word suffixes and prefixes, and to lose sight of reading as a purposeful, real-world activity.

The benefits of integrating L2 reading and writing in the same classroom thus seem undeniable and, since reading and writing draw upon the same cognitive text world (Carson, this volume; Kucer, 1985), reciprocal. The chapters of this book detail the ways in which reading in the composition classroom sustains writing.

But writing, even beyond providing a purpose for reading, clearly also enhances reading. Anticipating in writing the content of a text, i.e., writing before reading (Spack, 1990), primes schemata and thereby facilitates reading a text. Interacting with the content of a text by annotating and engaging the text in dialogue brings home more clearly the reader's own understanding of the text, for it is often through the pressure of new or opposing ideas that our own ideas may become clear to us, just as it is often by expressing the ideas of others in our own words (in effect, translating them), that these other or new ideas begin to have meaning. Writing is a way of reading better "because it requires the learner to reconstruct the structure and meaning of ideas expressed by another writer. To possess an idea that one is reading about requires competence in regenerating the idea, competence in learning how to write the ideas of another" (Squire, 1983, cited in Sternglass, 1986, p. 2). (See Zamel, 1992, for a further discussion of writing to read.) Furthermore, as a student engages a reading text by responding or reacting to it in writing, in effect communicating with the writer through text, the essentially social nature of literacy becomes unmistakable.

Social Acts of Reading and Writing

Research on cognitive processes has had tremendous influence on reading and writing theory, on writing pedagogy, and to some degree on reading classroom practice. But writing classrooms have counterbalanced this emphasis on cognitive processes with an awareness of the social dimension of writing. Writing classrooms have, for example, been much concerned with audience, the discourse communities into which we hope to initiate our students as writers. The recognition of the social dimension of writing has also become commonplace in writing classrooms in the form of peer responding, which has helped to break down the isolation of the individual author and to work against the very notion of individual authorship (Allaei & Connor, 1990; Leki, 1990b; Mittan, 1989).

Like writing, reading is not only a cognitive process. It is intricately bound up in a social, historical, and cultural network, one we are only beginning to explore (Carson, 1992). As readers, we are members of discourse communities formed primarily through reading the same texts. It is this broad social dimension of reading that allows us teachers and textbook writers to agree on the main idea of a text, for example, and to make assertions about textual misinterpretations we think our students make. If we agree on the main idea of a text, it is not because the main idea mechanically signals itself in the text (it is obviously not always the last sentence of the introduction or the first sentence of some fixed paragraph), but because we share the writer's discourse community. An important key to helping our students read better may also lie in clearer classroom recognition of this social dimension of reading.

But reading is also an essentially social activity in the more immediate sense that the text is where a specific reader and writer meet. Reader response theory describes text as the locus of struggle over meaning, suggesting the importance not of the text (where meaning does *not* reside) but of the encounter between individual human beings mediated through the text (Dasenbrock, 1991; Fish, 1980; Nystrand, 1989; Robinson, 1991; Rubin, 1988). L2 reading research, particularly in an interactive view of reading, also does not locate meaning in the text and has shown us repeatedly that the meaning of a given text depends on who is reading it (Anderson *et al.*, 1977; Carrell, 1983a; Parry, 1987; Steffenson & Joag-Dev, 1984). Each reader's reading of a text is somewhat different. Different readings are created not only by different readers but also over time. Thus the Shakespeare we read today is not and cannot be the same work that people read in Shakespeare's time. (See Dasenbrock, 1991 for the L1 debate about the ontological status of historical texts.) In fact, we count on that very fluidity of meaning over time when we advise students to leave a draft aside for a few days before rereading it for revision.

Yet despite this recognition of the instability of meaning, we often seem to entertain only in theory the idea that meaning does not reside in the text. In practice, our insistent privileging of cognitive strategies betrays our view of the text as a puzzle. If meaning did reside in the text, then well-honed cognitive strategies would be sufficient to unravel meaning. But a text is not a puzzle or a dictator; it is a partner in a dialogue, in a negotiation. Yet little is done to give students practice in negotiating meaning mediated by text or to foster the notion that meaning is created by the interaction of a specific reader and a text. In our reading classes a single, privileged interpretation of a text dominates, as is made clear by post-reading comprehension checks with their predetermined answers, ones that the teacher knows and the students must guess.

Ironically, this cognitive bias may be increased by reading theory's current view of reading as interactive, locating meaning in the interaction between the reader and the text, but with no clear role for the writer. The interactive view does, however, leave room for a social dimension in terms of the individual reader's formation as a social being. Schema theory, on which interactive views of reading are based, clearly views schema formation as the result of individual experience *within* a social context. (See, for instance, Anderson *et al.*, 1977, Flynn, 1983, Kintsch & Greene, 1978, and Steffenson & Joag-Dev, 1984 for descriptions of different stances taken before texts by different genders and sociocultural groups.)

Nevertheless, we seem consistently to ignore the social dimension of reading. The usual practice in our reading classrooms, for example, has worked against the idea of the classroom as an interpretive community and instead often sends our students home to read, alone, already published texts, by authors they do not know, writing about settings with which they are not familiar. Significantly, it is only when they return to class that they learn, from the teacher, how well their personal struggle with the text went. Certainly, the struggle with meaning is internal, and cognitive, but this struggle can also be made external, public, and social. By so doing, we can balance the action of individual cognition with the power of social interaction to shape and restructure meaning.

On the Brink of a Change:
The Transactional Reading/Writing Classroom

While the attitudes and activities described above persist in reading classes, we seem now to be on the brink of a shift in reading pedagogy similar to the one that oc-curred in writing over the last ten years and at least partly occasioned by the growing interest, of which this volume is evidence, in bringing reading systematically into writing classrooms. If we use reading and writing reciprocally in L2 classrooms, fo-cusing less on teaching language, reading, or writing and more on allowing students to engage intellectually with text, this engagement with text fosters a view of reading and writing as active construction of meaning. The text can now legitimately be read with varying degrees of attention since the text has peaks and valleys of importance for the reader; comprehension of each section of the text is no longer necessary; the significance of main ideas and details becomes clearer as the student determines which ones further his or her purposes; structures of knowledge are built that can be used to read/write other texts on the same subject; and the student reader/writer must come to terms with the transformation of old knowledge and incorporation of new knowledge into existing schemata (Bereiter & Scardamalia, 1987). Most importantly, teaching reading in the composition classroom no longer defers real reading until the future; reading is done for present, legitimate purposes.

Reading in composition classrooms may also give reading a social dimension that we have ignored by operating as though reading can only be individual and by directing our students to read at home alone and then answer questions about the text. Our students' facility in reading need not improve only through reading pub-lished texts. By reading each other's texts in a reading/writing class, students di-rectly confront the elusive, slippery nature of meaning. A writer intends a meaning; a reader perceives something else. When the reader and writer are face to face (es-pecially with the support of a teacher's expert guidance), a real negotiation over meaning can take place.

If we are convinced by an interactive view of reading, we need to permit and en-courage our students to become more active in reading—not merely to be led by the text, but to make it their own by responding to whatever is salient *to them* rather than merely pursuing the writer's meaning. This means that for some texts, the author's main idea may be entirely irrelevant to the reader's purpose and will play no role in the reader's use of the text. In this way we might see the metaphor of interactive as extending beyond its cognitive dimension, i.e., beyond the idea that both top-down and bottom-up strategies interact in reading. In a reading/writing class, interactive takes on a transactional meaning, implying an essential interface of reading and writing (Sternglass, 1986), by which we understand (1) that reading and writing in-teract, or function reciprocally; (2) that the reader can interact more actively with the text by viewing reading as dialogic and by writing to the text (responding to it, for example, with notes in the margin or in a reading journal); and (3) that in reading, the reader is also interacting with a writer who wrote for genuine purposes of communication.

In many writing classrooms these days, students read each other's writing and respond to it to help the writer improve that draft. In a reading/writing classroom, this activity can take on a new role, not only the one of various kinds of text repair or editing but of students using each other's writing as sources for their own writing, considering and addressing their classmates' points of view, and citing each other, not only published work, in their bibliographies.

Even with published texts, by reading them together in groups and interpreting as they go, students witness competing meanings and clarify their own understandings through discussion, debate, and the need to translate their understandings into their own words. By ultimately forming joint interpretations of their readings rather than learning from the teacher what the meaning of a text is, students experience the social dimension inherent in communicating through a text, a dimension too long neglected in ESL reading instruction. By making reading social, we externalize the process and demonstrate, or allow students to demonstrate to each other, that reading is meaning construction, that competing meanings are generated by texts read by different people or even by the same people at different times. (See Section III of this volume, on Social Perspectives, for further examples of ESL reading instruction that aims at these goals.)

The notion of meaning as negotiation and text as the locus of struggle suggests another insight that current views on writing may have to offer reading specialists. In post-reading comprehension questions, reading classrooms maintain an emphasis on error that many writing classrooms have chosen to downplay. Writing research has emphasized the futility and the negative, stifling effect of marking all the errors L2 students make in writing (Leki, 1990a; Zamel, 1985). As writing specialists tried to come to terms with the problem of errors in L2 students' writing, it became increasingly clear that it makes more sense to focus on what students can do well, rather than constantly reminding them of what they know they cannot do well, and to intervene in their writing process to help them do what they cannot do. In many writing classes these days, students show their drafts to others, including the teacher, as the drafts are developing in order to get guidance and feedback on their writing. Most writing teachers are convinced of the value of that kind of intervention. How might such an attitude be adopted in reading instruction in order to promote the goals of helping L2 students learn to read with ease, pleasure, and understanding? How can we intervene in our students' reading processes?

In a first step, again by analogy to procedures in writing classes in which teachers refuse to appropriate their students' writing, reading teachers might consider refraining from appropriating the meaning of the texts their students read. In other words, in helping students read, the question should not be "What is the author saying here? What is the author's main idea?" but rather "What did you get out of this? What do you make of this part? How does it happen that different class members understand this text differently?" While students lose little by not getting the main idea of an ESL reading passage about dreams or animal behavior, they gain a great deal if they are able to make some portion of that text their own, linguistically, rhetorically, or conceptually.

A de-emphasis of error also implies our acceptance of the idea that our students cannot understand everything they read and that they do not need to. They need to read actively and selectively, picking out what they can use to advance their own agendas. Furthermore, since any individual act of understanding is a reconstruction and in that sense necessarily a misreading (see Bartholomae, 1986), we must also accept that our students will not interpret texts the same way we do.[8] But negotiating through their understandings of a text with other students requires the struggle with meaning that leads to the ability to engage in constructing meaning with power and confidence.

We can also make our own struggle with meaning visible by letting students see our reading processes. Many writing teachers write with their students and share their drafts to demonstrate their writing processes (Spack, 1984). In teaching reading we might consider doing more reading out loud in our classes and doing so in a way that demonstrates our reading processes, thinking aloud as we read, as subjects are asked to do in protocol analyses (Davey, 1983). Rather than only giving individual students individual exercises in chunking, we might show them by reading out loud how we ourselves chunk groups of words together, how we use intonation to get us through heavy embedding, how we backtrack when we have lost the thread of the text, how we ignore incongruities or puzzling words for as long as possible before interrupting the flow of our reading, and, most importantly, how we work to tie the incoming text to patterns of information we already know. To help our students read faster, instead of timing them and pushing them to read faster individually, by reading out loud we keep them to a brisker pace than they might normally adopt when reading silently, and yet through intonation, pauses, and backtracking we also give them additional cues on how we are interpreting a text. By the same token, like writing conferences, reading conferences in which individual students reveal and demonstrate their reading processes to us may also uncover unproductive or self-defeating approaches to reading and allow us to intervene directly in the students' construction of meaning from a text.

Conclusion

While the research findings in reading and writing echo each other, teaching practices have not kept pace with each other, especially not in helping advanced ESL students read. The separation of reading from writing may be the result of our natural inclination to divide things up in order to deal with them, or it may be that the inclination to divide language up is a legacy of the ALM days, but, as this volume demonstrates, the time seems to have come for a new reintegration of reading and writing classrooms rather than a division of language into atomized, learnable bits or skills. The fact that reading and writing processes can be isolated does not mean that teaching those isolated processes is the best way to help our students read and write with greater ease. The construction of meaning, whether through reading or writing, is a messy, organic, and holistic task, perhaps less amenable to generic attempts to preempt problems than we once thought. Bringing the world of text together in one classroom gives every promise of enhancing our ESL students' ability to both read and write English through the cross-fertilization of reading and writing pedagogy, research, and theory.

Notes

1. Evidence from studies of inefficient L1 readers also shows the opposite tendency, excessive and inaccurate guessing about the meaning of a text without enough bottom-up information (Kimmel & MacGinitie, 1984).
2. The picture is actually more complex than this. L1 studies consistently show this pattern of allotting attention (Bereiter & Scardamalia, 1987; Perl, 1979), but at least one L2 study shows that even less-proficient writers also attend to meaning (Raimes, 1985).
3. Among the odd historical divisions within higher education in this country, we might also mention the division in English departments between literature and writing instruction, in certain ways analogous to the division between writing and reading courses: the first in each pair considered more prestigious and more appropriately a concern of higher education.
4. This is not to suggest in any way that there should be exit exams in reading. The wisdom of exit exams in writing is already questionable enough.
5. ESP, adjunct, and sheltered writing courses are the exceptions to this pattern.
6. In the same way, excessive attention to details in inexperienced writers is the symptom, not the cause, of difficulty with the task.
7. These techniques have been used for some time to teach reading to native English speaking children. For more information on these techniques, see Heimlich & Pittelman (1986), Stahl & Vancil (1986), and Au (1979).
8. It is interesting to note that in certain domains, such as in reading literature, idiosyncratic readings are often prized as more illuminating than pedestrian interpretations of a text. What we admire in the best literary critics and the best scientists is not that they understand texts well but that they extend our understanding of the meaning of a text by moving beyond the standard interpretation rendered by the discourse community for which it is intended.

Works Cited

Allaei, S.K. & Connor, U.M. (1990). Exploring the dynamics of cross-cultural collaboration in writing classrooms. *The Writing Instructor, 10,* 19-28.

Anderson, R.C. & Pearson, P.D. (1984). A schema-theoretic view of basic processes in reading comprehension. In P.D. Pearson (Ed.), *Handbook of reading research* (pp. 255-287). New York: Longman.

Anderson, R.C., Reynolds, R.E., Schallert, D.L., & Goetz, E.T. (1977). Frameworks for comprehending discourse. *American Educational Research Journal, 14,* 367-381.

Arndt, V. (1987). Six writers in search of texts: A protocol-based study of L1 and L2 writing. *ELT Journal, 41,* 257-267.

Au, K.H.-P. (1979). Using the experience-text-relationship method with minority children. *The Reading Teacher, 32,* 677-679.

Bartholomae, D. (1986). Wanderings: Misreadings, miswritings, misunderstandings. In T. Newkirk (Ed.), *Only connect: Uniting reading and writing* (pp. 89-118). Upper Montclair, NJ: Boynton/Cook.

Bartholomae, D. & Petrosky, A., (1990). *Ways of reading.* New York: St. Martin's.

Bartholomae, D. & Petrosky, A., (1986). *Facts, artifacts, and counterfacts: A reading and writing course.* Upper Montclair, NJ: Boynton/Cook.

Bazerman, C. (1980). A relationship between reading and writing: The conversational model. *College English, 41,* 656-661.

Bereiter, C. & Scardamalia, M., (1987). *The psychology of written composition.* Hillsdale, NJ: Erlbaum.

Blanton, L. (1987). Reshaping students' perceptions of writing. *ELT Journal, 41,* 112-118.

Carrell, P.L. (1988a). Introduction. In P.L. Carrell, J. Devine, & D. Eskey (Eds.), *Interactive approaches to second language reading* (pp. 1-7). New York: Cambridge University Press.

Carrell, P.L. (1988b). Some causes of text-boundedness and schema interference in ESL reading. In P.L. Carrell, J. Devine, & D. Eskey (Eds.), *Interactive approaches to second language reading* (pp. 101-113). New York: Cambridge University Press.

Carrell, P.L. (1983a). Some issues in studying the role of schemata, or background knowledge, in L2 comprehension. *Reading in a Foreign Language, 1,* 81-92.

Carrell, P.L. (1983b). Three components of background knowledge in reading comprehension. *Language Learning, 33,* 183-205.

Carrell, P.L., Devine, J., & Eskey, D.E., (Eds.). (1988). *Interactive approaches to second language reading.* New York: Cambridge University Press.

Carrell, P.L. & Eisterhold, J.C., (1983). Schema theory and ESL reading pedagogy. *TESOL Quarterly, 17,* 553-573.

Carrell, P.L., Pharis, B.G., & Liberto, J.C., (1989). Metacognitive training for ESL reading. *TESOL Quarterly, 23,* 647-678.

Carson, J.G. (1992). Becoming biliterate: First language influences. *Journal of Second Language Writing, 1,* 53-76.

Christison, M.A. & Krahnke, K., (1986). Student perceptions of academic language study. *TESOL Quarterly, 20,* 61-81.

Clarke, M. (1979). Reading in English and Spanish: Evidence from adult ESL students. *Language Learning, 29,* 121-150.

Cohen, A., Glasman, H., Rosenbaum-Cohen, P.R., Ferrara, J., & Fine, J. (1979). Reading for specialized purposes: Discourse analysis and the use of student informants. *TESOL Quarterly, 13,* 551-564.

Cumming, A. (1989). Writing expertise and second language proficiency. *Language Learning, 39,* 83-141.

Cziko, G. (1978). Differences in first- and second-language reading: The use of syntactic, semantic and discourse constraints. *Canadian Modern Language Journal, 34,* 473-489.

Dasenbrock, R.W. (1991). Do we write the text we read? *College English, 53,* 7-18.

Davey, B. (1983). Think-aloud: Modeling the cognitive processes of reading comprehension. *Journal of Reading, 27,* 219-224.

Devine, J. (1988). A case study of two readers: Models of reading and reading performance. In P. Carrell, J. Devine, & D. Eskey (Eds.), *Interactive approaches to second language reading* (pp. 127-139). New York: Cambridge University Press.

Devine, J., Carrell, P.L., & Eskey, D.E., (Eds.). (1987). *Research in reading in English as a second language.* Washington, DC: TESOL.

Dubin, F., Eskey, D.E., & Grabe, W., (Eds.). (1986). *Teaching second language reading for academic purposes.* Reading, MA: Addison-Wesley.

Elley, W.B. & Mangubhai, F., (1983). The effect of reading on second language learning. *Reading Research Quarterly, 19,* 53-67.

Eskey, D.E. (1986). Theoretical foundations. In F. Dubin, D.E. Eskey, & W. Grabe (Eds.), *Teaching second language reading for academic purposes* (pp. 3-21). Reading, MA: Addison-Wesley.

Eskey, D.E. & Grabe, W., (1988). Interactive models of second language reading: Perspectives on instruction. In P.L. Carrell, J. Devine, and D. Eskey (Eds.), *Interactive approaches to second language reading* (pp. 223-238). New York: Cambridge University Press.

Fish, S. (1980). *Is there a text in this class? The authority of interpretive communities.* Cambridge: Harvard University Press.

Flower, L., Stein, V., Ackerman, J., Kantz, M.J., McCormick, K., & Peck, W.C., (1990). *Reading to write: Exploring a cognitive and social process.* New York: Oxford University Press.

Flynn, E.A. (1983). Gender and reading. *College English, 45,* 236-253.

Gajdusek, L. (1988). Toward wider use of literature in ESL: Why and how. *TESOL Quarterly, 22,* 227-257.

Goodman, K. (1976). Reading: A psycholinguistic guessing game. In H. Singer & R. Ruddell (Eds.), *Theoretical models and processes of reading* (2nd ed.) (pp. 497-505). Newark, DE: International Reading Association.

Grabe, W. (1986). The transition from theory to practice in teaching reading. In F. Dubin, D.E. Eskey, & W. Grabe (Eds.), *Teaching second language reading for academic purposes* (pp. 25-48). Reading, MA: Addison-Wesley.

Hafiz, F.M. & Tudor, I., (1989). Extensive reading and the development of language skills. *ELT Journal, 43,* 1-13.

Hall, C. (1990). Managing the complexity of revising across languages. *TESOL Quarterly, 24,* 43-60.

Hatch, E., Polin, P., & Part, S., (1970). Acoustic scanning or syntactic processing. Paper presented at the meeting of the Western Psychological Association, San Francisco.

Heimlich, J.E. & Pittelman, S.D., (1986). *Semantic mapping: Classroom applications.* Newark, DE: International Reading Association.

Horowitz, D. (1986a). Essay examination prompts and the teaching of academic writing. *English for Specific Purposes, 5,* 107-120.

Horowitz, D. (1986b). Process, not product: Less than meets the eye. *TESOL Quarterly, 20,* 141-144.

Hosenfeld, C. (1984). Case studies of ninth grade readers. In J.C. Alderson & A.H. Urquhart (Eds.), *Reading in a foreign language* (pp. 231-244). New York: Longman.

Hudson, T. (1991). A content comprehension approach to reading English for science and technology. *TESOL Quarterly, 25(1),* 77-104.

Hudson, T. (1982). The effect of induced schemata on the "shortcircuit" in L2 reading: Non-decoding factors in L2 reading performance. *Language Learning, 32,* 1-31.

Janopoulos, M. (1986). The relationship of pleasure of reading and second language writing proficiency. *TESOL Quarterly, 20,* 763-768.

Johns, A. (1981). Necessary English: A faculty survey. *TESOL Quarterly, 15,* 51-57.

Johnson, D.M. & Roen, D.H., (Eds.). (1989). *Richness in writing: Empowering ESL students.* New York: Longman.

Jones, S. & Tetroe, J., (1987). Composing in a second language. In A. Matsuhashi (Ed.), *Writing in real time* (pp. 34-57). New York: Longman.

Kimmel, S. & MacGinitie, W.H., (1984). Identifying children who use a preservative text processing strategy. *Reading Research Quarterly, 19,* 162-172.

Kintsch, W. & Greene, E., (1978). The role of culture-specific schemata in the comprehension and recall of stories. *Discourse Processes, 1,* 1-13.

Krapels, A. (1990). An overview of second language writing process research. In B. Kroll (Ed.), *Second language writing* (pp. 37-56). New York: Cambridge University Press.

Krashen, S.D. (1988). Do we learn to read by reading? The relationship between free reading and reading ability. In D. Tannen (Ed.), *Linguistics in context: Connecting observation and understanding* (pp. 269-298). Norwood, NJ: Ablex.

Krashen, S.D. (1984). *Writing: Research, theory, and applications.* Oxford: Pergamon.

Kroll, B. (1991). Teaching writing in the ESL context. In M. Celce-Murcia (Ed.), *Teaching English as a second or foreign language* (2nd ed.) (pp. 245-263). New York: Newbury House.

Kroll, B. (Ed.). (1990). *Second language writing.* New York: Cambridge University Press.

Kucer, S. (1985). The making of meaning: Reading and writing as processes. *Written Communication, 2,* 317-336.

Leki, I. (1990a). Coaching from the margins: Issues in written response. In B. Kroll (Ed.), *Second language writing* (pp. 57-68). New York: Cambridge University Press.

Leki, I. (1990b). Potential problems with peer responding in ESL writing classes. *CATESOL Journal, 3,* 5-19.

McLaughlin, B. (1987). Reading in a second language: Studies of adult and child learners. In S.R. Goldman & H.T. Trueba (Eds.), *Becoming literate in English as a second language* (pp. 57-70). Norwood, NJ: Ablex.

Mittan, R. (1989). The peer review process: Harnessing students' communicative power. In D.M. Johnson & D.H. Roen (Eds.), *Richness in writing: Empowering ESL students* (pp. 207-219). New York: Longman.

Mlynarczyk, R. (1992). Student choice: An alternative to teacher-selected reading material. *College ESL, 1(2),* 1-8.

Nystrand, M. (1989). A social-interactive model of writing. *Written Communication, 6,* 66-85.

Parry, K.J. (1987). Reading in a second culture. In J. Devine, P.L. Carrell, & D.E. Eskey (Eds.), *Research in reading in English as a second language* (pp. 59-70). Washington, DC: TESOL.

Perl, S. (1979). The composing processes of unskilled college writers. *Research in the Teaching of English, 13,* 317-336.

Petrosky, A. (1982). From story to essay: Reading and writing. *College Composition and Communication, 33,* 19-37.

Radecki, P.M. & Swales, J.M., (1988). ESL students' reaction to written comments on their written work. *System, 16,* 355-365.

Raimes, A. (1986). Teaching ESL writing: Fitting what we do to what we know. *The Writing Instructor, 5,* 153-166.

Raimes, A. (1985). What unskilled writers do as they write: A classroom study. *TESOL Quarterly, 19,* 229-258.

Reid, J. (1987). ESL Composition: The expectations of the academic audience. *TESOL Newsletter, 21,* 34.

Rigg, P. (1977). The miscue-ESL project. In H.D. Brown, C.A. Yorio, & R.H. Crymes (Eds.), *Teaching and learning ESL: Trends in research and practice. On TESOL '77* (pp. 106-118). Washington, DC: TESOL.

Robinson, D. (1991). Henry James and euphemism. *College English, 53,* 403-427.

Rubin, D.L. (1988). Introduction: Four dimensions of social construction in written communication. In B.A. Rafoth and D.L. Rubin (Eds.), *The social construction of written communication* (pp. 1-33). Norwood, NJ: Ablex.

Rummelhart, D. (1977). Toward an interactive model of reading. In S. Dornic (Ed.), *Attention and performance,* vol. 6 (pp. 573-603). New York: Academic Press.

Sarig, G. (1987). High-level reading and the first and foreign language: Some comparative process data. In J. Devine, P.L. Carrell, & D.E. Eskey (Eds.), *Research in reading in English as a second language* (pp. 105-120). Washington, DC: TESOL.

Silva, T. (1990). ESL composition instruction: Developments, issues and directions. In B. Kroll (Ed.), *Second language writing* (pp. 11-23). New York: Cambridge University Press.

Smith, F. (1971). *Understanding reading: A psycholinguistic analysis of reading and learning to read,* 1st ed. New York: Holt, Rinehart, and Winston.

Spack, R. (1990). *Guidelines: A cross-cultural reading/writing text.* New York: St. Martin's.

Spack, R. (1988). Initiating ESL students into the academic discourse community: How far should we go? *TESOL Quarterly, 22,* 29-51.

Spack, R. (1985). Literature, reading, writing, and ESL: Bridging the gaps. *TESOL Quarterly, 19,* 703-726.

Spack, R. (1984). Invention strategies and the ESL college composition student. *TESOL Quarterly, 18,* 649-670.

Spack, R. & Sadow, C., (1983). Student-teacher working journals in ESL freshman composition. *TESOL Quarterly, 17,* 575-594.

Stahl, S.A. & Vancil, S.J., (1986). Discussion is what makes semantic maps work in vocabulary instruction. *The Reading Teacher, 40,* 62-67.

Stanovich, K.E. (1980). Toward an interactive-compensatory model of individual differences in the development of reading fluency. *Reading Research Quarterly, 16,* 32-71.

Steffensen, M.S. & Joag-Dev, C., (1984). Cultural knowledge and reading. In J.C. Alderson & A.H. Urquhart (Eds.), *Reading in a foreign language* (pp. 48-61). New York: Longman.

Sternglass, M. (1988). *The presence of thought: Introspective accounts of reading and writing.* Norwood, NJ: Ablex.

Sternglass, M. (1986). Introduction. In B. Petersen (Ed.), *Convergences: Transactions in reading and writing* (pp. 1-11). Urbana, IL: NCTE.

Tierney, R.J. & Pearson, P.D., (1983). Toward a composing model of reading. *Language Arts, 60,* 568-569.

Van Naerssen, M. (1985). Relaxed reading in ESP. *TESOL Newsletter, 19,* 2.

Zamel, V. (1992). Writing one's way into reading. *TESOL Quarterly, 26,* 463-485.

Zamel, V. (1985). Responding to student writing. *TESOL Quarterly, 19,* 79-101.

Zamel, V. (1983). The composing processes of advanced ESL students: Six case studies. *TESOL Quarterly, 17,* 165-187.

Toward an Understanding
of the Distinct Nature of L2 Writing:
The ESL Research and Its Implications
by Tony Silva

In recent years, ESL writing practitioners have frequently been advised to adopt practices from L1 writing. Underlying this advice, there would seem to be an assumption that L1 and L2 writing are practically identical or at least very similar. On a superficial level, such an assumption seems warranted. There is evidence to suggest that L1 and L2 writing are similar in their broad outlines; that is, it has been shown that both L1 and L2 writers employ a recursive composing process, involving planning, writing, and revising, to develop their ideas and find the appropriate rhetorical and linguistic means to express them. However, a closer examination of L1 and L2 writing will reveal salient and important differences drawn from the intuition of ESL writers (Silva, 1992), and ESL writing practitioners (Raimes, 1985), and from the results of the relevant comparative empirical research (the focus of this paper).

If such differences exist, then to make intelligent decisions about adopting and/or adapting L1 practices, ESL writing practitioners need to have a clear understanding of the unique nature of L2 writing, of how and to what extent it differs from L1 writing. One route to such an understanding is the consideration of the findings of empirical research comparing ESL and native-English-speaking writers (ESL/NES studies) and that comparing the L1 and L2 writing of ESL subjects (L1/L2 studies). (See Silva, in press, 1993, respectively, for separate treatments of the ESL/NES and the L1/L2 research.) Consequently, in this paper, I will review and synthesize the findings of this body of research in order to develop a coherent description of the differences between L1 and L2 writing, and I will draw implications from these findings for L2 writing theory, research, and practice. A comprehensive understanding of the distinct nature of L2 writing will require inquiry into writing in many L2s in addition to ESL. However, at the present time, ESL writing is by far the most developed area of scholarship in L2 writing; I expect that the findings of this analysis will be subject to revision in light of those from research on writing in other L2s.

Method

Procedures

For this study, all seemingly relevant reports of research that could be located were carefully screened. Included in this study were reports of empirical research involving a direct comparison of ESL and NES writing and/or the L1 and L2 writing of ESL subjects. Excluded were (a) ESL/NES studies that did not actually involve both ESL and NES writers and those which included ESL and NES writing that could not be fairly compared (e.g., impromptu writing by ESL students compared with the published work of professional NES writers) and (b) L1/L2 studies in which one group of nonnative English speakers wrote only in English and another group wrote only in their L1 (that is, only studies in which the same individuals produced written texts in their L1 and in English were included).

The chosen reports were then reread and analyzed. Noted especially were such features as research design, study focus, sample size, subject characteristics (L1, age, educational level, English proficiency, writing ability), writing tasks (number of tasks, genre, time constraints, writing context), methodological concerns (reporting of subject characteristics, data collection, data analysis, interpretation of findings), and most important, the studies' findings with regard to ESL/NES and L1/ESL comparisons.

Studies

Overall, 72 research reports met the criteria for inclusion mentioned above and were included in this examination. Forty-one involved ESL/ NES comparisons. Twenty-seven compared L1 and L2 writing. Four dealt with comparisons of both types (Appendix A lists ESL/NES reports; Appendix B, L1/L2 reports; Appendix C, reports involving both types of comparisons). A look at the publication dates of these reports indicates that comparative research of this kind is a fairly recent and ongoing phenomenon: More than 90% of all the reports examined were published in the past 10 years; 50% within the past 5. With regard to focus, reports looking at written texts outnumbered those dealing with composing processes by a ratio of more than 3:1. Of these text-based studies, more focused on rhetorical (discourse level) than on linguistic (sentence level and below) features. These differences were also reflected in the research design in which quantitative studies (typically text based) greatly outnumbered the qualitative (typically process based). Finally, with regard to subjects, the studies, in total, dealt with more than 4,000, with sample sizes ranging from 1 to more than 300.

Subjects

The subjects involved in this research came from a variety of language backgrounds. At least 27 different L1s were represented in the studies, with Arabic, Chinese, Japanese, and Spanish dominant. (See Appendices A, B, and C for the L1 backgrounds of the L2 subjects in the studies examined here.) Subjects were predominantly undergraduate college students in their late teens and early twenties, though educational levels ranged from high school to postgraduate. They had fairly advanced levels of English proficiency and exhibited a wide range of levels of writing ability. However, the statements here regarding the subjects' ages and levels of English proficiency and writing ability should be seen as tentative because these characteristics were not reported in a fairly large number of studies.

Writing Tasks

In this research, typically one (in the ESL/NES studies) or two (in the L1/L2 studies—one in English and one in the L1) writing tasks were assigned, though some used more. With regard to genre, most studies called for expository essays; argumentative and narrative tasks ran a far second and third. Subjects were normally given a range of from 20 min to as much time as they chose to take to complete their writing tasks; however, most studies allowed 30-60 min. Finally, with regard to contexts for writing, the majority of subjects in the studies did their writing in class; about half as many, under test conditions; a handful, under laboratory conditions.

Caveats

Before moving to a presentation of the findings of this research and a consideration of the implications of these findings, it is necessary to offer a few caveats with regard to this enterprise. First, as with any body of empirical research, the studies examined here, although generally sound, exhibit some limitations. These include some small samples (resulting in a low level of generalizability); some inadequate description (missing, partial, or imprecise reports) of subject characteristics, writing task features, and conditions for writing; some cases in which reliability estimates for data analyses and statistical tests of significance were not done where appropriate; and some overinterpretation of results (e.g., overgeneralization, unwarranted causal claims).

A second caveat relates to the focus of this paper: differences. This focus does not represent an attempt to ignore, deny, or trivialize the many important similarities between L1 and L2 writing; it stems from the belief that understanding these differences is crucial to comprehending and addressing ESL writers' special needs. Furthermore, the emphasis on differences should not be seen as an attempt to portray ESL writers in negative terms. My attempts at writing in an L2 and my experiences in teaching ESL writers have given me nothing but respect for ESL writers; I am frequently amazed and humbled by their efforts and abilities.

A third caveat has to do with the limitations of would-be synthesizers of research. Their constructions of the meaning of the findings are a function of their reading of the studies, their interests, their biases, and the limits of their knowledge and analytic and expressive abilities. It should also be recognized that any synthesis is reductive in nature; rough spots are smoothed over and details left out in order to present a coherent account of the data under examination. Consequently, it is not claimed that what follows is objective or disinterested. However, a serious attempt has been made to provide an account that is honest, fair, useful, and accessible, Furthermore, the conclusions that will be presented should not be seen as definitive; rather, they should be viewed as tentative, as a set of hypotheses in need of careful consideration and testing.

Findings

In this section, the findings of the studies examined will be presented. To enhance readability, in most cases, ESL/NES and L1/L2 studies (in all cases, the L2 was English) will not be distinguished, and the L1 backgrounds of the L2 writers will not always be provided. This information is available in Appendices A, B, and C. Further, the term L2 will be used to refer to the ESL writers and their writing in both types of studies. These findings, which will form the basis for generalizations made and implications drawn later in the paper, will be reported in two main categories: composing processes and written text features.

Composing Processes

A number of studies (Chelala, 1981; Krapels, 1990; Moragne e Silva, 1991; Schiller, 1989; Skibniewski, 1988; Skibniewski & Skibniewska, 1986; Whalen, 1988) reported that, in general terms, composing process patterns (sequences of writing behaviors) were similar in L1s and L2s. However, L2 composing was clearly more difficult and less effective; a closer look turns up some salient differences in the subprocesses of planning, transcribing, and reviewing.

Planning

It was reported that, overall, L2 writers did less planning, at the global and local levels (Campbell, 1987b; Dennett, 1985; Jones & Tetroe, 1987; Skibniewski, 1988; Whalen 1988; Yau, 1989). Whereas they devoted more attention to generating material (Hall, 1990; Moragne e Silva, 1989; Skibniewski, 1988), this generation was more difficult (Hildenbrand, 1985) and less successful in that more time was spent on figuring out the topic, less useful material was generated, and more of the generated ideas never found their way into the written text (Moragne e Silva, 1989). L2 writers did less goal setting, global and local (Skibniewski, 1988), and had more difficulty achieving these goals (Moragne e Silva, 1989). It was also reported that organizing generated material in the L2 was more difficult (Moragne e Silva, 1989; Whalen, 1988).

Transcribing

Transcribing (producing written text) in the L2 was more laborious, less fluent, and less productive. It was reported that L2 writers spent more time referring back to an outline or prompt (Moragne e Silva, 1989, 1991) and consulting a dictionary (Skibniewski & Skibniewska, 1986) and exhibited more concern and difficulty with vocabulary (Arndt, 1987; Dennett, 1985; Krapels, 1990; Moragne e Silva, 1991; Skibniewski, 1988; Yau, 1989). Findings indicated that, in L2 writing, pauses were more frequent (Hall, 1990; Hildenbrand, 1985; Skibniewski & Skibniewska, 1986), longer (Hildenbrand, 1985), and consumed more writing time (Hall, 1990). Furthermore, it was found that L2 writers wrote at a slower rate (Skibniewski & Skibniewska, 1986) and produced fewer words of written text (Moragne e Silva, 1989).

Reviewing

In general, L2 writing reportedly involved less reviewing (Silva, 1990; Skibniewski, 1988). There was evidence of less rereading of and reflecting on written texts (Chelala, 1981; Dennett, 1985; Gaskill, 1986; Silva, 1990; Skibniewski, 1988); however, Schiller (1989) found no difference in rereading in L1 and L2. With regard to revision, similar general patterns, systems, and/or strategies were reported in L1 and L2 writing (Gaskill, 1986; Hall, 1987, 1990; Tagong, 1991); however, differences in the frequency of revision were found. It was reported that L2 writing involved more revision (Gaskill, 1986; Hall, 1987, 1990; Schiller, 1989; Skibniewski & Skibniewska, 1986; Tagong, 1991)—though Skibniewski (1988) found that L2 writers revised less—more before drafting, during drafting, and between drafts (Hall, 1987). However, this revision was more difficult (Hall, 1987) and more of a preoccupation (Whalen, 1988). There was less "revising by ear," that is, making changes on the basis of what "sounds" good (Silva, 1990; Yau, 1989). Moreover, L2 revision seemed to focus more on grammar (Dennett, 1990; Hall, 1987, 1990) and less on mechanics, particularly spelling (Hall, 1990; Skibniewski, 1988).

Written Text Features

In this section, differences in the features of L1 and L2 written texts will be considered in terms of fluency, accuracy, quality, and structure.

Fluency

There is fairly strong evidence to suggest that L2 writing is a less fluent process. Sixteen studies (Benson, Deming, Denzer, & Valeri-Gold, 1992; Cummings, 1990;

Hall, 1990; Hirokawa, 1986; Kamel, 1989; Lin, 1989; Linnarud, 1986; Lux, 1991; Mahmoud, 1982; Moragne e Silva, 1991; Ragan, 1989; Reid, 1988; Silva, 1990; Tagong, 1991; Yau, 1989; Yu & Atkinson, 1988) found that L2 texts were shorter (i.e., contained fewer words). Four (Benson, 1980; Dennett, 1985, 1990; Hu, Brown, & Brown, 1982; Santiago, 1970) reported longer L2 texts; two (Frodesen, 1991; Skibniewski & Skibniewska, 1986) reported similar lengths in L1 and L2 texts.

Accuracy

The research clearly shows that L2 writers make more errors overall (Benson, 1980; Benson et al., 1992; Frodesen, 1991; Hirokawa, 1986; Silva, 1990; Stalker & Stalker, 1988; Terdal, 1985; Yu & Atkinson, 1988), more morphosyntactic errors (Benson, 1980; Benson et al, 1992; Campbell, 1987b; Frodesen, 1991; Hirokawa, 1986; Hu et al., 1982; Santiago, 1970; Silva, 1990; Stalker & Stalker, 1988), more lexicosemantic errors (Benson, 1980; Benson et al., 1992; Dennett, 1985; Frodesen, 1991; Hirokawa, 1986; Linnarud, 1986; Yu & Atkinson, 1988), and more errors with verbs (Benson, 1980; Benson et al., 1992; Hu et al., 1982; Silva, 1990), prepositions (Benson, 1980; Benson, 1992; Hafernik, 1990; Silva, 1990), articles (Benson, 1980; Benson et al., 1992; Silva, 1990), and nouns (Benson, 1980; Silva, 1990).

Quality

A number of studies (Campbell, 1987a, 1987b, 1990; Carlson, 1988; Connor, 1984; Hafernik, 1990; Park, 1988; Reid, 1988; Santiago, 1970, Xu, 1990; Yu & Atkinson, 1988) reported that (at least in terms of the judgments of native English speakers) L2 texts were less effective (i.e., received lower holistic scores).

Structure

General textual patterns. The studies that look at general textual patterns, typically in expository texts, can be fairly described as following from Kaplan's (1966) groundbreaking study, in which the "thought patterns" of the written English texts of NES and ESL writers are characterized and contrasted. Though Kaplan's study does not meet the criteria set forth for inclusion in this discussion, it is addressed here because it provides the theoretical basis for later studies which do. Kaplan described thought patterns as linear (for NESs), parallel (for native speakers of Semitic languages), indirect (for native speakers of "Oriental" languages), and digressive (for native speakers of Romance languages and Russian).

Norment's (1982, 1984) work corroborated Kaplan's claims, reporting distinct organizational patterns in the written English texts of NESs (linear), Chinese (centrifugal—symbolized by an inverted cone), and Spanish (linear with tangential breaks). Burtoff (1983) also reported distinct patterns of logical relations (which she described as culturally preferred rather than linguistically determined) in the written English texts of NESs (theme-rheme), Arabic (arguments of equal weight), and Japanese (causal chain), which she saw as corresponding in part to Kaplan's characterizations.

Kobayashi (1984a, 1984b) and Oi (1984) reported a tendency in written English texts toward a general-to-specific (deductive) rhetorical pattern for NES subjects and an inclination toward a specific-to-general (inductive) pattern for native Japanese speakers. Xu (1990), who reported no significant differences in the structure of expository paragraphs of ESL and NES subjects, provides a counterpoint to the foregoing studies.

Three studies (Norment, 1984, 1986; Santiago, 1970) comparing the L1 and L2 language writing of ESL subjects reported strong similarities in the patterns of logical relations between sentences (e.g., explanation, addition, illustration) and across languages (suggesting transfer of rhetorical patterns). Cook (1988), however, reported that her (native-Spanish-speaking) subjects wrote significantly more disunified (*digressive,* in Kaplan's terms) paragraphs in English than in Spanish (suggesting a possible L2 proficiency effect on L2 rhetorical patterns).

Argument structure.   A number of studies addressed the structure of L2 arguments. Mahmoud (1983) reported that his L2 subjects (native speakers of Arabic) did less reporting of conditions, less defining, and less exemplifying, but used more warning and phatic communion than their NES peers. He indicated that the L2 writers less often stated and supported their position fully and were inclined to develop their arguments by restating their position—NES subjects preferred to develop their arguments by stating a rationale for their position. Mahmoud also reported that the L2 writers' arguments exhibited less paragraphing, less rhetorical connectedness (position statements interrupted the flow of their texts), a looser segmental (introduction, discussion, conclusion) structure, less variety and more errors in the use of conjunctive elements, and less explicit formal closure.

Connor (1984) reported that her ESL subjects' texts had less adequate justifying support for claim statements and less linking of concluding inductive statements to the preceding subtopics of the problem. Oi (1984) found that her ESL writers (native speakers of Japanese) used more mixed arguments (arguing both for and against), more argument alternations (for-against-for-against), and more often ended their argument in a different direction (for or against) than it began. She also reported that her ESL subjects were inclined to be more tentative and less hyperbolic than their NES peers. Ouaouicha (1986), in the part of his study where the English arguments of L2 (native Arabic speakers) and NES writers were compared, reported that the L2 subjects provided more data but fewer claims, warrants, backings, and rebuttals. He also claimed that they less often fulfilled the task, used less ethos (ethical appeal), addressed the audience less often, and used more pathos (emotional appeal) in their texts.

Choi (1988a) reported that whereas all his NES subjects' texts included the elements of claim, justification, and conclusion, some elements were missing in the L2 subjects' (native speakers of Korean) texts. It was also found that the L2 subjects more often used indirect (inductive) strategies—going from evidence to conclusion (this corroborates the findings of Kobayashi, 1984a, 1984b; and Oi, 1984, with native speakers of Japanese). Choi (1988b) reports that his L2 subjects (again, native speakers of Korean) preferred a situation + problem + solution + conclusion pattern to that of the NES subjects (i.e., claim + justification + conclusion).

In two studies comparing L1 and L2 arguments, Kamel (1989) found fewer audience adaptation units, a lower percentage of claims, a higher percentage of data units, and a higher percentage of warrants in the L2 texts; Yu and Atkinson (1988) reported less effective linking of arguments in texts written in English.

Narrative structure. The features of L1 and L2 narratives were also compared. Harris (1983) asked his subjects to produce an account of a short cartoon film. He reported that the accounts written by L2 subjects had less to say on most of the narrative points, more often began in the middle of the story, less often referred explicitly to the film, and more often omitted essential scene setting elements than those of their NES counterparts. Indrasuta (1987, 1988) compared her native-Thai-speaking subjects' English narratives with those of their NES peers and with their L1 narratives. In the first comparison, she reported that the L2 subjects' texts exhibited more use of the first person singular, more backdrop setting (i.e., in which time and place are not important)—as opposed to the integral setting (i.e., in which characters, action, and theme are closely interwoven and thus setting is essential), less action, and more focus on mental states. In the second comparison, Indrasuta found more use of the pronoun *I,* more implicit (as opposed to explicit) themes, more real (as opposed to projected) scenes, and less description of mental states in the L2 texts. Overall, she found that her L2 subjects' narrative patterns in English were closer to those in their L1 than they were to those used by NES subjects. Lin (1989) reported that the English narratives of her L2 writers (native speakers of Chinese) contained fewer complete episodes and fewer mentions of entities in episodes (the latter presumed to reflect a smaller lexical repertoire in English) than their L1 versions.

Features of essay exam responses. Comparing the responses to essay questions on a final exam for a graduate course on L2 acquisition, Hirokawa (1986) reported that her L2 writers used more undefined terms, were less able to paraphrase concepts and less cognizant of expected essay answer forms, had more difficulty identifying the topic in the exam question and an appropriate discourse function for framing an answer, had a harder time presenting a reasoned argument and strong support, and had more unnecessary or irrelevant detail, information, and repetition of points.

Textual manifestations of the use of a background reading text. A couple of studies looked at background text use. Campbell (1987a, 1987b, 1990) reported that her L2 subjects' texts had fewer examples of information copied from the reading text, less backgrounding and foregrounding of examples, less use of information from the reading text in their first paragraphs and more use in their last, more documentation in footnotes and less in phrases acknowledging the author or text, more acknowledgment of quotations and paraphrases, and less smooth incorporation of material from the reading text. Frodesen (1991) found that her L2 writers had more difficulty in interpreting the background reading text and made less reference to the background text in their introductions.

Reader orientation.   Focusing on reader orientations (i.e., material preceding the introduction of a thesis statement), Scarcella (1984b) reported that her L2 subjects' orientations were longer and contained fewer and a smaller range of attention-getting devices. L2 writers also played down the importance of their themes more, used fewer sentences that signaled a following theme, used more clarifying devices to help readers understand their themes, and more often overspecified their themes and thus underestimated their readers' knowledge by introducing information readers considered obvious. In a similar vein, Atari (1983) reported that his L2 subjects (native Arabic speakers) more often preceded their topic sentences with a broad statement about a general state of affairs.

Morphosyntactic/stylistic features.   Numerous stylistic differences were reported. In general terms, L2 writing was found to be less complex (Park, 1988), less mature and stylistically appropriate (Yu, 1988), and less consistent and academic with regard to language, style, and tone (Campbell, 1987a, 1987b, 1990). In more specific terms, Hu et al. (1992) found their L2 subjects' writing to be more direct, explicit, and authoritative in tone and to involve more warning and admonition, less personal comparison, and more use of strong modals (*will, should, must*). Oi (1984) reported that her L2 subjects used more hedges and superlatives. Dunkelblau (1990) found that the L2 writing in her study exhibited less variety in stylistic device use, that it contained fewer set phrases, fewer interrogative sentences (rhetorical/lead questions), less analogy, less ornate language, less vocative exhortation (addressing the reader directly), less parallel structure, and more repetition of ideas.

A fairly large number of more strictly linguistic differences was reported. It was found that L2 writers produced sentences that had more (Gates, 1978; Silva, 1990) but shorter (Cummings, 1990; Dennett, 1985, 1990; Gates, 1978; Kamel, 1989) T units. These sentences also contained fewer (Gates, 1978, Hu et al., 1982) but longer (Gates, 1978; Hu et al., 1982; Silva, 1990) clauses. In terms of connections, they used more coordination (Silva, 1990) and simple coordinate conjunctions (Cummings, 1990; Reid, 1992) and less subordination (Hu et al., 1982; Park, 1988; Silva, 1990) and fewer subordinate conjunction openers (Reid, 1992). With regard to modification, it was claimed that L2 writers used fewer modifiers overall (Gates, 1978), more unmodified nouns and pronouns (Gates, 1978), fewer nonclausal/single word modifiers per T unit (Dennett, 1985, 1990; Gates, 1978), fewer adjectives (Gates, 1978), fewer possessives (Gates, 1978), fewer verb forms used as noun modifiers (Gates, 1978), fewer prepositions and prepositional phrases (Cummings, 1990; Gates, 1978; Reid, 1988, 1992), fewer definite articles (Oi, 1984), and fewer free modifiers (nonrestrictive phrasal and clausal elements) (Park, 1988). Additionally, L2 writers reportedly used more pronouns (Oi, 1984; Reid, 1988), more conjunctions (Oi, 1984; Reid, 1988), less passive voice (Carlson, 1988; Lux, 1991; Reid, 1988), and more initial and fewer medial transitional devices (Mann, 1988).

Lexicosemantic features. The use of cohesive devices was one area of Lexicosemantic difference. There was evidence that L2 writers used more conjunctive ties (Hafernik, 1990; Hu et al., 1982; Oi, 1984)—though Almeida (1984) found that they used fewer—and fewer lexical ties (Hu et al., 1982; Indrasuta, 1987, 1988; Mahmoud, 1983). They also reportedly used fewer synonyms (Almeida, 1984; Connor, 1984; Oi, 1984) and collocations (Connor, 1984; Mahmoud, 1983) and exhibited less variety in their use of lexical cohesion (Connor, 1984; Oi, 1984) and less control of over L2 cohesion resources overall (Almeida, 1984).

Another area of distinction was the subjects' lexical repertoire. It was reported that L2 writers used shorter (Reid, 1988) and vaguer (Carlson, 1988) words and that their texts exhibited less lexical variety and sophistication (Hu et al., 1982; Linnarud, 1986). Also, Webb's (1988) findings suggest the possibility of L2 effects of increased awareness of the metaphorical qualities of language and of reduced imagery but no L2 effect of metaphors used for catechresis (i.e., to fill gaps in the vocabulary caused by incomplete knowledge of the L2).

Discussion

Summary of Findings

The findings from this body of research suggest that, in general terms, adult L2 writing is distinct from and simpler and less effective (in the eyes of L1 readers) than L1 writing. Though general composing process patterns are similar in L1 and L2, it is clear that L2 composing is more constrained, more difficult, and less effective. L2 writers did less planning (global and local) and had more difficulty with setting goals and generating and organizing material. Their transcribing was more laborious, less fluent, and less productive—perhaps reflecting a lack of lexical resources. They reviewed, reread, and reflected on their written texts less, revised more—but with more difficulty and were less able to revise intuitively (i.e., "by ear").

In general, L2 writers' texts were less fluent (fewer words), less accurate (more errors), and less effective (lower holistic scores). At the discourse level, their texts often exhibited distinct patterns of exposition, argumentation, and narration; their responses to two particular types of academic writing tasks—answering essay exam questions and using background reading texts—were different and less effective. Their orientation of readers was deemed less appropriate and acceptable. In terms of lower level linguistic concerns, L2 writers' texts were stylistically distinct and simpler in structure. Their sentences included more but shorter T units, fewer but longer clauses, more coordination, less subordination, less noun modification, and less passivization. They evidenced distinct patterns in the use of cohesive devices, especially conjunctive (more) and lexical (fewer) ties, and exhibited less lexical control, variety, and sophistication overall.

Implications

Theory

There exists, at present, no coherent, comprehensive theory of L2 writing. This can be explained in part by the newness of L2 writing as an area of inquiry, but an equally important reason is the prevalent assumption that L1 and L2 writing are, for all intents and purposes, the same. This, largely unexamined assumption has led L2 writing specialists to rely for direction almost exclusively on L1 composition theories, theories which are, incidentally, largely monolingual, monocultural, ethnocentric, and fixated on the writing of NES undergraduates in North American colleges and universities. The findings of the research discussed above, however, make this assumption untenable. Clearly, L2 writing is strategically, rhetorically, and linguistically different in important ways from L1 writing. Therefore, L2 writing specialists need to look beyond L1 writing theories, to better describe the unique nature of L2 writing, to look into the potential sources (e.g., cognitive, developmental, social, cultural, educational, linguistic) of this uniqueness, to develop theories that adequately explain the phenomenon of L2 writing. Such theories would not only serve L2 writing practitioners but could also inform and enhance L1 theories of writing by providing them with a true multilingual/multicultural perspective, by making them more inclusive, more sensitive, and ultimately, more valid.

Research

The foregoing review of studies suggests a need for more, more balanced, and more rigorous research in this area. More comparative research is necessary to corroborate and enhance present findings and to fill in gaps. This research needs to be more balanced, that is, more evenly distributed in its treatment of strategic, rhetorical, and linguistic concerns; in its use of qualitative and quantitative designs; and in its consideration of subjects of different ages and levels of education, language proficiency, and writing ability. It is also important for future comparative researchers to continue to improve design, reporting, and interpretation by using larger samples to enhance generalizability; by including more writing tasks and making these tasks and the conditions under which they are done more realistic; by reporting on subject characteristics, writing task features, and writing conditions more fully; by providing reliability estimates for data analyses and information on statistical significance of findings, where appropriate; and by being reasonable and responsible when making generalizations and/or cause and effect claims based on their findings.

In addition to being more abundant, more balanced and more rigorous, research comparing L1 and L2 writing needs to be more accessible. As the bibliography of this paper indicates, most of the existing comparative research is available in the form of unpublished dissertations, ERIC documents, and articles in periodicals that are often difficult to locate. What are needed are more outlets for publication of research on L2 writing. Although some efforts have been made to increase the num-

ber of outlets, (e.g., the creation of the new *Journal of Second Language Writing*),
more needs to be done if significant progress is to be made. Mainstream (L1) writing publishers need to be more receptive to L2 writing scholarship, and generalist
publications in L2 studies need to allow for a greater focus on writing.

Practice

If these findings are valid, they have important implications for assessment,
placement, staffing, and instructional procedures and strategies. First, these findings cast doubt on the reasonableness of the expectation that L2 writers (even those
with advanced levels of L2 proficiency) will perform as well as L1 writers on writing tests, that L2 writers will be able to meet standards developed for L1 writers.
This suggests a need for different evaluation criteria for L2 writing and raises such
difficult but necessary questions as, When does different become incorrect or inappropriate? and What is good enough?

Second, the findings suggest that L2 writers, because they have special needs
(distinct from those of L1 writers, whether they be basic or skilled) might be best
served by being given the option of taking (credit-bearing, requirement-fulfilling)
writing classes designed especially for them, that is, not being forced, in
sink-or-swim fashion, into "mainstream" (i.e., native-speaker-dominated) writing
classes which may be inappropriate, and perhaps even counterproductive, for them.

Third, the findings support the notion that whether or not L2 writers find themselves in L2 writing classrooms, they should be taught by teachers who are cognizant of, sensitive to, and able to deal positively and effectively with sociocultural,
rhetorical, and linguistic differences of their students. That is, they should be taught
by teachers with special theoretical and practical preparation for teaching L2 writers. Significant levels of cooperation and collaboration between graduate programs
in composition studies and those in second language studies will be required to
graduate such teachers in needed quantities.

Fourth, the findings have numerous implications for instructional practices in
the L2 writing classroom. In the most general terms, L2 writers may need, as
Raimes (1985) suggests, "more of everything" (p. 250). (However, more of everything should not necessarily entail more work for L2 writing teachers at the same
rate of compensation; lowering class sizes and/or having fewer writing assignments
completed over longer periods of time are called for). In particular, it is likely that
L2 writing teachers will need to devote more time and attention across the board to
strategic, rhetorical, and linguistic concerns. They may need to include more work
on planning—to generate ideas, text structure, and language—so as to make the actual writing more manageable. They may need to have their students draft in stages,
for example, to focus on content and organization in one draft and on linguistic concerns in a subsequent draft or to separate their treatments of revising (rhetorical)
and editing (grammatical). In essence, teachers need to provide realistic strategies
for planning, transcribing, and reviewing that take into account their L2 students'
rhetorical and linguistic resources.

There also seems to be a clear need for more extensive treatment of textual concerns. At the discourse level, L2 writing teachers may need to familiarize their stu-

dents with L1 audience expectations and provide them with strategies for dealing with potentially unfamiliar textual patterns and task types they are likely to have to produce. It may also be necessary for L2 writing teachers to work to enhance their L2 writers' grammatical and lexical resources. Teachers might do this on a global level by using a set of assignments that look at one (student-chosen) theme or topic area from a variety of perspectives, thereby allowing students to build a syntactic and lexical repertoire in this area through repeated use (see Leki, 1991). On a more local level, teachers can provide individual L2 writers with syntactic and lexical options in the contexts of their own written texts.

In conclusion, the research comparing L1 and L2 writing, in my view, strongly suggests that, whereas they are similar in their broad outlines, they are different in numerous and important ways. This difference needs to be acknowledged and addressed by those who deal with L2 writers if these writers are to be treated fairly, taught effectively, and thus, given an equal chance to succeed in their writing-related personal and academic endeavors.

Acknowledgments

I would like to thank Margie Berns, Ilona Leki, Sandra Silberstein, and two anonymous *TESOL Quarterly* reviewers for their thorough readings of and valuable comments on the manuscript.

Works Cited

Almeida, J. (1984). The interplay of cohesion and coherence in native and nonnative written academic discourse. *Dissertation Abstracts International, 46* (5), 1263A.

Arndt, V. (1987). Six writers in search of texts: A protocol-based study of L1 and L2 writing. *ELT Journal, 41* (4), 257-266.

Atari, O. (1983). A contrastive analysis of Arab and American university students' strategies in accomplishing written English discourse functions. *Dissertation Abstracts International, 44* (11), 3307A.

Benson, B. (1980). A qualitative analysis of language structures in compositions written by first and second language learners. *Dissertation Abstracts International, 41* (5), 1984A.

Benson, B., Deming, M., Denzer, D., & Valeri-Gold, M. (1992). A combined basic writing/English as a second language class: Melting pot or mishmash? *Journal of Basic Writing, 11* (1), 58-59.

Burtoff, M. (1983). The logical organization of written expository discourse in English: A comparative study of Japanese, Arabic, and native-speaker strategies. *Dissertation Abstracts International, 45* (9), 2857A.

Campbell, C. (1987a). Writing with others' words: Native and non-native university students use of information from a background reading text in academic compositions. (ERIC Document Reproduction Service No. ED 287315)

Campbell, C. (1987 b). Writing with others' words: The use of information from a background reading text in the writing of native and non-native university composition students. *Dissertation Abstracts International, 48* (7), 1679A.

Campbell, C. (1990). Writing with others' words: Using background reading text in academic compositions. In B. Kroll (Ed.), *Second language writing: Research insights for the classroom* (pp. 211-230). New York: Cambridge University Press.

Carlson, S. (1988). Cultural differences in writing and reasoning skills. In A. Purves (Ed.), *Writing across languages and cultures: Issues in contrastive rhetoric* (pp. 227-260). Newbury Park, CA: Sage.

Carson, J., Carrell, P., Silberstein, S., Kroll, B., & Kuehn, P. (1990). Reading-writing relationships in first and second language. *TESOL Quarterly, 24* (2), 246-266.

Carson, J., & Kuehn, P. (1992). Evidence of transfer and loss in developing second language writers. *Language Learning, 42* (2), 157-182.

Chelala, S. (1981) The composing process of two Spanish speakers and the coherence in their texts: A case study. *Dissertation Abstracts International, 42* (12), 5045A.

Choi, Y. (1988a). Text structure of Korean speakers' argumentative essays in English. *World Englishes, 7* (2), 129-142.

Choi, Y. (1988b). Textual coherence in English and Korean: An analysis of argumentative writing by American and Korean students. *Dissertation Abstracts International, 50* (2), 429A.

Connor, U. (1984). A study of cohesion and coherence in English as a second language students' writing. *Papers in Linguistics, 17* (1-4), 301-316.

Cook, M. (1988). The validity of the contrastive rhetoric hypothesis as it relates to Spanish-speaking advanced ESL students. *Dissertation Abstracts International, 49* (9), 2567A.

Cummings, V. (1990). Speech and writing: An analysis of expository texts compared by native and non-native speakers of English at The City University of New York. *Dissertation Abstracts International, 51* (7), 2296A.

DeJesus, S. (1984). Predictors of English writing performance of native Spanish-speaking college freshmen. (ERIC Document Reproduction Service No. ED 256184)

Dennett, J. (1985). Writing technical English: A comparison of the process of native English and native Japanese speakers. *Dissertation Abstracts International, 46* (11), 3275A.

Dennett, J. (1990). ESL technical writing: Process and rhetorical differences. (ERIC Document Reproduction Service No. ED 322713)

Dunkelblau, H. (1990). A contrastive study of the organizational structure and stylistic elements of Chinese and English expository writing by Chinese high school students. *Dissertation Abstracts International, 51* (4), 1143A.

Frodesen, J. (1991). Aspects of coherence in a writing assessment context: Linguistic and rhetorical features of native and non-native English essays. *Dissertation Abstracts International, 52* (1), 150A.

Gaskill, W. (1986). Revising in Spanish and English as a second language: A process-oriented study of composition. *Dissertation Abstracts International, 47* (10), 3747A.

Gates, R. (1978). An analysis of grammatical structures in compositions written by four groups of students at Southern Technical Institute: Indo-Iranian, Latin-Romance, Sino-Tibetan, and American. *Dissertation Abstracts International, 39* (4), 2026A.

Hafernik, J. (1990). Relationships among English writing experience, contrastive rhetoric, and English expository prose of L1 and L2 college writers. *Dissertation Abstracts International, 51* (12), 4007A.

Hall, C. (1987). Revision strategies in L1 and L2 writing tasks: A case study. *Dissertation Abstracts International, 48* (5), 1187A.

Hall, C. (1990). Managing the complexity of revising across languages. *TESOL Quarterly, 24* (1), 43-60.

Harris, D. (1983). The organizational patterns of adult ESL student narratives: Report of a pilot study. (Eric Document Reproduction Service No. ED 275150)

Hildenbrand, J. (1985). Carmen: A case study of an ESL writer. *Dissertation Abstracts International, 46* (12), 3637A.

Hirokawa, K. (1986). An investigation of native/non-native speaker examination essays. *Papers in Applied Linguistics-Michigan, 1* (2), 105-131.

Hu, Z., Brown, D., & Brown, L. (1982). Some linguistic differences in the written English of Chinese and Australian students. *Language Learning and Communication, 1* (1), 39-49.

Indrasuta, C. (1987). A comparison of the written compositions of American and Thai students. *Dissertation Abstracts International, 48* (7), 1681A.

Indrasuta, C. (1988). Narrative styles in the writing of Thai and American students. In A. Purves (Ed.), *Writing across languages and cultures: Issues in contrastiue rhetoric* (pp. 206-226). Newbury Park, CA: Sage,

Intaraprawat, P. (1988). Metadiscourse in native English speakers' and ESL students persuasive essays. *Dissertation Abstracts International, 49* (7), 1720A.

Jones, S., & Tetroe, J. (1987). Composing in a second language. In A. Matsuhashi (Ed.), *Writing in real time: Modelling production processes* (pp. 34-57). New York: Longman.

Kamel, G. (1989). Argumentative writing by Arab learners of English as a foreign and second language: An empirical investigation of contrastive rhetoric. *Dissertation Abstracts International, 50* (3), 677A.

Kaplan, R. (1966). Cultural thought patterns in intercultural education. *Language Learning, 16* (1), 1-20.

Kobayashi, H. (1984a). Rhetorical patterns in English and Japanese. *Dissertation Abstracts International, 45* (8), 2425A.

Kobayashi, H. (1984b). Rhetorical patterns in English and Japanese. *TESOL Quarterly, 18* (4), 737-738.

Krapels, A. (1990). The interaction of first and second language composing: Processes and rhetorics. *Dissertation Abstracts International, 51* (12), 4045A.

Leki, I. (1991). Building expertise through sequenced writing assignments. *TESOL Journal, 1* (2), 19-23.

Lin, C. (1989). The structures of English and Chinese narratives written by college students in Taiwan. *Dissertation Abstracts International, 50* (7), 2036A.

Linnarud, M. (1986). *Lexis in composition: A performance analysis of Swedish.* Lund, Sweden: Liber Forlag Malmo.

Lux, P. (1991). Styles of Anglo and Latin American college student writers. *Dissertation Abstracts International, 52* (6), 2128A.

Mahmoud, A. (1982). A functional analysis of written compositions of Egyptian students of English and the implications of the notional functional syllabus for the teaching of writing. *Dissertation Abstracts International, 44* (5), 1439A.

Mann, R. (1986). A statistical survey of transitional device usage among writers of English as a second language and native writers of English. *Dissertation Abstracts International, 47* (5), 1636A.

Moragne e Silva, M. (1989). A study of composing in a first and second language. *Texas Papers in Foreign Language Education, 1* (2), 132-151.

Moragne e Silva, M. (1991). Cognitive, affective, social, and cultural aspects of composing in a first and second language: A case study of one adult writer. *Dissertation Abstracts International, 52* (12), 4249A.

Norment, N. (1982). Contrastive analysis of organizational structures and cohesive elements in English, Spanish (ESL), and Chinese (ESL) students' writing in narrative and expository modes. (ERIC Document Reproduction Service No. ED 269764)

Norment, N. (1984). Contrastive analyses of organizational structures and cohesive elements in native and ESL Chinese, English, and Spanish writing. *Dissertation Abstracts International, 45* (1), 172A.

Norment, N. (1986). Organizational structures of Chinese subjects writing in Chinese and ESL. *Journal of the Chinese Language Teachers Association, 21* (3), 49-72.

Oi, K. (1984). Cross-cultural differences in rhetorical patterning: A study of Japanese and English. *Dissertation Abstracts International, 45* (8), 2511A.

Ouaouicha, D. (1986). Contrastive rhetoric and the structure of learner-produced argumentative texts in Arabic and English. *Dissertation Abstracts International, 47* (9), 3339A.

Park, Y. (1988). Academic and ethnic background as factors affecting writing performance. In A. Purves (Ed.), *Writing across languages and cultures: Issues in contrastive rhetoric* (pp. 261-272). Newbury Park, CA: Sage.

Ragan, P. (1989). Applying functional grammar to teaching the writing of ESL. *Word, 40* (1-2), 117-127.

Raimes, A. (1985). What unskilled ESL students do as they write: A classroom study of composing. *TESOL Quarterly, 19* (2), 229-258.

Reid, J. (1988). Quantitative differences in English prose written by Arabic, Chinese, Spanish, and English students. *Dissertation Abstracts International, 50* (3), 672A.

Reid, J. (1992). A computer text analysis of four cohesion devices in English discourse by native and non-native writers. *Journal of Second Language Writing, 1* (2), 79-107.

Santiago, R. (1970). A contrastive analysis of some rhetorical aspects in the writing in Spanish and English of Spanish-speaking college students in Puerto Rico. *Dissertation Abstracts International, 31* (12), 6368A.

Scarcella, R. (1984a). Cohesion in the writing development of native and nonnative English speakers. *Dissertation Abstracts International, 45* (5), 86A.

Scarcella, R. (1984b). How writers orient their readers in expository essays: A comparative study of native and non-native English writers. *TESOL Quarterly, 18* (4), 671-688.

Schiller, J. (1989). Writing in L1—Writing in L2: Case studies of the composing processes of five adult Arabic-speaking ESL writers. *Dissertation Abstracts International, 50* (9), 2883A.

Silva, T. (1990). A comparative study of the composing of selected ESL and native English speaking freshman writers. *Dissertation Abstracts International, 51* (10), 3397A.

Silva, T. (1992). L1 vs. L2 writing: ESL graduate students' perceptions. *TESL Canada Journal, 10* (1), 27-47.

Silva, T. (1993). *Writing in two languages: Differences in ESL and L1 writing.* Manuscript submitted for publication.

Silva, T. (in press). Differences in ESL and native English speaker writing: The research and its implications. In J. Butler, J. Guerra, & C. Severino (Eds.), *Writing in multicultural settings.* New York: Modern Language Association.

Skibniewski, L. (1988). The writing processes of advanced foreign language learners in their native and foreign languages: Evidence from thinking aloud protocols. *Studia Anglica Posnaniensia, 21* (3), 177-186.

Skibniewski, L., & Skibniewska, M. (1986). Experimental study: The writing process of intermediate/advanced foreign language learners in their foreign and native languages. *Studia Anglica Posnanierzsia, 19* (3), 142-163.

Stalker, J. W., & Stalker, J. C. (1988). A comparison of pragmatic accommodation of non-native and native speakers in written English. *World Englishes, 7* (2), 119-128.

Tagong, K. (1991). Revising strategies of Thai students: Text-level changes in essays written in Thai and English. *Dissertation Abstracts International, 52* (8), 2849A.

Terdal, M. (1985). Learning to read and write in English: Case studies of two Southeast Asian students in a Northwest urban high school. *Dissertations Abstracts International, 46* (11), 3276A.

Watabe, M., Brown, C., & Ueta, Y. (1991). Transfer of discourse function: Passives in the writings of ESL and JSL learners. *IRAL, 29* (2), 115-134.

Webb, S. (1988). Using figurative language in epistemic writing: The purposes and processes of first and second language writers. *Dissertation Abstracts International, 49* (11), 3353A.

Whalen, K. (1988). Pilot study on the nature of difficulties in written expression in a second language: Process or product? *Bulletin of the CAAL, 1* (1), 51-57.

Xu, G. (1990). An ex post facto study of differences in the structure of the standard expository paragraphs between written compositions by native and nonnative speakers of English at the college level. *Dissertation Abstracts International, 51* (6), 1942A.

Yau, M. (1989, March). *A quantitative comparison of L1 and L2 writing processes.* Paper presented at the 23rd Annual TESOL Convention, San Antonio, Texas.

Yu, V., & Atkinson, P. (1988). An investigation of the language difficulties experienced by Hong Kong secondary school students in English medium schools: Pt. 1. The problems. *Journal of Multilingual and Multicultural Development, 9* (3), 267-284.

APPENDIX A
ESL/NES Studies: Native Languages of the ESL Subjects

Atari (1983): Arabic
Benson (1980): Arabic, Farsi, Ga, Japanese, Spanish, Thai
Benson et al. (1992): Amharic, Arabic, Cambodian, Chinese, Farsi, French, Gola, Gujartic, Hindi, Japanese,
    Korean, Portuguese, Somali, Spanish, Tagolog, Thai, Tigringa, Vietnamese
Burtoff (1983): Arabic, Japanese
Campbell (1987a): Chinese, Farsi, Hebrew, Indonesian, Korean, Lao, Spanish, Vietnamese
Campbell (1987b): Chinese, Farsi, Hebrew, Indonesian, Korean, Lao, Spanish, Vietnamese
Campbell (1990): Chinese, Farsi, Hebrew, Indonesian, Korean, Lao, Spanish, Vietnamese
Carlson (1988): Arabic, Chinese, Spanish
Choi (1988a): Korean
Choi (1988b): Korean
Connor (1984): Japanese, Spanish
Cummings (1990): Spanish
Dennett (1985): Japanese
Dennett (1990): Japanese
Frodesen (1991): Chinese, Korean, Spanish
Gates (1978): Farsi, Spanish, Thai
Hafernik (1990): Chinese, Japanese, Norwegian
Harris (1983): not specified
Hirokawa (1986): Arabic, Chinese, Indonesian, Japanese, Thai
Hu et al. (1982): Chinese
Intaraprawat (1988): Bengali, Chinese, French, Japanese, Thai
Kobayashi (1984a): Japanese
Kobayashi (1984b): Japanese
Linnarud (1986): Swedish
Lux (1991): Spanish
Mahmoud (1983): Arabic
Mann (1986): Arabic, Chinese, Spanish
Norment (1982): Arabic, Chinese, Spanish
Oi (1984): Japanese
Ouaouicha (1986): Arabic
Park (1988): Chinese
Ragan (1989): Chinese
Reid (1988): Arabic, Chinese, Spanish
Reid (1992): Arabic, Chinese, Spanish
Scarcella (1984a): Japanese, Korean, Romance, Taiwanese
Scarcella (1984b): Japanese, Korean, Romance, Taiwanese
Silva (1990): Chinese, Spanish
Stalker & Stalker (1988): not specified
Webb (1988): Spanish
Xu (1990): not specified
Yau (1989): Chinese

APPENDIX B
L1/L2 Studies: Native Languages of the Subjects

Almeida (1984): Portuguese
Arndt (1987): Chinese
Carson et al. (1990): Chinese, Japanese
Carson & Kuehn (1992): Chinese
Chelala (1981): Spanish
Cook (1988): Spanish
DeJesus (1984): Spanish
Dunkelblau (1990): Chinese
Gaskill (1986): Spanish
Hall (1987): Chinese, French, Norwegian, Polish
Hall (1990): Chinese, French, Norwegian, Polish
Hildenbrand (1985): Spanish
Jones & Tetroe (1987): Spanish
Kamel (1989): Arabic
Krapels (1990): Arabic, Chinese, Spanish
Lin (1989): Chinese
Moragne e Silva (1989): Portuguese
Moragne e Silva (1991): Portuguese
Norment (1986): Chinese
Santiago (1970): Spanish
Schiller (1989): Arabic
Skibniewski (1988): Polish
Skibniewski & Skibniewska (1986): Polish
Tagong (1991): Thai
Terdal (1985): Hmong, Vietnamese
Whalen (1988): French
Yu & Atkinson (1988): Chinese

APPENDIX C
ESL/NES and L1/L2 Comparisons: Native languages of the L2 Subjects

Indrasuta (1987): Thai
Indrasuta (1988): Thai
Norment (1984): Chinese, Spanish
Watabe et al. (1991): Japanese

Responding to ESL Students' Texts:
The Myths of Appropriation
by Joy Reid

Responding to students' texts has always been central to teaching writing. As we have embraced process writing, however, our methods of responding to student writing have changed. We used to treat students' texts as finished products, and we responded to and evaluated that product; now we usually intervene and respond at several points during the writing process. Because we comment on students' work in progress, the kinds of comments we traditionally made on the final draft are no longer sufficient and may even be counterproductive. In addition, many of us have discovered that product-based responses used during process-based intervention can result in the potential problem of appropriating students' texts.

I had been teaching ESL writing for nearly 20 years when I first encountered the phrase "appropriating student text" in two companion pieces about teacher response to native English speaker (NES) writing. In the first, "On Students' Rights to Their Own Texts: A Model of Teacher Response," Brannon and Knoblauch (1982) discussed the concept of authority in the classroom, and in so doing, defined the context for text appropriation:

> In classroom writing situations, the [teacher-reader] assumes primary control of the choices that writers make, feeling perfectly free to "correct" those choices any time an apprentice deviates from the teacher-reader's conception of what the developing text "ought" to look like or "ought" to be doing.... Student writers, then are put into the awkward position of having to accommodate, not only the personal intentions that guide their choice-making, but also the teacher-reader's expectations about how the assignment should be completed. (p. 158)

In the second article, Sommers (1982) used the word *appropriating* as she described the role of the teacher in a writing classroom: "The teacher appropriates the text from the student by confusing the student's purpose in writing the text with her own purpose in commenting" (p. 149).

Like many writing teachers, I was curious about and puzzled by the concept of appropriation. Greenhalgh (1992) summarizes the dilemma I faced in my composition classes:

> Teachers of writing regularly face the task of advising students about their work-in-progress. The task is problematic because it raises many practical and theoretical issues. Not least is the ethical issue of rights and responsibilities with respect to texts. Researchers recommend that a teacher must somehow make it possible for students to take control of their own writing. A responsible teacher, then, would be a responsive reader, one who helps students identify and solve writing problems but. . . . avoid[s] unwittingly appropriating the draft. Responsible students would, in turn, be their own best readers, taking responsibility for solving writing problems of their own making. (p. 401)

Greenhalgh argues that teachers must therefore find ways to comment on student writing while at the same time respecting the differences between teacher and student responsibility for an emerging text. As a partial solution, she states, instead of seeking the ideal text that exists in teachers' imaginations, teachers must negotiate with their students about the intentions of the text, and they must simultaneously broaden their expectations of successful student prose.

For ESL teachers, the issue of text appropriation during the last decade has been particularly complex, principally because it is entwined with several dichotomies: product versus process, accuracy versus fluency, and practical considerations of audience expectations versus creativity. In this article, I examine the question of text appropriation in the light of these dichotomies and propose that appropriation of student text is largely a mythical fear of ESL writing teachers. Instead of being worried about appropriating texts, I believe that teachers should accept their responsibility as cultural informants and as facilitators for creating the social discourse community in the ESL writing classroom.

Background

As I began to prepare this article, I realized I should investigate the reasons that appropriation became an issue in composition teaching. First, the revival of classical rhetoric described writing as an act guided by its situation—its purpose and audience (Bitzer, 1968; Faigley, 1986). If, in response to this perspective, teachers taught student writers to address readers and contexts outside the classroom, teachers could no longer measure student writing solely against their criteria for an ideal text. Next, a paradigm shift from product to process described by Hairston (1982) occurred as teachers and researchers began to practice teaching writing, as opposed to merely assigning and evaluating writing. As teachers began intervening in students' drafts, they realized the theoretical awkwardness of their position, the pedagogical gap between the need to teach writing and the need for students to develop their own intentions and purposes for writing. Finally, as students practiced invention heuristics, drafted, and revised their prose—often in expressive, writer-based classrooms—the question of authority and ownership of writing arose (Bizzell, 1990; Bruffee, 1986; Fish, 1980). If the writer owned the text, and therefore had authority for and over that text, what part could the teacher play without "stealing" (i.e., appropriating) that text? These three issues—rhetorical situation, process methodology, and authority concerns—converge at the moment teachers respond to students' drafts.

In retrospect, as a writing teacher, I could not see the larger picture of that paradigm shift; I was unable to distinguish between what Clark (1993) calls legitimate and illegitimate collaboration. Moreover, instead of understanding how the rights and responsibilities for making meaning in texts are shared by writers and readers, instead of responding to students' texts as a surrogate academic audience, I began to fear that I was appropriating my students' work. During the 1980s, appropriation became a buzzword for everything that was wrong with the old approaches to teaching writing; I could hardly go to a conference presentation without hearing about the evils of commenting on (i.e., intruding on) student papers; about the "tyranny" of teachers' responses; and about the student confusion that surrounded teacher response. These presentations ended by warning teachers not to get in their students' way, not to interfere with their writing, not to impose control or authority over their students' writing.

Appropriation seemed particularly serious when it occurred in the ESL classroom. One reason for this focus on text appropriation was the result of a distorted view of the product/process dichotomy. Although most ESL teachers regularly integrated process and product approaches in their writing classrooms, researchers often sought to castigate the product of writing (and its absolute focus on the mechanical, the accurate, the "recipe" rhetoric) in favor of the creative, intellectually stimulating autonomy of process writing (Taylor, 1981; Zamel, 1976, 1980, 1982). At its most extreme, teacher intervention in student writing processes was seen as culturally imperialistic, an attempt to teach ESL students that U.S. academic rhetoric was somehow superior to other cultural rhetorics (Kachru, 1982, 1985; Ouaouicha, 1986). Carried further, these attitudes inextricably linked process writing with personal and expressive writing and academic writing solely with product-based pedagogy.

Furthermore, researchers suggested that in the event of teacher intervention, students either slavishly responded to teacher comments, relinquishing their authority over their texts, or they misunderstood teacher response; the resulting revisions were therefore at best no more successful than the original texts (Cardelle & Corno, 1981; Freedman, 1987; Freedman & Sperling, 1985; Purves, 1986, 1992; Schwartz, 1984). Zamel (1985) noted that teachers should "no longer present ourselves as authorities but act instead as consultants, assistants, and facilitators" (p. 96).

Like any interested teacher, I thought about what I heard and read. The idea of text appropriation was intriguing and worrisome. What was appropriation? Correcting a spelling error? Underlining a syntax error? Possibly, because error correction establishes the authority of the teacher and leads students to give up ownership of their texts. If students acquiesce in matters of black and white grammar errors, they may transfer that acquiescence to more complex teacher responses about rhetoric, audience, and levels of evidence. Was appropriation asking a question about content? Mentioning the need for additional detail? Possibly, because depending on the question or the comment, the teacher might be substituting her intention for the student's. Directing the student to rearrange paragraphs, eliminate ideas, or add evidence? Probably, because the writing might then fulfill the purposes of the teacher rather than the student's intent. As a consequence, the student who revised the text might well cede control of the text to the teacher.

So I drew away from writing comments on my students' papers; after all, when might I interfere with their objectives or crush their creativity? In what ways might I assume control or ownership over their texts? What might I say that would deter them from becoming independent writers? The fewer comments I made and the less I tried to "interfere," however, the more fraudulent I felt as a teacher. And when I evaluated final drafts of student writing and wrote the summative comments that explained the grade, I often thought that I could have helped the students more if I had not been so worried about appropriating their texts. I began to resent my fear of appropriation because it had begun to affect my effectiveness as a teacher.

In time, I realized that I felt fraudulent because avoiding "appropriating" students' texts conflicted with my philosophy of teaching ESL writing. My teaching philosophy is based on two assumptions. First, education is change, and the teacher's primary responsibility is to provide opportunities for change in the classroom. In the ideal classroom, the students would have the foresight, knowledge, and perspective to approach, identify, and implement change in themselves. In reality, it is the ESL teacher who often acts as the change agent, who offers students a classroom atmosphere and cultural expertise that will allow them the choice of change (of education). Second, the major difference between isolated learning—through, for example, instructional television—and classroom education is the community of students and teacher whose goals are established and who work together to reach those goals. Communities are not ideal either, nor are they composed of clones; hierarchies, individual strengths and weaknesses, and different levels of commitment exist. In the ESL writing classroom, the teacher is responsible for establishing the classroom discourse community, for providing an atmosphere in which that community of writers can grow, and, especially at the beginning of the class, for providing the necessary scaffolding that will result in students' opportunities to work together to change—to learn.

In light of this philosophy, I now believe that many of the appropriation arguments are myths and that these myths of appropriation grew out of teachers' good intentions to withdraw from student texts in order to provide better learning experiences for their students. Two reasons account for the flawed theory of appropriation. First, the theoretical basis for defining text appropriation all but ignored the social contexts for writing: how writers negotiate meaning with their academic audience in mind, how peers are or are not able to make meaning from a student's text, and how readers in discourse communities outside the classroom might construct meaning successfully from students' texts. These situational contexts inside and outside the classroom were underrepresented and undervalued, particularly in light of the fact that many ESL writers are unable to identify the needs and expectations of U.S. audiences. Second, like most new perspectives on pedagogy, the idea of appropriating student text was embraced and then exaggerated; in application, teachers would not utilize their expertise as cultural informants and experienced academic readers for fear of changing (i.e., educating) their students. However, the teacher exists because of her expertise, and it is therefore the responsibility of the teacher to share her cultural and rhetorical knowledge with her students, to intervene in student writing in order to educate her students.

Appropriation and Social Context

As I began to examine the meaning of appropriation, I realized that the original definition of appropriation excluded the social context of writing. With the possible exception of some personal writing, the processes and products of writing do not occur in a vacuum, and, in Flower's terms (1979), most academic writing is reader based (i.e., written for someone other than the author), not writer based. Writing/reading theory has demonstrated that written communication has three interactive parts: the writer, the text, and the reader. The transaction that occurs among these three elements results in communication (Carrell, 1987; Meyer, 1982; Meyer & Rice, 1982; Rosenblatt, 1988, 1993). In order to communicate successfully, writers must therefore consider not only their purpose(s) but also the purpose(s) and expectations of their readers. The author's intentions, and the author's control (or ownership) of a text must be balanced by the increasing knowledge of the audience (Frank, 1992; Johns, 1992, 1993b; Schriver, 1992). Identification and analysis of audience is a complex process that involves more than a brief character sketch ("I'm writing this for novice skiers" or "to the President"): From discrete items like word choice to greater concerns with focus and with levels of evidence, to decisions about form and format—all these and more impact directly on the reader. As Arrington (1992) states,

> First, writers should usually try to reduce a reader's uncertainties about meaning as far as possible. Second, readers seem to need some conventions of written prose to help them reduce those uncertainties. These conventions aren't absolutely or historically fixed, but they do help writers address and affect readers they don't know and would likely never meet. (p. 327)

For academic prose, the audience outside the context of the writing classroom is U.S. academic readers who belong to various discourse communities: Each discourse community comprises a group of readers who share similar objectives, values, and expectations about (among other things) academic prose. In the ESL writing classroom, the teacher serves not simply as an evaluator of products, and not only as an expert in the skills of written communication, but also as the surrogate academic audience. She is a liaison between student and discourse communities, and it is in this role that she "conspires" with her students in order to "manage, in advance, the encounter between writer and reader" (Geisler, 1991, p. 26). As Newkirk (1989) states, "No one (I hope) condones the practice condemned by Knoblauch and Brannon in which students must guess at some Platonic text that exists in the teacher's imagination. But by the same token, the expectations of the teacher, the course, and the academy must interact with the intentions of the students" (p. 329). From this perspective, teachers collaborate with students not as gatekeepers but as coaches and discourse community experts who use their resources to help their students through the gate into those communities of writers.

A discussion of text appropriation must also include the social context of the ESL writing classroom. Within the class, written response to student drafts by teacher and peers also takes place in a discourse community; within the classroom community, teachers and students establish lines of communication. At the beginning of the class, when the community of the classroom is in a formative stage, teacher response to student writing parallels initial conversations between strangers. In my own classes, I begin that conversation by assigning writing that requires the students to analyze their writing in some way (through a description of the results of a learning styles survey, a discussion of individual writing rituals, or an observation of previous successful and/or unsuccessful writing). In this way, the essays themselves introduce the students. Still, because the students are strangers, my written comments on drafts tend to be more directional and more generic than my comments later in the course because I am striving to establish my place in the community of the classroom as I begin to represent the expectations of academic audiences. Students respond in the conversation by revising, and, during those revision processes, they discuss and negotiate possible changes with peers, with writing center tutors, and with me. As the processes of the developing conversation continues within the classroom community, members of this community of writers assume a variety of roles (as drafters, peer reviewers, revisers, and responders). As knowledge and experience within the community grows, students become more aware of their responsibilities to the classroom community, and of the need for intervention (by self, peers, and teacher) in their writing.

As the course progresses, the teacher accumulates knowledge of individual student strengths and weaknesses, expectations, and needs. In my classes, my responses to student writing tend to become more individualized and shorter, but in this case, less is often more. For instance, because students' writing processes and strengths differ, I approach each text with the writer in mind, becoming increasingly aware of the differing levels of language knowledge, background knowledge, and rhetorical experience of the writers. Consequently, within a single set of student papers, I may underline a particular stubborn grammar problem on one ("Again??"), praise the support in a paragraph on another ("Whoopee! This is great support"), and ask questions about audience awareness on a third ("How will the hostile audience [whom we have discussed in class and who is the assigned audience for this essay] respond?").

Yet research focusing on the efficacy and effectiveness of teacher comments on student drafts does not take into account this social context. Often the results of such research label teacher responses as strictly mechanical, unhelpful, and confusing (Purves, 1984; Schwartz, 1984) without considering the context in which the comments were written. After examining written teacher responses on student papers, Zamel (1985) castigated teacher-responders:

> ESL writing teachers misread student texts, are inconsistent in their reactions, make arbitrary corrections, write contradictory comments, provide vague prescriptions, impose abstract rules and standards, respond to texts as fixed and final products, and rarely make content-specific comments or offer specific strategies for revising the text. (p. 86)

Connors and Lunsford (1993) researching a corpus of teacher responses written on 3,000 NES student essays found a "large number of short, careless, exhausted or insensitive comments" (p. 215). According to Connors and Lunsford,

> The job that teachers felt they were supposed to do was, it seemed, overwhelmingly a job of looking at papers rather than students; our [research evaluators] found very little readerly response and very little response to context. Most teachers, if our sample is representative, continue to feel that a major task is to "correct" and edit papers, primarily for formal errors but also for deviation from algorithmic and often rigid "rhetorical" rules as well. (p, 2 17)

Whether or not these ESL and NES papers were representative, they had been isolated from the social context of the classroom community and evaluated in that isolation; the one-dimensional quality of such research, and the assumptions made by the evaluators concerning the misreading, contradictions, and insensitivity of the responders, at best weaken the results. Moreover, studies that asked ESL students to evaluate the efficacy of written teacher response have demonstrated that a great majority of students found the comments helpful, used the comments to revise, and particularly appreciated teacher response that led them to positive learning experiences in their revision processes (Cohen & Cavalcanti, 1990; Fathman & Whalley, 1990; Leki, 1990; McCurdy, 1992).

A researcher outside the social context of my classroom who examines just my written responses (above) on a midsemester set of ESL papers may classify my comments as erratic, useless, and/or appropriative. The researcher may miss the rationale and the result of the communicative negotiation between the student and the teacher, made within the established and mutually understood content and context of the classroom. Another example: Late in the semester, as my students begin drafting persuasive essays, they study logical fallacies. In peer review groups, they examine each other's essays to discover and revise hasty generalizations or inadequately supported opinions. Before they turn in their final drafts, they know that I, too, will be looking for the fallacies (among other features and factors). If I find one, I promise to circle it with yellow highlighter, and in the margin to label the fallacy: "hasty" or "oversimplification" or "post hoc." An outside examiner viewing those abbreviated remarks might conclude that I am being obtuse, negative, and appropriative. Instead, my students view it as a game; they fully understand the shorthand of the response, which reminds them of our classroom discussion and activates their background knowledge about logical fallacies.

This is not to say that misunderstanding, inadequacies, and contradictions do not occur in teacher comments, but rather that many teacher comments, seen within the context of a classroom or conference, are more communicative and more valuable than they seem when taken out of context. Furthermore, if a sense of community has been established and maintained in the ESL classroom, mutual respect and good will can overcome such errors. If, for example, a student does not know the correct verb tense, cannot identify the problem with focus in a paragraph, or is unable to answer a question about how an audience might respond to certain evidence, that student can consult with peers during a revision workshop, or the teacher during a conference, or a tutor during a visit to the writing center. Within the social situation of the classroom community, then, students and the teacher participate in the meaning-making process concerning intentions and communicative purposes that will be applied in student writing to the larger social context—the academic discourse community outside the classroom (Johns, 1993a; Johns, 1993b; Reid, 1989).

Appropriation and the Academic Audience

Research that considers the social contexts for academic writing has demonstrated that even many NESs must learn about academic discourse communities; they must be taught to identify, analyze, and fulfill audience expectations (see Faigley, 1985; Greenhalgh, 1992; Onore, 1989; Thompson, 1989). Interestingly, even in early appropriation discussions Brannon and Knoblauch (1982) did not believe that teaching takes place in a hands-off environment. Instead, they felt strongly that teachers should be intervening in student texts:

> The challenge we face as teachers is to develop comments which will provide an inherent reason for students to revise; it is a sense of revision as discovery, as a repeated process of beginning again, as starting out new, that our students have not learned. We need to show our students how to seek, in the possibility of revision, the dissonances of discovery—to show them through our comments why new choices would positively change their texts and thus show them the potential for development implicit in their own writing. (p. 156)

If this is true for NES classes, it is essential for ESL writers, whose cultural schema for writing differs, sometimes dramatically, from that of their NES audience. Because their linguistic, content, contextual, and rhetorical schemata differ, they often have problems with the identification and fulfillment of U.S. audience expectations. For these students, a writing class is more than practice of acquired skills; it is a content course about the rhetorical and contextual expectations of their academic audience.

These ESL students have extraordinary needs. Teachers must therefore act as cultural informants as well as surrogate audiences. They must investigate the requirements and expectations of academic assignments and then help their students analyze and understand U.S. academic assignments and readers (Canesco & Byrd, 1989; Horowitz, 1986; Reid, 1992; Smagorinsky & Smith, 1992). In my classes, we often examine actual academic assignments from across the curriculum, analyzing the parameters of the assignment, identifying the expectations of that academic reader/evaluator, and discussing strategies to meet those expectations. In addition, from nearly the first day of class, I begin educating the students about contrastive rhetoric. Importantly, the students understand that they have choices and that each choice involves consequences. If, for example, they choose not to modify their rhetoric to fulfill the needs of their U.S. discourse communities, they may encounter confusion and misunderstanding from their readers. If, on the other hand, they adapt their rhetoric, they might find it difficult to readjust their writing when they return to their countries of origin. I ask the students to experiment with their rhetorical presentation skills in the relatively unthreatening atmosphere of our class before they make decisions about their U.S. academic writing assignments outside the classroom.

Power and Empowerment

At the foundation of the text appropriation argument is the problem of power and empowerment in the classroom. Should students have exclusive power (and ownership) over their texts? What is (or should be) the influence of the social situation of the discourse communities and readers within the academic context? How can teachers help to empower student writers? What is the role, and what is the level of authority, of the teacher in student writing processes?

At the foundation of my teaching philosophy is a firm belief that power does not have a finite quality. The teacher does not have to give up power in order to empower her students. Instead, teachers must introduce situations and contexts in which students can feel empowered, some of which students may not have considered previously; we must introduce students to ways in which they can learn to gain ownership of their writing while at the same time considering their readers.

One of the problems with student empowerment lies in the definition of academic writing. Unlike much of the writing discussed in conference presentations and research, the audiences and purposes of academic writing rest on asymmetrical relationships among the elements of writer, text, and reader. First, in contrast to much personal writing—diaries, letters to familials, and the like—academic topics are usually assigned, and the written product is evaluated. Next, the audience for academic writing is often limited to the person who also designs, assigns, and assesses that writing, so the relationship between the writer and the reader does not approximate that of most other socially situated writing. Instead of writers having an expert-to-novice relationship, or a colleague-to-colleague relationship with their readers, the relationship is skewed: novice-to-expert, with the expert (teacher/reader) assessing the novice (student/writer) in ways that impact on the writer's life. Teacher/readers also face unusual social interactions in their responses to and evaluations of student writing. They often play several roles, among them coach, judge, facilitator, and gatekeeper as they offer more response and more intervention than an ordinary reader (Freedman & Sperling, 1985; Johnson, 1992; Moxley, 1989; Radecki & Swales, 1988).

As anomalous as academic writing seems, there are other academic parallels. Grant proposals are submitted for review, and articles, like this one, are examined and carefully reviewed. In each of these cases, authors write for a group of unknown readers whose expertise may be greater than theirs; in each case, there is an evaluation (and in some cases, even a grade) for the work. For each, there is a potential for written feedback, sometimes detailed with suggestions. If the writers are fortunate enough to be advised to revise and resubmit, surely those (experienced, academic) writers will strive to make the necessary changes for resubmission in order to appeal to and satisfy the expectations of the readers/evaluators. Because of their level of expertise and experience, they may question some of the comments, but generally they will revise with the readers/evaluators in mind. Finally, in each case, acceptance of the proposal or article results in some direct benefit to the writer (money, fame), while rejection sends the opposite real-life message.

Are the grant readers and the editors appropriating the text of the experienced academic writers? Are those writers abandoning their creativity and their independence as writers by revising their manuscripts? Is it any wonder that students look to teachers' comments and responses, striving to fulfill those expectations because in doing so they serve their own self-interest? When I receive a manuscript for revision (and the initial feeling of rejection has waned), I find that the comments by reviewers usually have been made to more carefully describe the parameters and constraints of the social context and to point out inconsistencies that might later prove embarrassing. Ideally, they offer me new perspectives, they open new areas for communication, and they allow me to see more clearly my writing through readers' eyes in the discourse community for whom I am writing. If the reviewers praise the work I have done well, make specific suggestions for improvement, and offer additional ideas and resources, I am grateful for the insights, and I am empowered to revise. If, on the other hand, the review is unhelpfully vague, if an article or grant proposal is rejected without comment, or if even one remark is off-handedly sarcastic, revision is much, much more difficult for me.

Therefore, when I respond to student texts in my classes, I try first to describe what those student texts seem to say, discuss the linguistic and rhetorical choices the students have made, and offer alternatives that are based on my knowledge of U.S. academic audience expectations. I think of these processes as intervention, as an effective use of my cultural knowledge that can assist my students in their entrance into the U.S. academic community. If this is appropriation, I am guilty. However, I see my intervention as a direct result of student needs, probably more directive (i.e., content based) than I might be with NESs. Although I try not to appropriate students' language by, for example, rewriting passages, I often indicate directly how academic readers might respond, and I offer rhetorically based choices. If, instead, I would refrain from intervention in order to avoid appropriation, I believe that I would abdicate my responsibilities as a cultural informant and an educator.

Intervention and Empowerment

So what about the appropriation of student work? Do ESL students expect and need directive teacher response? Because academic writing is a social endeavor, and because, as the teacher, I know more about the parameters and constraints of academic writing, I believe that it is my responsibility to intervene in my students' writing. The teacher is a resource and an authority as well as a facilitator and a member of the classroom community—which, like all communities, comprises a hierarchy. I agree with Mitchell (1992):

> My job is to orchestrate: I probe students to find out what they really want to focus on; help them find models of writing; discuss the elements of style and teach students to analyze style as a basis for designing their projects; ask questions that encourage deeper reading of models; comment on drafts; present evaluative workshops based on common patterns of error in each set of papers I read; push students to work beyond what they perceive as their capacities. (p. 400)

For those who feel that this view is too narrow, too teacher-centered, too formalistic, I offer the following: Some years ago, when I received an Exxon grant, I decided I needed to know more about statistics, so I enrolled in a class convenient to my teaching schedule. It turned out to be an Honors Statistics class, a dozen bright-eyed undergraduates and me. For fully 2 weeks I sat in class, trying with increasing desperation to understand the three languages: the ordinary English language of greetings and discussion, which made up about a third of the class; the language on the board, filled with symbols; and the simultaneous explanation of those symbols by the professor in statistics as a foreign language. The worst, though, was the freedom within the class. Regularly, the professor would demonstrate three ways to solve a problem; he would mention in passing that we were to determine, through analysis and trial, which of the three was preferable.

I couldn't. I didn't understand the statistics discourse community: I didn't have the necessary linguistic, content, contextual, or even rhetorical schemata that would allow me to function. Because I knew so little, I could not enter into the verbal analyses of the variations; in fact, I could not even follow them. And, as my affective filter rose, I was able to take in less and less. What I needed was a single way to solve a problem, one that I could understand linguistically and schematically, and then I needed adequate practice to make it my own. I needed the professor to pay attention to what I didn't know and to intervene in the problem-solving processes so that I could succeed. And secretly, what I believed was that the professor knew which of the ways to solve each problem was the best (for me? for the discourse community? for efficiency?), but that for reasons of his own (his choice to be the keeper of the secret answer? the culture of statistics as a mystery? his desire to be cruel to me?) he had chosen not to tell me. At the end of the third week of class, overwhelmed, I talked with the professor and changed into a different class, one in which the professor was willing to say "Here's the best [fastest, easiest, more accepted] way," and to offer worksheets, class discussion, and office hours (all in one language: classroom English). He has remained my statistics mentor to this day.

ESL writing classes, I believe, are no less disorienting than my experiences in the statistics class. Therefore, ESL writing classes should be pragmatic places in which students learn the essentials of academic writing. Written literacy does not come naturally, particularly for L2 writers, for whom the context for writing needs what Arrington (1992) calls a "social translation." I suspect that our students think that there is just one correct way to write, and that we teachers know but won't tell them. In order to demystify the writing process, I believe that teachers must intervene to provide students with adequate schemata (linguistic, content, contextual, and rhetorical) that will serve as a scaffolding for writing, then offer opportunities to discover coping styles and strategies that will result in effective communication (Harris & Silva, 1993). And because writing is an act of confidence, we must help students to see both the potential and the problems in their writing, and we must be able, through our intervention, to send our students back into the writing process with a concrete plan for improving their writing. I therefore show my students ways to fulfill audience expectations, but I remind them again and again that I am providing only a skeleton for effective communication. The muscles, the ligaments, the filling out of the skeleton comes only with experience, practice, and additional intervention.

Avoiding Appropriation

Can appropriation of student text occur? Of course. In fact, the greatest potential for appropriation is in the most process-based, writer-based classes, particularly those in which evaluation occurs solely on the final portfolio of writing. Although it may seem that appropriation of student texts is least possible in this situation because the power of the grade is not behind the teacher's comments, in fact the specter of the final grade looms large in students' minds, particularly when interim evaluation is not specific and therefore is unknown. In such classes, the teacher is simply one member of the writing community in which, supposedly, all members have equal status; students turn in draft after draft, and the teacher comments (orally or in writing) on each draft, encouraging students by making suggestions for improvement (or asking questions that are, in actuality, suggestions) but not evaluating the writing directly.

Unfortunately, the more assistance the teacher offers, the less responsibility the student needs to take. Students are not, generally, any more ideal than the texts they write; their objectives in the class may differ dramatically from the teacher's wishes that they become mature, experienced decision makers about their writing. Instead, for many students, the final grade is the bottom line, so these students will acquiesce willingly, reshaping their prose according to teacher comments with each successive draft. This ceding of responsibility for the text is easy in the expert-novice relationship between teacher and student; much more difficult for the teacher is working in tandem with a student while simultaneously requiring that all decisions be the purview of the student. The results are often predictable: If judgments concerning the improvement of student writing remain the sole province of the teacher, then the student may choose not to make choices, not to negotiate with the expert/teacher to solve problems. At the end of the course, when the final writing is assessed, the "owner" of the writing may be dual—the student and the teacher—but quite suddenly the teacher/collaborator is the evaluator. This sudden change in roles, from facilitative to evaluative, is at best confusing for both student and teacher, and the evaluation may easily focus on the collaborative success rather than on student achievement.

Fortunately, with substantial effort and self-discipline, we can assist our students without appropriating their texts. First, we need to bring our students into the conversation about response by discussing their expectations about the teacher's role. I work with the students to identify and describe criteria for successful U.S. academic writing, the criteria by which we will all respond to student papers. I ask students to write metacognitive memos or journal entries that reveal their intentions, describe their struggles, and analyze their rationales, for writing strengthens their investment (and ownership) in their writing. Second, we must teach students the skills and strategies to reread their own writing as the reader, not the writer, of the text; to do this, we must model for our students how U.S. academic audiences read, which discourse conventions they expect, and how they respond to texts. This training is more time-consuming and complex for me than simply reading and marking student drafts; however, the students gradually learn to be aware of the discourse communities for whom they write and to modify their intentions to fulfill the expectations of their audiences. The result of this training (this educating) may be students who grow into independent writers, capable of making effective choices in their future writing. My job as responder, as Elbow (1993) advises, is to look "hard and thoughtfully at [each] piece of writing in order to make distinctions as to the quality of different features or dimensions" (p. 91). As I read the student memos that accompany their writing, I gain insights into student intention that makes response and intervention more effective. As a consequence, I am both direct and directive as I suggest revision options. Finally, as I praise what each student does well, I try to individualize response: Which student needs additional support? Which "tough love"? Which a touch of humor?

Moreover, responding to student writing should be a learning process for the teacher as well as for the student (Bates, Lane, & Lange, 1994). As teachers of academic prose, we must first relinquish the concept of the ideal text and approach our students' texts with their intentions and authority in mind. Then we must meet each of our students at his/her developmental stage, intervening individually in ways that will allow the student to learn. Next, we can learn to respond responsibly by reexamining our intervention strategies and analyzing our goals by considering such questions as

- When and how frequently during the writing process should I respond?
- Who is the student, and in what ways can I best respond to this student?
- How can I respond to the student's writing so that the student can process the comments and apply the specifics of my response?
- Which role(s) should I play in this response: responder, consultant, describer, coach, evaluator?

- Where should I respond: in conference, in class? directly on the paper or in a written memo at the end of the paper?
- Who else should be responding to the student's text?
- What form(s) of response (written, oral, individual, group, formal or informal) would be most successful for the student)?
- When should my response be global (i.e., focusing mainly on the major strengths and/or weaknesses) or discrete (i.e., focusing on local concerns—single items) in the discourse?
- What are my objectives for this writing task? That is, what do I want the students to learn?

Finally, while the teacher is the expert resource concerning academic prose and discourse communities, students must be taught to authentically engage in choice making and problem solving, and to accept responsibility for their own writing. The teacher then becomes the respondent instead of the initiator in the response conversation, and, rather than a monologue, response becomes a dialogue in which teacher and student negotiate meaning (Murray, 1985).

Conclusion

Despite its sometimes extreme applications, the research on appropriation of student texts has provided some useful insights for teachers. It sensitized me to the differences between the summative evaluation of written products and the formative intervention in student drafts (Horvath, 1985). It also demonstrated the multiple roles that writers must assume as readers, responders, coaches, and expert members of the academic discourse community.

Articles on appropriation of student texts have all but passed out of the NES literature; instead, the focus is on empowering students to enter discourse communities. Yet distortions of the appropriation arguments still persist in some ESL writing classrooms. These myths of appropriation may give a very few teachers license to abdicate their responsibilities as cultural informants and surrogate academic audiences—as educators. For most teachers, however, seeing intervention in the wider context of discourse communities opens the door to a classroom in which teachers begin by responding to students' own purposes and goals and by negotiating text meaning through questions, conferencing, and written comments.

Works Cited

Arrington, P. (1992). Reflections on the expository principle. *College English, 54,* 314-332.

Bates, L., Lane, J., & Lange, E. (1994). *Writing clearly: Responding to ESL compositions.* Boston: Heinle & Heinle.

Bitzer, L. (1968). The rhetorical situation. *Philosophy and Rhetoric, 1,* 1-14.

Bizzell, P. (1990). Beyond anti-foundationalism to rhetorical authority: Problems defining "cultural literacy." *College English, 52,* 661-675.

Brannon, L., & Knoblauch, C. H. (1982). On students' rights to their own texts: A model of teacher response. *College Composition and Communication, 33,* 157-166.

Bruffee, K. (1986). Social construction, language, and the authority of knowledge: A bibliographic essay. *College English, 48,* 773-790.

Canesco, G., & Byrd, P. (1989). Writing required in graduate courses in business administration. *TESOL Quarterly, 23,* 305-316.

Cardelle, M., & Corno, L. (1981). Effects on second language learning of variations in written feedback on homework assignments. *TESOL Quarterly, 15,* 251-261.

Carrell, P. L. (1987, April). Readability in ESL: A schema-theoretic perspective. Paper presented at the 21st Annual TESOL Convention, Miami,

Clark, I. (1993). Portfolio evaluation, collaboration, and writing centers. *College Composition and Communication, 44,* 515-524.

Cohen, A., & Cavalcanti, M. (1990). Feedback on compositions: Teacher and student verbal reports. In B. Kroll (Ed.), *Second language writing: Research insights for the classroom* (pp. 155-177). New York: Cambridge University Press.

Connors, R. J., & Lunsford, A. A. (1993). Teachers' rhetorical comments on student papers. *College Composition and Communication, 44,* 200-223.

Elbow, P. (1993). Ranking, evaluating, and liking: Sorting out three forms of judgment. *College English, 55,* 187-206.

Faigley, L. L. (1985). Non-academic writing: The social perspective. In L. O'Dell & D. Goswami (Eds.), *Writing in a non-academic settings* (pp. 231-248). New York: Guilford Press.

Faigley, L. L. (1986). Competing theories of process: A critique and a proposal. *College English, 48,* 527-542.

Fathman, A., & Whalley, E. (1990). Teacher response to student writing: Focus on form versus content. In B. Kroll (Ed.), *Second language writing: Research insights for the classroom* (pp. 178-190). New York: Cambridge University Press.

Fish, S. (1980). *Is there a text in this class? The authority of interpretive communities.* Cambridge, MA: Harvard University Press.

Flower, L. (1979). Writer-based prose: A cognitive basis for problems in writing. *College English, 41,* 19-38.

Frank, L. (1992). Writing to be read: Young writers' ability to demonstrate audience awareness when evaluated by their readers. *Research in the Teaching of English, 26,* 277-298.

Freedman, S. (1987). *Response to student writing.* Urbana, IL: NCTE.

Freedman, S., & Sperling, M. (1985). Teacher-student interaction in the writing conference: Response and teaching. In S. Freedman (Ed.), *The acquisition of written language: Revision and response* (pp. 106-130). Norwood, NJ: Ablex.

Geisler, C. (1991). Reader, parent, coach: Defining the profession by our practice of response. *Reader, 25,* 17-33.

Greenhalgh, A. M. (1992). Voices in response: A postmodern reading of teacher response. *College Composition and Communication, 43,* 401-410.

Hairston, M. (1982). The winds of change: Thomas Kuhn and the revolution in the teaching of writing. *College Composition and Communication, 33,* 76-88.

Harris, M., & Silva, T. (1993). Tutoring ESL students: Issues and options. *College Composition and Communication, 44,* 525-537.

Horowitz, D. (1986). What professors actually require: Academic tasks for the ESL classroom. *TESOL Quarterly, 20,* 445-462.

Horvath, B. (1985). The components of written response: A practical synthesis of current views. *Rhetoric Review, 2,* 136-156.

Johns, A. (1992). Academic English: What can we do? *Journal of Intensive English Studies, 6,* 61-69.

Johns, A. (1993a). Writing argumentation for real audiences: Suggestions for teacher research and classroom practice. *TESOL Quarterly, 27,* 75-90.

Johns, A. M. (1993b). Reading and writing tasks in English for academic purposes classes: Products, processes, and resources. In J. Carson & I. Leki (Eds.), *Reading in the composition classroom: Second language perspectives* (pp. 274-289). Boston: Heinle & Heinle.

Johnson, H. (1992). Fossilizing. *ELT Journal, 46,* 180-189.

Kachru, B. (1982). Models of English for the Third World: White man's linguistic burden or language pragmatic? *TESOL Quarterly, 10,* 221-232.

Kachru, B. (1985). Institutionalized second language varieties. In S. Greenbaum (Ed.), *The English language today* (pp. 211-226). London: Oxford University Press.

Leki, I. (1990). Coaching from the margins: Issues in written response. In B. Kroll (Ed.), *Second language writing: Research insights for the classroom* (pp. 57-68). New York: Cambridge University Press.

McCurdy, P. (1992, March). *What students do with composition feedback.* Paper presented at the 26th Annual TESOL Convention, Vancouver, Canada.

Meyer, B. J. F. (1982). Reading research and the composition teacher. *College Composition and Communication, 33,* 37-39.

Meyer, B. J. F., & Rice, G. E. (1982). The interaction of reader strategies and the organization of text. *Text, 2,* 155-192.

Mitchell, F. (1992). Balancing individual projects and collaborative learning in an advanced writing class. *College Composition and Communication, 43,* 393-408.

Moxley, J. (1989). Responding to student writing: Goals, methods, alternatives. *Freshman English News, 17,* 3-11.

Murray, D. (1985). *A writing teacher teaches writing* (2nd ed.). Boston: Houghton Mifflin.

Newkirk, T. (1989). The first five minutes: Setting the agenda in a conference. In C. M. Anson (Ed.), *Writing and response: Theory, practice, and research* (pp. 317-331). Urbana, IL: NCTE.

Onore, C. (1989). The student, the teacher, and the text: Negotiating meanings through response and revision. In C. Anson (Ed.), *Writing and response: Theory, Practice and research* (pp. 231-260). Urbana, IL: NCTE.

Ouaouicha, D. (1986). *Contrastive rhetoric and the structure of learner-produced argumentative texts in Arabic and English.* Unpublished doctoral dissertation, University of Texas, Austin.

Purves, A. (1984). The teacher as reader: An anatomy. *College English, 46,* 259-265.

Purves, A. (1986). Rhetorical communities, the international student, and basic writing. *Journal of Basic Writing, 5,* 38-51.

Purves, A. (1992). Reflections on research and assessment in written composition. *Research in the Teaching of English, 26,* 108-122.

Radecki, P. M., & Swales, J. (1988). ESL student reaction to written comments on their written work. *System, 16,* 355-365.

Reid, J. (1989). ESL expectations in higher education: The expectations of the academic audience. In D. Johnson & D. Roen (Eds.), *Richness in writing: Empowering ESL students* (pp. 220-234). New York: Longman.

Reid, J. (1992). Teaching ESL writers. In L. Troyka (Ed.), *The Simon and Schuster handbook for writers* (pp. 35-44). Englewood Cliffs, NJ: Prentice Hall.

Rosenblatt, L. (1988). Writing and reading: The transactional theory. *Reader, 20,* 7-31.

Rosenblatt, L. (1993). The transactional theory: Against dualisms. *College English, 55,* 377-386.

Schriver, K. A. (1992). Teaching writers to anticipate readers' needs: A classroom-evaluated pedagogy. *Written Communication, 9,* 179-208.

Schwartz, M. (1984). Response to writing: A college-wide perspective. *College English, 46,* 556-562.

Smagorinsky, P., & Smith, M. W. (1992). The nature of knowledge in composition and literacy understanding: A question of specificity. *Review of Educational Research, 62,* 279-305.

Sommers, N. (1982). Responding to student writers. *College Composition and Communication, 33,* 148-156.

Taylor, B. (1981). Content and written form: A two-way street. *TESOL Quarterly, 15,* 5-13.

Thompson, D. P. (1989). Using a local network to teach computer revision. *Journal of Teaching Writing, 8,* 77-86.

Zamel, V. (1976). Teaching composition in the ESL classroom: What we can learn from research in the teaching of English. *TESOL Quarterly, 10,* 67-76.

Zamel, V. (1980). Re-evaluating sentence-combining practice. *TESOL Quarterly, 14,* 81-90.

Zamel, V. (1982). Writing: The process of discovering meaning. *TESOL Quarterly, 16,* 195-209.

Zamel, V. (1985). Responding to student writing. *TESOL Quarterly, 19,* 79-102.

Issues in ESL Writing Assessment: An Overview
by Liz Hamp-Lyons and Barbara Kroll

Introduction

For many second language college students, the writing they are most concerned with is writing that is part of the academy's gate-keeping practices, namely writing on placement, proficiency or exit exams. Several recent studies have investigated the difficulties faced by non-native English speaking students in passing required writing examinations at various institutions (Johns, 1991; Blot, 1994; Ruetten, 1994; Janopoulos, 1995; and Byrd & Nelson, 1995). Such studies illustrate the critical importance of the search for excellence in developing writing assessment instruments that provide the best possible information about student proficiency.

In this paper we present an overview of the variables that contribute to the complexity of writing assessment design. The development and validation of appropriate and excellent measures of nonnative writers' English language writing competencies is critical to assure optimally fair testing practices. This is true whether the context is large-scale testing or an assessment program at a single college. As soon as the assessment context extends beyond an individual teacher's classroom, many more aspects come into play than is the case when setting up an assessment in a single course. We assert that writing assessments in academic contexts need to be conducted with a thorough examination of all the component parts identified and discussed here. This kind of careful attention to the whole process of assessment design could ease some of the valid concerns about potential negative effects of gate-keeping practices on second language writers.

"Issues in ESL writing assessment: An overview" by Hamp-Lyons, L., & Kroll, B., first appeared in *College ESL, 6*(1), 52-72, 1996, published by the Office of Academic Affairs, City University of New York.

Variations in Existing Models in Writing Assessment

A variety of approaches can be used to structure writing assessment procedures, each of which yields a different framework for assessing writing. We briefly describe four such methods here, pointing to the aspects that test developers must attend to the most.

A Snapshot Approach

The single-sample text, written under limited time constraints, on a topic the test taker has not prepared him or herself to write about can be called a "snapshot" approach to testing. While quite typical, this method has a serious drawback: It cuts writers off from much that is part of their writerly skills, including their background knowledge and experience. A potential consequence of this is that the measurement of students' writing abilities will be compressed into a smaller score range than might occur if writers were able to find their own level either by writing on topics they feel comfortable with or in an amount of time that allows room for those with a good deal to say or with extensive composing skills to show what they are capable of. The snapshot approach reinforces the impression created by weaker writers that they have little to say or are constrained by limited language command from saying it.

A Growth/Multiple Competencies Approach

Currently in the field of education generally, and in educational assessment and composition pedagogy in particular, the use of portfolios is attracting great attention (Belanoff and Dickson, 1991; Yancey, 1992; McIntyre, 1995; Gillette & Nelson, 1995; Callahan, 1996). Portfolios have been heralded as a favorable assessment approach to the writing of ESL students (Valdés, 1991; Brookes, Markstein, Price, & Withrow, 1992). Portfolio assessment offers the benefits of extra writing time, promotes the use of support services such as writing centers, and offers other pedagogically enriching aspects, all of which help to create a portrait of an individual writer that displays personal growth and competency in multiple dimensions. And yet, there is a great deal still to be learned about the impact of portfolio assessment on ESL students, including some of the potentially negative effects of providing extensive revision opportunities (Hamp-Lyons, 1995a; 1996). Later, we will consider the complexities of portfolios as assessment instruments in light of the issues raised in this paper.

Assessing Writing as Academic Literacy

It is only when students use both reading and writing to engage in meaningful work within academic classes that they truly have the possibility of becoming part of the academic conversation. Writing texts that draw on a connection to already written texts (i.e., readings) signal students' responses to academic ideas and serve as invitations to others to respond to their ideas in turn.

The richness of such a view of academic literacy suggests that writing assessment designers might consider at least some integration of the skills of reading and writing. This could be done without prejudicing a fair measurement of pure writing skill and reading skill by, for example, using one reading text as content input to a writing prompt, or by following a "take a position" essay prompt with a reading text that takes one specific position on the same issue. While some studies have explored the ways in which ESL student writers use source texts in the production of papers (Campbell, 1990; Sarig, 1993; Bloch & Chi, 1995), at present there is little research about using source texts within a testing framework, except on a case study basis (Johns, 1991). Thus, selecting such an approach would require a major research effort to assure optimally conceived exams of this type.

Assessing Writing
Within Wider Academic Competencies

While reading and writing are often viewed as key language skills for success in the academy, speaking and listening are also vital. Lectures, for example, require formal listening abilities. Furthermore, any student whose spoken language command prevents a visit to a professor's office hours or inhibits asking questions about assignments will be at an extra disadvantage in the class. There is, then, *prima facie* validity to the notion of an integration of all skills in an assessment context. From the point of view of authentic testing of writing, this would make a great deal of sense, since academic classrooms and writing classrooms in academic contexts are multi-skill environments, where talk is the essential underpinning of all the work of writing. Indeed, verbal negotiation and the search for shared meaning characterize the process approach to writing instruction. However, creating assessment instruments to tap into the entire competency framework would be an especially complex task, and such tests would no longer be simply "writing" instruments.

Searching for An Idealized Mode
for Academic Writing Assessment

As we explore variations in approaches to academic writing assessment in the ESL context, our task is further complicated by consideration of questions that must inform our thinking.

1. What is the universe of writing skills needed to succeed in an academic context? How are these skills socially constructed? Are they the results of expressive and cognitive processes that are relatively de-centered from specific academic tasks or expectations? Do they require a social (re)construction of the writer's own cognitive and expressive processes to conform to genre or to faculty expectations or conventions?
2. How can we elicit samples of those writing skills in a way that is true to the nature of so-called "real" writing and to real writing in academia?

3. In examining performance expectations for the purpose of determining scoring procedures, whose expectations should be privileged: those of ESL instructors, of English (composition) instructors, or of faculty in the discipline areas? And if the latter, from which level—from general education courses or from courses in the major discipline?
4. How can we, and should we, prepare readers to judge writing that is appropriate to the writers' purposes and their constructed audience (as opposed to the actual audience, the test essay rater)?
5. If we succeed in eliciting and evaluating samples that are congruent with the expectations of the academy, how are we to avoid disadvantaging candidates without experience in the expectations of the academy?

It will easily be understood that these questions have more or less relevance, and more or less simple answers, depending on whether the writers whose writing is to be assessed are already within an academic community (a college; a classroom) or whether they are a larger and more mixed population from unknown backgrounds, as is the case on large-scale tests, such as the TOEFL program's Test of Written English, the University of Michigan's MELAB writing subtest, or the University of Cambridge Local Examinations Syndicate/British Council's IELTS writing sub-test.[1]

Similarly, we can see that testing instruments for ESL students will differ depending on which perspective their developers take. No such thing as a single idealized model exists. For example, a test that seeks to discover students' ability to demonstrate membership in a particular discourse community (for example, writing like a biologist or like a historian) would be different from a test that seeks to discover whether students use a whole range of writing processes or to find out what writing processes they do use. Choosing only one perspective will automatically fail to account for the entire context in which academic writing is produced. (See Blanton, 1995, for a discussion of how alternative philosophies of teaching shape the nature of curriculum as well.) Our aim is not to answer the questions posed above, but to call attention to all of them and begin conversation about them. The position we take echoes the sentiments of Johns (1990), who reminds us:

> . . . because world views among theorists, researchers and teachers in both the first language and ESL differ . . . no single, comprehensive theory of ESL composition can be developed on which all can agree. (p. 33)

Contextualizing the Academic Writing Situation

The academic writing situation is often referred to as though it were a single entity, a single set of skills that applies to all disciplines at all levels of study. Much evidence, however, suggests that this is not true. The issues of situational responsiveness become an important part of writing assessment design, particularly when comparing requirements of many ESL writing courses to the writing required in English composition courses (Atkinson & Ramanathan, 1995), and to the writing required in the disciplines (Leki & Carson, 1994). Nor can we overlook some of the critical distinctions identified in undergraduate versus graduate writing (Bridgeman & Carlson. 1983; Swales & Feak, 1994). With these factors in mind, we turn to issues related both to genre and to the writers themselves.

Writing Tasks and Genre Issues

The most concrete aspect of the academic writing situation, that which as test developers we can most hope to identify and respond meaningfully to, is the range and nature of academic writing tasks. Without a solid picture of the task types, variation, and frequency encountered "within" the academy (where "within" must be defined contextually, that is, relative to the position of the individual writer), it will be impossible to construct a test to meet even the minimum demands of face validity, namely requiring test candidates to produce one or more writing samples similar in nature to the writing each is asked to produce in courses they enroll in. Yet studies of academic writing tasks to date indicate a far more complex picture than is typically acknowledged in writing test design.

An additional complicating factor comes from the uncertain nature of disciplinary boundaries themselves. For example, it is increasingly common to talk of "disciplinary cultures" (Becher, 1986, 1987, 1994), to question the view that academics are members of a single profession, and instead to view "the academy" as a large number of different professions. There is, however, no grouping of academic disciplines into categories by research modes, language genres, or other clear types. At present, then, a problem with attempts to label disciplinary classifications is their lack of generalizability. In such a context, a more general model of academic language must be used to underpin test development.

Models of Academic Writers

Empirical studies may establish a model of academic writing proficiency that specifies the key characteristics of successful "apprentice writers" shown to be common across disciplines, but problems will always arise in applying such models to the wide range of ESL students in our institutions. One reason for this difficulty is suggested by Leki (1992), who discusses the extent to which North American faculty and their international students may be said to even inhabit the same world. She points out, for example, that faculty may feel comfortable challenging naive or inappropriate assumptions made by native English speakers, but that assumptions of ESL students may be "built on realities we have no experience with" (p. 74). This can create a disjunction between faculty interpretation and student intention, allowing for a situation in which what faculty might view as an inappropriate response to an assessment topic actually grows out of the socio-cultural norms of the writer's native culture.

Any idealized model of what writers should write like is further complicated not only by variability in discipline and culture, but also by the variablility in level of education of test takers. Bridgeman and Carlson (1983), for example, found considerable differences between undergraduate and graduate tasks and expectations. Indeed, expectations in key areas, such as breadth and depth of reading, ability to generate an original argument or thesis, amount of support required for an argument, and so on, all appear anecdotally to differ markedly at the graduate versus undergraduate level, and now some empirical evidence to support the validity of this view is beginning to appear (Hale, Taylor, Bridgeman, Carson, Kroll, & Kantor, 1996). Furthermore, we should not overlook the fact that undergraduates will probably have to complete one or more required writing courses as part of their undergraduate curriculum. They should not be held accountable on a placement exam, for example, for demonstrating the type of proficiency that they are first expected to be taught and to learn *after* the exam is behind them. Their exam results should be informative about what they do know and can do in academic writing, not solely about what they cannot yet do. Conversely, graduate students will not necessarily find institutions that either require or even have available writing courses designed to increase their proficiency; rather, they are often expected to have a threshold level of writing competence upon entrance to the program of their choice. A placement test for entering graduate students, then, is likely to have a different agenda than a placement test for undergraduates.

Add to all this that each writer is a complex of experience, knowledge, ideas, emotions and opinions, and that all of these things come with her or him to the essay test. In interpreting and responding to the topic of an essay test, each writer must create a fit between her world and the world of the essay test topic and she must interpret the task in terms which make sense to her before she can respond to it. Even when a topic or task appears to be quite specific, it is, as Labov (1969) said, "absurd to believe that an identical 'stimulus' is obtained by asking everyone the same 'question'" (p.108).

Balancing the Pieces in Designing Assessment Instruments

The basic elements that contribute to the complexity of writing assessment design must be resolved in any model—ideal or otherwise—chosen as the design template for a given assessment program. (These aspects are discussed in more detail by Hamp-Lyons [1990; 1991] in the context of ESL testing, and in the context of writing assessment in general by Ruth and Murphy [1988] and by White [1994]).

Prompt Development

In large-scale testing, it is critical for the validity of the test that the candidates should be given a test that is equivalent from one administration to the next. Here equivalent means that each person would receive a score not significantly different regardless of the occasion on which she or he took the test. In multiple-choice tests, several statistical strategies can be used to ensure equivalence from test to test. This is much harder to do with writing tests because items cannot be repeated (due to breaches of confidentiality and to the practice effect) and because we have not yet been able to construct forms of writing assessment that are truly equivalent in difficulty and accessibility. The reasons for these difficulties involve (1) the prompts, (2) the candidates, and (3) the scoring procedures used to rate the writing samples produced.

Prompts.   In addition to the linguistic features they exhibit, prompts also tap into the knowledge base of the candidates either through the wording or through the ancillary presentation of material (oral or visual) which focuses and restricts the possible content about which the candidate can write. The candidate comes into the testing room and is presented with a topic that may immediately tap into a well-known issue, or may not. When each candidate brings his or her own range of knowledge of the world to the exam and is asked to write on a topic that might fall at the periphery of that knowledge base, it seems unfair to offer a test that yields one sample and provides no options. Obviously, some candidates have more knowledge or experience than others. Designing assessments that offer equally accessible prompts is extremely difficult because of the wide range of variables that impact each individual writer's writing performance. Pollitt, Hutchinson, Entwhistle, and De Luca (1985), for instance, list 32 characteristics *just within the textuality of the prompt itself* that influence the difficulty of a prompt.

Prompt difficulty and accessibility are connected to the nature of the tasks the prompt asks the writer to perform. Critical questions include: Are the tasks cognitively easy or difficult? Are the tasks stated implicitly or explicitly? Is there more than one task in a prompt, and can all tasks be completed in the time allowed? Tasks here can be subdivided into the work required of the candidate at the cognitive level and the work required at the rhetorical level. Kroll and Reid (1994) provide a fuller discussion of the issues related to prompt development, as summarized in Table 1.

How Candidates and Prompts Interact.   Another avenue of research to pursue relates to how the candidates themselves view the difficulty and accessibility of particular topics. Writing tests often have pre-testing procedures that include an evaluation of the viability of every potential "live" topic. But while writing teachers and test administrators are routinely asked to comment on the prompts their students try out, the writers themselves are generally not asked to fill out questionnaire data or to participate in interview sessions to analyze their reactions to the topics they write about—data which could provide some critical information about how writers process and interpret prompts. A recent small-scale study by Polio and Glew (1996) sheds some light on students' perspectives regarding prompt choice on a timed writing assessment. In this case, a majority of participants preferred to be given a choice of prompts in order to choose the one which would "[allow] them to display their best writing ability" (p. 45), though the resulting products were not evaluated for quality in this study.

Certainly, data-based research based on student input can produce inconclusive and problematic results. There is some evidence that student writers cannot always make good choices for themselves (Peretz & Shoham, 1990; Schaeffer, 1993), and

Table 1
Prompt Design Guidelines

Context

    place of test in course, curriculum or program
    discriminant power of test
    criteria/reason for evaluation of product

Content

    within the experience (schemata) of the student writers
    culturally accessible to intended interpretation
    allows for multiple approaches

Language

    instructions
        comprehensible
        as brief as clarity allows
        unambiguous
        vocabulary and syntax appropriately simple or complex
    prompt
        culturally accessible
        transparent
        easy to interpret
        unambiguous

Task(s)

    appropriately narrow to accomplish within the external
        parameters of the task
    appropriately "rich" to allow more proficient students to
        demonstrate their true range

Rhetorical Specifications

    clear directions
    rhetorical specification at optimal level
    adequate rhetorical cues

Evaluation

    determines which criteria are most critical in judging
        performance
    criteria made manifest to test takers

Source: Kroll & Reid, 1994, p. 242

even experts do not agree on the notion of topic difficulty (Hamp-Lyons & Mathias, 1994). However, if we could learn more about what factors writers use when judging whether a test prompt will be difficult or easy to write on, we could design documentation for the test that would help writers think about prompts in ways that might be fruitful in their specific test environment.

Scoring Procedures and Prompts Must Interact. The most common method for scoring writing, and that includes the writing of nonnative writers in academic contexts, is holistic scoring. Traditional holistic scoring is characterized by impression marking and the use of multiple raters to compensate for interrater unreliability (Cooper, 1984). While a number of serious problems with this form of holistic scoring occur in any context (White, 1993), these problems are especially serious in ESL writing assessment contexts. In speeded, impressionistic holistic scoring many raters make judgments by responding to the surface of the text and may not reward the strength of ideas and experiences the writer discusses. Making a single judgment, readers might find it difficult to reach a reasonable balance among all the essential elements of good writing. Many studies have shown that L2 writers score less well in these contexts than L1 writers (Vann, Lorenz, & Meyer, 1991; Janopoulos, 1992; Silva 1993). In the ESL context, a detailed scoring procedure requiring the readers to attend to the multidimensionality of ESL writing may ensure more valid judgments of the mix of strengths and weaknesses often found in ESL writings. (See Hamp-Lyons, 1995b; and Jacobs, Zingraf, Wormuth, Hartfiel, & Hughey, 1981.)

The development of scoring guides and rating scales for all writing tests is a skilled, complex, and time-consuming activity. Furthermore, if a writing assessment is truly to assess *academic* writing, not only must the scoring criteria used in the scoring instrument realistically embody academic writing expectations, but additionally essay readers/raters must be experienced teachers and readers of *academic* writing and fully trained to reward effective academic writing when they see it.

In the ESL context, scoring is both complex and critical, since the way that ESL writing performance expectations are stated in the rating scale will both shape readers' judgments and influence the teaching of writing around the world. As these scales become known to writers around the world, conventional expectations about the features of good writing are gradually being developed. While the scoring for each writing test is separately developed, it seems probable that a study of all the available large-scale writing assessments (among them TWE, MELAB, IELTS, *access:*, OTESL, CanTEST,[2] and so on) would show significant agreement among them as to what constitutes good writing.

The way writing is scored directly relates to prompt difficulty because during rater training, raters will be asked either to strictly adhere to the ways in which candidates' writing samples instantiate particular features of the scoring guide (making a prompt more difficult), or to overlook and perhaps ignore instances of well intentioned but misguided interpretations of the prompt (making it easier). Also, an overly complex scoring guide, or a strict emphasis on scoring speed, will force raters to find strategies for appearing to conform to the rules while "getting the job done"—the same is true in situations where raters are required to score large numbers of essays over too long a period. On the other hand, an overly simple scoring guide gives no guidance to readers, no internal basis for training new raters, and its output in scores provides little information to students or their instructors (Hamp-Lyons, 1995b). As with so many things, finding a happy balance is essential.

Selection and Training of Readers

We also need to consider who will do the actual reading of ESL writing samples and how those readers will be trained. Where non-ESL writing specialists are used, they must be provided with opportunities to distinguish global errors (errors that interfere with communication) from local errors (errors that may be irritating but do not interfere with comprehension). Research studies regarding the writing of native versus non-native English speakers and ratings by teachers of native versus non-native English speakers have provided conflicting results. In a pilot project which explored the ratings assigned to essays produced for the English Placement Test administered by the Province of British Columbia in 1979, McDaniel (1985) concluded that raters did not respond "the same way towards essays written by ESL and non-ESL students" (p.15). Brown (1991) found that while essays written by University of Hawaii students enrolled in either English composition or ESL composition classes and rated by ESL and non-ESL teachers received similar scores, the teacher-raters did not agree on what components of the student texts could be classified as either the worst or the best features. More recently, Sweedler-Brown (1993) concluded that raters not trained to work with ESL students tend to judge essays on different criteria than they judge essays written by native English speaking students. O'Loughlin (1993) found that under some conditions English and ESL-trained raters rated ESL essays differently. The weight of the studies reported above suggests that ESL-trained readers are likely to give more valid (and reliable) readings of ESL essays. We must also not forget the need for readers to be sensitive to the special expectations of *academic* writing.

Test Constraints

Reliability.   Decisions about scoring procedures follow inevitably from decisions about prompts, test type, time allowed and all the other prior contextual constraints. Scoring must, of course, be reliable. We are now much more aware of the limitations of the traditional definition of reliability on writing tests as a coefficient based on two readers' scores (which as Eliot, Plata, and Zelhart have illustrated [1990, pp. 88-89] can be above .90 even when readers never give identical scores), or even as a percentage of agreement between readers. Such a definition fails to recognize that other factors work to lower the reliability of writing tests: variability of prompt difficulty which, as we have shown, is a serious and so far unsolved problem with writing assessments; variations in writers' background knowledge, and so on. We now have statistical tools, especially the FACETS program, which applies a multiple facet latent trait model to data analysis, that can compensate for some of these kinds of variability by allowing us to identify raters who are more or less severe, prompts that are more or less difficult, as well as writers that are more or less proficient. But, in many cases, the data needed for FACETS to help us are not available (for example, writing on more than one prompt by the same candidate; scoring of more than one prompt by each rater).

Validity.   We are always caught in a bind over reliability and validity. The psychometric wisdom is that no test can be more valid than it is reliable; if scores are not stable and consistent, then they are essentially meaningless and cannot be valid. But the knife cuts both ways: If a test is not valid, there is no point in its being reliable since it is not testing any behavior of interest. This is a modern view of validity based on the work of Anastasi (1982), Messick (1988), and Cronbach (1988), for example, which emphasizes construct validity. It is concerns about construct validity that have driven our discussion of prompts and of scoring procedures. Validity must be established for all the components of a direct test of writing—not only the prompt (including the task) and the scoring procedures, but also who the writers and readers are and how they are directed to take or score the test.

The Special Problem of Time.   Within the realistic constraints of large-scale writing assessments, it is hardly possible to create a testing situation in which students can have space for the full exercise of all processes; however, it seems important to insure sufficient time is available for students to make choices and decisions and to be able to follow them through. For example, on a two-hour writing test, it would be possible to have students do two or three different types of tasks, none of which required a long, essay-style response, therefore giving the students time to work through prewriting and revision or editing on at least one of the tasks, and more if they use time carefully. Some students would find the alloted time more than they know how to use, but two kinds of writers would have an advantage. First, intermediate to high intermediate writers who have been taught, or who intuitively possess, a good understanding of their own writing processes would have the time to apply their writing processes/strategies and show themselves at their best. And second, students who find timed testing situations particularly difficult would encounter less time pressure and (if time constraint is truly the source of their test anxiety) be able to spend time thinking through what they want to do before actually starting to write.

Test takers who do well on the highly time-constrained tests are likely to be not only those with a strong linguistic competence but also those with exposure to writing in timed test situations, who already possess a well-formed mental model of the test expectations including a model genre and text structure for responses. These demands are especially heavy ones for the commonly used 30-minute or 60-minute time period, and the fact that so many writers are able to write successfully under these conditions suggests that compensatory strategies are at work.

Portfolios as Assessments for ESL Learners

While portfolio assessment is not the subject of this paper, some general comments are appropriate in an overview such as this. It must be emphasized that portfolios are excellent pedagogical tools. Portfolios permit the display of growth and of multiple competencies; in appropriate contexts, they permit the assessment of writing as academic literacy in authentic environments; they not only permit, they demand contextualization of the academic writing situation; they enable teachers and learners to negotiate authenticity of tasks and genres on an individual as well as class level; they provide a rich source of data for developing models of academic writers. What is in doubt is whether portfolios are equally promising as assessment tools. The first requirement of any assessment measure is stability: The goalposts, whatever they may be, must be the same for all persons being assessed and for all persons asked to make judgments. But a portfolio by its nature permits each writer to create a personal portrait, a personal record, which is in important ways different from the portrait or record created by every other writer. The force of the portfolio is in the sense of uniqueness it gives each writer.

Looking back at our comments about the requirements for stability of prompt characteristics, and the performance of prompts from candidate to candidate and occasion to occasion, we can see that a measure that allows writers to create their own prompts and then to select among different pieces of writing on different prompts to create an assembly of work to be assessed will make judges' work very difficult. Further, it can be seen from our comments about the development of scoring guides and rating scales that specialized scoring instruments are needed for portfolios; few such instruments have yet been developed, let alone validated. Even when that is done, the training of judges (readers) will be a complex and time-consuming task. It is commonly claimed in the educational measurement literature (Wolf, Bixby, Glenn, & Gardner, 1991) that portfolios and other alternative assessments should not be required to meet the expectations of other types of tests—that, in fact, by their very nature they fall outside the traditional, formal parameters of tests. This is a complex and interesting debate that is by no means concluded. (See, for example, Messick, 1995.)

If portfolios do not meet the criteria we have discussed in this paper, then some alternative criteria for ensuring excellence must be found; this is an issue of great concern to the groups responsible for ethical standards for tests such as AERA/NCME and ILTA.[3] But a further problem is that portfolios may in fact be used as tests. Early evidence (Hamp-Lyons, 1995a) suggests that when portfolios are used as formal measures of progress or proficiency (for example, as exit measures from writing courses), they function, at least for some students in some classes, in the same ways tests do. In sum, at this stage much is not known about portfolios as assessments, and we advocate caution in bringing a portfolio approach into an "ideal assessment model" in the ESL context.

Conclusion

We understand a great deal less about our test takers from countries around the world than we need to: This is the great underresearched aspect of language testing.

From the field of contrastive rhetoric (see, for example, Connor, 1996), the remarkable paper by Fan Shen (1989) has revealed for us how conflicted a second language writer can be in the North American academic context—but Shen is clearly a successful, indeed an exceptional, student. Tucker's (1995) close case study analysis of several international students further underscores the need for a rich cultural understanding of our student populations.

Certainly, differences among test takers are both natural and desirable since tests are intended to discriminate, but these differences must be due to real differences in English-language writing ability by the test takers and not be due to either obvious or subtle bias in the test which fails to factor in the effect of these identifiable variables. In the research and development process, the ultimate stakeholders in this testing context—the test-takers—are almost always excluded from any role in the decision-making process itself. And yet, these are the very people from whom we can learn the most about what works, or doesn't, and why. Within the field of education there is a groundswell of interest in collaborative assessment and self-assessment. We hope to see these utilized in designing writing assessments for ESL students in academic contexts in the future.

Finally, in designing writing assessments at the most ideal level, we would want to select test parameters that call upon writers to apply their discourse, sociolinguistic, and metacognitive abilities as well as their linguistic and rehearsed genre competence in an entire package. We should aim to design a test that acknowledges on some level the writing processes that all written products depend on. If we fail in this, the test we design will only give information about some competencies, and those competencies may not be the ones we most need to know about in the academic context that is our focus. Furthermore, the design of future writing assessments should be responsive to the sociopolitical concerns that are raised about writing assessments (for example, Greenberg, 1986; Raimes, 1990) as well as to the best interests of the test candidates. As our discussion has shown, this is most certainly not an easy task. Given that "writing is a multidimensional, situational construct that fluctuates in a wide variety of contexts" (Greenberg, 1992, p. 18), it is perhaps inevitable that creating the best of all possible tests and testing situations remains a constantly shifting balancing act.

Notes

1. TOEFL = Test of English as a Foreign Language; MELAB = Michigan English Language Assesstment Battery; IELTS = International English Language Testing Service.
2. TWE = Test of Written English; MELAB = Michigan English Language Assessment Battery; IELTS = International English Language Testing Service; access: = language proficiency test for migrants to Australia; OTESL = Ontario Test of English as a Second Language; CanTEST = Canadian Test.
3. AERA = American Educational Research Association; NCME = National Council for Measurement in Education; ILTA = International Language Testing Association.

Works Cited

Anastasi, A. (1982). *Psychological testing.* (5th Edition). London: Collier Macmillan.
Atkinson, D. & Ramanathan, V. (1995). Cultures of writing: An ethnographic comparison of L1 and L2 university writing/language programs. *TESOL Quarterly, 29* (3) 539-568.

Becher, T. (1986). The disciplinary shaping of the profession. In B. R. Clark (Ed.), *The academic profession.* University of California Press.

Becher, T. (1987). Disciplinary discourse. *Studies in Higher Education, 12* (3) 261-274.

Becher, T. (1994). The significance of disciplinary differences. *Studies in Higher Education, 19* (2) 151-161.

Belanoff, P., & Dickson, M. (Eds.) (1991). *Portfolios: Process and product.* Portsmouth, NH: Boynton/Cook Heinemann.

Blanton, L.L. (1995). Elephants and paradigms: Conversations about teaching L2 writing. *College ESL, 5* (1) 1-21.

Bloch, J., & Chi, L. (1995). A comparison of the use of citations in Chinese and English academic discourse. In D. Belcher & G. Braine (Eds.), *Academic writing in a second language: Essays on research & pedagogy* (pp. 231-274). Norwood, NJ: Ablex.

Blot, D. (1994). Lessening the influence of the WAT in an ESL curriculum. *College ESL, 4* (1) 61-70.

Bridgeman, B., & Carlson, S. (1983). *Survey of academic writing tasks required of graduate and undergraduate students* (TOEFL Research Report #15). Princeton, NJ: Educational Testing Service.

Brookes, G., Markstein, L, Price, S., & Withrow, J. (1992, March). Portfolio assessment at Manhattan Community College, City University of New York. Paper presented at the 26th Annual TESOL Convention, Vancouver, Canada.

Brown, J.D. (1991). Do English and ESL faculties rate writing samples differently? *TESOL Quarterly, 25,* 587-603.

Byrd, P., & Nelson, G. (1995). NNS performance on writing proficiency exams: Focus on students who failed. *Journal of Second Language Writing, 4* (3) 273-285.

Callahan, S. (1996). Portfolio expections: possibilities and limits. *Assessing Writing, 2* (2) 117-151.

Campbell, C. (1990). Writing with others' words: Using background reading texts in academic compositions. In B. Kroll (Ed.), *Second language writing: Research insights for the classroom* (pp. 211–230). New York: Cambridge University Press.

Connor, U. (1996). *Contrastive rhetoric.* New York: Cambridge University Press.

Cooper, C. R. (1984). Holistic evaluation of writing. In C. R. Cooper and L. Odell (Eds.), *Evaluating writing: Describing, measuring, judging* (pp. 3-32). Urbana, IL: NCTE.

Cronbach, L. (1988). Five perspectives on the validity argument. In H. Wainer and H.I. Braun (Eds.), *Test Validity* (pp. 3-17). Hillsdale, NJ: Erlbaum.

Eliot, N., Plata, M., & Zelhart, P. (1990). *A program development handbook for the holistic assessment of writing.* Lanham, NY: University Press of America.

Gillette, S. & Nelson, E. (1995, March). Implementation of portfolio assessment in an EAP program. Paper presented at the 29th Annual TESOL Convention, Long Beach, CA.

Greenberg, K. L. (1986). The development and validation of the TOEFL writing test: A discussion of TOEFL research reports 15 and 19. *TESOL Quarterly, 20* (4) 531-544.

Greenberg, K. L. (1992). Validity and reliability issues in direct assessment of writing. *WPA: Writing program administration, 16* (1-2) 7-22.

Hale, G., Taylor, C., Bridgeman, B., Carson, J., Kroll, B., & Kantor, R. (1996). *A study of writing tasks assigned in academic degree programs.* (TOEFL Research Report #54). Princeton, NJ: Educational Testing Service.

Hamp-Lyons, L. (1990). Second language writing: Assessment issues. In B. Kroll (Ed.), *Second language writing: Research insights for the classroom* (pp. 69-87). New York: Cambridge University Press.

Hamp-Lyons, L. (Ed.) (1991). *Assessing second language writing in academic contexts.* Norwood, NJ: Ablex.

Hamp-Lyons, L. (1995a, March). Portfolios with ESL writers: What the research shows. Paper presented at the 29th Annual TESOL Convention, Long Beach, CA.

Hamp-Lyons, L. (1995b). Rating non-native writing: The trouble with holistic scoring. *TESOL Quarterly, 29* (4) 759-762.

Hamp-Lyons, L. (1996). Applying ethical standards to portfolio assessment of writing in English as a second language. In M. Milanovich & N. Saville, *Studies in language testing 3: Performance testing, cognition, and assessment.* Cambridge: Cambridge University Press.

Hamp-Lyons, L. (in press). The challenges of second-language writing assessment. In E. White, W. Lutz, & S. Kamasukiri (Eds.), *The politics and policies of assessment in writing.* New York: Modern Language Association.

Hamp-Lyons, L., and Mathias, S. P. (1994). Examining expert judgments of task difficulty on essay tests. *Journal of Second Language Writing, 3* (1) 49-68.

Jacobs, H., Zingraf, S.A., Wormuth, D.R., Hartfiel, V.F., & Hughey, J.B. (1981). *Testing ESL composition: A practical approach.* Rowley, MA: Newbury House.

Janoupoulos, M. (1992). University faculty tolerance of NS and NNS writing errors: A comparison. *Journal of Second Language Writing, 1* (2) 109-121.

Janopoulos, M. (1995). Writing across the curriculum, writing proficiency exams, and the NNS college student. *Journal of Second Language Writing, 4* (1) 43-50.

Johns, A.M. (1990). L1 composition theories: Implications for developing theories of L2 composition. In B. Kroll (Ed.), *Second language writing: Research insights for the classroom* (pp. 24-36). New York: Cambridge University Press.

Johns, A.M. (1991). Interpreting an English competency examination: The frustrations of an ESL science student. *Written Communication, 8,* 379-401.

Kroll, B., & Reid, J. (1994). Guidelines for designing writing prompts: Clarifications, caveats, and cautions. *Journal of Second Language Writing, 3* (3) 231-255.

Labov, W. (1969). *The logic of non-standard English.* Urbana, IL: National Council of Teachers of English.

Leki, I. (1992). *Understanding ESL writers: A guide for teachers.* Portsmouth, NH: Boynton/Cook Heinemann.

Leki, I., & Carson, J. G. (1994). Students' perceptions of EAP writing instruction and writing needs across the disciplines. *TESOL Quarterly, 28* (1) 81-101.

McDaniel, B. A. (1985, March). Ratings vs. equity in the evaluation of writing. Paper presented at the 36th Annual Conference on College Composition and Communication. Minneapolis, MN.

McIntyre, K. (1995, March). Classroom research: Portfolio assessment in an ESL writing class. Paper presented at the 29th Annual TESOL Convention, Long Beach, CA.

Messick, S. (1988). The once and future issues of validity: Assessing the meaning and consequences of measurement. In H. Wainer and H.I. Braun (Eds.), *Test Validity* (pp. 3-17). Hillsdale, NJ: Erlbaum.

Messick, S. (1995). Standards of validity and the validity of standards in performance assessment. *Educational Measurement: Issues and Practice, 14* (4) 5-8.

O'Loughlin, K. (1993, August). The assessment of writing by English and ESL teachers. Paper presented at the International Language Testing Research Colloquium, Cambridge, England.

Peretz, A.S., & Shoham, M. (1990). Testing reading comprehension in LSP: Does topic familiarity affect assessed difficulty and actual performance? *Reading in a Foreign Language, 7,* 447-55.

Polio, C., & Glew, M. (1996). ESL writing assessment prompts: How students choose. *Journal of Second Language Writing, 5* (1) 35-49.

Pollitt, A., Hutchinson, C., Entwhistle, N., & De Luca, C. (1985). *What makes exam questions difficult?* Edinburgh: Scottish Academic Press.

Raimes, A. (1990). The TOEFL Test of Written English: Causes for concern. *TESOL Quarterly, 24* (3) 427-442.

Ruetten, M. K. (1994). Evaluating ESL students' performance on proficiency exams. *Journal of Second Language Writing, 3* (2) 85-96.

Ruth, L., & Murphy, S. (1988). *Designing writing tasks for the assessment of writing.* Norwood, NJ: Ablex.

Sarig, G. (1993). Composing a study-summary: A reading/writing encounter. In J.G. Carson and I. Leki (Eds.), *Readings in the composition classroom: Second language perspectives* (pp. 161-182). Boston, MA: Heinle and Heinle.

Schaeffer, C. (1993). *Pragmatic sequencing: A comparative case study of a freshman composition class in English.* Unpublished master's thesis, California State University, Northridge.

Shen, F. (1989). The classroom and the wider culture: Identity as a key to learning English composition. *College Composition and Communication, 40,* 459-466.

Silva, T. (1993). Toward an understanding of the distinct nature of L2 writing: The ESL research and its implications. *TESOL Quarterly, 27* (4) 657-677.

Swales, J.M., & Feak, C. (1994). *Academic writing for graduate students: A course for nonnative speakers of English.* Ann Arbor: University of Michigan Press.

Sweedler-Brown, C.O. (1993). ESL essay evaluation: The influence of sentence-level and rhetorical features. *Journal of Second Language Writing, 2,* 3-17.

Tucker, A. (1995). *Decoding ESL: International students in the American college classroom.* Portsmouth, NH: Boynton/Cook Heinemann.

Valdés, G. (1991). *Bilingual minorities and language issues in writing: Toward profession-wide responses to a new challenge.* Technical Report No. 54. Berkeley, CA: Center for the Study of Writing.

Vann, R.J., Lorenz, F.O., & Meyer, D.M. (1991). Error gravity: Faculty response to errors in the written discourse of nonnative speakers of English. In L. Hamp-Lyons (Ed.), *Assessing second language writing in academic contexts* (pp. 181-195). Norwood, NJ: Ablex.

White, E.M. (1993). Holistic scoring: Past triumphs, future challenges. In M. A. Williamson and B.A. Huot (Eds.), *Validating holistic scoring for writing assessment* (pp.79-108). Cresskill, NJ: Hampton Press.

White, E.M. (1994). *Teaching and assessing writing.* Second edition. San Francisco: Jossey-Bass.

Wolf, D., Bixby, J., Glenn, J., & Gardner, H. (1991). To use their minds well: Investigating new forms of assessment. In G. Grand (Ed.), *Review of Research in Education,* Vol. 17. Washington DC: American Educational Research Association.

Yancey, K. (1992). *Portfolios in the writing classroom.* Urbana, IL: NCTE.

Contrastive Rhetoric in Context:
A Dynamic Model of L2 Writing
by Paul Kei Matsuda

Originally proposed by Kaplan (1966) as a pedagogical solution to the problem of L2 organizational structures, contrastive rhetoric has seen a significant growth as a field of inquiry. In the last three decades, several books have been published (i.e., Connor, 1996; Connor & Kaplan, 1987: Kaplan, 1972, 1983; Martin, 1992; Purves, 1988), and numerous articles and dissertations have been written on this subject. During the 1980s, the development of research approaches, such as text linguistics and discourse analysis, helped to improve the methodological orientation of contrastive rhetoric research (Enkvist, 1987; Leki, 1991). As a result, researchers have begun to study organizational structures of both L1 and L2 written discourse more vigorously and systematically (Martin, 1992), and contrastive rhetoric has come to be defined in a broader term, encompassing more than just the organizational structures (see Connor, 1996; Ostler, 1996).

Despite the initial pedagogical aim of contrastive rhetoric, however, the insights gained by research have not been effectively translated into the practice of teaching organizational structures (Raimes, 1991; Robinson, 1993). As Kaplan (1980) once wrote, the insights generated by scientific analyses of language yield "interesting results" but they may not become useful to language teachers immediately because "the needs of the language analyst are quite different from the needs of the language user" (p. 59). More recently. Leki (1991) pointed out that "the immediate practical uses of the findings of contrastive rhetoric for ESL writing teachers are not altogether clear" (p. 137). Grabe and Kaplan (1989) also warned ESL writing teachers that "contrastive rhetoric does not offer a curriculum" (p. 277), although the notion "will continue to make a significant contribution to L2 curricular decisions and writing instruction" (p. 278).

Reprinted from the *Journal of Second Language Writing, 6*(1), Matsuda, P. K., Contrastive rhetoric in context: A dynamic model of L2 writing, 1997, with permission from Elsevier Science.

241

The need for ESL writers to learn how to organize English written discourse still exists (Grabe & Kaplan, 1989; Kaplan, 1988; Leki, 1991, 1992; Reid, 1989; Severino, 1993), although the way to translate research insights into classroom practice is yet to be developed. My aim in this study, then, is to develop a model of L2 writing that can help teachers place insights from contrastive rhetoric studies into the practice of teaching ESL writing. I begin by identifying a static theory of L2 writing that incorporates findings of early contrastive rhetoric research, and then discuss how this theory has been limiting the potential contribution of contrastive rhetoric to L2 writing pedagogy. Finally, I propose an alternative model that can guide further research and the teaching of L2 textual organization.

A Static Theory of L2 Writing

Early in the history of contrastive rhetoric studies, some attempts were made to incorporate the insights from early contrastive rhetoric research into an approach to the teaching of ESL writing (see Raimes, 1983, 1991; Silva, 1990). The early contrastive rhetoric-based pedagogy, however, uncritically accepted what some researchers (e.g., Connor, 1996; Liebman, 1992) call "old" contrastive rhetoric, while failing to evolve with the subsequent development of "new" contrastive rhetoric research.

Viewing the problem of L2 writing essentially as the problem of negative transfer, the early pedagogical approach to textual organization, or what Raimes (1983) called "the paragraph-pattern approach" tended to focus on teaching "the particularly 'English' features of a piece of writing" (pp. 7-8). In this approach, students

> copy paragraphs, analyze the form of model paragraphs, and imitate model passages. They put scrambled sentences into paragraph order, they identify general and specific statements, they choose or invent an appropriate topic sentence, they insert or delete sentences. (p. 8)

Perhaps for lack of workable alternatives, this "current-traditional" pedagogy became one of the dominant approaches in the teaching of ESL writing (Silva, 1990). However, this pedagogical approach came to be severely criticized because of its prescriptive nature and its deterministic view of the influence of the L2 writer's background (Leki, 1991). The criticism of this pedagogy in turn limited the potential contribution of contrastive rhetoric to the teaching of L2 writing. Underlying this early pedagogical approach to the teaching of L2 textual organization is a static theory of L2 writing. This section elaborates on the static theory and discusses its limitations.

Explanations for L2 Textual Organization

One of the important contributions that contrastive rhetoric researchers have been making is the understanding of discourse-level structures that are observed in different languages (Grabe & Kaplan, 1989; Leki, 1991, 1992). The findings of contrastive rhetoric research have provided teachers with some insights that can guide their decisions in developing curriculum and in responding to ESL students' needs. At the very least, contrastive rhetoric suggests the need for the teachers to be aware of the differing cultural, linguistic, and rhetorical traditions that students bring with them (Leki, 1992).

Some contrastive rhetoric researchers have contributed to the teaching of ESL writing by identifying the possible sources of the apparent lack of coherence in ESL texts. The explanations that they have generated can be classified roughly into three types: linguistic, cultural, and educational explanations.

The following review is not intended to be a taxonomy of contrastive rhetoric studies per se, but a characterization of ways in which contrastive rhetoric has been incorporated into the static model of L2 writing. Whereas this type of classification scheme is necessarily a reductive generalization, it can nonetheless help teachers and researchers understand some of the guiding assumptions that underlie the early pedagogical theory of L2 textual organization.

The linguistic explanation emphasizes the prominence of the writer's L1 as an influencing—if not determining—factor in the L2 organizational structures (see Hinds, 1983, 1990; Kaplan, 1966; Ostler, 1987). Influenced by the Sapir-Whorf hypothesis to varying degrees, studies that support this explanation regard organizational structures of written discourse as above-sentence-level linguistic structures (Kaplan, 1987; Martin, 1992).[1] Grabe and Kaplan (1989) summarized the linguistic explanation generated by early contrastive rhetoric researchers as follows:

> Writers composing in different *languages* [italics added] will produce rhetorically distinct texts, independent of other causal factors such as differences in processing, in age, in relative proficiency, in education, in topic, in task complexity, or in audience. (p. 264)

Since the organizational structure of written text is considered as part of the linguistic structure, the linguistic explanation holds that the teaching of written English should also include the teaching of the "morphosyntax of the target language . . . at the intersentential level" (Kaplan, 1988, p. 278).

The cultural explanation maintains that organizational structures are strongly influenced, if not determined, by the cultural background of the writer (see Bickner & Peyasantiwong, 1988; Leki, 1992; Matalene, 1985; Purves, 1988; Söter, 1988). Studies that fall under this category support the view that the organizational structure of written discourse is a cultural phenomenon. Leki (1992) wrote, for example, "cultures evolve writing styles appropriate to their own histories and the needs of their societies" (p. 90). The pedagogical application of this view involves the teaching of organizational structures that fit the cultural conventions shared by the readers, because "the fact that the student knows the conventions of his or her own writing system does not mean the student understands the conventions employed in the target language" (Kaplan, 1988, pp. 296-297).

The educational explanation considers how writers acquire the patterns they use in their writing in the first place, and explains the structures of ESL texts in terms of educational backgrounds. Mohan and Lo (1985), for example, compared

ESL writing instruction in Hong Kong and British Columbia, and concluded that the organizational structure in ESL text may be a result of developmental factors. Similarly, Liebman (1992) argued that prior L1 writing instruction may also be a factor influencing different aspects of writing. In this view, the ESL text may seem to be organized inappropriately because the writer has either been taught differing organizational schemata or has not mastered the organizational patterns to produce structures that are acceptable in the discourse community in which the text is placed.

These three explanations are not mutually exclusive, as some contrastive rhetoric researchers have acknowledged (i.e., Hinds, 1983; Leki, 1992; Mohan, 1986; Mohan & Lo, 1985). At this point, little evidence exists to support the view that any one of them is most salient (Mohan, 1986; Mohan & Lo, 1985), and researchers (e.g., Taylor & Chen, 1991) are beginning to consider "cultural orientations toward self, others, society, and social interaction" (Connor, 1996, p. 41) as influencing factors. However, the accumulating evidence from contrastive rhetoric research warrants the view that linguistic, cultural, and educational backgrounds have some influence on the organizational structures of ESL text, although they are by no means the only factors (see Connor, 1996; Grabe & Kaplan, 1989).

The three major explanations for the organizational structures of ESL text come from different theoretical perspectives, leading to different conclusions about the nature of organization in ESL texts and the teaching of ESL writing. These explanations were incorporated into a static pedagogical theory of L2 writing, which has been widely used in ESL writing classrooms. This pedagogical theory provides a set of assumptions about what Silva (1990) called the elements of L2 writing: "the L2 writer," "the L1 reader," "the L2 text," "the contexts for L2 writing," and "the interaction of these elements in a variety of authentic ESL settings" (p. 18). The conceptual relationship among the elements of L2 writing in the existing theory is shown in Figure 1.

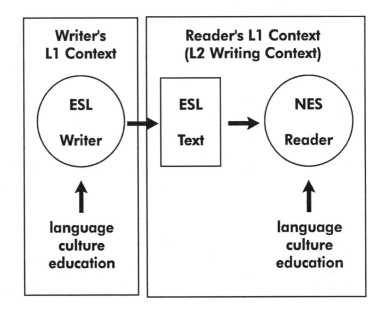

Some Underlying Assumptions

The static theory of L2 writing pedagogy holds a mechanistic view of the writer, which may have come from the behavioristic assumption that was dominant in oral approach and controlled composition (Silva, 1990). Under this view, the writer is not granted agency; he or she does not have the autonomy to make decisions in spite of the circumstance. Instead, the writer is seen as a "writing machine," as it were, that creates text by reproducing the pattern provided by his or her linguistic, cultural, or educational background. Take, for example, a Japanese student writing a letter to the editor of the campus newspaper about the quality of coverage on campus issues. The pedagogical theory based on this view of L2 writing explains features of the text only in terms of the influence from Japanese language, culture, or educational system. All other factors (e.g., the writer's past experience with the genre and with the particular discourse community) that might be influencing the textual features—beyond the fact that it was written as a letter to the editor—would be ignored.

Another important assumption underlying the static theory is that text is merely a linguistic code. Despite the increasing recognition of the negotiation and construction of meaning that take place both in the process of writing (e.g., Zamel, 1982) and in the process of reading (e.g., Tierney & Pearson, 1985), the textual structure is still construed as the direct representation of the writer's mental process, which is to be decoded by the reader. For this reason, some early contrastive rhetoric researchers assumed that the examination of text alone can reveal the "thought patterns" of the writer (Kaplan, 1966, p. 4) or the "rhetorical patterns" of the L1 written discourse (Hinds, 1983, p. 186).[2] However, I would argue, generalizations about the student's background that were made without consulting the student to understand his or her intentions in organizing the text do not provide useful information for the teacher.

If the text is seen as the embodiment of the schematic code prescribed by the writer's background, the reader's role is reduced to being the decoder of the schematic information along with the message. What makes communication fail in this model, then, is the discrepancy between the writer's and the reader's schematic expectations that come from differing backgrounds. The static theory would explain that the text is ineffective simply because it conforms to the typical pattern of organization in Japanese written discourse, with which NES readers are not familiar.

Finally, the most fundamental, yet least recognized assumption is the one about the context of writing. In the static model of L2 writing, the writer's and the reader's backgrounds—linguistic, cultural, and educational—are the only elements that constitute the context of writing, and they are construed as static entities—hence the term *static theory*—that determine the identities of the writer and the reader. Furthermore, L2 writing is expected to signify the reader's context and not the writer's. That is, the L2 writer is writing from the context with which he or she is familiar (e.g., the discourse community in his or her native country), while the L1 reader is reading from another context (e.g., the U.S. academic discourse community). The L2 text in this model is placed in the reader's context, from which the writer is excluded. In other words, the ESL writer is considered to be writing from the outside of the context of reading. Since the reader expects certain organizational structures that are commonly accepted in his or her language, culture, or educational system, the text that may be considered effective in the writer's context may still be perceived as incoherent in the reader's context.

Limitations of the Static Theory

Together, these assumptions about the writer, the reader, the text, and the context comprise the static theory of L2 writing on which the existing contrastive rhetoric-based approaches have been founded. This theory has limited the potential application of contrastive rhetoric research to the teaching of L2 writing. The assumption about the writer makes the static theory especially problematic because it denies the writer's agency. This theory assumes that ESL writers are more or less "programmed" to write in a certain way, and the lack of "appropriate" organizational structure in ESL text is considered to be the reflection of the lack of proper programming. In order to help the Japanese writer in the aforementioned example make her letter seem coherent to NES readers, approaches that are based on this pedagogical theory might try to "program" her properly by prescribing a typical organizational pattern of letters to the editor written in English.

The prescriptive nature of the teaching has been one of the central problems of contrastive rhetoric-based approaches. If, as the static model of L2 writing suggests, the appropriate organization of the text must conform to the reader's expectations that are determined by the static context, the view of organizational structures as "patterns" is justified, and the teaching of organizational patterns found in English-written discourse inevitably becomes the prescription of the value system of the NES writers.

Such a prescriptive application of contrastive rhetoric research has lead contrastive rhetoric-based approaches to be frowned upon by some teachers and researchers, who have characterized them as "ESL version[s] of current-traditional rhetoric" (Silva, 1990, p. 13; cf. Grabe & Kaplan, 1989). Indeed, many contrastive rhetoric-based approaches to the teaching of organizational structures have been reminiscent of current-traditional rhetoric, which assumes that the writer's thoughts "can be graphically displayed in discourse" (Crowley, 1990, p. 13). Just as the adherents of current-traditional rhetoric contended that "bad writing is nothing more than outward and visible sign of bad thinking" (Campbell, 1939, p. 179), so uncritical proponents of contrastive rhetoric-based approaches assume that the organizational structure of L2 text is the sign of the ways of thinking that are specific to the linguistic, cultural, or educational background of the writer.

Another problem associated with the static pedagogical theory is that textual features are equated with the personal background of the ESL writer, and the writer's linguistic and cultural background is viewed as a significant part of her or his identity. Thus, the teaching of a new cultural and linguistic identity—namely, that of the English language—has been equated with the violation of the writer's personal identity. Land and Whitley (1989) argued, for instance, that to demand students to construct texts that resemble ones written by native English speakers is to ask them to "situate themselves within a particular sociopolitical context, and we respond to and judge their writing according to how accurately they are able to do so" (p. 289). For this reason, they called the pedagogical approaches based an this static theory "composition and colonization" (p. 289). These negative characterizations of one form of contrastive rhetoric-based pedagogy have led some teachers and researchers of L2 writing to dismiss contrastive rhetoric-based approaches altogether, as well as the insights generated by contrastive rhetoric research.

The teaching of organization is indeed problematic if one accepts the proposition that the organizational structure of written discourse is determined wholly by the writer's background, which constitutes his or her linguistic and cultural identity. However, the teaching of organization need not be prescriptive or colonizing, because organizational structure of written discourse is not determined solely by who the writer is. The decisions about the organization may be influenced by the writer's cultural, linguistic, or educational background, as the static theory may indicate, but these three are not the determining factors. The organization of the text reflects the complexity of the process of decision making that writers go through as they respond to their own perception of the particular context of writing. The process of writing, then, can be seen as the process of deciding how to respond to the context of writing.

In order to understand the complex decision-making process involved in the organization of written text, a pedagogical theory of L2 writing needs to look beyond the background of ESL writers. In other words, an alternative theory of L2 writing is needed. In the following section, I propose an alternative model of L2 writing that accounts for the complexity of factors that influence the writer in the process of organizing L2 text.

A Dynamic Model of L2 Writing

The graphic representation of the interrelationship among the elements within a dynamic model of L2 writing is provided in Figure 2. In this alternative model, the

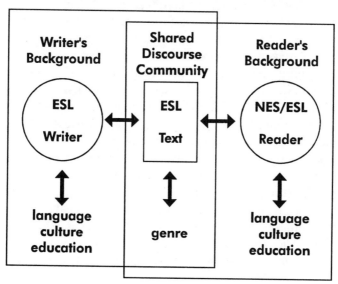

context of writing—which consists of all of the shaded areas—includes both the writer and the reader along with their backgrounds. Writing in this model is considered to take place in its own dynamic context, which is created as a result of the encounter of the writer and the reader—an encounter mediated through the text. The context of writing, then, is defined as the dynamic environment that surrounds the meeting of the writer and the reader through the text in a particular writing situation.

Three key features of the dynamic model of L2 writing are (a) the writer's and the reader's backgrounds, (b) shared discourse community, and (c) the interaction of the elements of L2 writing within the dynamic context. In the following sections. I explain each of these features.

An Expanded Conception of Backgrounds

Placing the writer within the immediate context of writing does not remove the three explanations generated by early contrastive rhetoric studies from the picture. On the contrary, writer's and reader's backgrounds are still differentiated in this model, although they are not conflated with the context of writing as it was in the static model. In the static model, the L1 reader's background alone constituted the context of writing whereas in the dynamic model, the context of writing includes both the writer's and the reader's backgrounds.

In this model, however, the backgrounds of the writer and the reader include more than just language, culture, and education in a broad sense. Although these three are still probably the most salient constituents of the writer's and the reader's backgrounds, there are other, perhaps more immediate, sources of influence. The writer's decisions may also be influenced by, for example, variations within his or her native language (i.e., dialect) and culture (i.e., socioeconomic class), his or her knowledge of the subject matter, past interactions with the reader, and the writer's membership to various L1 and L2 discourse communities.

To refer back to the example of the Japanese student writing a letter to the editor, her background as a writer is much more than growing up in Japanese culture, speaking the Japanese language, or being educated in Japanese school system. Her decisions as a writer may perhaps be influenced by, for example, her experience as an editor of a high-school newspaper in Japan. Her religious view may also affect how she reacts to the particular issue. She may try to present herself more indirectly if the editor she is criticizing lives in the same residence hall as she. Furthermore, she may approach the task of writing with more confidence if she has some prior experience in writing argumentative letters for the same newspaper.

The characterization of the backgrounds of interactants is only suggestive; defining the background of the writer or the reader is probably impossible, and even useless. Although writers from similar cultural, linguistic, and educational backgrounds may exhibit some similarities in the way they write, no two people from similar backgrounds share exactly the same experience. What is important is not to arrive at a clear definition of the background of the writer and the reader, but to understand that their backgrounds are complex and flexible—varying from person to person and from time to time—and that the context of writing is also dynamic.

Because of the possible diversity of the backgrounds even among writers and readers from similar linguistic, cultural, and educational traditions, a similar process of negotiation may occur between an ESL writer and an ESL reader or between an NES writer and an NES reader.[3] For instance, the ESL writer who has had ample exposure to the linguistic and rhetorical conventions of the target language may exhibit the ability to compose a letter more similar in quality to those written by the NES writer than ones written by other ESL writers. Conversely, the editor may have been exposed to many ESL texts and thus be able to tolerate a wider variety of textual features than average NES readers. It is also possible that the editor is an ESL reader, in which case he or she may react differently toward particular ESL errors (see Kobayashi, 1992).

The Shared Discourse Community

Unlike the static model, which conflated the reader's background and the discourse community in which the text was placed, the dynamic model sees the discourse community as shared by both the writer and the reader. The shared discourse community is the space that surrounds the text, which is placed at the intersection of the backgrounds of the writer and the reader. According to Swales (1990), a discourse community is a community that has, among other things, "a broadly agreed set of common public goals" (p. 24) and "mechanisms of intercommunication among its members" (p. 25). For the Japanese writer in my example, the campus newspaper acts as the mechanism which serves the community by disseminating potentially useful or important information for students, faculty, and staff members, and—to a lesser extent—facilitating discussions and communication among them by providing sections such as letters to the editor and classified ads.

As a member of the discourse community, the Japanese writer shares with her readers—and with other writers—"one or more genres" and "specific lexis" that are used for the "communicative furtherance of [the community's] aims" (Swales, 1990, p. 26). In this case, the student is using the genre of letter to the editor (or what is acknowledged in the particular discourse community as such) to communicate her view on the way the communication mechanism (i.e., editorial section of the newspaper) is serving the shared goals of the discourse community.

Before she can use the genre effectively, however, she still has to acquire "a suitable degree of relevant content and discoursal expertise" (Swales, 1990, p. 27; see also Bazerman, 1985; Berkenkotter, Huckin, & Ackerman, 1988) just as any new member of the community does (Bartholomae, 1985; Bizzell, 1982a, 1982b), regardless of his or her linguistic, cultural, or educational background. However, it is important to note that, in the proposed model, each writer's or reader's expertise as a member of the community influences the area of the shared discourse community. The writer can therefore negotiate his or her access to the discourse community by becoming familiar with the discourse-level conventions. The Japanese writer may increase the chance of having her letter published by studying the ways in which conventionalized discourse features are used by other members of the community.

Although these global conceptions of the discourse community are useful, the shared discourse community does not simply exist "out there." Rather, the shared discourse community is "local, historical, and interactive" (Casanave, 1995, p. 88); they are created or modified through the encounter of the writer and the reader who have differing levels of discourse expertise as well as different backgrounds. In other words, the reader can also help to enlarge the shared area by growing accustomed to the presence of the text which embodies differing assumptions, experiences, and levels of discourse expertise.

Bidirectionality of the Interrelationship

Another key feature of the dynamic model of L2 writing is the bidirectional nature of the interrelationship among its elements. The interaction of the differing backgrounds not only constructs the shared discourse community, but also transforms the writer's and reader's backgrounds. For this reason, the context of writing in this model is more than the sum of the writer's and the reader's backgrounds.

The writer is also capable of deviating from the influences of his or her background as well as transforming it by changing the way he or she perceives and relates to it. The Japanese student's experience of participating in the discourse community of the campus newspaper may influence the way she writes later in other discourse communities, such as local newspapers in her home town, thus contributing to the transformation of the conventions of those communities. In other words, the experience of participating in a new discourse situation becomes part of the writer's background.

In this model, ESL students are not solely responsible for becoming enculturated into existing discourse communities. The reader may also experience a similar process of negotiating his or her own background as a result of reading the Japanese student's text. Casanave (1995), for example, demonstrated how professors came to perceive their own discourse differently as a result of interactions with students from backgrounds that were different from their own. Having participated in the discourse with the Japanese writer, the reader in my example may have gained a new perspective with which to reevaluate and transform his or her own background.

Furthermore, the presence of L2 text can lead to the transformation of L1 discourse into a more pluralistic one, as Land and Whitley (1989) argued. Prior (1995) also showed that students, through their participation in local academic discourse communities, contributed to the dialogical construction of genres within those communities. Because the Japanese student's participation in the shared discourse community (i.e., writing a letter to the editor) adds to the network of texts within the discourse community, it may eventually influence the existing genre conventions.

The bidirectionality also applies to the text. The text can be seen as a medium through which the context of writing is negotiated rather than as a codified body of meaning that is structured according to patterns prescribed by the writer's background. As Kaplan (1991) wrote:

A text has no reality until it is instantiated by a receptor; that is, the meaning of the text lies not in the text itself, but in the complex interaction between the author's intent and his/her performance ability to encode that intent, and the receptor's intent and his/her performative ability not only to decode the author's intent but to mesh his/her own intent with the author's. (p. 203)

The text, then, creates a virtual world, as it were, in which the writer and the reader meet each other and construct a shared social reality (Brandt, 1986). To serve this purpose adequately, the organization of text must reflect the writer's understanding of the complexity of the context of writing.

With this view of text, the writer needs to learn more than just the organizational pattern preferred by the reader or the accepted genre conventions in the shared discourse community. In order to mediate the differing backgrounds that the writer and the reader bring to the context of writing, the text must also reflect the writer's understanding of the reader's background and the genres in the discourse community shared by the writer and the reader. The Japanese writer in the previous example needs to shape her letter according to her understanding of the readers (e.g., students, faculty, and staff) and their backgrounds (e.g., language, culture, education, relationship with the writer), as well as the genre (e.g., letter to the editor), and her own awareness of the ongoing discussions about the subject in the particular newspaper.

Teaching ESL students to organize L2 writing, then, does not mean imposing on them the cultural values of native English speakers or prescribing patterns. Rather, it should be considered as a way of raising ESL students' awareness of various factors that are involved in structuring the text, including the reader's expectations of certain organizational patterns. In other words, the act of organizing the text is not the same as using prescribed patterns or genre conventions that fit the subject, but should be seen as the process of complex decision making, which involves an understanding of the dynamic nature of the context of writing.

Implications

What I have presented is an attempt to construct a model that may be developed into a more empirically grounded theory of L2 writing pedagogy. At this point, I submit this model for further scrutiny, because not enough empirical evidence exists to help define the relationship between text and context, or to differentiate processes of L1 and L2 writing. This is not to say that writing in L1 and L2 are essentially the same. The difference between L1 and L2, however, lies not in what are involved in the general process of organizing a piece of writing but in how and to what degree elements of the dynamic model interact with one another. After all, even L1 writers may come from diverse cultural, educational, and sociolinguistic backgrounds. The difference needs to be determined through empirical studies that are conducted in a variety of authentic contexts and with L1 and L2 writers and readers from various backgrounds. Models of L2 writing such as this one can play a role in designing empirical studies and in interpreting their results.

The proposed model is offered as a heuristic, a tool for thinking about the dynamic nature of the context of writing and the complexity of decision-making processes that are involved in the construction of L2 text. It is my hope that this model will facilitate further inquiry into the process of organizing L2 text. As a heuristic, the model raises more questions than it answers. For example:

1. How does the L2 textual organization reflect the writer's understanding of the context of writing?
2. What types of textual features are used in the process of negotiating the context?
3. What is involved in the decision-making process that L2 writers go through as they organize their texts? How is the process reflected in the textual features?
4. How do experienced and inexperienced writers use the text differently to establish and develop the shared discourse community?
5. How do answers to these questions differ between L1 writers and L2 writers?

To answer these questions, contrastive analysis of written discourse in itself will not be sufficient. Organizational structures of L2 text should be analyzed in context; that is, in light of the writer's mental representation of the context of writing, the reader's actual reactions to the text, and the outcome of the interaction of the two. One way to yield such understanding may be to combine discourse analysis and qualitative analysis of the writing and reading processes through interview-based research methods. Context-sensitive text analysis, as proposed by Huckin (1992), is especially useful for this purpose.

The dynamic model of L2 writing also has some implications for the teaching of L2 textual organization. Because an effective organization of text must reflect the decisions that the writer makes based on his or her perception of the context of writing, the teaching of organization necessarily involves the teaching of the awareness of the context of writing (see Liebman, 1988, for an example of awareness-raising pedagogy).

Students need to learn how to negotiate the context of writing by actually experiencing the process. For this purpose, each writing assignment needs to be placed in a real context of writing, involving a discourse community shared with real readers. Writing assignments such as asking students to write a critical review of one another's essay, and then to share it with the whole class, including the author of the essay, allow the writer to see how the intended readers react to his or her text and how other people approach the same task.

The teacher's responses to students' writing can foster the same goal by emphasizing the importance of the awareness of the context of writing, and of the negotiation that occurs at the intersection of the writer's and the reader's backgrounds. The teacher who assigned the review of a classmate's essay might express how she might feel about the directness of the criticism if she were the author of the essay.

Evaluation of organization might include considering the possible reactions of the intended reader. The teacher might also consider how the writer of the review incorporated the responses from the author of the essay and other classmates in revising the review. Only by taking into consideration the context in which the student intended to write, can the teacher accurately evaluate the effectiveness of the organizational structure of L2 text in negotiating the context.

The study of organization in written discourse has been, and will continue to be, an important part of L2 writing research. Pedagogical implications of contrastive rhetoric studies should not be dismissed because of the problems with the early attempts to apply the findings of contrastive rhetoric research. Because textual organization is one of the areas with which ESL students have most difficulties, it needs to be taught in ESL writing classrooms, but it needs to be taught in ways that are informed by an appropriate theory of L2 writing.

Acknowledgments

I thank Ulla Connor, Akiko Fujii, Aya Matsuda, and the editors and anonymous reviewers of the *Journal of Second Language Writing* for their thoughtful comments on earlier versions of this article.

Notes

1. The Sapir-Whorf (or Whorfian) hypothesis is the notion that human perception is affected by the language spoken by the individual. See Connor (1996, pp. 28-29) for a succinct review of the Sapir-Whorf hypothesis and its variations.
2. The notion that the textual organization directly reflects the "thought pattern" of the writer has been denounced by many contemporary contrastive rhetoric researchers, including Kaplan himself, to be too deterministic.
3. Since both the writer and the reader can be either NES or ESL speaker, this dynamic model of writing may also be applicable to the teaching of L1 writing. Although the way the context of writing influences L1 and L2 textual organization will be different, the way and the degree of the difference need to be determined through empirical research. For my realization of the potential inclusiveness of this model, I am especially indebted to Margie Berns.

Works Cited

Bartholomae, D. (1985). Inventing the university. In M. Rose (Ed.), *When a writer can't write: Studies in writer's block and other composing problems* (pp. 134-165). New York: Guilford Press.

Bazerman, C. (1985). Physicists reading physics: Schema-laden purposes and purpose-laden schema. *Written Communication, 2,* 3-24.

Berkenkotter, C., Huckin. T. N., & Ackerman, J. (1988). Conventions, conversations, and the writer: Case study of a student in a rhetoric Ph.D. program. *Research in the Teaching of English, 22,* 9-44.

Bickner, R., & Peyasantiwong, P. (1988). Cultural variation in reflective writing. In A. C. Purves (Ed.), *Writing across languages and cultures: Issues in contrastive rhetoric* (pp. 160-174). Newbury Park, CA: Sage.

Bizzell, P. (1982a). Cognition, convention, and certainty: What we need to know about writing. *Pre/Text, 3,* 213-241.

Bizzell, P. (1982b). College composition: Initiation into the academic discourse community. *Curriculum Inquiry, 12,* 191-207.

Brandt, D. (1986). Toward an understanding of context in composition. *Written Communication, 3,* 139-157.

Campbell, O.J. (1939). The failure of freshman English. *English Journal: College Edition, 28,* 177-185.

Casanave, C.P. (1995). Local interactions: Constructing contexts for composing in a graduate sociology program. In D. Belcher & G. Braine (Eds.), *Academic writing in a second language: Essays on research and pedagogy* (pp. 83-110). Norwood, NJ: Ablex.

Connor, U. (1996). *Contrastive rhetoric: Cross-cultural aspects of second-language writing.* New York: Cambridge University Press.

Connor, U., & Kaplan, R.B. (Eds.). (1987). *Writing across languages: Analysis of L2 text.* Readings. MA: Addison-Wesley.

Crowley, S. (1990). *The methodical memory: Invention in current-traditional rhetoric.* Carbondale: Southern Illinois University Press.

Enkvist, N.E. (1987). Text linguistics for the applier: An orientation. In U. Connor & R.B. Kaplan (Eds.), *Writing across languages: Analysis of L2 text* (pp. 23-43). Reading, MA: Addison-Wesley.

Grabe, W., & Kaplan, R.B. (1989). Writing in a second language: Contrastive rhetoric. In D.M. Johnson & D.H. Roen (Eds.), *Richness in writing: Empowering ESL students* (pp. 263-283). White Plains, NY: Longman.

Hinds, J. (1983). Contrastive rhetoric: Japanese and English. *Text, 3,* 183-195.

Hinds, J. (1990). Inductive, deductive, quasi-indictive: Expository writing in Japanese, Korean, Chinese, and Thai. In U. Connor & A.M. Johns (Eds.), *Coherence in writing: Research and pedagogical perspective* (pp. 89-260). Alexandria, VA: TESOL.

Huckin, T.N. (1992). Context-sensitive text analysis. In G. Kirsch & P.A. Sullivan (Eds.), *Methods and methodology in composition research* (pp. 84-104). Carbondale: Southern Illinois University Press.

Kaplan, R.B. (1966). Cultural thought patterns in inter-cultural education. *Language Learning, 16,* 1-20.

Kaplan, R.B. (1972). *The anatomy of rhetoric: Prolegomena to a functional theory of rhetoric.* Philadelphia: Center for Curriculum Development.

Kaplan, R.B. (1980). On the scope of linguistics, applied and non-. In R.B. Kaplan (Ed.), *On the scope of applied linguistics* (pp. 57-66). Rowley, MA: Newbury.

Kaplan, R.B. (Ed.). (1983). Annual review of applied linguistics (Vol. 3).

Kaplan, R.B. (1987). Cultural thought patterns revisited. In U. Connor & R.B. Kaplan (Eds.), *Writing across languages: Analysis of L2 text* (pp. 9-21). Reading, MA: Addison-Wesley.

Kaplan, R.B. (1988). Contrastive rhetoric and second language learning: Notes toward a theory of contrastive rhetoric. In A. Purves (Ed.), *Writing across languages and cultures: Issues in contrastive rhetoric* (pp. 275-304). Newbury Park, CA: Sage.

Kaplan, R.B. (1991). Concluding essay: On applied linguistics and discourse analysis. *Annual Review of Applied Linguistics, 11,* 199-204.

Kobayashi, T. (1992). Native and nonnative reactions to ESL compositions. *TESOL Quarterly, 26,* 81-112.

Land, R. E., Jr., & Whitley, C. (1989). Evaluating second language essays in regular composition classes: Toward a pluralistic U.S. rhetoric. In D.M. Johnson & D.H. Roen (Eds.), *Richness in writing: Empowering ESL students* (pp. 284-293). New York: Longman.

Leki, I. (1991). Twenty-five years of contrastive rhetoric: Text analysis and writing pedagogies. *TESOL Quarterly, 25,* 123-143.

Leki, I. (1992). *Understanding ESL writers: A guide for teachers.* Portsmouth, NH: Boynton/Cook.

Liebman, J. (1988). Contrastive rhetoric: Students as ethnographers. *Journal of Basic Writing, 7,* 6-27.

Liebman, J.D. (1992). Toward a new contrastive rhetoric: Differences between Arabic and Japanese rhetorical instruction. *Journal of Second Language Writing, 1,* 141-165.

Martin, J.E. (1992). *Towards a theory of text for contrastive rhetoric: An introduction to issues of text for students and practitioners of contrastive rhetoric.* New York: Peter Lang.

Matalene, C. (1985). Contrastive rhetoric: An American writing teacher in China. *College English, 47,* 789-807.

Mohan, B.A. (1986). On evidence for cross-cultural rhetoric. *TESOL Quarterly, 20,* 358-361.

Mohan, B.A., & Lo, W.A-Y. (1985). Academic writing and Chinese students' transfer and developmental factors. *TESOL Quarterly, 19,* 515-534.

Ostler, S.E. (1987). English in parallels: A comparison of English and Arabic prose. In U. Connor & R.B. Kaplan (Eds.), *Writing across languages: Analysis of L2 text* (pp. 169-185). Reading, MA: Addison-Wesley.

Ostler, S.E. (1996, March). *Contrastive rhetoric: Myths, facts, and pedagogy.* Paper presented at the 30th Annual TESOL Conference, Chicago.

Prior, P. (1995). Redefining the task: An ethnographic examination of writing and response in graduate seminars. In D. Belcher & G. Braine (Eds.), *Academic writing in a second language: Essays on research and pedagogy* (pp. 47-82). Norwood, NJ: Ablex.

Purves, A.C. (1988). Introduction. *Writing across languages and cultures: Issues in contrastive rhetoric* (pp. 9-21). Newbury Park, CA: Sage.

Raimes, A. (1983). *Techniques in reaching writing*. New York: Oxford University Press.

Raimes, A. (1991). Out of the woods: Emerging traditions in the teaching of writing. *TESOL Quarterly, 25,* 407-430.

Reid, J.M. (1989). English as second language composition in higher education: The expectations of the academic audience. In D.M. Johnson & D.H. Roen (Eds.), *Richness in writing: Empowering ESL students*. New York: Longman.

Robinson, J.H. (1993, April). *Contrastive rhetoric and the revision process for East Asian students.* Paper presented at the 27th Annual TESOL convention, Atlanta.

Severino, C. (1993). The "doodles" in context: Qualifying claims about contrastive rhetoric. *The Writing Center Journal, 13,* 44-61.

Silva, T. (1990). Second language composition instruction: Developments, issues and directions in ESL. In B. Kroll (Ed.), *Second language writing: Research insights for the classroom* (pp. 11-23). New York: Cambridge University Press.

Söter, A.O. (1988). The second language learner and cultural transfer in narration. In A. Purves (Ed.), *Writing across languages and cultures: Issues in contrastive rhetoric* (pp. 177-205). Newbury Park, CA: Sage.

Swales, J.M. (1990). *Genre analysis: English in academic and research settings.* New York: Cambridge University Press.

Taylor, G., & Chen, C. (1991). Linguistic, cultural, and subcultural issues in contrastive discourse analysis: Anglo-American and Chinese scientific texts. *Applied Linguistics, 12,* 319-336.

Tierney, R.J., & Pearson, P.D. (1985). Toward a composing model of reading. *Reading Research Quarterly, 9,* 135-147.

Zamel, V. (1982). Writing: The process of discovering meaning. *TESOL Quarterly, 16,* 195-209.

Author Index

A

Ackerman, J., 120, 127, 175, 176, 249
Allaei, S.K., 182
Allen, E.D., 28
Allen, H.B., 9
Almeida, J., 200, 208
Anastasi, A., 235
Anderson, R.C., 176, 183
Applebee, A.N., 96, 103
Applebee, R.K., 33
Arapoff, N., 29
Arndt, V., 173, 174, 195, 208
Aronowitz, S., 170
Arrington, P., 213, 220
Atari, O., 199, 207
Atkinson, D., xiv, xix, 228
Atkinson, P., 196, 198, 208
Au, K.H.-P., 187

B

Ballard, B., 128
Bander, R.G., 92
Bannai, H., 117
Bardov-Harlig, K., 78
Barnes-Felfelli P., 125
Bartholomae, D., 173, 175, 177, 178, 186, 249
Bateman, D.R., 32
Bates, L., 221
Bazerman, C., 93, 96, 101, 175, 249
Beach, R., 37, 76
Becher, T., 229
Becker, H.S., 96
Behrens, L., 94
Belanger, M., 137
Belanoff, P., 226
Belcher, C.L., 96, 98
Belcher, D., xvii, xviii, xix,
Benesch, S., xviii
Bennett, S., 117
Benson, B., 195, 196, 207
Benson, M.J., 129
Bereiter, C., 125, 174, 175, 184, 187
Berkenkotter, C., 120, 127, 249
Berlin, J., 160, 162
Berns, M., 253
Biber, D., 78, 82
Bickner, R., 243

Billows, F.L., 9, 28
Bitzer, L., 210
Bixby, J., 236
Bizzell, P., 91, 92, 94, 101, 160, 163, 167, 211, 249
Black, K., 122, 127
Blanton, L., 175, 176, 181, 228
Bloch, J, 227
Blot, D., 225
Boyd, R., 113
Boyle, J., 110
Braddock, R., 31, 32
Braine, G., xvii, 109, 111
Brandt, D., 125, 251
Brannon, L., 209, 216
Brice, C., xviii
Bridwell, L.S., 76
Bridwell-Bowles, L., 161
Bridgeman, B., xvii, 94, 118, 124, 129, 229, 230
Brier, E.M., 124, 125
Briere, E.J., 27, 30
Brinton, D.M., 121
Brookes, G., 226
Brooks, C., 24
Brooks, N., xiv, 8, 9
Brossell, G., 119
Brown, C., 208
Brown, D., 196, 199, 200, 207
Brown, G., xvi, 77
Brown, J.D., 234
Brown, L., 196, 199, 200, 207
Bruffee, K., 160, 161, 163, 211
Burtoff, M., 196, 207
Butler, J.E., xix
Byrd, P., xx, 217, 225

C

Calkins, L.M., 38
Callahan, S., 226
Campbell, C., 167, 194, 196, 198, 199, 207, 227
Campbell, O.J., xv, 246
Cambell, R.R., 9
Canale, M., 137
Canesco, G., 217
Cardelle, M., 211

Carey, L., 119, 120, 123, 124, 125, 127
Carlson, D., 117
Carlson, S.B., xvii, 94, 118, 124, 129, 196, 199,
    200, 207, 229
Carr, D.H., 29
Carrell, P.L., 79, 84, 86, 121, 137, 173, 174,
    175, 176, 181, 183, 208, 213
Carson, J.G., xiv, xix, xx, 121, 127, 182, 208,
    228, 230
Casanave, C.P., xix, 250
Casanova, S., 117
Castell, S. de, 130
Cavalcanti, M., 21
Cave, G.N., 30
Cepeda. R., 117
Cerniglia, C., 80
Chafe, W., 65, 120
Chang, S.J., 137
Chapman, L.R.H., 9
Charnofsky, H., 117
Chastain, K., 28
Chelala, S., 194, 195, 208
Chen, C., 244
Chi, L., 227
Choi, Y., 197, 207
Christensen, F., 25
Christison, M.A., 175
Clanchy, J., 128
Clark, G., 152
Clark, H.H., 71, 72
Clark, I., 211
Clarke, M., 137, 173
Cleverly, J., 141, 142, 155
Clifford, J., 165
Coe, R.M., 105
Coffey, B., 96, 100
Cohen, A., 174, 215
Cole, K.C., 93
Coles, N., 103
Connolly, F., 25
Connor, U., xv, xvi, xvii,72, 78, 79, 80, 82, 83,
    84, 111, 124, 137, 159, 182, 196, 197,
    200, 207, 237, 241, 242, 244, 253
Connors, R.J., 93, 215
Cook, M., 197, 208
Cooper, C. R., 233
Cooper, M., 40, 160
Corbett, E.P.J., 25
Corno, L., 211
Crews, F., 165
Cronbach, L., 235
Crowell, T.L., Jr., 9
Crowley, S., 246
Cumming, A., 118, 173
Cummings, V., 195, 199, 207
Cummins, J., 137
Currie, P., xix
Cziko, G., 137, 173

D

Dai, B-Y., 149
Danes, F., 77
Daro, P., 117
Dasenbrock, R.W., 183
Davey, B., 186
Davidson, D.H., 141, 143
Davis, T., xiii
de Beaugrande, R., xvi, 79
DeFrancis, J., 155
Degenhart, R.E., 155
DeJesus, S., 208
Della-Piana, G.M., 38
DeLuca, C., 119, 231
Dennett, J., 194, 195, 196, 199, 207
Denzer, D., 195, 196, 207
Deming, M., 195, 196, 207
de Pruna, R.D.G., 9
Devine, J., 173, 179
Dick, J.A.R., 96
Dickson, M., 226
Doheny-Farina, S., 152
Dorfman, C.H., 138, 139, 141, 144
Dressel, P., 31
Dressier, W.U., 76
Dressler, W., xvi
Dubin, F., 102, 103
Dufrenne, M., 24
Duhamel, P.A., 25, 67
Duke, B., 138, 139, 140, 145, 148
Dunkelblau, H., 199, 208
Dykstra, G., 29
Dyson, A.H., 120

E

Edelsky, C., 38, 137
Eggington, W.G., 137
Eisterhold, J.C., 84, 88, 121,176
Elbow, P., 128, 160, 221
Eliot, N., 234
Elley, W.B., 178
Elson, B., 9
Emig, J., 33, 37, 38, 46
Enkvist, N.E., xvi, 76, 79, 241
Entwistle, N., 119
Erazmus, E.T., xv, 8, 30
Ericsson, K.A., 40, 41
Esch, R.M., 96
Eskey, D.E., 102, 103, 176, 178, 180
Evensen, L.S., 78, 79

F

Faigley, L., 38, 40, 53, 78, 82, 97, 98, 99,129,
    160, 167, 210, 216
Farmer, M., 78, 79, 80

Fathman, A., 215
Feak, C., 229
Ferrara, J., 174
Ferris, D.R., xx
Fine, J., 174
Finocchiaro, M., 28
Firbas, J., 77
Fish, S., 183, 211
Flavell, J.H., 128
Flower, L.S., 38, 40, 41, 55, 76, 93,119, 120,
        122, 123, 124, 125, 127, 160, 175,
        176, 213
Flynn, E.A., 183
Fox, T., 160
Frank, L., 213
Freedman, C., 165
Freedman, S.W., 120, 211, 218
Frenette, N., 137
Fries, C.C., xiv
Frodesen, J., 196, 198, 207
Frogner, E., 32
Fry, D.J., 32
Fuller, H.R., 9
Fulwiler, T., 96

G

Gajdusek, L., xvii, xviii, 109, 110, 111, 112,
        113, 114, 175
Gardner, H., 236
Gaskill, W.H., 38, 195, 208
Gates, R., 199, 207
Geisler, C., 214
Gilbert, G.N., 96
Gillette, S., 226
Glasman, H., 174
Glenn, J., 236
Glew, M., 231
Goetz, E.T., 183
Goodman, K., 176, 181
Gorman, T.P., 155
Grabe, W., xxi, 78, 82, 102, 103, 174, 175, 176,
        178, 241, 242, 243, 244, 246
Graves, D.H., 38
Green, J.F., 29
Greenberg, J.H., 63
Greenberg, K.L., 237
Greene, E., 183
Greenhalgh, A.M., 210, 216
Grimes, J., 83
Guerra, J.C., xix
Guth, H.P., 25

H

Haas, C., 119, 120, 123, 124, 125, 127
Hafernik, J., 196, 200, 207
Hafiz, F.M., 178

Hairston, M., xvi, 75, 163, 210
Hale, G., 230
Hall, C., 173, 194, 195, 196, 208
Hall, E.T., xvii
Halliday, M.A.K., xvi, 77, 82
Hamilton-Wieler, S., 160
Hamp-Lyons, L., xx, 91,117, 119, 124, 226,
        230, 233, 234, 236
Hansen, K., 97, 98, 99,129
Harklau, L., xix
Harris, D.P., 84, 198, 207
Harris, M., 220
Hartfiel, V.F., 37, 39, 93,159, 233
Hasan, R., xvi, 77, 82
Haswell, R.H., xx
Hatch, E., 174
Haviland, S., 71, 72
Hayes, J.R., 38, 40, 41, 76, 93,119, 120, 123,
        124, 125, 127, 160
Hearn, G.W., 96, 98
Heimlich, H.E., 187
Henderson, C.A., 32
Herrington, A.J., 98, 100, 103, 124
Herzberg, B., 160
Heuring, D.L., 38
Hildenbrand, J., 194, 195, 208
Hilgers, T.L., 38
Hill, L.A., 9
Hill, S.S., 98
Hillocks, G., Jr., 101
Hilyard, A., 65
Hinds, J., xvii, 67, 68, 70, 72, 84, 137, 152,
        159, 243, 244, 245
Hinds, W., 72
Hirokawa, K., 196, 198, 207
Hirvela, A., xviii, xix, 110
Hoetker, J., 119
Holzman, M., 40, 160
Homberg, T., 118
Horowitz, D.M., xvi, xvii, xviii, 91, 94,
        103,110, 111, 121, 129, 166, 167,
        175, 176, 217
Horvath, B., 222
Hosenfeld, C., 174
Hu, Z., 196, 199, 200, 207
Huckin, T.N., 120, 127, 249, 252
Hudson, T., 173, 181, 182
Hughes, R. E., 25, 67
Hughey, J.B., 37, 39, 93,159, 233
Hunt, K.W., 32
Hunting, R., 31
Hutchinson, C., 119
Hymes, D., 166

I

Indrasuta, C., 198, 200, 208
Intaraprawat, P., 207

J

Jacobs, H.L., 37, 39, 93, 159, 233
Jacobs, S.E., 38
Janopoulos, M., 178, 225, 233
Jenkins, S., 84
Jiang, S., 146, 149, 151, 155
Joag-Dev., C., 183
Johns, A.M., xv, xvii, xviii, xx, 78, 79, 94, 104,
    109, 110, 111, 115, 121, 123, 124,
    130, 152,160, 161, 167, 175, 213,
    216, 225, 227, 228
Johnson, D.M., 161
Johnson, H., 218
Johnson, M., 112
Johnson, N.S., 84
Jolliffe, D.A., 124, 125
Jones, C.S., 38, 39, 42, 54, 173, 194, 208

K

Kachru, B., 211
Kamel, G., 196, 198, 199, 208
Kantor, R., 230
Kantz, M.J., 175, 176
Kaplan, R.B., xv, xvi, xxi, 25, 29, 67, 72, 137,
    196, 241, 242, 243, 244, 245, 246,
    250
Keyes, J.R., 39
Kimball, R., 165
Kimmel, S., 187
Kinosita, K., 155
Kintsch, W., 76, 79, 83, 183
Klauser, E.L., 32
Knepler, M., 39
Knoblauch, C., 209, 216
Kobayashi, H., 197, 207, 249
Koclanes, T.A., 9
Krahnke, K., 175
Krakowian, B., 109
Krapels, A.R., xvi, 173, 194, 195, 208
Krashen, S.D., 38, 52, 54, 101, 178
Kraus, S.A., 32
Kroll, B., xvii, xx, 94,121, 137, 175, 176, 178,
    181, 208, 30, 231, 232
Kroll, B.M., 160
Kubota, R., xix
Kucer, S., 182
Kuehn, B., 121, 137, 208
Kuno, S., 67
Kutz, E., 168

L

Labov, W., 230
Lado, R., xiv
Lakoff, G., 112
Land, R.E., 161, 246, 250

Lane, J., 221
Lange, E., 221
Lauer, J., 84
Lautamaati, L., 78, 79, 80, 81
Lay, N.D.S., 38, 39, 93
Lee, S-Y., 153
Leki, I., xiv, xv, xix, 159, 182, 185, 200, 203,
    215, 228, 229, 241, 242, 243, 244
Leong, C.K., 146, 148, 149
Leong, K.K., 148, 149
Lester, M., 32
Li, B., 146, 149, 151, 155
Li, C.N., 64, 66
Liberto, J.C., 181
Liebman, J.D., 242, 244, 252
Liebman-Kleine, J., 91
Lin, C., 196, 198, 208
Lindeberg, A., 79, 84
Lindell, E., 78, 82
Linnarud, M., 196, 200, 207
Liu, S.B.F., 145, 149
Lloyd-Jones, R., 161
Lo, W.A.-Y., xix, 243, 244
Loban, W., 33
Lokke, V.L., 34
Longacre, R.E., xvi
Lorenz, F.O., 233
Lorenzen, P., 13
Losey, K.M., xix
Lu, J-P., 149
Lu, M., 104
Luke, A., 130
Lunsford, A.A., 160, 161, 215
Lux, P., 196, 199, 207

M

Macaulay, T.B., 14
MacDonald, S.P., 93
MacGinitie, W.H., 187
Maher, J., 96, 98
Mahmoud, A., 196, 197, 200, 207
Maimon, E.P., 95, 96, 98, 104
Maize, R.C., 34
Makita, K., 139, 144, 146, 147
Mandler, J.M., 84
Mangelsdorf, K., xx
Mangubhai, F., 178
Mann, R., 199, 207
Marckwardt, A.H., 9
Markstein, L., 226
Martin, J.E., 241, 243
Martin, J.R., 84
Matalene, C., 243
Mathias, S.P., 233
Matsuda, P.K., xiii, xiv, xv, xviii, xxi
Matsuhashi, A., 38
Maynard, S., 68

McCagg, P., xvii, 83, 84, 87, 137
McCarthy, L., 120
McColly, W., 34
McCormick, K., 175, 176
McCurdy, P., 215
McDaniel, B.A., 234
McGillivray, J. H., 8
McIntyre, K., 226
McKay, S.L., xviii, 167
McKee, M.B., 103
McLaughlin, B., 174
Medsker, K., 80
Mellon, J.C., 32
Merrit, K., 117
Messick, S., 235, 236
Meyer, B.J.F., 83, 84, 213
Meyer, D.M., 233
Mischel, T., 38
Mitchell, F., 219
Mittan, R., 182
Mlynarczyk, R., 175
Moberg, G., 165
Moffett, J., 160
Mohan, B.A., xix, 243, 244
Monane, T., 64, 72
Moody, K.W., 29
Moragne e Silva, M., 194, 195, 196, 208
Moxley, J., 218
Mulkay, M., 96
Murphy, J.M., xx
Murphy, S., 230
Murray, D.M., 38, 160, 222
Myers, G., 96,124

N

Naotsuka, R., 65
Nelson, E., 226
Nelson, G., xx, 225
Nelson, J., 124, 128
Newkirk, T., 214
Nodine, B.F., 96, 98
Norman, J., 155
Norment, N., 196, 197, 207, 208
Nystrand, M., 183

O

O'Connor, F.B., 96, 98
Odell, L., 38
O'Donnell, R.C., 32
O'Hare, F., 32, 33
Oi, K., 197, 199, 200, 207
Oliver, R.T., 24
O'Loughlin, K., 234
Olson, D.R., 65
Onore, C., 216
Ostler, S.E., xvii, 94, 137, 241, 243
Ouaouicha, D., 197, 207, 211

P

Park, Y., 196, 199, 207
Parker, L., 117
Parry, K.J., 179, 183
Part, S., 174
Patterson, A., 78, 82
Paulston, C.B., 29
Pearson, P.D., 176, 180, 245
Pearson, S., 97
Peck, S., 128
Peck, W.C., 175, 176
Peirce, B.N., 160
Pennycook, A., 160
Perdue, V., 161
Perelman, C., 111
Peretz, A.S., 231
Perl, S., 37, 38, 40, 42, 43, 46, 48, 49, 51, 52,
    54, 55, 187
Petroski, H., 93
Petrosky, A.R., 101, 102, 173, 175, 177, 178,
    180
Pettit, S., 117
Peyasantiwong, P., 243
Peyton, J.K., 129
Pfingstag, N., 38
Pharis, B.G., 181
Phelps, L.W., 75, 79
Pianko, S., 38, 42, 46, 52
Piche, G.L., 127
Pickett, V.B., 9
Pincas, A. xiv, 29
Pittelman, S.D., 187
Plata, M., 234
Polanyi, M., 24
Polin, P., 174
Polio, C., 231
Pollitt, A., 119
Potter, R.R., 33
Povey, J.F., 30,
Power, S.G., 161
Price, S., 226
Prior, P., xix, 250
Prochnow, S., 117, 119
Purves, A.C., xv, 155, 211, 215, 241, 243

R

Radcliffe, T., 33
Radecki, P.M., 218
Rafoth, B.A., 122, 160
Ragan, P., 196, 207
Raimes, A., xvi, 38, 76, 93, 94, 159, 160, 173,
    174, 187, 191, 202, 237, 241, 242
Ramanathan, V., xiv, xviii, 228
Reichelt, M., xviii
Reid, J.M., xx, 78, 91, 129, 167, 168, 174, 175,
    176, 196, 199, 200, 207, 216, 217,
    231, 232, 242

Remstad, R., 34
Reynolds, R.E., 183
Rice, G.E., 213
Richardson, G., 129
Rigg, P., 173
Rivers, W., xiv, 28
Roberts, P., 9
Robinson, D., 183
Robinson, J.H., 241
Robson, A.E., 109, 110
Roen, D.H., 161
Rogers, L. 64, 72
Rojas, P.M., 29
Rose, M., 38, 94, 99, 105
Rosenbaum-Cohen, P.R., 174
Rosenblatt, L., 213
Ross, J., 29
Rothery, J., 84
Rouse, J., 161
Roy, A., xiv
Rubin, D.L., 122, 127, 160, 183
Ruetten, M.K., 225
Rummelhart, D., 176
Russell, D.R., 95,129
Ruth, L., 230

S

Sadow, C., xvi, xvii, 39, 102, 176
Sakamoto, T., 139, 144, 146, 147, 155
Salvatori, M., 101
Santiago, R., 196, 197, 208
Santos, T., xiv, xviii, 167
Sapir, E., 25
Sarig, G., 181, 227
Saville-Troike, M., 120
Scarcella, R.C., 84, 199, 207
Scardamalia, M., 125, 174, 175, 184, 187
Schaeffer, C., 231
Schallert, D.L., 183
Scheiber, H.J., 95
Schiller, J., 194, 195, 208
Schriver, K.A., 119, 120, 123, 124, 125, 127,
        213
Schwartz, M., 211, 215
Schwartz, S., 25
Selenker, L., 54
Selzer, J., 38, 96
Severino, C., xviii, xix, xx, 242
Shanghai, Zhejiang, Beijing, and Tianyin Joint
        Writing Group for the Design of Edu-
        cational Materials, 149, 150
Shaughnessy, M., 94
Shen, F., 237
Sheridan, E.M., 151, 155
Shih, M., 93, 95, 96, 103
Shoham, M., 231
Silberstein, S., 121, 137, 208

Siegal, M., xix
Siegel, F., 165
Silk, M., 99
Silva, T., xiv, xvi, xviii, xx, 174, 191, 195, 196,
        199, 207, 220, 233, 242, 244, 245,
        246
Simon, H.A., 40, 41
Skibniewska, M., 194, 195, 196, 208
Skibniewski, L., 194, 195, 196, 208
Sledd, J., 163
Smagorinsky, P., 217
Smith, F., 181
Smith, M.W., 217
Snow, M.A., 121
Sommers, N.I., 38, 76, 210
Soppelsa, B.F., 96
Soter, A., 84, 243
Spack, R., xvi, xvii, xviii, xix, 39, 91, 101, 102,
        104,109, 110, 111, 112, 113, 114,
        160, 166, 175, 176, 177, 182, 186
Spencer, D.H., 29
Sperling, M., 211, 218
Spitzer, L., 24
Squire, J.R., 33
Stahl, S.A., 187
Stalker, J.C., 196, 207
Stalker, J.W., 196, 207
Stallard, C.K., 38
Stanovich, K.E., 174, 176
Staton, J., 129
Steffenson, M.S., 183
Stein, V., 175, 176
Steinberg, D.D., 155
Sternglass, M., 174, 177, 182, 184
Stevenson, A.W., 153
Stevick, E.W., 9
Stewart, D.C., 163
Stigler, J.W., 153
Stokes, E., 39
Strode, H., 25
Stygall, G., 84
Suggs, L.R., 32
Susser, B., xix,
Suzuki, T., 66
Swales, J., xvii, 94, 96, 100,110, 111, 112, 128,
        166, 218, 229, 249
Swarts, H., 41
Swartz, S., 20
Sweedler-Brown, C., 130, 234

T

Tagong, K., 195, 196, 208
Takala, S., 84
Takemata, K., 70
Tannacito, D.J., xviii
Taylor, B.P., xvi, 39, 211
Taylor, C., 230

Taylor, C.V., 78, 82
Taylor, G., 244
Terdal, M., 196, 208
Tetroe J., 38, 39, 173, 194, 208
Thomas, L., 93
Thompson, D.P., 216
Thompson, S.A., 64, 66
Tierney, R.J., 180, 245
Tirkkonen-Condit, S., 84
Tobin, J.J., 141, 143
Tomlinson, B., 122
Topping, D.M., 109
Toulmin, S., 84, 124
Trimbur, J., 160, 161, 162, 163, 164
Truscott, J., xx
Tucker, A., 237
Tudor, I., 178

U

Ueta, Y., 208
Unger, J., 142, 143, 150, 151

V

Valdés, G., xiv, xix, 226
Valeri-Gold, M., 195, 196, 207
Valette, R.M., 28
Vancil, S.T., 187
van Dijk, T.A., xvi, 76, 79, 83
vanDommelen, D., xviii
Vann, R.J., 233
Van Naerssen, M., 178

W

Wall, S.V., 103
Wardhaugh, R., 32
Warfel, H.R., 9
Warren, R.P., 24
Wasell, F.F., 9
Watabe, M., 208
Watson, C.B., xvi
Webb, S., 200, 207
Werlich, E., 77
Wesche, M.B., 121
West, G.K., 98
Whalen, K., 194, 195, 208

Whalley, E., 215
White, E.M., 230, 233
White, L., 117
White, M., 139, 140, 141, 155
White, R.H., 32
Whitley, C., 161, 246, 250
Widdowson, H.G., 55, 56, 110, 111, 112
Wiener, H.S., 162, 163
Wikborg, E., 78, 79, 82, 159
Wilkinson, A.M., 97
Wilson, J., 117
Winfield. F.E., 125
Withrow, J., 226
Witte, S.P., 38, 40, 53, 78, 79, 80, 82
Wolf, D., 236
Wolf, M., 34
Wolfram, W., 129
Woodford, F.P., 99
Wormuth, D.R., 37, 39, 93, 159, 233
Wu, D.Y.H., 141, 143
Wykoff, G.S., 34

X

Xu, G., 196, 197, 207

Y

Yamada, J., 155
Yancey, K., 226
Yau, M., 194, 195, 196, 207
Yearley, S., 99
Yoshikawa, M., 66
Yu, V., 196, 198, 199, 208
Yule, G., xvi, 77

Z

Zamel, V., xv, xvi, xxi, 38, 39, 42, 51, 53, 54,
    55, 76, 91, 93, 94, 101,159, 173, 174,
    182, 185, 211, 215, 245
Zeiger, W., 105
Zelhart, P., 234
Zhang, S., xx
Zhang, J., 151
Zhao, H., 155
Zidonis, F.J., 32
Zingraf, S.A., 39, 233

Subject Index

Academic writing,
    defining, 92-95
    discourse communities, 109; 114-115
    and ESL students, 100-109
    and literature, 109-115
    teaching academic writing for other disciplines, 95-100
Assessment,
    and appropriation of student texts, 209-222
    competency examinations, 117-130
    writing assessment design, 226-236
Audio-lingualism, see Behaviorism
Behaviorism,
    habit formation, 1-2; 29
Collaborative learning, see Ideology
Composing processes,
    in a second language, 38-39
    of native speakers of English, 37-38
    of unskilled ESL writers, 40-56
Composition, see Composing processes and Pedagogy
Contrastive rhetoric,
    cultural thought patterns,
        in English, 12-14
        in other languages, 15-21
    as dynamic model of second language writing, 247-252
    as static theory of second language writing, 242-247
    reader/writer responsibility, 65-72
Development of field,
    instruction, xiv-xv; xvii-xviii
    scholarship, xv-xvii; xviii-xxi
ESL writing, also see Composing processes and Contrastive rhetoric
    and other language skills, 28-29
ESP (English for Specific Purposes), see Academic writing
Grammar, see Pedagogy
Ideology,
    in first language composition theory, 159-165

in second language composition theory, 165-170
Japanese, 67-72
Language,
    typologies, 63-64
Literacy,
    acquisition in Japan and China, 138-151
    biliteracy, 151-154
Methodology, see Pedagogy
Organization, see Contrastive rhetoric
Pedagogy, also see Ideology and Literacy
    controlled composition, 28-30
        multiple substitution, 2-8
        for paragraphing, 22-24
    and first-language research, 30-33
    process approach, 159-160
        call for, 34
    transfer from first language to second language, 191-192
    and use of literature, see Academic writing
Process approach, see Pedagogy
Reading, also see Academic writing
    and writing instruction, 176-186
    reciprocal themes in reading/writing research, 173-176
Research, 27-28, also see specific areas of interest
    in composing processes, 194-195
    implications of second language research, 202-203
    methods,
        think aloud protocols, 40-41; 56
    in written text features, 195-200
Social constructionism, see Ideology
Theory, also see Contrastive rhetoric, Development of field, and Ideology
    integration of, 75-76
    lack of in second language writing, 201
    transfer from L1 to L2, 159-160
Text linguistics, 76-77
    sentence-based approach, 77-82
    process-centered approach, 82-87

AEA-0192